DE QUINCEY TO WORDSWORTH

DE QUINCEY TO WORDSWORTH

A Biography of a Relationship

With the
LETTERS OF THOMAS DE QUINCEY
TO THE WORDSWORTH FAMILY

John E. Jordan

UNIVERSITY OF CALIFORNIA PRESS
BERKELEY AND LOS ANGELES 1963

UNIVERSITY OF CALIFORNIA PRESS
BERKELEY AND LOS ANGELES, CALIFORNIA
CAMBRIDGE UNIVERSITY PRESS
LONDON, ENGLAND
© 1962 BY THE REGENTS OF THE UNIVERSITY OF CALIFORNIA
SECOND PRINTING, 1963
LIBRARY OF CONGRESS CATALOG CARD NUMBER: 62-9013
MANUFACTURED IN THE UNITED STATES OF AMERICA

*To My Mother
and the memory of My Father*

FOREWORD

The letters of Thomas De Quincey to the Wordsworths record with peculiar eloquence an interesting association which left its mark in literature. De Quincey's letters alone, however, cannot tell the whole story, and my original plan of letting them stand with only a brief introduction proved to be unsatisfactory. For here are letters spanning more than forty years of De Quincey's life, eventful years of change and development. Over these years he avoided tutors in Oxford, "worshipped" nature in Westmorland, plagued printers in London, and dodged bailiffs in Edinburgh. He loved—and lost, became broken in fortune and in health, and learned to know the pleasures and pains of opium. He also developed from a stilted schoolboy rhetorician to a master of English prose, serving on the way as newspaper editor, magazine critic, and author of countless articles calculated to amuse the English public, while instructing them in everything from the theory of economics to the merits of Wordsworth's poetry. William Wordsworth, moreover, was not merely a correspondent before whom these changes were paraded; he probably had more influence upon the whole pattern of development than did any other individual.

To understand the fateful relations between these two men, we must not only put De Quincey's letters in the context of those they answered and prompted but we must also ask why they were written; we must interpret them by whatever flickering biographical light is vouchsafed us. If to do this we must sometimes deal in gossip, hearsay, and innuendo; if we must sort a multitude of details often trivial in themselves, our reward is finally a narrative of the impact of two superior, creative individuals on one another. Our history is now comic, now pathetic, and now touched with tragedy. In it we come close to the human beings who were Thomas De Quincey and William Wordsworth; we see into their shallows and get some hints of their depths. And if our concern is more with the men than with the artists, we find the two aspects ultimately inseparable, and learn something of both in this biography of a relationship.

In this effort I have been given hearty coöperation and much help by many people, to whom my sincere thanks. I am especially grateful to the Trustees of Dove Cottage for permission to print the bulk of De Quincey's letters to the Wordsworths and to quote from other manuscript materials in their collection. For permission to publish and cite manuscript materials in their possession I am also grateful to the Curator of the Cornell Wordsworth Collection, the Trustees of Dr. Williams's Library, the Trustees of the British Museum, the Keeper of the Victoria and Albert Museum, the Trustees of the National Library of Scotland, Mr. Carl H. Pforzheimer, Jr., Mr. M. Ronald Brukenfeld, Miss Joanna Hutchinson, Miss Maude de Quincey Craig, and Miss Clare Craig. It is a particular pleasure to record my appreciation of the friendly help of the Misses Craig in going over their great-grandfather's papers. Quotations from certain De Quincey letters are reprinted with permission from the Carl and Lily Pforzheimer Foundation, Inc., on behalf of the Carl H. Pforzheimer Library.

I want also to acknowledge the kindness of the staffs of

the many libraries in which I have found pieces of the picture, particularly the British Museum, the National Library of Scotland, the Bodleian Library, the Dr. Williams's Library, the Carlisle Public Library, the Bristol Public Library, the Sheffield Public Library, the University of Leeds Library, the New York Public Library, the Pierpont Morgan Library, the Cornell University Library, the Folger Shakespeare Library, the Library of Congress, the Houghton Library, and the University of California Library. I am especially indebted to Colonel C. H. Wilkinson of Worcester College, Oxford, for extending to me the materials of not only that library but also his own private collection. J. G. Lightburn, editor of the *Westmorland Gazette,* graciously made available to me the files of his journal; and Miss Phoebe Johnson, librarian of the Dove Cottage Collection, made this whole project possible by generous response to inconvenient requests over several years.

Special acknowledgment must also be made to the publishers and authors of the following works:

J. M. Dent & Sons, Ltd.: Edith J. Morley, ed., *Henry Crabb Robinson on Books and Their Writers* (London, 1938).

Home and Van Thal, Ltd.: Arthur Aspinall, *Politics and the Press* (London, 1949).

Routledge & Kegan Paul: Kathleen Coburn, ed., *The Letters of Sara Hutchinson* (London, 1954).

Cornell University Press: Leslie N. Broughton, ed., *Some Letters of the Wordsworth Family* (Ithaca, 1942); Leslie N. Broughton, ed., *Wordsworth and Reed: The Poet's Correspondence with His American Editor: 1836–1850* (Ithaca, 1933).

The Clarendon Press: E. de Selincourt, ed., *The Early Letters of William and Dorothy Wordsworth* (Oxford, 1935); *The Letters of William and Dorothy Wordsworth: The Middle Years* (Oxford, 1937); *The Letters of William and Dorothy Wordsworth: The Later Years* (Oxford, 1939); Edith J. Morley, ed., *The Correspondence of Henry Crabb Robinson with the Wordsworth Circle, 1808–1866* (Oxford,

1927); Mary E. Burton, ed., *The Letters of Mary Wordsworth, 1800–1855* (Oxford, 1958); Earl Leslie Griggs, ed., *Collected Letters of Samuel Taylor Coleridge* (Oxford, 1956–1959). Through the kindness of Miss Helen Darbishire and the Clarendon Press I have also had access to and permission to quote from unpublished Wordsworth letters in the Lonsdale and Latymer manuscripts which are to appear in the revised edition of the *Letters of William Wordsworth*.

My manifold obligations to other writers on Wordsworth and De Quincey appear from the footnotes. Also, for offering encouragement, answering queries, allowing me to quote from their published works, and reading drafts of this study, I am most grateful to the late Miss Helen Darbishire and the late Mrs. H. D. Rawnsley, to Mrs. Mary Moorman, Professor C. O. Brink, Professor Arthur Aspinall, A. Halcrow, Dr. Ian Jack, Miss Ruth I. Aldrich, Professor Kathleen Coburn, Professor Mary E. Burton, Professor Earl Leslie Griggs, Professor Horace A. Eaton, Howard P. Vincent, Mrs. Dorothy Dickson, Sir John Murray, the Reverend R. C. Tait, Professor Theodore Hornberger, Professor Wilfred Dowden, and my colleagues, Professors Travis Bogard, James R. Caldwell, Bertrand Evans, Josephine Miles, and Wayne Shumaker. For yeoman help in preparing typescript and checking references, I wish to express my thanks to Mrs. Elizabeth Edwards, Mr. and Mrs. Jerry James, and the late Mrs. Beatrix Hogan, whose untimely death is a loss to all Wordsworthians.

I also gratefully acknowledge the financial assistance from the Ford Foundation, the John Simon Guggenheim Memorial Foundation, and the University of California, which made possible the necessary work in Great Britain, as well as funds from the Research Committee of the University of California, which aided in the preparation of the typescript.

Finally, my obligations to my wife are such as will be understood by all married readers.

The letters are printed in chronological order, and supplied with headings indicating the source of the copy and
its more important previous publications, if any. Although
De Quincey frequently copied his letters over before sending them (some of his drafts are printed herein), the sent
versions often show evidence of revision. I have regularly
transcribed the corrected form, reproducing words scratched
out only when they have some special interest. I have
endeavored to follow De Quincey's spelling, except that
I have not thought it worthwhile to reproduce the regular superscription of terminal letters in abbreviations. De
Quincey's early practice was to use parentheses for the
interpolated material so characteristic of him; later he made
marks which are halfway between parentheses and brackets,
and finally he seemed to prefer brackets. I have normalized
all these into parentheses, reserving the bracket for editorial additions. Roman type within brackets is used for
editorial expansions and for conjectural readings, which are
preceded by a question mark. Italic type within brackets
indicates editorial explanation.

De Quincey usually filled his paper, sometimes even
squeezing in upside-down passages; these are marked [*inserted inverted*]. His afterthoughts are printed as post-
scripts unless they were clearly intended to be read earlier,
but their location elsewhere is shown in brackets if necessary.
He frequently drew lines across his paper to separate sections of a letter; these are suggested by printers' rules.

Notes to my text are given at the end of the book. Ex-
planatory notes to the letters are at the foot of their respective pages.

CONTENTS

LIST OF LETTERS

ABBREVIATIONS

Books   *Henry Crabb Robinson on Books and Their Writers,* ed. Edith J. Morley (London, 1938)

Circle   *The Correspondence of Henry Crabb Robinson with the Wordsworth Circle, 1808–1866,* ed. *Edith J. Morley* (Oxford, 1927)

Craig Mss.   Manuscripts in the possession of Miss Maude de Quincey Craig and Miss Clare Craig

Diary   *A Diary of Thomas De Quincey for 1803,* ed. Horace A. Eaton (London: Noel Douglas, 1927)

Dicey   *Wordsworth's Tract on the Convention of Cintra,* ed. A. V. Dicey (London: Humphrey Milford, 1915)

Eaton   Horace A. Eaton, *Thomas De Quincey* (London: Oxford University Press, 1936)

EL   *The Early Letters of William and Dorothy Wordsworth (1787–1805),* ed. E. de Selincourt (Oxford, 1935)

Elwin   *Confessions of an English Opium-Eater, in Both the Revised and the Original Texts, with Its Sequels, Suspiria de Profundis and the English Mail-Coach,* ed. Malcolm Elwin (London: Macdonald, 1956)

Japp   A. H. Japp, *Thomas De Quincey: His Life and Writings* (London, 1890)

Lake Poets   *Letters from the Lake Poets to Daniel Stuart,* ed. Mary Stuart and E. H. Coleridge (London, 1889)

Lit. Rem.   *Literary Reminiscences.* Vols. [V and VI] of *De Quincey's Writings,* (Boston: Ticknor and Fields, 1859)

LY   *The Letters of William and Dorothy Wordsworth: The Later Years,* ed. E. de Selincourt (Oxford, 1939)

M   *The Collected Writings of Thomas De Quincey,* ed. David Masson (London, 1896)

Memorials *De Quincey Memorials,* ed. A. H. Japp (London, 1891)

MY *The Letters of William and Dorothy Wordsworth: The Middle Years,* ed. E. de Selincourt (Oxford, 1937)

Poetical Works *The Poetical Works of William Wordsworth,* ed. E. de Selincourt and Helen Darbishire (Oxford, 1940–1954)

Pollitt [Charles Pollitt], *De Quincey's Editorship of the Westmorland Gazette* (Kendal and London, 1890)

Prose Works *The Prose Works of William Wordsworth,* ed. A. B. Grosart (London, 1876)

SH *The Letters of Sara Hutchinson, from 1800–1835,* ed. Kathleen Coburn (London, 1954)

STC *Collected Letters of Samuel Taylor Coleridge,* ed. E. L. Griggs (London, 1956–1959)

The following standard abbreviations are also used:

DNB *Dictionary of National Biography*

ELH *A Journal of English Literary History*

JEGP *Journal of English and Germanic Philology*

MP *Modern Philology*

N & Q *Notes and Queries*

PMLA *Publications of the Modern Language Association of America*

SP *Studies in Philology*

CHAPTER ONE

✐ APPROACH

"It is a bad thing for a boy to be, and to know himself, far beyond his tutors, whether in knowledge or in power of mind." When Thomas De Quincey wrote this revealing sentence in the 1821 version of his *Confessions of an English Opium-Eater,* he was explaining his vexation in 1802 at being almost seventeen and still a schoolboy at Manchester Grammar School instead of the gownsman he fancied himself. His contempt for his headmaster, the "coarse, clumsy, and inelegant" Charles Lawson, only reflected De Quincey's general dissatisfaction with his Manchester life. There his health suffered from the lack of exercise and from the ministrations of an apothecary whose whole wit was exhausted in the concoction of one shattering "tiger-drench." There his spirits drooped, as he wrote his mother, at the crass mercantile atmosphere which dissipated "the whole train of romantic visions" he had conjured up.[1] It fell to William Wordsworth to take, all unwittingly, an important role in those visions: he became to the boyish imagination an ideal tutor who more than supplied poor Mr. Lawson's deficiencies, one to whom De Quincey could look up in reverence, and who was capable of appreciating his worth. The poet's home in the romantic Vale of Grasmere likewise gleamed as the ideal opposite to "cotton-bag" Manchester.

The unhappy boy, determining at last that he "had nothing to hope for" from his guardians in improving his frustrating situation at Manchester, took matters in his own hands and fled, in July, 1802. His first intention, he later admitted, was to head for the Lake District, drawn by the "deep, deep magnet" of William Wordsworth. But he could not present himself to his idol in the character of a runaway schoolboy—his "principle of 'veneration' " was too strong.[2] He went, instead, by his family's home at Chester, and then to Wales, and finally to London, in pathetic pursuit of independence through futile, dragged-out applications to money-lenders. He nearly starved to death, found a "benefactress" in the "noble-minded" prostitute, Ann of Oxford Street, and at last—probably through the good offices of a family friend—returned ignominiously home to Chester in March, 1803. In that time of misery and misunderstanding, Wordsworth was the cynosure; and it is impossible to understand the whole pattern of the relationship between the two men without recognizing that a very important part of that relationship was the boy's "expectation, and desire, / And something evermore about to be" of those "romantic visions"—years before he knew Wordsworth, and even some time before he dared to begin a correspondence with the poet.

It *is* a bad thing for a boy to know himself beyond tutors placed over him by arbitrary authority, and to live in an atmosphere where there can be no praise he values; it is perhaps even worse for the man who as a boy chose his own tutor, enthroned his own idol, and finally came sadly away feeling that his worship was wronged and his just reward stinted. That is the larger pattern of the relationship between De Quincey and Wordsworth. As De Quincey sorrowfully wrote many years after the fact, there was an error on someone's part, "either on Wordsworth's in doing too little, or on mine in expecting too much." But the design is much more complicated: Wordsworth came to

feel that he had done too much, and certainly his anticipa-
tions were not realized either.[3] Expectations and disap-
pointments were great on both sides.

Certainly the sixteen-year-old boy who turned his
thoughts longingly toward Westmorland expected a great
deal—of himself and, more vaguely, of Wordsworth. He
needed a great deal. He was proud and he was lonely.
"Naturally, I am fond of solitude; but everyone has times
when he wishes for company," the schoolboy wrote his
mother plaintively. What he really wanted was a "fit
audience . . . though few." He could visit the Manchester
house of John Kelsall, formerly his father's clerk and now
the family business adviser, but "Mr. K. and I have not
one idea in common." [4] There was more satisfaction to be
found in the quiet library of the Reverend John Clowes,
and Lady Carbery, a family friend who flattered him by
learning Greek from him at Laxton in 1800, had unexpectedly brightened his Manchester life by a visit. But her
presence also embittered his schoolboy role. When she and
her friends came to hear him recite at the Christmas
speeches, "frantic" was his "inner sense of shame at the
childish exhibition." [5] Her departure in the spring left him
even more miserable in the isolation of his pride, and ripe
for rebellion.

Behind the rebellion lay a boyhood of feast or famine
of sympathetic appreciation. He was born August 15,
1785, the fifth child and second son of a prosperous but
sickly Manchester merchant who was usually absent on
business. Since his four-years-older brother William was
generally away at school after Thomas came to the age of
awareness, and since his other brothers, Richard and Henry,
were four and eight years younger, respectively, than he,
De Quincey later wrote that his "infant feelings were
moulded by the gentlest of sisters, and not by horrid,
pugilistic brothers." [6] Certainly he spent his early years in
a predominantly feminine atmosphere. He was a fragile,
pink-and-white little fellow (he still appeared so in a minia-
ture made when he was sixteen) who was petted by sisters,

maids, and even the factory girls he met on his way into Manchester, where he went to study with one of his guardians, the Reverend Samuel Hall. Without being at all effeminate, he had a feminine quality of delicacy and sensitiveness which established a rapport with women all his life. The first shock to his sense of superiority came when, after their father's death in 1793, brother William returned home, "very naturally despised" him, and "took no pains to conceal that he did." Although De Quincey protests that he was eager to be despised, since thus he was left alone, his whole account of his "Introduction to the World of Strife" reveals his need for recognition. He suffered especially at William's communicating to the housekeeper, Mrs. Evans, his disgraces in battle with the factory lads. Mrs. Evans, too, Thomas was sure, "detested" him.[7]

These are, of course, the later reflections of the man; it is hard to say to what extent they represent the actual feelings of the eight-year-old. Since, however, De Quincey was writing with a definite "Child is father of the Man" philosophy, certainly he was describing what retrospectively seemed important about his boyhood. The portrait of the proud, sensitive, lonesome little fellow, hungry for love and admiration, rings true. Not only did his brother and Mrs. Evans "despise" him, but his mother gave him little warmth and affection. Elizabeth Penson De Quincey was a proud woman herself: she added the aristocratic "de" to the family name, would hold no converse with her domestics, spent more than she could afford in architectural improvements on her various residences, moved in social circles a bit above her rank, and would have liked Thomas to go to Eton. Later she came under the influence of Hannah More and put away the "de" as worldly vanity, but her whole demeanor makes it plain that her son came by his pride honestly. She conscientiously did her duty by her children, but it seemed to De Quincey that "she delighted not in infancy, nor infancy in her." The most significant thing in De Quincey's memory of her was her austere refusal to praise her children, or hear them praised: "Usually mothers defend their own cubs, right or wrong; and they also think favourably of any pretensions to praise which these cubs may put forward. Not so my mother." Mrs. De Quincey's letters bear out her son's boyish impression. "You are wrong to blame Mr. Pratt," she wrote about some now mysterious episode. The "you are wrong" was characteristic. She lectured him for appearing at Frogmore in traveling dress, accused him of "want of resolution" in accepting an invitation to go to the theater, and sent him an elaborate "steering chart" to get himself and his younger brothers from Manchester to Liverpool, implying little confidence in him. De Quincey was convinced that she removed him from Bath Grammar School because the master praised him. Her sentiments in these matters are confirmed by her comment on having the boy prodigy Thomas Macaulay as a house guest: "He says such extraordinary things that he will be ruined by praise." [8] That fate would not befall her Thomas if she could help it.

Mrs. De Quincey was a good, sensible woman, undoubtedly a better mother than De Quincey gave her credit for being, and some of his later animus probably stemmed from the fact that she lived on into her nineties, effectively defrauding him of an inheritance he thought rightly his. Still, her sprinkling children with lavender water, kissing them ceremoniously on the forehead, and conjuring them solemnly by their filial duty—all this left an emptiness in the heart of a boy who believed he had inherited an "expansive love" from a father not there to satisfy it.

From the contempt of William, the austerity of Mrs. De Quincey, and the required sermon memorizing of the "dull, dreadfully dull" Reverend Samuel Hall, Thomas escaped at the age of eleven into the boys' world of Bath Grammar School. De Quincey expanded under the genial praise of Headmaster Morgan. His talents were appreciated, and the salve to his pride was still pungent as late as the first version of *The Confessions of an English Opium-Eater,* in which he recalled Morgan's praise of his Greek. Morgan, significantly, is hailed as "a scholar, 'and a ripe and good one:' and of all my tutors . . . the only one whom I loved or reverenced." [9] Unfortunately, De

Quincey was not allowed to remain in the happy, challenging life of Bath Grammar School. A prefect's cane, intended for another boy's shoulder, unaccountably landed on Thomas' head, resulting in a three-week siege of leeches and in Mrs. De Quincey's deciding that Bath was not a fit place for her son. She sent him instead, in the fall of 1799, to join his younger brother Richard at a private school, Mr. Spencer's Academy at Winkfield, Wiltshire.

Spencer's proved unbearable. De Quincey complained, "I had no one to praise me, to spur me on, or to help me." [10] The need to be among one's peers and to be praised, a universal human drive, was especially strong in young Thomas De Quincey. Miserable, he fought to go back to Bath Grammar School. When it was suggested that he go to Eton, he vetoed the idea cleverly by writing his mother horror tales of the deplorable morals of the Etonians— boys were thrown into the Thames and porters beaten up. Thomas' real reason for disliking Eton came out incidentally: the prospective humiliation of his "situation as a Boy on the foundation." Late in 1800 Mrs. De Quincey and the guardians finally compromised on Manchester Grammar School, with a canny view to the exhibitions at Brasenose open to Manchester boys of three years' residence. Once again, unfortunately, Thomas found himself in an unappreciative atmosphere. Although De Quincey later made the worthy Headmaster Lawson seem dull and ridiculous, one suspects that much of the master's alleged incapacity lay in his failure to put a proper value on his new pupil. True, at the boy's entering examination Mr. Lawson paid him a compliment, but it was the "very last." [11] This neglect of impatient merit was the more intolerable by contrast with the experiences of the summer of 1800, which De Quincey had spent with his young friend Lord Westport at the family estate in Ireland. Westport's father, the Earl of Altamont, was interested by the bright young English lad, and paid him flattering attentions: Thomas pronounced him a "very sensible man." With Westport, Thomas had even met George III, and proudly informed him that the De Quinceys were no recent Huguenot refugees but had arrived at the time of the Conquest. From Ireland he had gone to Laxton to bask in Lady Carbery's approbation. What a descent was this to be back at Manchester Grammar School! He felt himself, and no doubt with reason, out of place. He had at grammar school the same reaction that Wordsworth had at college—"A feeling that I was not for that hour, / Nor for that place" (*Prelude*, III, 81–2).

Yet there was something more working on him. On the boat coming back from Ireland he had been slighted by a pretentious lady as a "humble friend" of Lord Westport. When Lady Carbery had ordered her husband's gamekeeper to give young Thomas instructions in the manly accomplishments of her circle, the inept pupil had come to the conclusion that his "destiny was not in that direction which could command the ordinary sympathies of this world." He did not belong in these aristocratic circles: his attainments were intellectual and imaginative. He was disappointed at even Lady Carbery's "constitutional inaptitude for poetry," [12] and shocked by her calling the Ancient Mariner "an old quiz." De Quincey's pride was for a time nourished by the coronets of Westport and Laxton, but he soon felt his native superiority. If he could not command the "ordinary sympathies" of the world, he believed that he could those "not in the roll of common men." Thus his imagination flew to Westmorland, to his chief of poets, his surrogate for the master he could not respect and the father he did not have.

Wordsworth had probably appeared above young De Quincey's horizon by 1799. There is considerable evidence that when the boy was only fourteen he had an experience of Wordsworth's poetry, which produced a delayed reaction about two years later. The earliest contemporary documents which attest to the boy's interest in the poet date from 1803: De Quincey's *Diary*, which he kept at Everton from March to June, 1803; and his first letter to Wordsworth, finally sent on May 31, 1803. These documents suggest, however, that the poet had long been a luminary:

the letter asserts "the hope of your friendship has sustained me through two years." Probably De Quincey had not reached the stage of desiring Wordsworth's friendship until he had had some acquaintance with his works. Years later, in the revised *Confessions,* he said: "In 1799 I had become acquainted with 'We Are Seven' at Bath. In the winter of 1801–2 I had read the whole of 'Ruth.' " [13]

De Quincey may have read Wordsworth at Bath in 1799 with particular attention, because he was probably about that time deciding upon poetry for his own vocation. Some time before 1803 at any rate, he had determined to be a poet—an ambition which undoubtedly had considerable influence on the roots of his relation with Wordsworth. This ambition probably took form at Bath, for it was at the Bath Grammar School that the master particularly admired Thomas' Latin verses. De Quincey thought it worth telling Woodhouse, some twenty years later, how he frequently used to see Morgan pointing him out with his cane to the boys of the upper class.[14] When he unwillingly transferred to Spencer's Academy, he continued his verse making, although the efforts we hear of now were in English. A schoolmate, Edward Grinfield, wrote De Quincey's daughter, just after her father's death in 1859, of De Quincey's contributions to a student paper called the *Observer:* "I can even now recall some lines he composed in answer to a challenge from a neighboring school:—

"Since Ames's skinny school has dared
To challenge Spencer's boys,
We thus to them bold answer give
To prove ourselves 'no toys.'

"Full thirty hardy boys we are,
As brave as e'er was known;
We will nor threats nor dangers mind
To make you change your tone!"

There is no telling how much longer this went on, for Thomas Grinfield, Edward's brother, reminded De Quincey in 1847, "Your own favorite stanza began—'Haply you chance to meet our little band so brave.' " [15] These lines hardly deserve enshrinement in the memory for fifty or sixty years, but they have a homely energy. They may well be a boy's idea of the ballad simplicity of some of the *Lyrical Ballads*. Certainly they display some of "the real language of men"—or, rather, boys. The meter is that of "The Rime of the Ancient Mariner," and the mock heroic tone with low language is similar to that of "The Idiot Boy."

Less Wordsworthian, but probably more influential in making De Quincey think of himself in the ranks of modern poets, was the next poem of his which has survived. This was a translation of Horace's Ode I.22, entered in a contest sponsored by the *Juvenile Library* in June, 1800:

> Fuscus! the man whose heart is pure,
>   Whose life unsullied by offence,
> Needs not the jav'lines of the Moor
>   In his defence.
>
> Should he o'er Libya's burning sands
>   Fainting pursue his breathless way,
> No bow he'd seek to arm his hands
>   Against dismay.
>
> Quivers of poisoned shafts he'd scorn,
>   Nor, though unarmed, would feel a dread
> To pass where Caucasus forlorn
>   Rears his huge head.
>
> In his own conscious worth secure,
>   Fearless he'd roam amidst his foes,
> Where fabulous Hydaspes pure
>   Romantic flows.
>
> For, late as in the Sabine wood
>   Singing my Lalage I strayed,—
> Unarmed I was,—a wolf there stood:
>   He fled afraid.

Larger than which one ne'er was seen
    In warlike Daunia's beechen groves,
Nor yet in Juba's land, where e'en
                    The lion roves.

Send me to dreary barren lands
    Where never summer zephyrs play,
Where never sun dissolves the bands
                    Of ice away:

Send me again to scorching realms
    Where not one cot affords a seat,
And where no shady pines or elms
                    Keep off the heat:

In every clime, in every isle,
    Me Lalage shall still rejoice;
I'll think of her enchanting smile,
                    And of her voice.

For a fifteen-year-old this was promising work—neat, controlled, imaginative: it compares favorably with the fifteen-year-old Wordsworth's lines in celebration of the bicentenary of Hawkshead School. Young Thomas won the third prize, which was in itself an unexpected distinction for Spencer's small academy. But there were those then, and have been since, who affirmed that his ode was as good as or better than that of Leigh Hunt, who won the first prize. As De Quincey put it, in the estimation of his friends he not only came to wear the laurel, "but also with the advantageous addition of having suffered some injustice." [16]

His *Diary* proves that the boy was meditating other poems at this time. Included in a "list of the works which I have, at some time or other, seriously intended to execute" was this item: *"A poetic and pathetic ballad* reciting the wanderings of two young children (brother and sister) and their falling asleep on a frosty-moonlight night among the lanes . . . and so perishing. (I projected this at Bath;— I think, a few weeks before my going to Ireland)." [17] In Ireland, as it happened, he found further encouragement for his muse. The Altamont party stopped at the Arch-

bishop of Tuam's palace, where occurred a pleasing event
which Thomas reported to his mother on August 20, 1800:
"Lord Altamont having read my Translation of the Ode
in Horace desired me to show it to the Company. The
Book, after a great deal of Search, could not be found: but,
as I could say it by heart, I wrote it out and Mr. Murray
read it. They then desired me to translate for them another
ode at Westport which I am going to do." The scene is
amusing. The Earl of Altamont, later to become the Marquis of Sligo, a "very fat Man, and so lame that he is
obliged to have 2 Servants to support him when ever he
stirs," giving the diminutive Thomas a chance to shine; the
vain searching for the book; De Quincey knowing the
verses by heart, of course, but refusing to recite them like
a schoolboy, rather writing them out so that they can be
appreciatively read by an adult; the delighted company
begging for more; and the modest author simply assenting
to their wish. What with the Westport routine of "Reading, Hunting, Riding, Shooting, bathing, and Sea excur-
sions," which Thomas wrote his sister Jane on September
3 "have taken up all my time," the promised second ode
probably never materialized. De Quincey had told his
mother, however, that he was "teaching Lord Westport
every day to make verses" in Latin (August 12, 1800).
The confidence of more poetic composition remained un-
shaken in De Quincey's mind, as we know fom Sligo's
letters after the boy had returned to England. On September 22 the Marquis wrote, "I shall receive your ode or
anything else from your pen with particular pleasure." The
"long-promised ode" was still anticipated on January 12
and May 5, 1801. Apparently De Quincey was not succeeding in writing poetry, but he was still expecting to. Twenty
years later he told Woodhouse that he was translating
some of Horace's Odes! [18]

In later years De Quincey played down his early poetic
ambitions. "I was inclined," he wrote in 1834, describing
the response to his prize ode, "even in those days, to doubt
whether my natural vocation lay towards poetry." By this
time, however, the record of his achievement must have

encouraged him, like Charles Lamb, to reckon himself "a
dab at prose" and leave verse to his "betters." In "those
days" he felt quite differently. He recorded in his *Diary*
on May 26, 1803: "I have besides always intended of
course that *poems* should form the corner-stones of my
fame." That "of course" is revealing. The *Diary* does not,
curiously in view of this easy assumption, contain any original verse: it is not a poet's notebook. It does, however,
contain a list of De Quincey's intended projects, including
three dramas marked "Poetic and pathetic," a *"poetic and
pathetic ballad,"* a *"pathetic poem,"* an *"ode,"* and an
"essay on poetry." [19] It also contains what were possibly
some of the materials for the essay on poetry, in the form
of interesting speculations on the difference between the
pathetic and the poetic, two types of nature poetry, and
the character of poetic composition. The last suggests
Wordsworth's "spontaneous overflow of powerful feeling," if it is more Bardic in its overtones:

Poetry has been properly enough termed inspiration: the connection is
natural; and the resemblance may be traced in more points than one.
A man of genius (whether addressing the imagination or the heart)
pours forth his unpremeditated torrents of sublimity—of beauty—of
pathos, he knows not—he cares not—how; he is rapt in a fit of enthusiasm or rather a temporary madness and is not sensible of the
workings of his mind any more than the ancient seer—"wrapt into
future times"—during the tide of prophetic frenzy—or a man in the
wild delirium of a fever—is conscious of the words he utters (*Diary,*
I, 169).

So young De Quincey wrote on "Saturday morning, May
14, 1803," the day after he started an abortive draft of his
first letter to Wordsworth.

To be sure, neither poetry nor Wordsworth dominates
the *Diary.* De Quincey was reading much light fare; he was
a returned runaway, rusticated in Everton (a village outside Liverpool), waiting for his guardians to decide what
to do with him after his London escapades. He went duti-
fully through Cowper's translation of the *Iliad,* and relaxed
with Sophia Lee, Ann Radcliffe, Mary Robinson, Jane

West, Monk Lewis, Clara Reeve, and Charlotte Smith. He even intended to write two "pathetic tales," but his serious interest seems to have been poetry. First on his list of "The sources of Happiness" was "Poetry." He meant, even then, the "new" and "natural" poetry he associated with Wordsworth. Although he was hospitably entertained in the Liverpool literary circle of Roscoe, Currie, and Shepherd, he made an ungracious return in his 1837 article called "Literary Novitiate" because "to me, who . . . already knew of a grand renovation of poetic power—of a new birth in poetry, interesting not so much to England as to the human mind—it was secretly amusing to contrast the little artificial usages of their petty traditional knack with the natural forms of a divine art." [20]

Of these renovating poets Southey is actually mentioned in the *Diary* more frequently than is Wordsworth. Although De Quincey does not speak of being then engaged in reading Wordsworth's poetry, he records that on May 25 he bought a second-hand volume of Southey's poems and that he even read them aloud to "the ladies" he visited, gaining a reputation as a "Southeian." Southey, Coleridge, and Wordsworth sometimes seem to have been on the same plane in his thinking: "My imagination flies, like Noah's dove, from the ark of my mind . . . and finds no place on which to rest the sole of her foot except Coleridge—Wordsworth and Southey." Once Coleridge seems to have received the supreme accolade: "I walk home thinking of *Coleridge;*—am in transports of love and admiration for him;—read a few pages of 'Recess'; go to bed . . . still thinking of Coleridge . . . I begin to think him the greatest man that has ever appeared and go to sleep." Still De Quincey affirms that "there is no good pastoral in the world but Wordsworth's 'Brothers,' " [21] and the *Diary* list of "Poets" shows exclamation points after no name except Wordsworth's; his has three! These voluble exclamation points suggest why it was to Wordsworth instead of to Southey and Coleridge that Thomas finally appealed. In this context his appeal must be understood not only as a proud, lonely boy's reaching for an ideal mentor-father, but also as a tentative effort of a

young would-be poet to associate himself with the poets of
his day whom he most admired. Probably one of the reasons
that De Quincey was so long in following up his overture,
even after Wordsworth's warm response, was that his poetic
hopes did not materialize and he could not appear in the role
he had cast for himself, just as he probably abandoned his
correspondence with the marquis because the "long-promised
ode" was never forthcoming.

Drafts in his *Diary* reveal how De Quincey labored over
that all-important first letter to Wordsworth.[22] He began
on May 13, in a routine fashion: "I take this method of
requesting," but immediately scratched that out as too
prosaic. Then he polished another opening sentence, sensi-
tively changing "What I am going to say would seem strange
to most men," to read "To most men what I am going to say
would seem strange." He went on to write out a full draft,
complete with signature and address. But he clearly considered too self-derogatory the section which admitted that
Wordsworth might find "more congenial" minds than his.
He struck a line through that passage, and at the end tried
another version: "What ["claim" struck out] pretensions
can I urge to be admitted to a fellowship with genius so
wild and magnificent as that which illumines your society?
I dare not say that—" Then, finding it difficult to say what
he dared not say, he broke off. Not until May 31 did he
write a letter which satisfied him.

This letter, too, was hardwrought. Not only does the
draft show much revision, but the *Diary* records: "Rise
about 9 o'clock;—write—copy—seal—take to office two
letters—one to Wordsworth—and a second to my mother;
finish these letters at 20 minutes before 4 by Miss B's
clock." [23] Since the letter to his mother was a note of six
lines dashed off with one correction, most of the day must
have gone to polishing Wordsworth's letter. The differences
between this letter and the abortive draft are interesting.
Not only is the acceptable version longer and more elabo-
rately laudatory; it is also in some ways more tactful. It is
amusing to see the boy work in a quotation from *Henry IV,
Part 1,* "in the roll of common men," to certify his literate-

ness and to complement the not-too-subtle flattery of the
later quotation from Wordsworth's own "Ruth": "Are
dearer than the sun" (p. 28). In the first version De Quincey had stressed his many futile efforts to reach Wordsworth. Perhaps the boy decided that these statements were
not literally true or that they seemed to emphasize his fail-
ures; his revision strikes a more positive note. The first
draft, as we have seen, was disturbingly frank about De
Quincey's unworthiness to join Wordsworth's society. Although the final form is still becomingly modest, there is a
definite hint that he believes himself to "have some spark of
that heavenly fire which blazes there" (p. 31). This is as
close as De Quincey then came to revealing his own poetic
ambitions to Wordsworth. He doubtless sensed that Wordsworth would hesitate to put himself in the position of possibly being urged to "revise and retouch." De Quincey also
softened the statement of the first version which might raise
a question about his personality: "friends I have none" (p.
29). What he meant is that he had "no connexion" (Letter
2) which might disturb Wordsworth's tranquillity.

The revised version, nevertheless, is in some ways not so
good a letter as the first draft: it shows more strain, more
exaggeration, more patent dramatization of the situation.
De Quincey added, with appropriate disclaimers as to the
value of his "feeble" applause, an assertion that his pleasure
from the *Lyrical Ballads* had infinitely exceeded the aggregate he had received "from some eight or nine other poets
that I have been able to find since the world began." He first
said "nine or ten other English poets"—after all, the *Diary*
lists twelve "Poets," all English, and, although he had by
this time gone back and struck off one name, he still had ten
English poets in addition to Wordsworth. But he would not
be thought to be so provincial or to restrict his acclaim. The
final draft also harps more persistently and insistently on
his desire for Wordsworth's "friendship"; the word appears
four times, along with "intimacy" and "fellowship." Although De Quincey originally wrote, in the draft of the
final version, of steps "for obtaining your notice and friendship," he decided to strike out the "and friendship." It is

revealing that when he made a fair copy of his letter he first wrote "obtaining your friendship" and then struck it out to conform to his draft. He also asserted that "hope" of Wordsworth's "friendship" had sustained him and been the subject of "morning and . . . evening orisons," and went on to declare that he would "sacrifice even his life" to promote Wordsworth's "interest and happiness."

Certainly the curtain to this personal drama went up with a flourish. What did Wordsworth make of this theatrical letter? He could not know that behind it lay the influences of an absentee father, an unsympathetic mother, a dull master, a tiger-drenching apothecary, delaying money-lenders, and helpful prostitutes. Wordsworth probably dismissed the "lethargy of despair," the "painful circumstances" and "bitter recollections," as part of the Gothic dressing of the letter. He must, however, have seen that this was no ordinary boy. Indeed, if he read carefully—as he seems not always to have done with De Quincey's letters—he must have sensed the fierce pride of the grand conclusion: "And I will add that, to no man on earth except yourself and *one* other (a friend of your's [certainly Coleridge]), would I thus lowly and suppliantly prostrate myself." This is reverence, but in truth the worship of the acolyte proud of his humility. De Quincey recalled in 1838 that "Miss Wordsworth in after years assured" him they believed the letter "to be the production of some person much older" than he represented himself.[24]

Whatever Wordsworth thought, he wrote a good answer, a very good answer indeed—kind and wise. Although just turned thirty-three, he was nearly twice De Quincey's age and could be paternal. Although a poet ten years before the public, he had not achieved such reputation as to scorn even the most modest admirer. The copyright of the 1798 *Lyrical Ballads* had actually been given back to him because when its publisher, Joseph Cottle, sold out, it was declared worthless. And now that the "Preface" to the 1800 edition had announced what Francis Jeffrey of the *Edinburgh Review* considered a pernicious "system," he had most of the critics snorting at him. Of course the 1802 edition had been called for, and he had his appreciative circle—Coleridge, Lamb, Basil Montagu, Francis Wrangham, Sir George Beaumont— and just the year before young John Wilson (the larval "Christopher North") had sent him such an admiring letter as De Quincey's.[25]

Wordsworth's reply was thoughtful and mindful of his responsibility. Because the publisher Longman, through whom De Quincey had sent his letter, had delayed forwarding it, the poet did not get the May 31 letter until July 27. He showed a sympathetic appreciation of the boy's anxiety by answering within two days. He was, he said frankly, pleased and "kindly disposed" toward De Quincey, but he gently added, "My friendship it is not in my power to give." He remonstrated against De Quincey's depreciation of "the great names of past times," prepared the boy for not expecting too much by humorously describing himself as "the most lazy and impatient Letter-writer in the world," told him of a projected trip into Scotland, and ended with an invitation for him to visit Grasmere. Then, thinking the invitation sounded perfunctory, he added a long postscript emphasizing that he would be "very happy" to see the boy. The poet had married Mary Hutchinson the previous October and had brought his wife to Dove Cottage, in Grasmere, where he and his sister Dorothy had lived since 1799. Now he had a month-old son, John (born prematurely on June 18), and was established frugally but happily in his first real, domestic home. Tasting the joys of hospitality and patronage, he was in an effusive mood as he urged his young admirer to come. Coleridge fumed the same October that Wordsworth was "living wholly among *Devotees*—having every the minutest Thing, almost his very Eating & Drinking, done for him by his Sister, or Wife." [26] Perhaps it seemed to Wordsworth natural enough to welcome another "devotee" in young De Quincey. Not even so sensitive a lad could have wished for more. Here was the praise, the spur, the help he had been missing since Bath Grammar School; the tutorial tone was probably just what he wanted.

At any rate, the correspondence was fairly launched. It bumped along irregularly for four years before the parties

met in November, 1807. In that time De Quincey wrote at
least seven letters, of which five and part of the sixth are
known to have survived. Wordsworth also certainly wrote
seven, three or four of them hardly more than notes, and
probably at least one more; and Dorothy Wordsworth
wrote one letter which has been lost. The second letters on
each side are among the most interesting. Having despaired
of a reply to his first letter, De Quincey was so overwhelmed
by Wordsworth's kindness when the answer came—he said
later that it kept him awake all night "from mere excess of
pleasure" [27]—that he outdid himself in return. His second
letter, of August 6, 1803 (pp. 32–35), is if anything more
hyperbolical than the first. He grows lyrical over "the unspeakable pleasure" he has derived from "those wonderful
poems"—none others have given him "such permanent and
increasing delight," and "from the wreck of all earthly
things" belonging to him he would "endeavor to save that
work by an impulse second to none but that of self-preservation." Certainly he will visit Grasmere: "the bowers of
paradise could hold out no such allurement." At this distance
the adulation seems more than a little ridiculous.

It did not seem so to Wordsworth; obviously he liked it.
His next reply was long delayed, not being written until
March 6, 1804; but when it came it displayed a warmth and
familiarity surprising in a letter to a stranger, and a mere
boy at that. After profuse apologies for his procrastination,
he praised the boy's stilted letter: "Your last Letter gave
me great pleasure; it was indeed a very amiable one; and I
was highly gratified in the thought of being so endeared to
you by the mere effect of my writings." [28] Wordsworth had
struck this note in his first letter, remarking on his satisfaction that his poems had given a favorable impression of
his "character as a man." Possibly one reason for his warm
response to De Quincey's letters was that, although he attached no importance to the boy's critical judgment, he was
pleased at the personal appeal to himself, the man speaking
to men. Possibly another reason was that the poet who
"wanted to be considered as a teacher, or as nothing" responded to the opportunity of having so perceptive a pupil.

He became homiletic, and naturally denied it: "I do not mean to preach: I speak in simplicity and tender apprehension, as one lover of Nature and of Virtue speaking to another." His didactic impulse had been brought out by the news that De Quincey was going to Oxford. He urged upon the undergraduate "virtue and temperance, and, let me add chastity." Although he took no notice of De Quincey's hint about "some slight metrical trifles," he discussed his own work almost as if with a fellow poet, talking of "the poem on my own earlier life," which it would give him "great pleasure to read" to De Quincey, and a "larger and more important work," a "moral and philosophical Poem." [29] He complained of the plagiarism and parody of one Peter Bayley in a style curiously prophetic of his later request to De Quincey to defend him against Jeffrey and his ilk. Wordsworth even signed himself "your very affectionate Friend." That friendship which he had sagely said was the "growth of time and circumstance" had come in two letters!

This remarkable letter had been so long delayed that De Quincey had written again on March 14, before it arrived. His letter is apparently lost; but what is certainly a copy of most of it survives in a curious and significant fashion: it was transcribed by Dorothy into William's "Commonplace Book." [30] Why should a letter from an unknown undergraduate be thought worthy of being recorded along with passages from the poet's reading? The answer is amusingly traceable to De Quincey's incorrigible procrastination. He was fearful as to what construction had been put on his seven-month silence; for, although he may have been half-hopefully waiting for the overdue answer to his last letter, he had earlier magnanimously declared that he was grateful just to be heard without presuming to expect replies. His explanation of this letterless interval led him to superlatives about the Wordsworth circle which, in typical De Quincey fashion, he then felt he must also explain. It was certainly this second explanation, dealing with the absorbing matter of how he had become so strongly attracted to Wordsworth, which prompted Dorothy to take the trouble to copy the letter. Indeed, almost as soon as that subject was finished

she broke off in the middle of a sentence, without bothering
to complete the letter or even to indicate its author. The
passage echoes, in what must have been to the Wordsworths
a surprising way, one of the themes of that autobiographical
poem on which William was then at work, later called *The
Prelude:* the ethical influence of nature. It also records what
Dorothy was later to call De Quincey himself, "a remarkable instance of the power of my brother's poem." [31] De
Quincey had, he said, been dazzled by feverish aspirations
to personal renown, until amidst "surrounding nature" he
"felt her mild reproach"; then, looking round "for some
guide who might assist to develope & to tutor my new feelings," he remembered having heard "We are Seven," and
turned to Wordsworth's poetry, by which he had been "delivered," "purified & uplifted" (p. 37). This could not
but be welcome testimony to a man who was writing of a
not-too-dissimilar experience, and to a poet who hoped his
not-yet-appreciated verses might have just such an effect.
Wordsworth got off a hasty note within "a day or two" of
reading this letter, obviously agitated that his own rich
epistle of March 6 had not been received, and urging De
Quincey to track it down, even to the Dead Letter Office.
Understandably this note carries a tone of real gratitude:
"I cannot express to you how much pleasure it gave me to
learn that my Poems had been of such eminent service. . . .
Such facts as you have communicated to me are an abundant
recompense for all the labour and pains which the profession
of Poetry requires." [32] It is equally comprehensible that the
poet should exclaim cautioningly—and presciently: "May
God grant that you may persevere in all good habits, desires,
and resolutions."

    None of Wordsworth's other surviving letters to De
Quincey matches the intimacy and heartiness of that March
6 letter, although the poet ought to have been even better
pleased by the answer which came to him from the Oxford
undergraduate on March 31. Sure of his ground—he now
signed himself "your grateful and affectionate friend"—De
Quincey struck a somewhat more authoritative note, but the
way in which he said the right thing is almost uncanny.

Probably knowing nothing of Wordsworth's own experiences at Cambridge except the little the poet had told him, he pronounced what might almost have been an echo of Wordsworth's sentiments: Oxford was "singularly barren" of "either virtue or talents or knowledge" and he was resolved "to pass no more . . . time there than is necessary." He could hardly have done better than to say, "the poem on your own life is the one which I should most anxiously wish to see finished," or to pity the "delusions" and "disordered taste" of the captious critics and parodists (pp. 39–41). Wordsworth's interest in De Quincey heretofore must have owed much to the poet's gratification at evidence of the influence of his work and the validity of his ideas; now his interest must have taken on more intellectual respect for the boy himself—unless he bridled a bit at the independence of his young admirer. The poet evidently answered this letter, for when De Quincey next renews the correspondence he sounds as if the interruption was all his fault; it would be interesting to know what Wordsworth said.

We have, however, no more letters of Wordsworth's until May 5, 1806—a brief note in answer to a very strange letter written on April 6, which must have given the poet cause to wonder what manner of young man he was dealing with, and probably led Wordsworth, consciously or unconsciously, to consider a retreat to those walls of reserve which were ever ready to him. De Quincey was again in Everton and planning a tour of the Lakes, but wanted reassurance that he would still be welcome at Grasmere after his "long silence." Since he spoke of "the last two years" of his life as a blank, he may not have written since March 31, 1804. What De Quincey told Wordsworth was that he had been ill and disturbed over the running-away to sea of his younger brother Richard, whose loss reinforced his feelings of desertion and loneliness. At last he had let Wordsworth see clearly into his proud isolation. What he did not tell Wordsworth was that on a rainy Sunday afternoon in the autumn of 1804 he had received from the beatific druggist his first dose of laudanum, to relieve neuralgia, and had become so entranced by the "celestial pleasures" that he began passing deliberate "opium evenings" in London at intervals of three weeks or so.[33] That part of him which was a dreaming thing gloried in the opiate. There he found also in new colors the exclusiveness which his pride had made a habit of mind. Opium-eating was both a product and, ultimately, a flaunt of his independence. But now it was still secret.

He did not tell Wordsworth either that he had gone into the Lake Country to visit the poet, and faintheartedly turned back. He may have made such an effort, nevertheless. In 1839 he wrote: "twice I came so far as the little rustic inn . . . at Church Coniston; . . . once I absolutely went forwards from Coniston to the very gorge of Hammerscar, from which the whole Vale of Grasmere suddenly breaks upon the view." [34] He could even see the gleaming white dot of Dove Cottage! "This," he said, "was in 1806." It is not clear whether he means both or one of the visits was in 1806, and it is hard to know where to fit them in. Conceivably in the spring of 1806 De Quincey went up to Coniston, became too diffident to go farther, retired to Everton to write the April 6 letter asking for reassurance, was disappointed to learn from a letter of Dorothy's [35] that William was in London, and then was delayed by the daily expectation of news from his brother Richard (as he says in his letter of June 9), so that his visit had to be deferred. Apparently, however, even after Wordsworth's assurance in May that he was most welcome, he still could not then bring himself any closer to the presence than Coniston.

For there is an interesting document labeled "Constituents of Happiness" and dated "Coniston, Monday Morning, August 18, 1806," with additions dated inconsistently "Everton, Saturday Morning, August 22, 1806." [36] Several of these "constituents" are curiously Wordsworthian and seem to reflect De Quincey's current Grasmere orientation. The very first is "a capacity of thinking—i.e. of abstraction and reverie." Next comes "cultivation of an interest in all that concerns human life and human nature"; years later De Quincey was to write that "the great distinction" of Wordsworth's poetry was "his sympathy with what is *really* permanent in human feelings." The third constituent, "a fixed and not merely temporary, residence in some spot of eminent beauty" obviously shows the influence of the Lake Country. His reasoning about his "infant attachment" to a place "from associating with its scenery the pleasure derived from thinking, or reading, or other pleasures" is quite like Wordsworth's discussion in *The Prelude* of his youthful associations, and suggests that De Quincey had looked into Associationism.[37] Also Wordsworthian are "interchange of solitude and interesting society," "some great intellectual project," and "the education of a child"—the last of which curiously De Quincey was to undertake with one of Wordsworth's children, young Catharine. More characteristically De Quinceyan are items number five, "<u>Books</u>" (the only one underscored), and twelve, "a personal appearance tolerably respectable." This last is given much more space than any other on the original list, and seems to have been a sore spot with De Quincey. He concludes that where "moderate advantages" are lacking, they may be compensated for by "temperate and unostentatious dignity" and by "acquiring a high literary name."

There was the rub. De Quincey was quite small. Dorothy Wordsworth described him as "very diminutive in person, which, to strangers, makes him appear insignificant." To Carlyle he was "a pretty little creature," of whom Jane Welsh said "What wouldn't one give to have him in a box, and take him out to talk!" Southey called him "Little Mr. De Quincey," and wrote: "I wish he were not so little." [38] De Quincey's consciousness of such reactions to his appearance undoubtedly helped to cause him to hesitate at Coniston, especially since he had not yet acquired a "high literary name," or even done anything to justify his secret claims in that direction. The reason De Quincey gave in his 1839 article for not going on to Dove Cottage was "mere excess of nervous distrust in my own powers for sustaining a conversation with Wordsworth," because when he was young he had a great talent *"pour le silence."* [39] His *Diary,* however, shows him fairly outspoken in Everton society. The real nature of his distrust appears in a passage which he left out when he revised the essay:

. . . no doubt my conduct was very absurd; and I began to think so myself. . . . Still I witnessed a case where a kind of idol had, after all, rejected an idolator that did not offer a splendid triumph to his pride; . . . And, although I thought better of Mr. Wordsworth's moral nature than to suppose it possible for him to err in this extent . . . yet I could not reconcile myself to the place of an humble admirer, valued, perhaps, for the right direction of his feelings, but practically neglected in behalf of some more gifted companion, who might have the power (which much I feared that I should never have) of talking to him on something like equal terms, as respected the laws and principles of poetry (*Lit. Rem.,* I, 265–266).

He did not want to be an "humble admirer"—he wanted to discuss poetry with Wordsworth on "something like equal terms"! The proud undergraduate's premonitions at Coniston were accurate. Of William Wordsworth no doubt this was expecting too much.

Although it was another year before De Quincey got to Grasmere and finally saw Wordsworth face to face, the remaining correspondence before their meeting is brief and hasty. It has the air on both sides of impatience. Wordsworth wrote notes: on May 5, 1806, asking De Quincey to defer his trip: "I cannot bear the thought that you should be in the North and I not see you"; on June 3, "we have been disappointed in not seeing you"; on April 25, 1807, in answer to a letter now apparently lost, "I shall be most happy to see you"; on April 28, announcing his departure from London, "I am very happy at the prospect of seeing you, for believe me I have been much interested in you." [40] We can well believe that after so much preamble Wordsworth was anxious to meet De Quincey, from curiosity if nothing else.

What finally removed the psychological obstacles in the road to Grasmere was De Quincey's successful approach to the other author of the *Lyrical Ballads.* "Late in 1804 or early in 1805" De Quincey obtained a letter of introduction to Charles Lamb "with a view to some further knowledge of Coleridge," [41] who was then in Malta. This maneuver was unsuccessful. Lamb welcomed De Quincey cordially, but was so amused at his worshipful attitude toward Coleridge that he could not resist teasing him by mocking the *Ancient Mar-iner*. De Quincey put his hands to his ears at the sacrilege and went away not liking Lamb. The sensitive little man did not care to be made fun of. Contemplating the direct approach, De Quincey then "began to inquire about the best route to Malta." One wonders whether he would have arrived in the harbor and not have been able to get off the ship—not waiting, as did Lord Byron, for a salute from the guns of the fort, but restrained by that overactive "organ of veneration" of his. It was, however, not to be put to the trial. Coleridge returned from Malta, and on July 26, 1807, De Quincey was given a curious passport to him: a letter from Joseph Cottle, first publisher of the *Lyrical Ballads,* to Thomas Poole, who was a Nether Stowey neighbor and friend of Coleridge. The letter began: "The bearer, Mr. De Quincey, a Gentleman of Oxford, a Scholar and a man of Genius, feels a high admiration for Coleridge's character, and understanding that he was either with you or in the neighbourhood, Mr. De Quincey felt disposed to pay him a passing visit." [42] Under the protective insouciance of a "passing visit" and the comforting colors of a "man of Genius" (one wonders what persuaded Cottle in 1807 to such an appellation) De Quincey was emboldened to advance. Coleridge proved not to be with Poole; but once on the track, De Quincey followed it to Bridgewater, where he found Coleridge standing under a gateway "in a deep reverie." [43] De Quincey "made two or three trifling arrangements at an inn-door"—a delicious give-away as to the "best-foot-forward" character of the approach—and bearded the metaphysician in his reverie. He was graciously received, invited to dinner, and frigidly introduced to Mrs. Coleridge.

De Quincey's admiration of Coleridge may have seemed to Lamb ridiculous, but it soon proved to have real substance in it. De Quincey made himself useful at once. He played with the Coleridge children, taking Hartley "at the risk of our respective necks—through every dell and tangled path of Leighwood." More significantly, through Cottle he anonymously presented Coleridge with £300, hoping—in vain—that it "might have the effect of liberating his mind from anxiety for a year or two." This service was, as De Quincey admitted to his mother years later, for one of his modest means an immoral act.[44] But it must have been a very satisfying act for the young man. His fourth letter to Wordsworth had contained an offer to go to Bath to make arrangements for Coleridge if he wished to try the waters, alleging that the distance from Oxford to Bath was "so trifling"— which sixty-odd miles was not in those days. His constant desire to be of service is a little pathetic, revealing as it does his wish to become in some way important to his idols.

It was this desire that finally got him to Grasmere. Mrs. Coleridge, with three small children, was about to set out for Keswick, and De Quincey offered his services as escort. Sara was happy to have "the great convenience of travelling all the way in Chaises, and under the protecting wing of kind Mr. de Q.—." [45] Apparently De Quincey's purse as well as his protection was offered. Thus he approached Grasmere, not as a runaway schoolboy or a petitioning undergraduate, but as the friend to whom Coleridge had entrusted his family. He did not then know that Coleridge and his wife were virtually separated; Dorothy highlights the subsequent wry comedy at Dove Cottage, describing Mrs. Coleridge's anxious pretense: "When we were alone together she entreated us to say nothing to Mr. De Q. that should make him suspect anything amiss." [46] What De Quincey did not know did not hurt him; on November 4, 1807, he came running down the hill from White Moss Common with the Coleridge boys, and was suddenly upon the shrine which had been so unapproachable. The experience he later described almost as a mystic revelation: "I heard a step, a voice, and, like a flash of lightning, I saw the figure emerge of a tallish man, who held out his hand, and saluted me with most cordial expressions of welcome." That memorable night, said De Quincey,

was marked by a change even in the physical condition of my nervous system. Long disappointment—hope forever baffled (and why should it be less painful because *self*-baffled?)—vexation and self-blame, almost self-contempt, at my own want of courage to face the man whom of all since the Flood I most yearned to behold:—these feelings had impressed upon my nervous sensibilities a character of irritation—agitation—restlessness—eternal self-dissatisfaction—which . . . in one hour, all passed away.[47]

At long last he had met Wordsworth. The first chapter of their relationship was over.

LETTERS, 1803–1806

1. *To William Wordsworth*

Ms. photostat. Pub. Diary, pp. 167–168. Draft not sent; for final version see next letter.

Everton, May 13. [1803]

Sir,

—To most men what I am going to say would seem strange; and to most men therefore I would *not* say it; but to you I will, because your feelings do not follow the current of the world.

From the time when I first saw the "Lyrical Ballads" I made a resolution to obtain (if I could) the friendship of their author. In taking this resolution I was influenced (I believe) by my reverence for the astonishing genius displayed in those delightful poems, and, in an inferior degree, for the dignity of moral character which I persuaded myself their author possessed. Since then I have sought every opportunity—and revolved many a scheme of gaining an introduction into your society. But all have failed; and I am compelled either to take this method of soliciting your friendship (which, I am afraid, you will think a liberty), or of giving up almost every chance for obtaining that without which what good can my life do me? Now have I decided on this alternative, you see, Sir. Indeed on such a point it could not cost me much trouble to decide; for I have accustomed myself so long to look forward to the accomplishment of this wish, that it appears to me almost half accomplished already: this wish has, under every circumstance, been the ruling one in my heart: my dull and vacant hours it has served to animate; and from many painful circumstances—many gnawing anxieties—and many many bitter recollections—it has been my only solace. Your image is so linked to all the goodly scenes of nature that I never view the one without thinking of the other; and not only yourself—but every place and circumstance and character sung by you—and each dear soul in that enchanting community of yours—to me

"Are dearer than the sun." [1]

Letter 1:
[1] Wordsworth's "Ruth," l. 90.

Between the certainty of losing what I looked for so ardently—and the uncertainty of offending you by a liberty which will perhaps be its own excuse, what contest could there be? And hence it is that I take so strange a step. But to you, who are not "in the common roll of men,' it may not appear so.

As to all externals, I believe there are none which would [or] could make you scruple to grant me some share of your acquaintance. And do not think, Sir, that I shall ever attempt to interrupt your hallowed solitude by making interest for any friend: for friends I have none: I am yet but a boy, and have formed no connexions which can tie me to this busy world; so that, by suffering me to share in your society, you will have gone not one step farther from the sweet retreats of poetry to the detested haunts of men. But, alas! what allurements can my friendship, unknown and unhonoured as I am, hold out to you? [*Everything from here through the address has a line through it.*] This only thing can I say—that, though you may find minds more congenial with your own—and therefore more worthy of your regard than mine, you will never find one more zealously attached to you—more willing to sacrifice every low consideration of this earth to your happiness—one filled with more admiration of your genius and of reverential love for your virtues than the author of this letter. And I will add that to no man upon earth except yourself and one other (a friend of your's)—would my pride suffer me thus lowly to prostrate myself.

I am, Sir,

Your's for ever and ever,

Mrs. Best's, Everton, near Liverpool   Thomas de Quincey.

[*Address:*] William Wordsworth, Esqr. / To the care of Mr. N. Longman, / Paternoster-Row, / London.

What pretensions can I urge to be admitted to a fellowship with genius so wild and magnificent as that which illumines your society? I dare not say that [*breaks off*]

2. *To William Wordsworth*

Ms. Dove Cottage. Pub. ELH, III, 16–18. Diary, pp. 185–188, pub. rough draft from which this letter was carefully copied.

[Everton]
May 31, 1803.

Sir,

I suppose that most men would think what I am going to say—
strange at least or rude: but I am bold enough to imagine that, as you
are not yourself "in the roll of common men," [1] you may be willing
to excuse anything uncommon in the liberty I am now taking.

My object in troubling you, Sir, is that hereafter I may have the
satisfaction of recollecting that I made one effort at least for obtaining your [friendship *scratched out*] notice—and that I did not,
through any want of exertion on my own part, miss that without
which what good can my life do me? I have no other motive for
soliciting your friendship than what (I should think) every man,
who has read and felt the "Lyrical Ballads," must have in common
with me. There is no need that I should express my admiration and
love for those delightful poems; nor is it possible that I should do
so. Besides, I am persuaded that the dignity of your moral character
sets you as far above the littleness of any vanity which could be soothed
by applause feeble and insignificant as mine—as the transcendency
of your genius makes all applause fall beneath it. But I may say in
general, without the smallest exaggeration, that the whole aggregate
of pleasure I have received from some eight or nine other poets that
I have been able to find since the world began—falls infinitely short
of what those two enchanting volumes have singly afforded me;—
that your name is with me for ever linked to the lovely scenes of
nature;—and that not yourself only but that each place and object
you have mentioned—and all the souls in that delightful community
of your's—to me

"Are dearer than the sun!"

With such opinions, it is not surprising that I should so earnestly and
humbly sue for your friendship;—it is not surprising that the hope of
that friendship should have sustained me through two years of a life
passed partially in the world—and therefore not passed in happiness;
—that I should have breathed forth my morning and my evening
orisons for the accomplishment of that hope;—that I should now consider it as the only object worthy of my nature or capable of rewarding

Letter 2:
[1] *Henry IV, Part I*, III, i, 42.

my pains. Sometimes indeed, in the sad and dreary vacuity of worldly intercourse, this hope will touch those chords that have power to rouse me from the lethargy of despair; and sometimes, from many painful circumstances—many many bitter recollections, it is my only refuge.

But my reasons for seeking your regard—it would be endless to recount and (I am afraid) useless; for I do not forget that the motives to any intimacy must be mutual: and, alas! to me, unknown and unhonored as I am, why should anyone—the meanest of God's creatures —extend his friendship?—What claim then can I urge to a fellowship with a society such as your's—beaming (as it does) with genius so wild and so magnificent? I dare not say that I too have some spark of that heavenly fire which blazes there; for, if I have, it has not yet kindled and shone out in any exertion which only could entitle me to your notice. But, though I can shew no positive pretensions to a gift so high, I may yet advance some few negative reasons why you may suffer me, if but at a distance, to buoy myself up with the idea that I am not wholly disregarded in your sight—when I say that my life has been passed chiefly in the contemplation and altogether in the worship of nature—that I am but a boy and have therefore formed no connection which could draw you one step farther from the sweet retreats of poetry to the detested haunts of men—that no one should ever dare, in confidence of any acquaintance he might have with me, to intrude on your hallowed solitude—and lastly that you would at any rate have an opportunity of offering to God the pleasant and grateful incense of a good deed—by blessing the existence of a fellowcreature. As to all external points, I believe that there is nothing in them which would disgrace you.

I cannot say anything more than that, though you may find many minds more congenial with your own—and therefore proportionately more worthy of your regard, you will never find any one more zealously attached to you—more full of admiration for your mental excellence and of reverential love for your moral character—more ready (I speak from my heart!) to sacrifice even his life—whenever it could have a chance of promoting your interest and happiness—than he who now bends the knee before you. And I will add that, to no man on earth except yourself and *one* other (a friend of your's), would I thus lowly and suppliantly prostrate myself.

Dear Sir!
Your's for ever,
Thomas de Quincey.

Mrs. Best's, Everton, near Liverpool.

[*Address:*] William Wordsworth, Esq. / To the Care of Messrs. N. Longman
         and O. Rees, / Paternoster Row, / London. /
[*Stamp:*]   Liverpool

3. *To William Wordsworth*

Ms. Dove Cottage. Pub. ELH, *III, 18–21.*

                                                    Chester, August 6, 1803.
Dear Sir,
     This is the first morning I have been completely at leisure since I
received your letter, or it should not have remained unanswered until
now. It is impossible to express how much I was delighted and surprised with it. To obtain that, which one has so long and so ardently
wished, at the very moment when one has ceased to expect it—is a
happiness which falls to the lot of few men. Many days before your
letter arrived, I had given up almost every hope of having succeeded in
my object;—one stay of hope still remained; and that, it appears, was
well-founded. But thoughts were continually rising to shake this; for I
had doubted, before I wrote, whether I was not likely to offend you
by obtruding myself on your notice; and afterwards I recollected that,
from having written during a fit of languor and despondency, I had
expressed myself in a tone of egotism which (I was afraid) might be
disgusting. I had thus ceased to expect an answer; and yet I am sure
that I felt no anger but only sorrow at being (as I then thought)
neglected: I had spent many hours in devising other plans for com-
passing my point—and had at length determined to send you some
slight metrical trifles;—I thought of such a scheme however only
when I despaired of succeeding by any other. At last, on Tuesday
evening—when I hoped no longer (for it was the last evening of my
stay at Everton), all my fears and schemes were put to flight by your
kindness: I am utterly unable to express my deep sense of it; but I
assure you, Sir, that, if you knew what great and lasting pleasure you
have afforded me—how you have made me rise in my own estimation,
you would think your purpose (or what I suppose to be a great part of
your purpose) in writing to me—fully answered; for I know how

much more of that favor I should attribute to your goodness than to any merit of my own.

When you say that you are *kindly disposed* towards me, you say a great deal more than I dared to expect. What foolish thing I said of friendship, I cannot now recollect: but, if (as I gather from your remarks on it) I asked for *your* friendship, I must have written without consulting my understanding;—to think only that my name should meet your eyes—was sufficient to animate me; and the marks of kindness you have already shewn me—are far above what, in my most sanguine moments, I looked for.

On the subject of poetry above all others, he must be a bold man that should venture to combat one opinion of your's; and certainly I am the last person in the world to think myself capable of maintaining even the shadow of an argument against what you have said on that point. I am not attempting therefore to justify—but only to explain myself in what I reply to that part of your letter where you express your concern at 'The very unreasonable value I set upon your writings compared with those of others.' Nothing, I am sure, was farther from my intention than to breathe a syllable of disrespect against our elder poets;—from my youth up I have revered them: Spenser—Shakespeare —Milton—Thomson (partially)—and Collins were the companions of my childhood: I well remember that it was Milton who first waked me to a sense of poetry, and I think there are only two names which I honor above his: but it would be mere hypocrisy in me to say that even his works are so 'twisted with my heart-strings' as the *Lyrical Ballads.* I could be more diffuse on this subject; only that I know it would weary you and betray my ignorance in the philosophy of the mind if I should attempt to explain what I suppose to be the sources of the unspeakable pleasure which I derive from those wonderful poems. But, —even though abstractly I *did* think it possible for the imagination of man to run forth in more delightful wanderings—or the heart in wilder passion—even though I should reason myself into a belief that anything, which the world has yet seen, can so well claim the title of pure poetry,—yet my feelings would contradict the cold deductions of my understanding: for I have felt more than once that I can hear other poems talked of by worldly men without such exquisite torture;—I am daily made sensible that I rest on no other poems with such permanent and increasing delight;—I feel that, from the wreck of all earthly things which belong to me, I should endeavour to save that work by an impulse second to none but that of self-preservation.

I must repeat that I say all this not with so foolish and vain a purpose as that of justifying myself against your opinion—but merely with a view to shew that I was not betrayed, by any sudden warmth of gratitude for the pleasure I had received, into an exaggerated estimate of it—but that it was the result of my feelings—and that those feelings still continue in full force: but I am not so arrogant as to suppose that no revolution will take place in my sentiments—and that I shall never raise any other poems nearer to the level of the *Lyrical Ballads:* on the contrary, I believe that, to some degree, such a revolution will happen—because you tell me so; and I see that you say it from such profound observations of the progress of the mind in this point—as it would be folly in me to question.

To that part of your letter, in which you invite me to see you when I visit Grasmere, I scarcely know how to reply: it did indeed fill up the measure of my joy; because, though your kindness alone might have induced you to humor me by answering my letter, nothing less than your really thinking me in some measure worthy of your notice—could (I think) have made you run the risk of being pestered with an hour of my company. Henceforward I shall look to that country as to the land of promise: I cannot say how many emotions the land of lakes raises in my mind—of itself: I have always felt a strange love for everything connected with it; and the magic of The *Lyrical Ballads* has completed and established the charm. But,—when, to these inducements for visiting it, is added the hope of seeing those whom no danger (but that of being an unwelcome visitor) could have withheld me from seeking out, —I believe that the bowers of paradise could hold out no such allurement. Unfortunately however I am not yet my own master; and (in compliance with the wishes of my Mother and my guardians) I am going, in a month or two, to enter myself at Oxford. I had myself an intention of making a tour in the Highlands this autumn; but now, just at the time when I find that I should have a chance of meeting you there, my plans (I fear) will be traversed. 'Many a northern look' however I shall cast to the country of your wanderings; and (in the mean time) I shall be cheered with the hope that, when summer returns —and I bend my course to the lakes, I shall have the happiness of seeing those persons whom above all the world I honor—and amidst those scenes too which, delightful as they are in themselves, are much more so on their account.

> I remain, dear Sir,
> With the deepest veneration, ever your's,
> Thomas de Quincey.

St. John's Priory.

P.S. Your aversion to letter-writing, at the same time that it enhances the value of a letter from you, forces me to beg that you will not give yourself the trouble of writing at all oftener than you feel disposed— in answer to those which I shall send you as long as you give me leave and as often as I think it will not be disagreeable to you. Be assured too that I shall never feel slighted by the shortness of your letters;—I shall think myself abundantly honored by a single line: indeed, Sir, I am not worthy of such another letter as your first. In saying this, I am plead- ing violently against my own interest and wishes; for certainly no present can be so acceptable to me as a letter from you: but I cannot bear that you should put yourself to any inconvenience on my account —or that you should imagine I can think you capable of any unkind- ness to me. [*Across folded back, inverted:*] You mention Miss Words- worth (I speak at a venture) and Mr. Coleridge; and this emboldens me to use the privilege of a friend and take a liberty which I should not otherwise have done—when I beg you to convey my most sincere and respectful good wishes to them both.

[*Address:*] William Wordsworth, Esqr. / Grasmere, / Near Kendal, / *West-moreland.* /
[*Stamp:*]   Chester / [?] AUG 1803

4. *To William Wordsworth*

Ms. copy by Dorothy Wordsworth. Dove Cottage. Unpub. Qtd. by Mary Moorman in "Wordsworth's Commonplace Book," N & Q, Sept., 1957, pp. 400–405.

> village of Littlemore—near Oxford—March 14 [1804]

Dear Sir,

After a long interval I write to you again with more pleasure than ever—mix'd, however, with a little anxiety as to the construction you will have put upon my long silence. As you gave me your permission to write you must have wondered, (whenever you remembered me) that I made so little use of it; but when you hear my reason[s] for abstaining from writing to everybody whom I value (except upon business) you will see how strongly they must have influenced me with respect to yourself. In the latter part of last year I came up to College; and there, when I found myself unable to abstract my thoughts entirely from all those little, & till then unknown cares which fastened themselves upon me (& I suppose upon every man of small fortune, with any independence of mind at this first entrance) I determined rather to defer writing to those whom I loved and honoured untill I could [?] my mind in some retirement than to abate any thing of that delightful awe with which I had been accustomed to approach them by mixing their images with the debasing ideas of those painful employments which then engrossed my time. Now therefore (having kept the short term) I have retired to this little village, & having endeavoured with some success to marshal my thoughts afresh, I bring the first fruits of returning moral health to that circle of human beings in whom half my love, & all my admiration are centred.

These last words I am tempted to alter because I am afraid that you should not think them perfectly sincere. I know that some other expressions of admiration which I have used before, would to many appear rather out of proportion to any created excellence whether moral or intellectual. But I should be very sorry if I thought you viewed them in that light,—both because I am sure it is not in my character to exaggerate, & still more because you must be pained & offended at receiving what you suspect to be hyperbolical tributes of admiration. The best explanation I can give on this subject will be a sketch of the circumstances attending my first acquaintance with your poems.

Some years ago spending my holidays at Bath [1] I was shewn the poem of We are Seven which was handed about in manuscript. Between this period & that when I afterwards discovered the volume from which it was taken a long time intervened. During this interval I gradually

---

Letter 4:

[1] De Quincey's mother lived in Bath from August, 1796, to October, 1801. This holiday must have fallen within that period. Later statements place his first acquaintance with the *Lyrical Ballads* in about 1799 (see above, pp. 7–8).

came under the dominion of my passions, & from frequent meditation on some characters of our own, & some of ancient story, & afterwards on some of the German Drama, I began to model my conduct & my aims on theirs: by degrees, being dazzled by the glory thrown on such objects by the voice of the people, & miserably deluding myself with the thought that I was led on by high aims, & such as were most worthy of my nature I daily intoxicated myself more & more with that delirious & lawless pleasure which I drew from the hope of elevating my name in authority & kingly splendour above every name that is named upon earth. For I felt myself unable to live in the pursuit of common objects, & unfettered by any ties of common restraint—& I felt, too, or imagined myself able to compass any plans capable of gratifying that stimulating class of desires which I then thought ebullitions of the highest state of moral improvement, but which I now consider as only a less degrading species of sensualism. Yet admidst all these feverish & turbulent dreams of meditation, it was not possible that I, maintained from my infancy in the Love of Nature, should not, at times relent & resign myself to a confused feeling of purer & more permanent pleasure flowing from other sources—therefore during my long & lonely rambles through many beautiful scenes sometimes in the stillness & silence of surrounding nature, & sometimes in her merest sights & sounds I felt her mild reproach, and so, gradually prepared for being weaned from my temporary frenzy, I looked round for some guide who might assist to develope & to tutor my new feelings, & then it was that from a recollection of the deep impression made on me by the short poem I have mentioned I knew where to seek that guidance, & where I sought, I found it.

And now dr Sir at this day I—once so bewildered & wretched find myself delivered from much undue influence or rather bondage, & many wrong tendencies of passion which involved in themselves the needs of infinite misery. I feel every principle of good within me purified & uplifted—& above all I have such visions of future happiness opened to me as, in my deepest fits of gloom are sufficient continually to sustain & cheer me for since that time I have prayed for the hour when I shall become my own Master, as that in which I shall assert my perfect freedom, & I look forward, after some years travelling to no less happiness (for higher surely cannot be) than to live with those of my Brothers & Sisters who still remain to me, in solitary converse with

Nature, & (as the consumation of all earthly good), to enjoy if not an intimate connexion yet perhaps (if it is your good pleasure) [*breaks off*]

5. *To William Wordsworth*

Ms. Dove Cottage. Pub. ELH, *III, 23–25.*

[Littlemore]
Saturday, March 31. [1804]

Dear Sir,

I had given directions to have all my letters forwarded to Littlemoor; but, on not receiving any for some weeks, it occurred to me that they had been carried to the college; and accordingly, when I sent there to inquire on last Thursday evening, I received a number among which were both yours. The first of them had come round by Bath, and both must have lain some days in college. I mention this circumstance to account to you for my delay in answering them—which must have surprised you.

I was greatly sorry to find that your first letter, which in every other respect gave me a degree of pleasure that I have not enjoyed for many weeks, should cloud it with the news of Mr. Coleridge's illness and your own. Your own you do not speak of as systematic;—Mr. Coleridge's, I rather gather from what you say, is so—but still, I hope not dangerous. If he is advised to try Bath waters (which, I believe, are of great benefit in rheumatic complaints) and he has no friend there whose services he would prefer on such an occasion, I hope that I may be permitted to procure lodgings and all other accommodations for him. I can never have any engagements here important enough to detain me from such an office; besides that the distance from Bath to Oxford is so trifling and the time it would take to execute such a commission so short that the inconvenience to me, even on a less interesting occasion, would be none at all. I trust that you will consider this offer not as mere form but as proceding from a sincere desire to shew a small mark of the affection and great reverence I bear to Mr. Coleridge both on his own account and as your friend.

To me, who am so much interested in the least anecdote relating to you, you may imagine, Sir, how welcome that information must be which you have condescended to give me of your projects in poetry. Any person, who is not a perfect stranger to you, must wish most earnestly to see that work completed which you [*struck out:* are pleased to] call the least important of the three: but to the world at large I suppose that the greater work to which it is attached must, from the more comprehensive range of it's subjects and from the more universal connexion it has with the condition of man, be at the same time more extensively useful and more delightful; and for my country's sake therefore I am bound to offer my first and most fervent petitions for the completion of that poem. But, with a view to my individual gratification, the poem on your own life is the one which I should most anxiously wish to see finished; and I do indeed look with great expectation for the advent of that day, on which I may hear you read it, as the happiest I shall see. I should not have presumed to form any such expectation if some words in your letter had not suggested it.

The wretched man, who has parodied your poems,[1] I have never before even heard of by name: but that is not extraordinary; for latterly I have left off looking into the reviews from which I used to gain a general knowledge of the current English literature. Indeed, if I had seen any account of his work, I should not have read it; for I have studiously avoided reading any attempts at a ludicrous parody of real poetry whenever I have met with them—and especially of your poems. The harmless critiques of the reviewers, as they were generally not conceived in a spirit of ridicule, I read; and, for the same reason, I generally felt real pity for them. Wherever indeed (as in the solemn and *profound* analysis of your poetry by the Scotch reviewers) I have seen men impressed with a sincere belief that you had founded a school of poetry adverse to the canons of true taste, I have always felt any momentary indignation at their arrogance overbalanced by compassion for the delusions they are putting upon themselves and the disordered

---

Letter 5:
[1] Wordsworth had complained to De Quincey that Peter Bayley, after "pillaging" his poems, had "had the baseness to write a long poem in ridicule of them"; and he had grieved especially that anyone could combine "an admiration and love of those poems, with moral feelings so detestable" (*EL,* p. 371). The offending work is *Poems,* by Peter Bayley, Jun. (London, 1803). The "long poem in ridicule" is "The Fisherman's Wife, Dedicated to all admirers of the familiar style of tale-writing, so popular in 1800," which Wordsworth recognized as a parody of "The Idiot Boy."

taste which such a belief argues; but for this miscreant who, having himself felt their beauty, would belie his own convictions and with unparalleled depravity seek to mislead the tastes of a numerous class of his fellow-creatures that under happier guidance might have had their minds half hallowed by their salutary influence, I can scarcely feel the pity which yet his miserable state of mind demands; for, in such wanton wickedness, there seems to me the malignant temper of an evil spirit.—I lament this affair very deeply;—not that I suppose such an attempt or the attempts of any man or any faction of men can ever take from you the least part of that 'kingly style' which must hereafter be yours—but because I fear (which, I know, would grieve you much more) lest, if this book should have an extensive circulation, it may with low minds turned to ridicule and satire obstruct the beneficial effects which your poems might otherwise produce even on such distempered tastes.—I feel much curiosity to see this man's book; but the same fear, which has always hitherto made me turn away from burlesque imitations of what I love, operates with tenfold force on this occasion.

The interest—so very gratifying to me, which you are kind enough to take in my welfare, would be of itself a sufficient check upon me if I were unhappily disposed to licentiousness: but I have been through life so much restrained from dissolute conduct by the ever-waking love of my mother—and of late years so purified from dissolute propensities by the new order of pleasures which I have been led to cultivate that I feel a degree of confidence (not arrogant, I hope) that, even with greater temptations, I should not by my *conduct* at any rate make you repent the notice you have taken of me. The college however, which I am at, holds out no very powerful temptations: it has indeed the character of being very riotious; but I cannot see that it deserves such a character preeminently—though it's discipline is certainly less strict than that of any other college. But it is singularly barren (as far as my short residence there will permit me to judge) of either virtue or talents or knowledge; so that the intemperance I see practiced, coming unrecommended by any great qualifications, is doubly disgusting to me. And, even though I should meet with these debauched habits in the person of a man of genius, it would be difficult for me to be so much seduced as lightly to exchange the high and lasting pleasures which I have found in other paths for such as, exclusively of their vast intrinsic inferiority and the train of evils which attend them, bring along with them the seeds of their own destruction. And besides, from the great aversion I have to a college life, I shall pass no more of my time there than is necessary; and, for that reason as well as for the little attraction I have found in the society, I have lived almost alone since my entrance; and, until I see something greater or better, I shall continue to do so.—With respect to my conduct therefore during the time I have been at college, I have not much to reproach myself with. But I hope that you will give me credit for not wishing to claim any praise for avoiding those intemperate pleasures for which I have so few opportunities from the secluded manner in which I live and so little inclination from the better direction which has been given to my pursuits. In all that relates to the government and cultivation of my mind I am very deficient and fully conscious of my own unworthiness; and it is only upon the perpetual hope and assurance of something better that I shall be hereafter that I found any pretensions to your regard.

Sunday morning.

Not having room to enter on any other subject I must here close my letter with the warmest wishes for Mr. Coleridge's and your recovery —taking the liberty of repeating my request to be made useful in any way which occurs to you—and begging my respectful acknowledgments to Miss Wordsworth for her kindness in remembering me.

Thanking you, dear Sir, for your great goodness in writing to me I remain, with the deepest devotion,

Your grateful and affectionate friend,
Thomas de Quincey.

Littlemoor.

[*Address:*] William Wordsworth, Esqr. / Grasmere, / Near Kendal, / Westmoreland.

[*Stamp:*]   Oxford

6. *To William Wordsworth*

Ms. Dove Cottage. Pub. ELH, *III, 28–30.*

[Everton]
April 6, 1806.

Dear Sir,

I have come up here from the south with the intention of visiting

Westmoreland this spring; but I cannot resolve to advance any farther until I know whether it would be agreeable to you that I should call at your cottage in my tour: I feel unspeakable sorrow that I myself should have put this into doubt; for, I cannot tell how far the kindness which you formerly shewed me and which led you then to desire that I would do so—has been alienated from me by my long silence.—That any intermission of a correspondence which I held one of the first privileges of my life should have arisen on my part—must have seemed strange; but you had, I think, an assurance in the very constitution of my mind (with which it could not but be that my veneration for you should be coeval) that no influence short of at least a moral necessity could have driven me to the suspension of such an intercourse as I always thought my pleasure and my interest more involved in cultivating than they could have been in an intercourse with any other of all the men that have lived from the beginning of time. To say then that the deep interest I took in all that related to you has suffered no pause—is, I hope, unnecessary: but, as a debt of respect to you and of justice to myself, I will briefly sketch the history of the long interval of pain between this letter and my last during which my faculties have been so withered and such gloom thrown upon my spirits that I have written none but a few letters of business and form.

Through the greater part of this interval I have been struggling with an unconfirmed pulmonary consumption which I inherit and which the sedentariness of a college life greatly aided: in this early state my symptoms might easily have been corrected; but the neglect with which I treated them at first from ignorance of their nature and a fever which flung me back after I had made some progress in recovery—have made my reestablishment a work of time and difficulty.—But my great affliction was the loss of my brother—a boy of great promise who, in disdain of the tyranny exercised over him at school, went to sea at a time when I was incapable of giving him any assistance or advice: this has grown heavier and heavier as the chance of my hearing any tidings of him has diminished.[1] In losing him I lost a future friend; for, be-

---

Letter 6:

[1] De Quincey's brother Richard (whom he called "Pink") returned safely (see pp. 203–204), but he was much away at sea and finally disappeared in Jamaica about 1815, so that the "friendship" of allied minds never flourished. Indeed, Thomas' feelings were probably compounded of a sense of guilt, encouraged by his mother, that his own running away had set the example for Richard.

sides what we had of alliance in our minds, we had passed so much of
our childhood together (though latterly we had generally been
separated) that we had between us common remembrances of early
life. It has never happened to me before or after to meet any one among
the many young men I have slightly known with whom I had such a
community of thought and feeling on subjects most interesting to me
as might serve for the basis of a friendship: this indeed has been my
primal affliction through life and especially through my college life
that I have lived under a perpetual sense of desertion and have felt,
on any demand which my situation made for a service higher than mere
youthful generosity could prompt, that I was walking alone in the
world: in sickness I felt this severely; for then, from the exhaustion
and wasting which wait upon the hectic fever, my mind lost it's energy
so much that it was passive to whatever noxious influence I fell under
for the time; and so by turns it was half palsied by total solitude or
disentranced from its native mood by heartless society.

These things have shed blight upon my mind and have made the two
last years of my life so complete a blank in the account of happiness
that I know not whether there be one hour in that whole time which
I would willingly recal: I have had intervals of bodily health but
never any respite from sickness of the mind; for books, which might
in part have supplied the place of all other pleasures, my small income
diminished by the expences of illness &c. and sometimes my situation
would not permit me to procure in any tolerable quantity.

And thus, as I could not endure to dissociate pleasure from my correspondence with you—and resolved therefore never to write under
depression of spirits with shattered health and a famished intellect, I
deferred writing from month to month—always calculating on the
near approach of some period of pleasure and renovation which was
never to arrive: how this could be, I can now scarcely understand;
and, if I could have foreseen the long term to which these alternations
of pain and apathy would extend, I should have put violence on my
feelings of reluctance and have written a few lines explaining my
situation: but I [*torn*] petually in prospect some change of life
which I thought [*torn*] state me in a capacity of writing more at
length; and in some way or other I was perpetually disappointed.

Even at this time, though completely restored to health, I write by
no means at ease—restlessly anxious to learn what interpretation you
have put on my silence and not knowing whether I am not utterly re-

jected from your thoughts. Nevertheless the recollection of the great kindness which you shewed me even in your first letter—which is so strongly recalled to me at this moment by the place in which I write— gives me confidence that you will not, for a failure in the forms of respect (scarcely indeed within the control of my will), withdraw from me your notice at a time when it has become trebly necessary to me and when I have learned (if that were possible) yet more to value it.

I remain, dear sir, with great veneration, your affectionate friend,

Thomas de Quincey.

If you should find it convenient and should be disposed to write a single line in answer within a week, it will find me here; and at my departure I shall leave directions to have it sent after me.

Mrs. Best's, Everton, near Liverpool.

[*Address:*] William Wordsworth, Esqr. / Grasmere near Kendal / West-moreland [2]

7. *To William Wordsworth*

Ms. Dove Cottage. Unpub.

Everton—June 9. [1806]

Dear Sir,

A hurried answer which I wrote last night to your letter from Grasmere [1] being too late for the post, I can now explain more clearly my present situation and my reasons for not giving an earlier answer to your first letter.[2]

I am at present waiting here in daily expectation of hearing some final account of the Cambridge—the ship in which my brother sailed; and, other circumstances having made it difficult for me to say anything positive as to the time of my visit to Westmoreland, I thought

---

[2] Dorothy and Mary forwarded this letter to William in London, at Sir George Beaumont's, and added notes to it (*MY*, I, 18–19).

Letter 7:

[1] June 3, 1806 (*MY*, I, 29).

[2] May 5, 1806, written from London (*MY*, I, 22–23).

it better to wait until I could than to trouble you with a letter so unsatisfactory in all respects as any letter written under my present feelings must be; especially as I thought and have now reason to expect that, before the end of this week, my anxiety on most of the subjects I allude to will be removed. I had calculated besides on your reaching Grasmere not quite so soon as I learn from your letter that you have; though, on referring to your letter from London, I find that you left the term of your further absence from home indefinite. I had also, to escape from the unpleasant feelings attached to my present situation and the review of so much time lately lost, employed myself in arranging all such affairs as might otherwise call upon me for attention at any time hereafter when I should more unwillingly pay it; and, as I felt that in the state of mind growing out of such employment I could not write anything which it would be pleasant to you to receive except my sense of your kindness in continuing your favor to me (to which I could not do justice), my extreme reluctance to trouble you with a letter lightly—urged me to wait until I should hear something which would set me at liberty from my present indecision of purpose; and, on some of those circumstances which have detained me here, I must certainly hear something decisive in a few days. But now, finding that you have been at Grasmere for a full fortnight, I am sorry that I did not at any rate communicate my change of plan before.

I think it now almost certain that I shall come into Westmoreland before the end of this month; as soon as I hear anything conclusive on the circumstances which at present hold me in suspense, I will not fail to write immediately. At present I am obliged to conclude; begging you to pardon the shortness of this letter and whatever else may bespeak hasty thought or inattention in my letters at this time and to ascribe them to that feverishness and distemperament of mind which my mode of life for some time past has generated and with which all calm thoughts and actions are out of harmony.

I owe many acknowledgments to the ladies of your family for their kindness in informing me of your absence from home: besides that that information relieved me from much anxiety, I felt greatly pleased and honored by such a mark of attention from them.

My health, I ought to add in answer to your kind inquiries, is [seal]ly restored so as to make it unnecessary for me to pay any further attentions to it.

Believe me, dear sir, with great affection and veneration, your sincere friend, Thomas de Quincey.

[*Address:*] William Wordsworth Esqr. / Grasmere / near Kendal / Westmoreland. / Single sheet /
[*Postmark:*] JUN 10

CHAPTER TWO

✎ OPPORTUNITY

No contemporary record attests to just what the disciple and master thought of each other that November in 1807. Although expectation such as De Quincey's was doomed to some disappointment, he was (if we may credit his account written some thirty-two years later for *Tait's Magazine*) generally pleased. This first visit lasted a week, putting some strain on the Dove Cottage accommodations. "By lodging two at Peggy Ashburners," wrote Dorothy, "we contrived to harbour the whole party, not excepting Mr. de Quincey." [1] The latter was not among those shunted to Peggy's: he was given the best bedroom although, as he discovered the next morning, a corner of it was also occupied by four-year-old Johnny Wordsworth!

De Quincey was surprised and delighted at many things. The conversation at tea was "superior by much" to any he had heard, except Coleridge's. William and Dorothy promptly did the honors of the vale, taking him in the rain on a walk around Grasmere Lake and Rydal Water. They also proposed that the trip on to Keswick, where he was to deliver Sara Coleridge and her children into Southey's hands at Greta Hall, be made by the scenic route via Patterdale.

Already a bit shocked by the rather primitive simplicity of the Wordsworths' way of life, De Quincey was more startled when, on the third day, the party set out through Ambleside and Kirkstone Pass in a common farmer's cart driven by a local lass. But he loyally decided, "What was good enough for the Wordsworths was good enough for me." [2] The next day De Quincey had Wordsworth all to himself, as the two left the women and children and walked through the woods of Lowther. What did they talk about? Did they discuss poetry on "something like equal terms"? Hardly. Dorothy describes De Quincey at the time as "so modest, and so very shy"; and he spoke of himself as "far too diffident" to take part in Wordsworth's and Southey's surprisingly disloyal political discussion two days later. Somewhere along Ullswater, however, Wordsworth read to De Quincey the introduction to *The White Doe*. De Quincey made no mention of this in his *Tait's* essay, but in 1854 when he was revising it— and chiefly cutting it—he added significantly: "On this day, which must have been the Sunday next after the 5th of November in 1807, I may record it as an incident most memorable to myself, that Wordsworth read to me the 'White Doe of Rylstone.' " [3]

The two men who walked to Penrith getting acquainted with each other that day were both gentlemen, of about the same social rank and education, but their backgrounds had been significantly dissimilar. The tall, mountain-bred poet with the rough edge had lost both his parents by the time he was thirteen and had felt the chill of genteel poverty. He was now turned cautious. The diminutive city-bred disciple with the courtly manners carried, despite the early death of his own father and his self-imposed agonies in London, an aura of mercantile prosperity. He had not too long before come into his modest inheritance, still looked forward (how mistakenly!) to a gentlemanly competence, and was still expansive—his £300 gift-loan to Coleridge was then in process of negotiation through Cottle. Differences in temperament even more significant were probably just beginning to make themselves manifest, if the young man was not too "diffident"—essentially those differences between a constructive mind and a critical mind, between a bias toward "the common growth of mother-earth" and a penchant for "subtleties of all sorts and degrees." [4]

Yet if the young pilgrim revealed any of the history of his escapades after his flight from Manchester Grammar School, Wordsworth must have recognized something of a kindred spirit. For De Quincey wandering in Wales, a refugee from his guardians' plans for his education, was not much different from a somewhat older Wordsworth wandering in France in 1791–1792, fending off his uncles' sensible plans for a career in the church. Or if he let the poet see into the near-mystical side of his nature, that part of him which "demanded mysteries" and communicated by dreams "with the shadowy," Wordsworth had a similar side which could respond. The boy who came upon the site of an ancient gibbet and needed

> Colours and words that are unknown to man,
> To paint the visionary dreariness
> Which, while I looked all round for my lost guide,
> Invested moorland waste, and naked pool,
> (*The Prelude,* XII, 255–259)

was kin to the boy who by the side of the bier of his sister heard "a wind that might have swept the fields of mortality for a thousand centuries . . . the one great audible symbol of eternity." [5] Such moments, however, were fleeting with both men, and by the time they met had become infrequent in Wordsworth's life.

Like Wordsworth, De Quincey felt the pull of solitude, once remarking curiously, "in order that I *might* like all men, I wished to associate with none." He also advertised himself congenially in his early letters to the poet as a great lover of nature. In his way perhaps he was, but it was rather more analytic and intellectualized than Wordsworth's way. Only a month or so before his first meeting with the poet he wrote his sister of his

speculation on the essential differences of savage and civilized life and their causes; as, e.g. how much of the virtue and moral elevation found

amongst the Northern Indians is due to the influences of beautiful
natural scenery; how far amongst civilized men, the seclusion from
such scenery in large towns is compensated by the visual representation
of it in pictures and the intellectual suggestions of it (or pictures in
visions) in poems—romances &c.

This notion of vicarious nature, if it came into the Ullswater
conversation, probably struck the poet as wire-drawn. And
what could he think of a nature lover capable of confessing
"universally I am a poor hand at observing"? [6]
    Characteristics the two men had in common were chiefly
fervent admiration for Wordsworth's poetry and its world;
a tendency to value those solitary experiences in which the
"light of sense" went out or was distorted; in varying degrees and kinds a real feeling for nature; and—danger-
ously—rebellious and proud independence of mind. Would
those be capable of sustaining a personal relationship?
    Curiously, in his *Tait's* article De Quincey did not say
anything about that conversation on the way to Penrith, nor
did he seem particularly surprised that the poet took him to
the house of Captain Wordsworth and went about some
business of his own, leaving his guest to go on to Greta Hall
to meet Southey by himself the next day. De Quincey did
take occasion to describe Southey as "in the lesser moralities
—those which govern the daily habits, and transpire through
the manners . . . certainly a better man . . . than Wordsworth." [7] It was to Dorothy's "fervent and hospitable
temper" that he attributed his being asked to join the
brother and sister in a long-standing dinner invitation on
his last night in Westmorland—a Barmecide feast amusingly
described in "The Saracen's Head." It was Dorothy, also,
who wrote to Lady Beaumont on December 6 of De Quincey
in these terms:

I think of this young man with extraordinary pleasure, as he is a remarkable instance of the power of my brother's poems over a lovely
and contemplative mind, unwarped by any established laws of taste
(as far as it is in my power to judge from his letters, and the little I
have seen of him)—a pure and innocent mind! (*MY*, 159–160)

And it was to Dorothy that De Quincey addressed his next surviving letter, and almost all of his letters thereafter— even when answering one from William—until after his marriage.

The pilgrim went back to finish the Michaelmas term at Oxford, and promptly became ill. His bread-and-butter letter to Grasmere, which seems to have been lost, was written in a brief period of "abatement"; but by the time of his next letter, March 25, 1808, he had another long tale of suffering to account for his failure to answer two letters from Dorothy. As soon as the term was over he went up to London, where he met Wordsworth, who had come down on February 24, worried by reports that Coleridge had become so ill that he had been able to give only two lectures of his series at the Royal Institution.[8] Apparently relations between the poet and the undergraduate in London were affable; they had, for one thing, their common interest in Coleridge's welfare.

De Quincey had been visiting Coleridge in his quarters at the *Courier* office in the Strand almost daily. In January the ailing Coleridge "sent for Abernethie, who has restored Mr. Dequincey to Health." Recommending a physician was only a small part of the young man's services. So dependent had Coleridge come to be upon him, that, when De Quincey absented himself for a few days, Coleridge was much disturbed. On Tuesday, February 2, he wrote: "I have suffered considerable alarm at not having seen you for so many days," adding somewhat lamely, "I have had Bodings utterly out of all Proportion to the exact number of Days that you have been absent." [9] An entry possibly dating from about this time, in one of Coleridge's notebooks, lists under "Bibliological Memoranda": "To have a long Morning's Ramble with De Quincey, first to Egerton's, and then to his Book Haunts." He had been using De Quincey to get books for him—"*De Emendatione* . . . Longus, Heliodorus, & D'Orville's Chariton"—and to listen to his doleful docket of maladies and his frequent convictions of imminent dissolution, and probably—ironically enough—to hear his confessions and self-incriminations over the opium habit. Years later Coleridge wrote to Cottle that "with flowing tears, and with an agony of forewarning" he had pleaded with De Quincey: "He utterly denied it, but I fear that I had even then to *deter* perhaps not to forewarn." [10]

Without question De Quincey made the *Courier* office a steppingstone to Grasmere. That Wordsworth came frequently into the conversation is indicated by the close of Coleridge's February 2 letter to his young friend: "That there is such a man in the World, as Wordsworth, and that such a man enjoys such a Family, makes both Death and my inefficient Life, a less grievous Thought to me." When Wordsworth arrived in town he and De Quincey no doubt met frequently at Coleridge's rooms. It was perhaps there that De Quincey heard Wordsworth read "the whole of the White Doe in London," for Wordsworth had brought the poem to town with an intention of publishing it and, apparently, decided against it partly because Coleridge had offered to alter some passages.[11]

De Quincey left the city first, returning to the university on March 5, and the poet seems to have intended to visit him in Oxford on his way home. Dorothy wrote to William on March 23, care of De Quincey at Worcester College, and said, "Remember me affectionately to Mr De Quincey and tell him that we hope to hear that he intends coming into the North this summer." [12] But William, hurrying back to Grasmere on news that his sister-in-law, Sara Hutchinson, was sick, did not go by Oxford. Curiously, De Quincey's March 25 letter to Dorothy does not mention the possibility of a visit from the poet. It does hint at his later complaints that Wordsworth did not listen attentively to his long explanations, and tempts one to speculate that perhaps De Quincey's vague suspicions of Wordsworth's limited sympathies were strengthened by Coleridge. For Coleridge wrote to his young friend, asking for his frank comments on his work, and remarking:

It would have been indeed far, far better for me—in some little degree perhaps for society—if I could have attached more importance, greater warmth of feeling, to my own Writings. But I have not been happy enough for that.—So however it is, that the pleasure, the sincere pleasure, of receiving that proof of friendship—'I cannot say, that this or that satisfied me—I did not like this for such and such reasons—it appeared to me slight, not the genuine *Stuff,'* &c—has often blinded me so far as to believe at once, & for a long season, more meanly of what I had done, than after-experience confi[rmed] (*STC,* III, 48 f.).

This complaint probably refers to Coleridge's growing conviction that Wordsworth had not really appreciated and encouraged his friend's muse; that he was always glad to receive praise, but slow to give it. On May 12 he finally exploded to Wordsworth about his "cowardly mock-prudence relatively to his Friends." [13] Perhaps he let some of this feeling show to the perceptive young man who was fast uncovering his idol's feet.

Possibly De Quincey carried back to Oxford from his sojourn with poets some encouragement, given wittingly or not, to scorn academic accolades. What more natural than for Wordsworth to ask De Quincey about his work at college, and to reveal in the course of the conversation that he himself took only a pass degree at Cambridge, and had little patience with the system of honors competition? Certainly De Quincey is more outspoken in his March 25 letter about the "approaching prizefighting" for honors than he would have been if he thought Wordsworth were in sympathy with such things. Some of this disdain may be protective coloration, for De Quincey—through illness, procrastination, or iconoclasticism—had got so far behind in his academic reading that he could allow only a week for going through thirty-three Greek tragedies. His attitude, however, seems remarkably similar to Wordsworth's:

> of important days,
> Examinations, when the man was weighed
> As in a balance! of excessive hopes,
> Tremblings withal and commendable fears,
> Small jealousies, and triumphs good or bad,
> Let others that know more speak as they know.
> Such glory was but little sought by me,
> And little won.
>
> (*Prelude,* III, 68–75)

De Quincey was honest enough to admit that he would like to be "Illustrious," but he was shamefaced about it. His next note, a harried one on May 8, declared that he was reading eighteen hours out of twenty-four, because he was motivated by a desire not to disappoint his college.

What made De Quincey interrupt his violent cramming for even a note was his wish to contribute to the fund for the children of George and Sarah Green, whose tragic loss in a snowstorm he later recounted in "Recollections of Grasmere." He sent £5, deprecatingly, declaring that he was "not one of the rich"; but Lady Beaumont and Lady Fleming sent no more, and his gift probably made the desired impression at Grasmere. "William's name cuts a great figure in the List of subscribers," wrote Dorothy, because, although he gave nothing himself, all the gifts he had solicited were marked, *through* Mr. Wordsworth." [14] Thus De Quincey was still serviceable, as he was anxious to be. He went back to his Greek plays.

Of all lost letters, one laments especially the next that De Quincey wrote the Wordsworths. For when he was finally called to be examined—after succeeding in getting the day deferred by having his name listed with the Q's—he did brilliantly on the written part, but simply left Oxford without taking the oral examination. What did he tell the Wordsworths? Did he elaborate on his contempt for the "prize-fighting," as he did later in describing to Woodhouse [15] his disgust that the answers to the Greek examination were suddenly directed to be given in English instead of Greek? Or did he have another long story of physical illness, such as might well have been the result of his not going to bed and and probably, although he would not have said so, taking opium?

Whatever he said, his physical illness must have loomed large, because Dorothy's next letter, July 7, sympathized: "I will not speak of our sorrow for your illness. You are recovered now, and we rejoice in thankfulness." De Quincey, then back in London, was apparently seeing a great deal of Coleridge, attending his lectures and even helping him with them. He later wrote, immodestly, that Coleridge's illustrations were not particularly effective, "except two or three, which I myself put ready marked into his hands." [16] When Coleridge left London about the middle of June, De Quincey stayed on because he was requisitioned to take part in the wedding of an Oxford friend. Meanwhile he was reveling in the bookshops, and wrote to offer to buy books for Wordsworth. Indeed, he more or less appointed himself book buyer extraordinary to the poet. In 1809 he was delighted to report that he had found the missing eleventh volume of *State Trials,* thus completing Wordsworth's set and making it worth twenty guineas! [17] The response to his 1808 offer gave him at the outset some notion as to the conditions under which he was to work: the answer came not from William, but from Dorothy; and although they had numbered over many wanted books on their walk the previous night, Dorothy had forgotten most of them and advised generally: "he wants all that is valuable and can be procured *very cheaply.*" She was, however, less vague about inviting De Quincey to visit them in their new home, Allan Bank: "At any time, and as soon as ever it suits you, we shall be most glad to see you . . . You may always have a sitting-room below stairs, and a bedroom above to yourself." When the time arrived that he wrote to say that he was coming, however, this expansive hospitality was not available. William sent a very brief note to say that although they would be "very happy to see" him, they could not even offer him a bed, because Coleridge was with them and the house was full. Wordsworth took off some of the curtness, however, by signing "very affectionately yours." [18] De Quincey was evidently in as good odor at Grasmere as if he could write himself B.A. He came on, anyway, and apparently shared John Wordsworth's bed.

De Quincey stayed from early in November, 1808, until the following February 20, one of the Allan Bank family, a menage which now numbered—counting servants and Coleridge's children, who were down from Keswick on the weekends—fifteen people. Life must have been hectic. The house was newly built and the chimneys all smoked horribly, ruining the eyes and doubling the housework. Dorothy wrote

wheedlingly to her lawyer brother Richard begging an oil-
cloth carpet for the white stone passage that could not be
kept clean. Sara Hutchinson was just recovering from a
serious illness, and De Quincey himself apparently got sick
again, for Dorothy wrote to Mrs. Coleridge early in 1809:
"Mr De Quincey sends his kind remembrances to you and
the Children. If he is well enough he will accompany Coleridge to Keswick." [19] Years later the experience does not seem
to have been warmly remembered by any of the parties.
Wordsworth twice wrote that De Quincey had been seven
months an "inmate" of his house. Unless he was adding up all
of De Quincey's visits, the reference must be to this stay in the
winter of 1808–1809, and apparently it dragged on in
Wordsworth's thinking until it seemed twice as long as it
was. De Quincey seems to have forgotten it entirely in 1834
when he wrote his articles on Coleridge, for he said: "The
next opportunity I had of seeing Coleridge [after London],
was at the Lakes, in the winter of 1809, and up to the
autumn of the following year"—skipping or telescoping the
winter of 1808. In a *Tait's* article of 1839, he remembered
chiefly the smoking chimneys, and reported acidly that the
poet tried to talk the landlord out of charging him any rent
on that score, for "whilst foolish people supposed him a
mere honeyed sentimentalist, speaking only in zephyrs and
bucolics, he was in fact a somewhat hard pursuer of what
he thought fair advantages." [20]

Both men had their memories soured, however, by later
events. At the time Dorothy painted for her friend Catherine Clarkson a much pleasanter picture of an almost idyllic
moment on December 8:

Mr. De Quincey, whom you would love dearly, as I am sure I do, is
beside me, quietly turning over the leaves of a Greek book—and God
be praised we are breathing a clear air, for the night is calm, and this
room (the Dining-room) only smokes very much in a high wind. Mr.
De Q. will stay with us, we hope, at least till the Spring. We feel often
as if he were one of the family—he is loving, gentle, and happy—a very
good scholar, and an acute logician—so much for his mind and manners
(*MY*, 255 f.).

A few days earlier Sara Hutchinson wrote what offers an interesting cross-reference:

Mr de Quincey has been here 3 weeks & I daresay will make a long stay—he is a good tempered amiable creature & uncommonly clever & an excellent scholar—but he is very shy & so reverences Wm & C[oleridge] that he chats very little . . . —he looks like only 18 but is nothing like either helpless or dissipid as Joanna said: but then he is in much better health than when she saw him.[21]

Among the women and children—except Joanna—De Quincey seems to have been well regarded. And since the women probably reflected in some measure the opinion of the male contingent—certainly they would hardly feel qualified on their own to comment so positively on De Quincey's scholarship—the "very little man" was certainly on a better footing in the household than later records suggest.

He ought to have been in his glory, under the same roof with both his idols and mingling in the society of the Lakes. Southey wrote on November 12: "Little Mr. De Quincey . . . was here last week, and is coming again." On November 29 De Quincey and Wordsworth dined at Elleray with John Wilson.[22] He had opportunities for intimacy with Wordsworth in those "lovely scenes of nature" which the boy said in his first letter he had devoted himself to worshiping: he "several times" walked with Wordsworth under the splendid trees on Nab Scar (end of Letter 31). There were also interesting things going on in which, shyly, reverently, and eager to be of service, he could have a part. Coleridge was getting started on the *Friend,* and the Wordsworths, with fingers crossed, were sending his prospectus around to their friends. One of the most revealing indications of De Quincey's closeness to the Wordsworths at this time is that they apparently admitted to him their doubts about Coleridge's carrying through the project. Dorothy wrote him on March 7 of her wish that Coleridge had not felt obliged to go to Penrith to make arrangements for printing the periodical: "If he had been able to stay quietly here, the trial would have been a fair one—and should he have failed, in future one

could never, in case of any other scheme, be vexed with
hopes or fears." [23] The implication, a bit cold-blooded, is
that Coleridge will fail and that it would be better if he
could do so in a way that would give him no excuse for
pestering them again with similar impractical schemes. By
now De Quincey must have been allowed to see all the
skeletons.

De Quincey sniffed an opportunity to help both of his
poets: he would set up a press at Grasmere. In February
Coleridge outlined the plan to Daniel Stuart:

Independently of 'The Friend,' we had intended to do this. I believe,
you have seen Mr De Quincy at the Courier office with me. Ho!—
He was the very short & boyish-looking modest man, whom I introduced to you in Cuthell's Shop, and afterwards gave you his character
&c. . . . Besides his erudition, he has a great turn for manual opera-
tions, and is even to something of old batchelor preciseness accurate,
and regular in all, he does. It is his determination, to have printed
under his own Eye immaculate Editions of such of the eminently great
Classics, English and Greek as most need it—and to begin with the
poetic Works of Milton. [24]

A respectable Kendal printer approved the idea, and it was
a talked-of project for some time. On May 25 De Quincey
was still writing, albeit rather jocularly, of prospective pro-
ductions of "the Grasmere Press." Then, however, he was
in London on Wordsworth's errand; Coleridge finally had to
print the *Friend* in Penrith. Nevertheless, the Grasmere
printing scheme was not without fruit of a sort. Wordsworth's son John, to his father's chagrin, was slow at his
letters, and De Quincey used the proposed press to stimulate
him. Sara wrote on March 27 that the boy said he was "to
be a *printer* with Mr de Quincey (who talks of having a
Press for his amusement) and must stay to learn to be a
good Scholar for that purpose—the hope of being with
Mr de Q. would stimulate him to anything for he loves him
better than anything in the world!" From London De Quincey wrote about how easy it was to be a printer, and even
went to the trouble of hand printing a letter to the boy. So
fond a father as Wordsworth must have been grateful. Aunt

Dorothy thought De Quincey's conversation "of very great use to John." [25]

One thing that was happening on this long visit, then, was that De Quincey's relations were being established with the Wordsworth household more than with the poet. Dorothy loved him "dearly," John was "passionately fond of him," and he was almost "one of the family." De Quincey always loved children—the pathetic little girl in Greek Street who slept in his arms, the boy his *Diary* shows him romping with at Everton, Coleridge's children in Bristol ("Derwent still continues my favourite"),[26] and now Wordsworth's in Grasmere. He was later to be godfather to William Junior, and to become much attached to Cathy. The "very little man" undoubtedly felt more at ease with young children. Moreover, in his eagerness to serve he gladly joined the satellites around Wordsworth and probably savored the intimacy of his domestic relationship. He was, however, falling into the role of the amiable young man of means who made nice presents, had pleasant manners, and was so good to the children. He had a somewhat more important role in mind for himself. He was no more content to sit by Dorothy turning the leaves of a Greek book than he had been to be the darling of his sisters in the nursery. His pretensions were intellectual: he wanted to be taken seriously in the world of men and poets. And Coleridge's comment to Stuart—"Ho!—He was the very short & boyish-looking modest man"—suggests the difficulty he was having in being so accepted. That "Ho" has a frosty sound. So sensitive a man as De Quincey would know when he was being laughed at. This may be part of the reason that, although he continued to see Coleridge for several years, their association did not develop and De Quincey later insisted that they had never been friends.[27]

While Wordsworth may not have laughed at De Quincey, he probably snorted at the "old batchelor preciseness," and he, too, obviously was not interested in the same things as his young admirer. One reason the Grasmere Press never materialized was perhaps that Wordsworth did not really care about "immaculate Editions." De Quincey later quoted approvingly Southey's dictum, "To introduce Wordsworth into one's library is like letting a bear into a tulip garden," and told with tolerant horror of the poet's cutting the pages of one of his books with a buttery knife. He was to write half-humorously from London that his exploits in the bookshops were unappreciated: "no applause ensued." [28] Under the jocularity was a note of hurt. But if Wordsworth was not interested in a press to turn out fine books, he was interested in politics; De Quincey became interested in politics, too.

De Quincey's 1803 *Diary* indeed shows him talking about war and Napoleon, but never with much sense of involvement. He later claimed that until he sat deferentially at Greta Hall in the fall of 1807 and heard Wordsworth and Southey talk "treason," he had been so little interested in political affairs that "for some years" he had "never looked into a newspaper." [29] During the Peninsular War, however, he often walked with Wordsworth up to Dunmail Raise at midnight to get Coleridge's complimentary copy of the *Courier* coming down from Keswick by carrier, so that they could read the latest reports from Spain. Wordsworth, of course, had long been interested in politics, probably since his Cambridge days, and at least since 1792, when in Orléans Beaupuy had stirred him to a participation in the social ideal of the French Revolution. His enthusiasm for the French cause had survived The Terror, but not the invasion of Switzerland and the threat of "Boney's" barges at Boulogne. Then Wordsworth had joined the Ambleside volunteers and written patriotic sonnets. Now he was exercised over the conduct of the Peninsular War. The Convention of Cintra, wrote Dorothy on December 4, 1808, "has interested him more than words can express. His first and his last thoughts are of Spain and Portugal." The day before William had described himself as "very deep in this subject, and about to publish upon it." [30]

The Convention of Cintra was an agreement signed on August 30, 1808, after the English victory of Vimeiro, between Sir Hew Dalrymple for the British army in Portugal and General Andoche Junot for the French army in Portugal. Under the terms of the convention the French troops evacuated Portugal and were transported, with all their arms and possessions—including apparently a good deal of booty—back to France in English ships. From a military point of view the convention may have been advantageous to England and her allies. Most of the generals thought so. Junot had not been decisively defeated, largely because Wellesley was restrained from following up his advantage after his superiors Sir Harry Burrard and Dalrymple arrived. The historian William Napier argues that Junot could not have been evicted without serious difficulty and losses, and would have wreaked great damage on Lisbon. Napoleon is supposed to have said that he would have court-martialed Junot for accepting such an agreement if the English had not spared him the pain of humiliating an old friend by trying their generals. Whatever the military aspects, however, from a propaganda and political point of view the convention was an English mistake. It slighted England's allies, the Portuguese, by giving them no part in the treaty; and it appeared to reward iniquity by sending the French and their spoils home with honor—whence they could march back again. English reaction was not favorable. The Government first proclaimed a celebration, then called a Court of Inquiry, which split on the propriety of the Convention but upheld the "unquestionable zeal" of the officers involved. Coleridge denounced the Court as a "process to kill the quicksilver of popular feeling by the saliva of drivellers." Southey wrote to Landor on November 26:

I did not meet a man who was not boiling over with shame & rage. I am sure that for the first week after the news arrived had Sir Hew D. appeared in any part of England he would have been torn in pieces. My cry was break the terms, & deliver up the wretch who signed them to the French, with a rope round his neck, & this is what Oliver Cromwell would have done. Oh Christ—this England, this noble country,—that hands so mighty & a heart so sound should have a face all leprosy, & a head fit for nothing but the vermin that burrow in it!—[31]

Wordsworth's reaction was equally unequivocal: "We are all here cut to the heart . . . For myself, I have not suffered

so much upon any public occasion these many years." Two
days later he was "all in a rage." He went to Keswick to
join Southey in efforts to hold a county meeting and send in
a petition. On November 6, when that seemed hopeless because of Lord Lonsdale's opposition, he "went home to
ease his heart in a pamphlet," as Southey put it—"a pamphlet upon this precious convention, which he will place in
a more philosophical point of view than anybody has yet
done." By December 6 he was hard at work on the pamphlet,
then to be called *The Convention of Cintra brought to the
Test of Principles; and the People of Great Britain vindi-
cated from the Charge of having prejudged it.* The last part
of the title obviously refers to King George III's reply to
the London Common Council's petition for inquiry and
punishment of "misconduct and incapacity," in which he reproached them for pronouncing judgment without previous
investigation. Thus Wordsworth's work was at its inception
an attack on the government. As time went by he became
more and more convinced of "the incapacity and guilt and
folly both of the man at the head of the ministry and the
army and the two Houses of Parliament." [32]

It was into this highly charged political atmosphere that
the generally conservative De Quincey moved when he came
to Allan Bank in November. Soon he was embroiled in the
project, which became a family affair: Wordsworth ground
out his weighty paragraphs; Coleridge rewrote and "in
some parts recomposed" when the two friends stayed up
until three in the morning to replace copy lost in transit;
Mary, Sara, and Dorothy served as secretaries; and De
Quincey was charged with correcting the punctuation and
perhaps writing parts. Coleridge remarked on De Quincey's
"marvellous slowness in writing a note to the Pamphlet
when at Grasmere," and De Quincey's daughter vaguely
remembered having heard that Wordsworth gave her father
"intolerable trouble" to write a note to the Pamphlet and
then canceled it "without a word." [33] Evidently De Quincey
threw himself into the business and became enough of an
authority on Spanish affairs to have been capable of writing
a note. Dorothy called him "so knowing an expounder of

the state of Nations" and said the Wordsworths were agreed that there was probably no one "in all England . . . so well qualified." William once wrote him, "I know that you have accurately in memory all the events of the campaign." He himself later claimed that he had brought his knowledge of the Spanish campaign "to as much accuracy as anybody can —who was not personally engaged in them." [34] Thus rigorously did he prepare to serve.

Anxious to get before the public, Wordsworth took Coleridge's advice to send the work to his friend, Daniel Stuart, for publication in the *Courier*. The first installment accordingly appeared on December 27, 1808, and the second on January 13, 1809. Coleridge expected a whole "series of most masterly Essays" [35] to appear in the *Courier*, and evidently four were sent, although only two were published. Wordsworth's subsequent "advertisement" to the work blamed the cessation of *Courier* publication on the loss of manuscript and lack of space; the fact of the matter is that he had begun to have higher aspirations for his work than to have it appear to be mere newspaper ephemera. His attitude is revealed by his urging Stuart to put some of the publisher's own writings "in a separate shape which might ensure their duration." Thus on February 3 Coleridge told Thomas Poole, "The whole . . . is now publishing as a Pamphlet." [36] Wordsworth wanted to write for posterity, but he wanted to ride the already fast-subsiding wave of popular interest in the Convention of Cintra. On the horns of his dilemma De Quincey was nearly impaled.

Wordsworth decided to entrust his pamphlet to his regular publisher, Longman, even though he thought him "an arrant Jew, like most of his Brethren." [37] The printing was to be done by the London firm of C. and R. Baldwin, publishers of the *St. James Chronicle*. To London, then, the manuscript began to go, so that by the end of February ninety-six pages had been set. But postage was expensive, and mail between Grasmere and London took at best three full days and sometimes as long as ten days. Wordsworth chafed at the delay. What an opportunity for De Quincey to be of service! He had soaked up Wordsworth's ideas and

was generally well informed on the whole Spanish situation;
he had also been helping read the proofs and had been im-
posing his system upon Wordsworth's chaotic punctuation.
He was eminently qualified to go to London to superintend
the printing.

As Wordsworth explained the situation later to Thomas
Poole, it sounds as if De Quincey were going to be in London
anyway:

> Mr. De Quincey, some time before the time I have mentioned [March
> 30], took his departure from my house to London; and, in order to
> save time and expense, I begged that instead of sending the sheets down
> to me to be corrected, they should be transferred directly to him for
> that purpose; and I determined to send the remaining portions of the
> MSS to him as they were finished, to be by him transmitted to the
> Press (*MY*, I, 320).

De Quincey, however, hardly allowed himself a day's stop
in Liverpool on the way, to eliminate the merest possibility
of delaying the anticipated manuscript from Grasmere. Over
the months he became lonely and unhappy in the capital
where he had no friends, and apparently would not have
stayed except for his charge. That is not to say he would not
soon have brought his Allan Bank visit to a close anyway. He
wanted to see his family and make various arrangements for
transferring his belongings to the Lakes, for he had already
determined to follow Wordsworth as tenant of Dove Cottage. Still, there is little question that De Quincey went to
London primarily to shepherd the pamphlet through the
press. He went with a high sense of mission and was obviously pleased with himself and his responsibility. The last
time he had been in London it was as a refugee from a university examination, ill in body and depressed in spirit. Now
he went on the "king's business," as it were—the trusted
agent of Wordsworth himself. Earth really had nothing
more fair to show him. He magnified his office into "editing
a pamphlet" (p. 199).

Although De Quincey was in London, he was still tied to
Grasmere. With an almost ridiculous exclusiveness and pro-

tective possessiveness he cherished his relations with the
Wordsworths. He hesitated, for instance, to have Dorothy
deal directly with Manchester merchants in furnishing Dove
Cottage for him, because he did not want them to be able
"to say that they had 'corresponded' " with the Wordsworths. He spent solitary evenings rather than accept invitations from coffee-house acquaintances which might expose him to curiosity-seeking visits (Letters 12 and 31).
His own sustaining connection with the Grasmere shrine
which he was anxious to keep inviolate was a steady stream
of letters, swirling around the pamphlet but eddying to anything which he thought might interest the Wordsworths. On
April 29 when the "vexations of the Press" were beginning
to make it difficult for him to write, he voiced his own amaze-
ment at his unprecedented "epistolary labors." These labors,
however, were to continue with slight abatement until the
end of May in London, and a few more letters were to come
from Wrington before De Quincey finally got back to Grasmere. From the whole episode twenty-six letters to the
Wordsworths have survived, and at least two apparently
have not. Several of these were fairly long, journal-type
letters, and one was well over five thousand words. He con-
tracted that if the Wordsworths would walk to Rydal on
Friday nights they would be sure to find a letter from him,
and until the pamphlet was out he generally got off a letter
on Tuesday nights to keep his promise. In the same period
the Wordsworths—chiefly Dorothy but also William and
Mary—and Sara Hutchinson wrote to De Quincey eighteen
letters now known, and at least eleven others which seem to
have been lost. Wordsworth put four letters to De Quincey
in the post on one day, and the next understandably wrote,
"I have been not a little jeered this morning when it was
seen that I meant to trouble you with another letter." [38]
De Quincey's letters are sensitive barometers of his reading of the weather back at Grasmere. At the beginning his
exhilaration over his mission and the confidence reposed in
him was reflected in high-spirited epistles, gay and witty,
full of all kinds of chitchat. As the pamphlet dragged and
he suspected dissatisfaction in Westmorland, the letters got

shorter, duller, and more defensive. Once the pamphlet was published, there was a spurt of relief at the burden lifted and his own wishful sense of the job well done. After it became apparent that Wordsworth was not entirely pleased, there was again some of the defensive note, soon dismissed for a coloring of the old status—but the letters grew farther apart.

The sprightly character of De Quincey's early letters to Grasmere derives not only from his high spirits, but also from a self-conscious desire to amuse. In the 1853 general preface to his collected works he remarked that one large class of his writings proposed "primarily to amuse the reader"; for very special readers he was trying to do the same thing in 1809.[39] He picturesquely described the burning ruins of Drury Lane Theater, commented on the blood of the *Quarterly Review* lately sprung up, relayed any interesting tidbit of news, and even expounded upon the "artificial ears" to be had in London town. When the vicissitudes of the pamphlet made his reports dull, he apologized and promised "to make atonement by a more amusing letter" or "to brighten up soon," and, when by March 14 he had heard nothing from his long, chatty letter mailed March 7, he expressed concern because he had "put into it all which had any chance of amusing" (Letters 21, 23, and 14). Dorothy was flatteringly appreciative of his first letter, mailed March 2:

I then hastened with my prize to William, and sat down beside him to *read* the letter; and truly a feast it was for us— You were very good in being so particular in your account of your journey and that feeling of your goodness made the entertaining description of your Fellow-travellers far more delightful (*MY,* I, 260).

Even William went so far as to scrawl across the back of a section of the pamphlet manuscript—probably sent in early March—"Many thanks for your very interesting letter which was a great delight to us all." [40]

As far as Wordsworth was concerned, however, De Quincey was not in London to write interesting letters—and that the young legate very well knew. When William walked down with De Quincey to Ambleside when the young man was to take the post chaise which would connect with the southern coach at Kendal—probably on February 20—their talk was of the pamphlet, and Wordsworth bethought himself of a last-minute correction and begged his emissary to make an alteration. This De Quincey remembered to do, although Wordsworth apparently forgot about it until, in a flurry of apprehension over the possibility of opening himself to a libel prosecution, he sent a reminder on May 10.[41] Thus De Quincey's first letter, although it was full of "entertaining gossip" about his fellow passengers and other experiences since the morning of February 21 when he caught the coach, was also full of the Spanish business. He hastened to reassure the impatient author that his subject was not out of date, but, indeed, the time for the appearance of the pamphlet could hardly have been better chosen.

De Quincey had come to London on an errand a wiser man would have shunned. He was in the perfect position to be blamed for everything. The pamphlet was of little interest to the printers and publishers: they knew that it would not make any money. One of Longman's partners finally told De Quincey that only one political pamphlet in twenty was expected to clear expenses, and that this printing of 500 copies could not cover the costs even if all were sold. To Wordsworth, however, this was no mere political pamphlet. Coleridge was not far wrong in "feeling that a considerable part is almost a self-robbery from some great philosophical poem." The work was engrossing most of Wordsworth's energy—"Verses have been out of my Head for some time," he wrote in April—and enlisting his fiercest loyalties. He earnestly desired that it be translated into Spanish.[42] This pamphlet was in the noble tradition of Milton and Burke, a work of originality and profundity, and Wordsworth knew it. But it is a difficult thing to be a midwife to genius. How could De Quincey mediate between the enthusiasm of Grasmere and the apathy of London? He was a plenipotentiary without power.

Wordsworth gave De Quincey broad authorities with one hand, and took them back with the other. On March 6 he wrote, "As to the mode [of] publishing, advertising, etc. do not wait to consult me in anything. Mr. Stuart and you will do everything together." On March 26 he was writing: "The paragraph in the Advertizement must stand thus." Frequently he appealed to his disciple's judgment: "do as you think best," "do this, or let it alone, just as you like," "you may, if you think proper, add a footnote of two words," "You will therefore act exactly as you think proper; either make a comment on these papers, or not." But when De Quincey added a footnote on his own he was told peremptorily: "It will therefore be necessary to *cancel* the page with the footnote." When he wanted to send a copy of the pamphlet to Sir Arthur Wellesley: "Let it not be done on any account." [43] The naturally diffident and cautious De Quincey realized fully the delicacy of his situation. Although Wordsworth gave carte blanche on March 6, "Make any verbal alteration according to your better judgment," De Quincey sent back a list of five minor changes, pointing out the painstaking care which had gone into them. But even care was not guaranteed to please, for it smelled of delay, and the impatient author wrote: "I am truly sorry for the trouble you are put to, and beg that you would not be so anxious, particularly as to a misspelt word or so." [44]

To get some sense of the scope of this undertaking, we need to remind ourselves that this "pamphlet" was really a short book; that, with appendices, it ran to 216 pages in its first edition. When De Quincey arrived in London on February 25, copy for only ninety-six pages had been sent, and that was not yet all printed. It was not until March 4 that he received two packets of manuscript from Grasmere, and not until March 9 that the first "winding-up of the pamphlet" reached him. Despite the fact that so much was left to do, De Quincey was at the beginning most naïve about the difficulties he would face and the time it would take to get the pamphlet published. In the first two packets of copy he came across an obviously lame sentence for which he furnished a reading on March 5, offering to cancel it should Wordsworth disagree, and the pamphlet not be published before he could reply. This possibility is almost ludicrous in the face

of the reality: notice of publication finally appeared in the
Courier on May 27,[45] two and a half months later. De Quincey remained incorrigibly optimistic that the date of publication was just around the corner. On March 11 he asked for a
list of persons to whom Wordsworth wanted copies sent, as if
the need for such information were imminent. For three
weeks, when much was obviously yet to be set and the copy
was not even all in, the rosy expectations ceased. Then on
March 29 he thought the pamphlet might be published by
April 10 or 11; on April 5 he reported, although with a de-
veloping scepticism, the printer's promise to have it out by
April 10; and on April 15 he was saying that it was vain to
hope for it before April 19. On April 29 he was confident
that it would "advance regularly" and hoped it would be
out by May 3. By May 9 he expected it to be in Longman's
hands within two days; on May 12 he hoped to send Wordsworth a copy the next night; on May 16 he thought for a
while it would be published the next day. Thus the will-o'-
the-wisp danced ever before him. To read only Wordsworth's letters is to get the impression that the author fum-
ing at Grasmere founded his expectations on his impatience,
and compounded his frustration. But De Quincey was even
more impatient, and in his naïveté gave Wordsworth con-
tinual false encouragement.

De Quincey's natural and ostensible functions in London
were, as Wordsworth outlined them to Poole, to transmit
copy and read proof. There was enough involved in these
chores; but his commission also turned out to include keeping
abreast of the affairs in Spain, researching on matters of
fact and references for the isolated author, keeping a sharp
eye for libelous passages, and prodding the recalcitrant
printers. Even just "transmitting the copy" involved more
than the phrase suggests.

The copy was generally good, most of it having been
written by Dorothy or Sara. But there are references to
"interlineary corrections" and insertions in the margin which
confused the printers, and at least one passage had to be
transcribed. There were also cruxes in the manuscript, which
De Quincey sought to get cleared up, not always with suc-

cess. March 7 he sent off a letter inquiring about a defective
sentence; the same query was repeated on March 11, and
anxious references made to it on March 25 and again on
March 28. By April 1 he had received Wordsworth's answer, that the emendation he had proposed was correct; but
as he had suggested alternative corrections, he was no wiser.
This sort of indication that the poet was not careful in reading his letters rankled, as shows through De Quincey's jocu-
lar admission on May 12 that the passage had finally gone
to print by guess because Wordsworth had a second time
sent an ambiguous reply.

Of course these "alterations and insertions" complicated
the problem. No sooner did Wordsworth send off copy than
he began to fret about it: as Dorothy said, "You know he
never likes to trust anything away fresh from the Brain."
The last of the original version was sent off on March 5;
the day after Wordsworth was at it: "I do not mean to
pester you with more alterations; but two suggested themselves to me this morning which must be adopted." He
pestered on. The very next day Dorothy asked De Quincey
how he liked the "conclusion," but added that her brother
was then "engaged in making an addition to one Paragraph,"
to be transcribed on the back of her letter. William, however, came upstairs to say he could not get it done in time,
and she postscripted, *Stop the Press* at the words 'career
in the fulness of.' " [46] It was probably the following day,
March 8, that William sent, not "an addition to one Paragraph," but what De Quincey called "the supplementary
intercalation" (Letter 12) and which may have been substantial, since De Quincey later spoke of "the delay after
I first came to Town (occasioned by the insertion)" (Letter
25). In the same letter in which he acknowledged the receipt
of this "intercalation," De Quincey remarked that things
were going slowly because of the press' preoccupation with
the memoirs of Mrs. Clarke, former mistress of the Duke
of York. Wordsworth seized the "opportunity to add general matter to the Pamphlet." He wrote a great deal, trying
to say "all that was necessary," then suppressed half of it,
and sent the last sheets to De Quincey on March 26. The

next day, however, he was "haunted" with fears that he had
not made himself clear, and shamefacedly wrote with exaggerated politeness: "I must be permitted to submit to your
judgment the following two sentences to be added." [47]

These anxious afterthoughts doubly complicated the trans-
mission of copy because they were sometimes hard to fit in.
Wordsworth himself did not always know just where they
went: "The great body of additions sent, since the conclusion was sent, will begin in this manner, after some expression like this which I cannot recollect . . . I cannot find
the passage in my MS." [48] If any cobbling was necessary to
make the insertion fit, De Quincey would "be so good" as
to do it. Considering the length of the manuscript, it was
almost expecting De Quincey to know it by heart to give
such directions as:

There is one passage which would stand better thus (the sentence
would be clearer . . .), 'The tendency of such education to warp, and
therefore weaken the intellect,' omitting what is said about 'shutting
out from common sympathies and genuine knowledge.' I have said
'deposited in the Escurial.' Was that the Place? (*MY*, I, 269)

No wonder De Quincey gingerly expressed "some doubt" as
to the place of an addition, and Wordsworth admitted, "I
am afraid you will have endless trouble about the alterations,
small and great." [49]

That question about the Escorial—"Was that the Place?"
—is indicative of the range of De Quincey's chores beyond
merely transmitting copy and reading proof. This same
March 26 letter, which Wordsworth ruefully called a
"miserable jumble" and trusted to De Quincey's "habits of
order" to correct, also asked him to do the following things:
add some remarks in the Appendix on the "iniquitous"
French Bulletin if he thought it "advisable"; look up and
insert in the Appendix such parts as he "might approve of"
of a speech made to Bonaparte by "some Italian deputies"
and his answer; correct if necessary any quotations Wordsworth might have made from the proceedings of the Board
of Inquiry; change a reference to Norway as an independent
nation if he were in error in thinking her one; add a note

remedying an injustice done to General Ferguson; find and quote a passage in the *Courier* copied from the *Moniteur;* and send copies of the pamphlet to the Spanish and Portuguese ambassadors with Latin notes (as De Quincey had volunteered to do) as well as to a list of other prominent individuals. He also wanted to know what had been done about his request at Ambleside that De Quincey put in a note on the Government's rebuke of the City of London's petition for inquiry, comparing it with the conduct of Parliament in the time of Charles II. The next day, in another letter, he added piteously: "Do mend that stupid part of the Note, which I sent you; in fact my brains were utterly dried up when I wrote it." [50]

More substantial than any of these tasks was that which Wordsworth imposed on March 29 by asking De Quincey to write a note on Sir John Moore's letters, refuting his low opinion of the spirit of the Spanish people. Wordsworth prefaced his request with flattering remarks on De Quincey's knowledge of the campaign which would enable him to "find no difficulty" in making appropriate comments—and then proceeded to "just set down at random two or three thoughts such as struck me as a skeleton," [51] for about three printed pages. De Quincey put this note in a postscript, conscientiously holding it open until the last minute in case any other letters of Moore's might be published in the meantime, and so that he could adjust the length of his note to the number of pages left in the sheet. But it is not surprising that he "wrote under a sense of constraint," attempting to use Wordsworth's ideas "and sometimes his words" (Letter 28). It is perhaps not too much to say that everything De Quincey did about this pamphlet he did "under a sense of constraint." He was trying hard to please.

In his eagerness De Quincey sometimes voluntarily added to his load by anticipating revisions which would be required by changing events, or by questioning the accuracy of the copy. Before Wordsworth asked him to take account of the publication of the proceedings of the Board of Inquiry he had begun remodeling Appendix A, and he pointed out that Lord Cochrane's return required a change in the text (Letters 14 and 16). Such active concern for the welfare of the pamphlet was doubtless pleasing to Wordsworth, but it could get out of hand. When, on March 21, De Quincey was forced to accept the news that the valiant defense of Saragossa had finally collapsed, he thought it necessary to put in a note to bring Wordsworth's remarks about the noble city up to date. Wordsworth wrote back peremptorily instructing him to cancel the sheet, for it was impossible to keep the pamphlet current, and "Besides, you will see by what is now sent that so far from thinking that Saragossa has broken her bond, in my estimation she has discharged it to the Letter." [52] Wordsworth meant only that the footnote was anticipating what he himself said in the passages just sent, but the supersensitive De Quincey took the remark to be a rebuttal. He was deeply hurt, not so much at the cancellation of his note as at the "very great injustice" done him by Wordsworth's apparently supposing that he thought Saragossa had broken her bond. The sense of injury was vivid enough at Grasmere that, although William was away, Dorothy got off a soothing letter saying that she did not know what her brother had written, but she knew that she had heard him utter no sentiment which could give De Quincey "the slightest pain" and she must conclude that he had "expressed himself negligently" and been misunderstood. Two days after Wordsworth returned he wrote more stiffly, expressing concern that De Quincey should have suffered such mortification and describing his own feelings, but refusing much explanation for fear of "furnishing new matter for misconception." [53] De Quincey was not much mollified. He waited five days to answer; then he disavowed any unkind feelings which might make him imagine new grounds for misconception, reaffirmed his "love and veneration for all at Grasmere," and asserted that he was sure that the misapprehension was his; all was outwardly smoothed over.

What Wordsworth probably considered De Quincey's officiousness never again provoked the clash of orders to cancel a sheet, but it doubtless continued to be a small annoyance. De Quincey was irritatingly meticulous about trifles. It was perhaps only amusing when he looked into Asiatic

research to determine "the most learned and *ineffable* orthography" (Letter 20) of Ghengis Khan. But it was an-
noying when he vigorously questioned Wordsworth's statement that British troops were broken at Corunna and in
Egypt, investigated, discovered the author was correct about
Egypt but not Corunna, and decided to expunge the latter
reference. Wordsworth defended himself a little peevishly,
but was unwilling to make an issue of the matter and un-
graciously concluded, "Therefore, the word 'Corunna' may
be omitted." It was definitely going too far when De Quincey
took it upon himself to change the motto, taken from Bacon's
defense of "bitter and earnest writing" which expressed
"hate or love," to read "zeal or love." Wordsworth was
"sadly grieved about that error," [54] and directed that it be
included in the errata. Then he learned that De Quincey
had checked the passage in the best editions of Bacon and
found that it there stood "zeal," and was holding up the
errata until he could consult the edition from which Wordsworth had quoted, and another to verify that! Wordsworth's
sentiments on reading this have not survived, but one doubts
if he were properly grateful for De Quincey's care.

Thus De Quincey's duties, imposed or assumed, were
legion, and were assiduously performed for a somewhat
testy taskmaster. For Wordsworth's relation to the pamphlet was conspicuously umbilical. It was very hard for him
to let go of the work; still he was anxious to see it published,
and not very realistic about what he was expecting of his
representative at the press. His unreasonable impatience is
evident in his writing Lord Lonsdale on May 25 that the
pamphlet "was finished, and ought to have appeared, two
months ago." [55] Actually, De Quincey did not even receive
the last of the copy from Wordsworth until March 30, and
not until April 5 his instructions to begin writing the substantial note on Sir John Moore. Yet to the author's impatient retrospect the work ought to have appeared by the
end of March.

Maybe it really ought to have appeared by the end of
April. That it did not, undoubtedly cast a shadow between
Wordsworth and De Quincey. Exactly why it did not is a

vexed question. The causes of delay are a half-ridiculous, half-pathetic compound of meticulousness, ineptitude, and mischance. De Quincey was probably miscast in his role, despite all his obvious qualifications. Daniel Stuart, the proprietor of the *Courier* and friend of Wordsworth and Coleridge, who was supposed to look after the business end of publishing the pamphlet, may have expressed some doubts. For Coleridge wrote to Stuart on May 2:

I both respect and have an affection for Mr De Quincey; but saw too much of his turn of mind, anxious yet dilatory, confused from over-accuracy, & at once systematic and labyrinthine, not fully to understand how great a plague he might easily be to a London Printer, his natural Tediousness made yet greater by his zeal & fear of not discharging his Trust; & superadded to Wordsworth's own Sybill's Leaves blown about by the changeful winds of an anxious Author's Second-thoughts.[56]

Coleridge's observations were quite astute, about both the anxious author and the zealous disciple. De Quincey certainly did have trouble with the printers, as he was to have on his own copy years later. Yet he began with glowing praise for the accuracy of the printing. On March 11 he wrote happily that he could not "detect a single error" in the first ninety-six pages. He must, however, have taken a closer look, for on March 28 he declared that in these same pages the printers had made many mistakes in punctuation and had ignored the "interlineary corrections" (Letters 12 and 16). Quite possibly the jaundiced view reflects a change in De Quincey's relations with "Baldwin's fiends," as he liked to call them. In his March 21 letter he had complained that a new compositor had been put on the pamphlet who was making such "monstrous errors" that he was insisting on second proofs. By March 25, even more scrupulous in collating the proof three or four times with the manuscript and also reading *verbatim et literatim,* he had become so incensed at the "extreme carelessness" that he had begun to demand a third proof, and was holding up galleys the printers wanted to strike off and redistribute.

Undoubtedly De Quincey's insistence on exact adherence

to his system of punctuation was also a thorn to the press.
It seems a curious thing for an author to do, but Wordsworth himself explained to Thomas Poole, "as the subject
of punctuation in prose was one to which I had never attended, and had of course settled no scheme of it in my own
mind, I deputed the office to Mr. De Quincey." [57] De Quincey's intention was to make the punctuation "a representation
of the logical divisions—and a gamut of the proportions
and symmetry of the different members—of each sentence"
(Letter 16). This logic he had a hard time impressing upon
the compositor, but he persisted in demanding "minute attention" to his punctuation, and probably made himself increasingly obnoxious.

From the beginning, however, De Quincey complained
about the delays of the press. When he first arrived he found
copy unset. On March 11 he remarked that things had "gone
on rather slowly," and offered the first of a remarkable
series of explanations for the lack of progress: all the presses
were neglecting other business to publish Mrs. Clarke's
memoirs. On March 21 it was the "stupid" new compositor
who was to blame; on April 5 the Easter week holiday; on
April 15 he was incensed that the printers dropped their
regular work to turn out "bills &c," and he threatened to
call on Mr. Baldwin—as he had already done once. On
April 21 he complained bitterly of a drunken compositor he
could not get changed, and four days later, angry that the
compositor showed up only two days in six and must have
been drunk then, he saw no help except to get another printer.
By April 29 he had learned that Baldwin was working over-
time to publish a property of his own, and he suspected
that the "absentee" compositor had all the time been at work
on that in another room—anyway, "Mr. B. must be a
rascal."

The increasing vehemence of De Quincey's criticism of
the press corresponds not only with the accumulation of
delay, but also with his dawning recognition that he was
suspected in Grasmere of being the cause of it. Wordsworth
had been half-glad at the early delays, which gave him an

opportunity to extend the pamphlet by long insertions, but he seems to have made no changes after March 28, and he expected the pamphlet soon thereafter: on March 30 he wrote to Poole, "I suppose it will be out in less than a fortnight." As the printing dragged on, he first accepted without question De Quincey's explanations of the causes. Thus on April 26 he sent off a peremptory letter begging Stuart to use his exertions "to procure the immediate finishing of the work, which has been most shamefully and injuriously delayed by a drunken compositor whom Mr. De Quincey cannot get changed." [58] Stuart, apparently, got from Baldwin quite a different story, and feeling the matter a little delicate, enlisted Coleridge's help in dealing with Wordsworth. Coleridge agreed that De Quincey could be a plague in a print shop and wrote Wordsworth that he doubted if the printers would be found so much at fault as he imagined. The author took the suggestion a bit stuffily and wrote Stuart:

I find, from Coleridge, that the Printers accuse Mr. de Quincey and myself of being the cause of the delay of the publication, by the chopping and changing that has taken place. As for myself, the charge gives me no concern; whatever harm has been occasioned by the delay cannot now be remedied. Mr. de Quincey will be happy [to] lay before you his opinion of the causes of the delay (*MY,* I, 297).

The effect of Coleridge's letter seems to have been to include Wordsworth with De Quincey in the printer's indictment, and thus to produce a solid front of defense against the charge of "chopping and changing." Wordsworth took the same line with Stuart when the pamphlet finally reached him: "It is now printed exactly as I sent it . . . how could any alterations of his [De Quincey's] in the text have caused this long delay?" [59] Evidently Wordsworth did not even honor the accusations to the extent of repeating them to De Quincey. It would perhaps have been better if he had, for De Quincey sensed a silent treatment from Grasmere. He complained of receiving no "cheering" letters, and he was vaguely aware that he was charged with something, he knew not what. His letters take on a desperate defensive tone as he insists, "I am truly sorry that I cannot make my anxiety for the early appearing of the work *manifest* itself more in the progress of the printing" (Letter 22).

De Quincey suspected that Stuart was blaming him for the delays. Perhaps he had always been a little jealous of Stuart's position as senior adviser. Not only had the work begun to appear in the *Courier,* but apparently the older man had also served as the author's agent in London until De Quincey's arrival; for Wordsworth wrote Stuart that he had put the pamphlet in his young friend's hands partly to save Stuart trouble. Probably Stuart, too, had remembered the character which Coleridge had given him of the "boyish-looking modest man" and thought "old batchelor precise-ness" had no place in a topical political pamphlet.[60] He seems to have urged Wordsworth early in the business to hurry up and print, and leave his second thoughts to a second edition. On March 29 he visited De Quincey to ask about the progress of the pamphlet. The sense of rivalry, if not felt by Stuart, was at least projected onto him by De Quincey, for he wrote Wordsworth that he feared the business adviser thought his privileges were being encroached upon (Letter 30). Probably De Quincey reflected some of his own animus in telling Wordsworth that the *Courier* was too "Canningly" and "Castlereaghy" for him, and regretting that the paper was mentioned in the Preface of the pamphlet (Letter 26). It was a petty little drama, but important to De Quincey, for he was conscious of Stuart as a critical observer who might report unfavorably and unfairly to Grasmere.

On April 25 he wrote with a confidence he did not feel, trusting that Stuart would satisfy himself "as to the real cause of the delay" and defending the rigor of his attention to punctuation because no time had been lost thereby, and if it had, it would have been worth it! He was certain that the printers covered themselves by making one set of excuses to Stuart and another to him, and he insisted finally, as he wrote on May 9, that they "confront" the pressmen together. He was uneasy that he had been "misrepresented" about the business. Still uneasy, the next day he got off a "long letter—wondrously dull!—being all in defence of myself," in which he gave the dates at which he delivered manuscript to the press and explained that he had always kept ahead of their need for copy and why he held the post-script on Moore until last. It is all quite plausible, and pathetic. He wrote, he said, "not as thinking that you would readily believe that the pamphlet had been delayed thro' my means" (Letter 25). But the "readily" was added as an afterthought, and the "delayed" was a substitution for an original "neglected."

The double irony of this long-winded defense is that it was just the kind of "fending and proving" which alienated Wordsworth, and besides he had suddenly shifted his priority from speed to caution. Wordsworth had been badly scared by reading of several court sentences for libel, and had written to Stuart on May 3 asking him to look over the pamphlet and cancel any suspected passages—"as to the expense, that I disregard in a case like this." When he did not hear promptly from Stuart, he panicked. On the same day that De Quincey was penning his apologies for the delay, Wordsworth was writing him "my anxiety to have it out has much abated," [61] and urging that no pains be spared to prevent the possibility of prosecution. De Quincey made the mistake of failing to understand how terribly earnest Wordsworth was about this, how completely fear had rooted out impatience. He indeed canceled one passage on Wordsworth's direct orders, and made a list of possibly suspect sections for Stuart's consideration; but he spoke of being willing to insure the pamphlet against prosecution and joked about "no hope of Newgate." Even worse, he withstood Stuart's desire to cancel a passage which was not on his list, arguing that it was not libelous, and with Baldwin's backing talked Stuart out of his intention. Nervous Wordsworth was irked; he wrote Stuart that he would be "most grievously vexed" if the experienced publisher's judgment had been overborne by De Quincey's perseverance instead of convinced by his arguments.[62] De Quincey felt obliged to write another dreary defense, insisting that Stuart had voluntarily withdrawn his objections. Worst of all, however, was De

Quincey's letter of May 24 describing dramatically his chagrin on learning on Thursday that the pamphlet, although
done, would take until Monday to dry and be published, and
the success of his bold proposal that fifty copies go immediately to Longman's to be dried before the fire and circulated
within two hours. He was obviously pleased with himself
and expected applause. But he dropped in casually the information that the last sheet had apparently been struck off
without waiting for Stuart's approval. The jittery author
was totally unappreciative of even Herculean efforts to get
out a pamphlet which he feared might land him in jail.
"This has angered me much," he wrote to Stuart. When he
learned a few days later that all this dangerous haste had
been pointless, for the pamphlet still languished at Longman's unpublished, it was too much. As he told Stuart, "I
have kept my temper till last night, but I must say that Mr.
De Quincey's letter of last night, ruffled me not a little." To
Poole he fumed, "Now is not this provoking?" [63] The cross
purposes are in retrospect merely ludicrous, since there was
no prosecution and no tragedy ensued except an intangible
one of human relations. To Wordsworth it seemed almost
that "there was a fatality attending" the pamphlet; De
Quincey wrote sadly and presciently of the troubles which
beset a delayed and repacked box for Grasmere: "I did not
like *always* to be making blunders" (Letter 32).

Thus the long-promised pamphlet finally came off the
press. On May 17 De Quincey had four advance copies
specially struck and sent to Grasmere, and anxiously awaited
the reaction. When by May 27 Wordsworth still had not said
a word, De Quincey wrote expressing his alarm at the
silence, and supposing—since he had submitted his revisions
for approval—that his postscript did not please. That, he
declared with a pathetic plea for recognition of his sacrifices
to the cause, was as good as he could make it under the
circumstances, especially the oppression of three months'
"solitariness." [64]

Actually the pamphlets did not arrive in Grasmere until
May 23. The next day William and Sara wrote a letter which

apparently did not reach the wistful De Quincey until May 29—a letter which seemed mainly concerned with errata, although Wordsworth graciously supposed the faults were in the manuscript and was "surprised" that De Quincey had been able to get it printed "so correctly." He pronounced the note on Moore "very well done," and offered "sincere thanks for all the trouble"; but he did not even mention the punctuation, and the whole tone of the letter was not warm enough to satisfy the young agent.[65] He boldly quoted Revelation: "I would thou wert cold or hot" (Letter 32). But he did not admit this until after he had received another, more conciliatory letter inspired by Mary, who asked her husband why he did "not use stronger language of approbation." With this May 26 letter, De Quincey professed himself much pleased. To the objective eye, the second letter seems scarcely better than the first. Mary appended a longish chat about domestic affairs, but William's part was brief and ambivalent. True, he said the "punctuation pleases me much," but he added "there are trifling errors in it"; he was glad De Quincey treated Moore with such gentleness, but his own feelings would not have allowed him to do so; he wished something nice had been said about Frere; he deplored the "error" in the Motto; and he wished now that he had had the foresight to ask that the proof sheets be sent to him for review—the very thing which De Quincey's presence in London was supposed to make unnecessary! [66] This is faint praise indeed, and De Quincey could have been satisfied with it only as the wish was father to the thought.

In truth Wordsworth was not happy, and although he did not wish to hurt De Quincey's feelings, his honesty could not allow him more hearty praise. As he wrote to Stuart with an attempt at resignation:

But it avails nothing to find fault, especially with one [who] has taken such pains (according to the best of his judgement) to forward this business—that he has failed is too clear, and not without great blame on his own part (being a man of great abilities and the best feelings, but, as I have found, not fitted for smooth and speedy progress in business) (MY, I, 319).

Somewhat unreasonably, he blamed De Quincey for the delay at Longman's in getting the pamphlet out, a delay caused, he conjectured, by Stuart's not having been informed: "what proof had Mr. De Quincey that this message was sent, much less that you had received it?" It seems not to have occurred to Wordsworth that Stuart was a man of many affairs of his own which may have taken precedence over the ill-fated pamphlet, and that the blame may have rested with him or Longman's. Somewhat more fairly, before he had been "ruffled" by this last delay, he told Stuart, "I have no doubt that Mr. De Quincey was *the occasion,* though I am at the same time assured that he neither was, nor could be, the necessary *cause* of the delay." And he speculated plausibly as to this occasion, both to Stuart and to Poole: "He had been so scrupulous with the Compositor, in having his own plan rigorously followed to an iota, that the Man took the Pet, and whole weeks elapsed without the Book's advancing a step." [67] Some of the monstrous errors which De Quincey complained of suggest that the compositors may have been teasing him: "they had introduced a *not* in the followg. place—'Done and concluded *not* the year and day above-mentioned' " (Letter 27). Although he was sure that the overseer, Mr. Westray, was his good friend, "bait De Quincey" may have become a print-shop sport. The printers may even have made up the story of the drunken compositor, but there were drunken proof sheets to match, and the responsibility was not De Quincey's. Possibly he was an occasion of delay, and it was a delicious understatement to say that he was "not fitted for smooth and speedy progress in business." Did this add up to "great blame on his own part"? It did to Wordsworth when he was exasperated, and he was even more exasperated on June 4 when he discovered that at least two of the ten stitched copies which De Quincey had sent him contained the sheet with the possible libel which was supposed to have been canceled; he could not speak for the other eight because he had already sent them off when he made the discovery—it was like finding half a worm in an apple. Angrily he wrote to Stuart: "I do earnestly entreat that you would do all in your power to have this remedied—

it has mortified me more than I can express." It was, he exclaimed, "a must culpable inattention on the part of some one." [68] He added that he had addressed a letter to the same purpose to De Quincey. Whether or not De Quincey was explicitly the culpable one, the letter was unlikely to have been pleasant. It must have arrived, for on July 7 De Quincey expressed to Dorothy fears that his last letter, written sometime in June, and containing among other things "some words about the canceled sheet," had not been received. Wordsworth's letter to De Quincey, however, seems not to have survived. Did the young disciple, goaded too far, hold it to the candle?

The grand mission had not been a success, although De Quincey tried to put a good face on it. He reported that by June 30 the pamphlet had sold 170 copies and he expected a second edition would be required, even hoped that it might become "*the rage*—and produce some thousand pounds." For such a cause he gladly volunteered, not knowing that Wordsworth had already made arrangements with Stuart to superintend a second edition if one should be called for. The need never arose, for although, as Dorothy put it, the pamphlet "made considerable impression . . . among a few," an unappreciative public remained apathetic. Even for this the unlucky De Quincey was apparently blamed at Grasmere. Not only was his finicky punctuation believed responsible for holding up the pamphlet until the iron was cooled, but that same punctuation was accused of making the work less readable. On June 13 Coleridge wrote Stuart from Grasmere that he feared the style was not accessible to common readers "partly from Mr De Quincey's strange & most mistaken System of punctuation—. The Periods are often alarmingly long perforce of their construction; but De Quincey's Punctuation has made several of them immeasurable, & perplexed half the rest. Never was a stranger whim than the notion that , ; : and . could be made logical symbols expressing all the diversities of logical connection." Southey also wrote Scott that Wordsworth's sentences were long and involved and "his friend, De Quincey, who corrected the press, has rendered them more obscure by an unusual system of punctuation." To John May (July 1, 1809) Southey seemed to blame the obscurity entirely on "the way in which his friend De Quincey has punctuated it." [69]

These complaints are somewhat difficult to understand: the punctuation does not seem peculiar; and where De Quincey's work can be gauged by comparison with the part of the pamphlet published in the *Courier,* it appears that he broke up some involved sentences and generally wrought improvement.[70] The charge may stem from Coleridge, whose critical, even antagonistic attitude toward De Quincey invites speculation. Is it the friction of similar natures, the irritation at being indebted to and exposed to a younger and inferior counterpart? Or is it half-jealousy of De Quincey for aspiring to the kind of intimacy Coleridge had enjoyed with Wordsworth but was losing? In any event, if Coleridge and Southey thought De Quincey's punctuation was a drag on the pamphlet, Wordsworth undoubtedly was at least aware of that point of view, and he would have been more than human entirely to have resisted that "flattering unction" to his author's vanity. Considering the provocation of his frustration, and the encouragement he had to take it out on De Quincey, Wordsworth's surviving letters to the young man are gentler than might have been expected. He was probably, like Lady Catherine, "seriously displeased," but he sent grudging compliments.

The whole *Convention of Cintra* episode left De Quincey just where he had been: on better footing with the women and children of the household than with the poet. Dorothy had been most sympathetic: "Oh, how I shall rejoice for your sake, and for the sake of your poor head and eyes, when the pamphlet is fairly *published!*" Tactfully she had written, "I do not think it likely that you would have 'Author of the L.B. etc.' printed in the title-page, which must by no means be done." She praised, "You have indeed been a Treasure to us," and "Thank you again and again for writing such 'nice letters.' " Sara wrote him about his cottage and his orchard, and once, "Mary desires her love to you." [71] Mary urged William to be more appreciative and, half-ashamed of her simplicity, sent to De Quincey domestic chat about the children. This situation is the more interesting because when the break finally came between Wordsworth and De Quincey, he blamed the women. Now Wordsworth was kind enough, regularly addressing De Quincey as "my dear friend," signing himself "affectionately," and saying in the letter which De Quincey would spit out as neither hot nor cold, "I must beg to hear when you purpose to return to Grasmere . . . We shall all be most happy to see you." Nevertheless, when he wrote to Coleridge he noted, "Mr. De Quincey says in his last letter" [72]—the young man was still *"Mr.* De Quincey," not one of the inner circle.

L E T T E R S , 1808–May, 1809

8. *To Dorothy Wordsworth*

Ms. Dove Cottage. Pub. in part, Eaton, pp. 126–128.

Worcester College
March 25, 1808.

Dear Madam,

I mentioned to Mr. Wordsworth in London (though I believe not very fully) the nature of the complaint in my head which had forced me to forbear writing altogether and reading in a great measure since my last letter. I hope that what I said then will have been sufficient (if he has recollected it) to account for what must else have appeared so strange an inattention to your two letters:[1] but, for fear that he may have forgotten what I said or may not yet have returned to Grasmere, I will repeat what I said or meant to say to him.—On my journey to this place from Grasmere I left Manchester for Birmingham soon after midnight in a very rapid mail; and in two hours after reaching Birmingham came on to Oxford in another: the feverishness which followed went off (as usual) after sleeping; but either that or the uneasy doze in which I had passed the night between Manchester and Birmingham left behind a strange affection in my head almost like lethargy so that I frequently fell asleep in the middle of the day: this gradually abated; and it was during this abatement (which I then hoped was leading regularly on to a close) that I wrote last: but in a few days after it finally settled into the complaint which I had before my visit to Grasmere—called, I believe, a determination of blood to the head: after getting through the term as well as I could, I went up to London; and there, by paying strict attention to the advice of my able surgeon—namely drinking no wine and never bending my head downwards, I recovered very soon so far as to be able to read very well by holding the book up in my hand; but still, fearing to do anything which might fling me back (having so much occasion for sanity of head at this particular time), I never ventured to write anything but a letter of business containing only a few lines.—I came down to col-

---

Letter 8:

[1] These letters seem not to have survived.

lege last Saturday fortnight almost entirely recovered; and found
your letter (as Mr. Wordsworth had given me reason to hope) lying
here: ever since then however until within a day or two (either from
having walked part of the way from London frequently without my
hat or from sleeping with my head too low) I have been wholly incapacitated from writing by a return of my complaint strengthened by
an inability to sleep until about morning when mere exhaustion forces
me into sleep: this attack would no doubt have yielded sooner to the
remedies prescribed to me in London but the anxiety which I could
not subdue as to the public examination for a degree urged me perpetually to attempt reading though I found that I could read to no
purpose; so that, finding the whole university on tiptoe for the approaching prize-fighting and myself in a state of palsy as to any
power of exertion, I felt very much as in dreams which I recollect
where I have been chaced by a lion and spellbound from even attempting to escape. Within these two days however I have recovered almost
entirely and having just received from my mother a reading-stand very
ingeniously constructed, I find myself able to read and write even with
advantage to my head from the necessity of looking up; so that I should
now have no doubt of mastering the quantity of labor if I could reconcile myself a little better to it's quality; but for the most part it consists
of learning by heart immense (*systems* they are called but in reality)
collections of unassorted details which, not being dependencies on any
common law—so that, the law in which they were involved being
known, the tributary parts—corollaries—illustrations &c. might be
elaborated by an extempore process of intellect during the examination
—but having almost as slight logical relations as the names of the men
living in a given street, must be gained by separate acts of memory.
And even that part of the labor which would of itself be pleasant becomes painful from the necessity of hurrying through it; as with respect
to reading the Greek tragedies; for, having now to do before about the
10th. of May what I doubted about being able to do between December
and that day, I have been obliged in my distribution of labor for the
next six weeks to crowd the reading through all the 33 tragedies into
one week; so that I must pass with such speed from grief to grief that
they are to me in prospect like the *woes* in the Revelations, only that
between those woes I remember some breathing-space is allowed which
mine will hardly admit of.—The motives to all this labor are besides
inadequate; for the difference between success and non-success are the

being placarded on all the college walls as the *Illustrious* Mr. A.B.C.
or 2ndly. as the *Praiseworthy* Mr. A.B.C. or 3rdly. the not being
placarded at all; and also the gratifying or displeasing one's own college; each of which motives is powerful enough with me, whilst I am
living with University men, to make me wish to be *Illustrious* at the
beginning of May next—but not powerful enough to transfer pleasure
on the means of atchieving that end.

I have wandered into a very long account of myself and my present
engagements which I began with the purpose of explaining the reason
for which I have been compelled to defer answering your letter; for,
though I have been repeatedly urged to attempt it from the presence
of painful feelings whenever I thought for any length of time what
interpretation you could give to such seeming negligence, I have been
compelled to leave off before I had finished the first sentence not merely
from the instant gathering of blood about my head but from an absolute
inability to give any coherent account of myself whilst in the uneasy
state of feeling which it caused.—I have hoped however all along that
you would suppose I was not in college and had not received your
letter.

Mr. Coleridge was at Bristol during the first week or two of my
stay in London; and gave his first lecture so soon after his return that
I did not know of his being in Town until some days after: that lecture
therefore I did not hear: of the second (and last), which was given a
fortnight afterwards, I meant to have dictated all that I remembered
to some acquaintance and to have sent it to Grasmere; but I found that
Mr. Coleridge considered it a very imperfect execution of his plan—
and that therefore, when he published his lectures (which he said he
should do immediately), so far as it differed from the spoken lecture
it would be improved; for Mr. Coleridge—being exceedingly ill on the
day he delivered that lecture—gave only one extempore illustration, I
believe, of which he will most probably be reminded by a note. I thought
besides that this lecture, from its very subject as a purely historical one,
would be less interesting to you than the philosophical ones which
[*torn*] ceed: it's general purport was to clear the ground for a just
estimate of Shakespeare by separating what he had individually from
what he had as a member of a particular nation in a particular age:
in order to which the progress of the drama was traced from the
mysteries downwards to Shakespeare; and it was shewn that the Fool

and the Clown were a bequest to the Shakespearian age from the mysteries—being the representatives of the Vice and the Devil degraded into secondary parts; that these parts of Shakespeare were therefore to be considered as necessary concessions to the lower part of the audience; but that, out of even this bad metal, he had wrought excellent workmanship: then a parallelism was noticed (though this part stood first, I believe, in order of time) in the Greek drama where the chorus, from being a whole in itself, passed into the relation of a part—first as a principal to an accessory—then as an accessory to a principal. The first lecture must have been very interesting as a general reconoitering of the ground before the engagement: it stated the question as to the existence of positive beauty; and distinguished the permanent tastes from the factitious ones introduced by commerce &c.: but this lecture I did not hear or see: and Mr. Coleridge said that he should expand it into an octavo volume and send it to the press immediately.[2]

I beg my kindest respects to Mrs. Wordsworth of whose continued ill health I was much concerned to hear frequently from Mr. Coleridge and afterwards from Mr. Wordsworth: when you are kind enough to write again, you will (I hope) say whether she has found any benefit from the advice which Mr. Wordsworth intended to ask in London.

I do not think that I can now be visible even in the twilight of Dorothy's memory or even of John's;[3] and therefore to desire my love to them would be to send them a message from a cluster of vowels and consonants having no more connexion with their feelings than the A.B. illustration of a logician or the Sophion and Philalethes of dialogues have with mine: but *I* shall be very glad to hear of *them;* which I mention, because you say nothing of them in your last letter. I must mention that I heard the whole of The White Doe read in London excepting the Introduction which, as you perhaps know, Mr. Wordsworth read to me on the Sunday we spent on Ulleswater.—I will not attempt to say in my present hurry how much I was de-

---

[2] De Quincey describes a lecture given on Feb. 5, the second of Coleridge's 1808 series at the Royal Institution. Coleridge did not forthwith bring out the octavo volume, but a part of his material can probably be found in the fragment "The Definition of Taste." (See T. M. Raysor, *Coleridge's Shakespearean Criticism* [London: Constable & Co., 1930], I, 176–184.)

[3] Dorothy Wordsworth (later called Dora) was born Aug. 16, 1804; John was born June 18, 1803.

lighted.—The Ariosto I need not say anything about, as Mr. Wordsworth told me in London that he wished to keep it for revision on
account of some harshness in the versification.[4]

Considering my own tardiness hitherto, it seems almost audacious to
ask you to write; but I may say very sincerely that the one single morning of pleasure which I expect to see for the next six weeks is that
hypothetical morning on which I *may* receive a letter from Grasmere.

I remain, dear Madam, most affectionately and respectfully yours,
Thos. de Quincey.

[*Across folded back:*] I am afraid that you will hardly be able to read
this letter; but the truth is that, this being here a beautiful spring
morning succeeding to some inclement days, the whole college are gone
out to see a military show; and I have been therefore obliged to refit
an old disabled hulk of a pen which under a press of sail goes most
crazily.

[*Address:*] Miss Wordsworth / Grasmere / near Kendal / Westmoreland /
        Single Sheet
[*Stamp:*] Oxford

9. *To Dorothy Wordsworth*

Ms. Dove Cottage. Unpub.

Worcester College
May 8th, 1808.

Dear Madam,

I write a few lines in acknowledgement of your kind and most welcome letter. You will, I am sure, excuse my not writing *more* than a
few lines, when I mention that I am now reading every day for 18
hours out of the 24—and never go at all to bed but only fall asleep on
a sofa when I can keep awake no longer. I am afraid you will think
this very foolish; but, having been treated with great kindness by my
college, I cannot endure to disappoint their expectations if the time I
have remaining will enable me to do what I have undertaken.

---

[4] Probably Wordsworth's translation of *Orlando Furioso,* two books of
which he had completed by 1805 (*EL,* p. 529), but only a fragment of
which survives (see *Poetical Works,* IV, 367–369, 472).

I am very much obliged to you for the interesting history contained in your letter [1] and inclose 5£. You will guess that I am not one of the rich; but I will mention it to my sisters and mother (who comes nearer to that class of people) the next time I write:—at present I have a drawer full of letters which I am quite unable to answer.

The examinations are already begun; and a great many criminals are already *turned off;* but, having prevailed on the proctor to insert my name as a *Q.* in the calendar, I am respited until about next Friday week.

I beg to be most kindly and respectfully remembered to Mr. and Mrs. Wordsworth—and am, dear Madam, very affectionately and gratefully yours,

Thos. de Quincey.

Sunday night.—

[*Address:*] Miss Wordsworth / Grasmere / near Kendal / Westmoreland /
[*Stamp:*]   Oxford

10. *To Dorothy Wordsworth*

Ms. Dove Cottage. Pub. in part, Eaton, pp. 151–153.

82, Great Titchfield St.—Cavendish Square [London]
[March 2, 1809]

My dear Madam,

Having very little time to *select,* I think it best to put down anything at all noticeable in the form of a Diary.—Tuesday morng. Feb, 21st.—*Rose at half past 4!;*—breakfasted by 9 in Lancaster;—here took up a foreigner who railed at the Spaniards—attributing to them all the disasters and hardships of OUR army (as he had the audacity to call it): I suggested that he must first prove the fact that Gallicia *had* failed our army in any express or implied engagements made to it;—2nd. if she had he must prove that this was not a *necessary* consequence of her own poverty;—3rd. he must prove, if this were not so—but a *voluntary* witholdg. of assistance, that Gallicia, who had not created but adopted the war, was to be held an evidence of what might be

---

Letter 9:
[1] Dorothy's letter seems to have been lost. The "history" was of the Green tragedy; see above, p. 54.

expected fr. the South.—In answer he said that, as to the 1st. point he had lately seen 60 English soldiers who had served in Spain—and agreed that of 2 evils—French and Spaniards—the French were far the least;—that, as to the 3rd., he had lived within 20 miles of Bayonne, and *therefore* must be allowed to understand the Spanish character.—A Farmer, who sat opposite approved of all that the foreigner said—adding, by way of confirmation, 'Why, it was but the other day that a Portighee (and that's all one with a Spaniard) killed an Englishman at Plymouth with a knife—(here telling a story which was in the Papers some months ago).—After it was agreed that *Portighees* and Spaniards were '*all one,*' I thought it better to say no more—At Preston took up, among others, a man lookg. like a lawyer—and an intelligent lookg. young man. Something being said, when the coach stopped for a few minutes, about Spain—the young man asked me how the war there was going on; and to my great surprise I found that he knew literally nothing of *what* had happened in Spain since last summer—not even that Bonaparte had entered it. The next time the coach stopped, I began—at his desire—to give him a sketch of the campaign; I had just got to the skirmish of Tudela—when he interrupted me with—"Well, but the English have an army there?"—at this moment the coach began to move . . . and, the road fm. Lancastr. to Lipool being all paved made such a rattling that I who sat at a distance fm. the young man (it was a *long* coach), could not go on; —but unfortunately the lawyer, who sate opposite to him, took upon himself to answer this question; and I had the misery for a whole quarter of an hour of sitting without being able to hear what he said but catching here and there—'*Sir J. Moore*'—'*Corunna*'—etc.—and not doubting that the whole was a horrid compost fm. English Gazettes—private letters—French Bulletins etc. However I resolved what to do; and accordingly, when we arrived at Liverpool (about dusk) instead of going to the house of an acquaintance—I went into the Inn coffee-room, guessing that the young man—who seemed a stranger—would come in also:—he soon did; and I had the pleasure of seeing him making his way up to the place where I sate:—there I disabused him of all the lies which no doubt the lawyer had told him —by expounding to him from the beginning all which had happened in both Spain and Portugal.—When I had finished, I could not help expressing to him my surprise that, anything of what I had told him should be news to him: he unriddled the matter by telling me that he

was an American who had just come over in one of the ships which
had broke the Embargo.—He told me that in America they were
absorbed in their own domestic feuds too much to take any interest in
any European News which did not bear directly on their interests. He
gave me some anecdotes about Maddison's election which, he said,
was carried by the Irish votes—and in two states by fradulent means;
—the Irish making it their single inquiry—What will distress England?—*Gallatin* [1] is not, as Mr. Coleridge (I think) supposed a
Frenchman, but a Swiss . . . and has qualified himself by the stat-
utable residence—Englishmen are still in most states better received
than men of any other nation.—He seemed, from the style of his
answers, very well able to have given me a great deal of useful information—if I had not been too sleepy to extract it.—The next morning,
when I came down to breakfast (though it was really not 10 o'clock),
I was sorry to meet the American at the door of the coffee-room just
going out on business; and I had no opportunity of seeing him again.—

Wednesday—Feb 22. Calculating that, if the M.S. were sent off from
Grasmere as soon even as Mr. Wordsworth proposed, it could not
reach London before Saturday,—I thought I might venture to stay
until the next day—particularly as I had some arrangements to make
about my books in Liverpool (supposing I might not return through
L. but by the Eastern road).

Thursday—Feb 23.—The coach was to set off exactly at 6 in the
evening:—I found the horses harnessed—and no place to be had (for
I had neglected to take one—from irresolution on collating the merits
of the different coaches) :—at length it was discovered that one passenger was going only 36 miles;—I agreed therefore to go so far on
the outside.—We did not reach Knutsford—which is only 30 miles
fm. L.—till 12 o'clock; and on inquiry it was thought certain that
nobody would be up when we got to Chelford: this was bad news for
me who had with great difficulty kept myself warm by borrowing one
of the coachman's coats—the night being piercingly cold—and latterly
with still greater difficulty kept myself fm. falling asleep. 'However,'
said the landlord at Knutsford, 'you have only to tell them at Chelford
that a gentleman for Col. Parker's is in the coach; and, if they were all

Letter 10:
[1] Albert Gallatin (1761–1849), then U. S. Secretary of the Treasury.

as fast as tops, I'll warrant they'll hear!'—We reached Chelford soon
after one; and tho' Col. Parker's name did not certainly operate any
magical effect until it was enforced by a general storm fm. guard-
coachman–and passengers—against doors and windows, yet—when it
was heard—it is but justice to allow that it had all the effect of
Orlando's name when muttered to the warden—by makg. the doors
&c. all fly open in an instant. Lodgings however they had none un-
occupied which would suit a visitor of Col. P's;—we were therefore
to try a mile or two farther on;—here luckily they had; and accordingly the passenger got out;—I took his place; and, for the first time
in my life, slept for some hours without pain in a coach. Friday—Feb.
24th.—In the morning I studied the faces of my 5 companions:—2 of
them we dropped before we reached Birmingham;—the other 3 were,
as I discovered by degrees, a *femme de chambre* of the Marchioness of
Donegal—a young Irishman about 23—apparently not a gentleman
but very frank and engaging in his manners—and another about 16
(as he told us)—who received pay as a Surgeon in the army and was
now going up to attend lectures in London. In the waiting-woman
one might easily discover that she had been a piece of furniture to a
woman of fashion:—she had met with the Irishmen in the packet coming over fm. Belfast—and, having received attentions fm. one of
them, appeared to think that gratitude required of her to be gracious
and condescending: nevertheless, by her stories about 'my ld. Belfast
—ld. Francis—and Ld Spencer Chichester'—etc. she reminded us not
to abide her condescension.—She said nothing worthy of mention except that she gave us an interesting account of the storms at a house
of Ld. Donegal's in East Lothian—where she had once passed some
months:—it stood upon the sea-shore; and upon some occasions a single
night's storm was sufficient to break all the windows on the sea-side;
so that, at the last, they were obliged to nail up oil-cloth for their protection.—At Stone we took up a boy of 15 who was going out as a
Cadet to the East Indies;—he had been educated at the Military
Academy at Marboro—of which all the account we could obtain fm.
him was—that the number of students ought to be 300; but that from
great interest made lately, 8 more than the proper complement had
been admitted—of which 8 he had been one;—that they kept guard as
in a garrison;—and finally that, in his opinion, it was a damned place.
He appeared to have no one anxiety on leaving England but lest his
stock of clothes should not be completed by the time the fleet sailed.—

We reached Birmingham about 5 to dinner; and left it at 6.—Here a
man, who talked to me about philology and Dr. Adam Clarke[2] (who,
he told me, was 'a universal genius'), took the sixth place—2 having
been vacated in the course of the morning.—We passed through Oxford early in the morning: and the philologist, who wanted to see the
colleges, had nearly lost his place by neglecting the directions I gave
him.

Saturday—Feb. 25th.—We began to discover that our lumbering
coach would not reach London till night instead of noon as we had
been promised.—When we came to Henley the day being very beautiful—we all got out, except the waiting-maid, to walk up the hill.—
I walked on considerably before the rest:—when they came up, they
told me that a horseman—whom they had just met—had informed
them that Drury-lane Theater was burnt down.—Not seeing any
smoke, as the horseman had told them we should, when we got to
Maidenhead—we agreed that it was a lie.[3]—Passing through Houns-
low, we saw parties of the 18th. Dragoons who annoyed the French
so much in Spain.—They seemed in very good health and made a most
splendid appearance.—At dusk—soon after the lamps were lit—we
entered Piccadilly.—Here I shook hands with my 2 Irish friends and
the philologist—and drove to my former lodgings:—found them occupied;—left my trunk;—and, being much fatigued, went immediately
to the Old Hummums[4] in Covent Garden;—here however no beds
were to be had for 2 hours.—This not suiting me, I went away; but,
being so near Drury Lane, I determined to look at the ruins.—

Here I am compelled to break off—it being now 5 o'clock.—I shall
write again to-morrow; and I calculate that you will receive this letter
no sooner than that: however I will give it a chance.—Up to this day

---

[2] Probably Adam Clarke (1762?–1832), editor of *A Bibliographical Dictionary containing a Chronological Account, alphabetically arranged, of the
most Curious, Scarce, Useful and Important Books, which have been published from the Infancy of Printing to the Beginning of the XIXth Century. With Biographical Anecdotes of Authors, Printers and Publishers.* 6
vols. (1802–1806).

[3] As De Quincey later shows, he soon recognized the truth of the report.
Fire broke out at the Drury Lane Theater at about 11:15 on Friday night,
Feb. 24.

[4] A hotel, originally a bathhouse, in Covent Garden, on the southwest
corner of Russell Street.

—Thursday March 2nd.—nothing of any kind, letter or *copy,* has reached me; though I have gone regularly to my old lodgings to inquire and am sure that they would be very careful of any letters.—I begin to be anxious because, if it had been kept back, I think it likely that you wd. have let me know. I do not find that the Convention of Cintra is at all out of date: everybody is so much dissatisfied with the wretched trifling in the H. of Commons on Ld. H. Petty's motion [5] that it may on the whole be of service to a pamphlet that it did not appear until the time for catchpenny works appearing—(and in general for all those who wd. make a party matter of it) is gone by—I found the copy which had been sent, not printed when I came to London:—I got yesterday one proof more for correction.—With my kindest love & respects to Mr. & Mrs. Wordsworth—Mr. Coleridge—and my best love to dear Johnny, I remain, dear Madam, your most affectionate friend, Thos. de Quincey.—[*Across back:*] I shall take the liberty of paying for all future letters and parcels;—but this, I must give to the Bellman, as it is not safe taking them to an office after 5; and therefore cannot pay for it.—

Where is Miss Monkhouse—that I may get the poem?—[6]

[*Address:*] Miss Wordsworth / Grasmere / near Kendal / Westmoreland / Single Sheet / March 2nd. 1809

11. *To Dorothy Wordsworth*

Ms. Dove Cottage. Unpub. Qtd. Eaton, pp. 154, 169, 180.

82, Gt. Titchfield St. Cavendish Square—Sunday night,
March 5th. [-7th, 1809]

Dear Madam,

Before I resume my Diary, I must mention that yesterday I received

---

[5] On Feb. 21 Lord Petty moved (according to the *Times* report), "That it is the opinion of this House that the Convention of Cintra, signed on the 30th August, and the maritime Convention of the Tagus, signed on the 3d of September, 1808, have disappointed the hopes and expectations of the public." Lord Castlereagh moved the previous question, and Petty's motion lost 203 to 153.

[6] Mary Monkhouse, Mary Wordsworth's first cousin, was in London at 21 Budge Row; but De Quincey was not informed. Wordsworth wrote him on March 26, "The Poem you need not call for; it is come" (*MY*, I, 271; misdated March 27).

2 packets (containing 4 *M.S.* sheets) from Grasmere. I did not hear of their having arrived until 8 at night when I returned home from dinner (probably owing to the mistress of the house in Northumberland St., who had offered on Thursday to send letters up by her nephew—whenever they arrived, having been at market when the post came round) :—I mention this, to account for my not having written last night to relieve the anxiety about them which my last letter would perhaps raise;—though *when* that last letter (which was also the *first*) was written, I have utterly forgotten.—After tea last night, I read the sheets through with great delight; and this day I have pointed the greatest part of them: to-morrow morning they will be given to the compositor with injunctions to set them immediately.—One sentence is left imperfect; and unfortunately there is nothing to *determine* me in the correction:—it is this:—'The former source of weakness,—namely, the want of appropriate and indispensible knowledge,—has, in the past investigation been reached,—and shall be further laid open; not without a hope of some result of *immediate* good by a direct application to the mind; and in full confidence that the best and surest way to render operative that knowledge which is already possessed, or to increase the stock of knowledge,' —the last member is evidently imperfect: there is a *lacuna,* as the critics say; and no man, short of an Oedipus, can tell how it shall be supplied. One hypothetical reading is:—'and in full confidence that (*it is* (i.e. the further laying open)) the best and surest way' etc; another—which I am inclined to think the true reading—is—'and in full confidence that the best and surest way to render operative that knowledge which is already possessed—*is* to increase the stock of knowledge'—This reading, unless I make some happier guess tonight, I shall send to the press: [1]—but, if it is not the true reading, I will have it canceled as soon as I hear from you; i.e. if the pamphlet should not be ready for publication before I hear fm. you; but, if it should, I shall take it for granted that you would not wish one single invalid to delay the march of the army.—One alteration I ventured to make for sake of euphony—viz. in the clause—'for reasons which may be added to those (which I have) already given'—I struck out the words within the brackets, as it seemed to be overladen with *whiches.*—Nothing is now to be heard in the streets but

Letter II:
[1] The second reading finally appeared. See *Wordsworth's Tract on the Convention of Cintra,* ed. A. V. Dicey (London, 1915), p. 131.

songs about Mrs. Clarke and *"one whom I will not name"*:[2] the pictures are of course very numerous; and one, I believe, is 'by authority': if you feel any curiosity about her face (which is really more pleasing than the Courier chose to allow), I will send it together with the portraits of Sir D. Baird[3]—and Sir J. Moore—when I send the copies of the pamphlet. Of Sir A. Wellesley there are no cheap portraits— nor indeed any picture at all but one sumptuous engraving at the expense of his family: this seems to prove that, in spite of all the base sycophancy and fawning of the H. of Commons, he is no favorite with the people: and as to this picture—which is no doubt a very good likeness—I can vouch that it contains a plenary justification and indemnity for the severest things that can have been said of him in the pamphlet: the rudiments of all wickedness lie in his features: there is a bill of indictment—with at least a billion of counts—in his mouth alone: if I was a despotic prince, I would not hesitate to hang any man who owned such a face—without any questions.—When I said *wickedness,* I meant *'scoundrelism';* for there is such a native meanness and cowardice in the expression—and in every element—of his face, that I could not help thinking him a fair representative of Jonathan Wild reversed—i.e. a man transfering upon the affairs of nations the laws and spirit of pick-pockets.[4]—In coming along the Strand last Wednesday, when all the new monthly publications had just appeared, I saw *'The Cabinet'*[5] lying open with a portrait by way of a frontis-

[2] Mary Anne Clarke (*ca.* 1776–1852) in 1803 became mistress of Frederick, Duke of York, and exploited her connection by accepting bribes for allegedly using her influence with the Duke, who was then Commander-in-Chief of the Army. The scandal had just then come out through Colonel Wardle's motion in Parliament on Jan. 27, 1809, that the house appoint a committee "to investigate the conduct of his royal highness the duke of York, the commander-in-chief, with regard to promotions, exchanges, and appointments to commissions in the army, and in raising levies for the army." The House sat as a committee of the whole, and the investigations lasted, with interruptions, until March 20.

[3] Sir David Baird, then a lieutenant-general, succeeded briefly to the command when Sir John Moore was killed at Corunna, Jan. 16, 1809.

[4] De Quincey was antagonistic toward Sir Arthur Wellesley because of his participation in the Convention of Cintra: he signed the preliminary armistice and supported the Convention before the Court of Inquiry. Later De Quincey withdrew his opinion of the portrait, but not of the general; see below, p. 187. Wellesley was made first Duke of Wellington in 1814.

[5] *The Cabinet, or Monthly Report of Polite Literature,* I, new series (Feb., 1809), had an article on "Samuel Turner Coleridge, Esq." (pp. 99–104) "embellished with a Portrait."

piece which I discovered fm. the label to be meant for Mr. Coleridge: —there is of course a *'Life'* added, which I have not yet had an opportunity of seeing; but I was informed within an hour afterwards by an acquaintance at a coffee-house, to whom I mentioned the circumstance, that his friend—Mr. Field—was the Editor of that work and would (he was sure) be very happy to contradict anything there stated— which might not be altogether agreeable or true—in the next number: —Such is Mr. Field's mode of composing *Lives!*—Having spoken of periodical works, I am put in mind to mention that the new Review (*'The Quarterly Rev.'*), which is to run in opposition to the Edinburgh Rev., started on Wednesday: [6] I have not yet read any part of it; but I must say that, in point of outside, it is a thousand times more *tasty* (as the ladies say) than the Edinb.; so that, if they provide plentifully for party malice and personal malice, there is little fear of their destroying the poor Scotchman; since the single advantage, which the Edinb. can have over them:—viz. that of being already established (which secures the continued purchase of all who do not like to have an imperfect work),—will, I suppose, be a great deal more than counterbalanced by the pleasure yielded in Novelty—in seeing the tables turned upon Mr. Constable's authors (for it is a fact now generally asserted that the Edin. Rev. praises every work printed by their printer Constable—and, since their quarrel with the Longman house,[7] go to the utmost limit of their daring in baiting Longman's authors: —this statement appears so ludicrous that I cannot forbear laughing as I write it; but I am seriously assured that it is true, though, from not having read the Ed. Rev. extensively or attentively enough, I do not—as the H. of C. say—'know it of my own knowledge')— and finally in opposite or different politics:—They will therefore so reduce the sale of the Ed. that it must fall into the ranks with the other reviews; and this will be to destroy them of course by making them *confessedly* contemptible; even if the mere act of commencing an avowed opposition to them fails of making their hearts burst with a paroxysm of *venomous fever* (I suppose, there is such a fever?). To be

---

[6] The first number of the *Quarterly Review*, edited by William Gifford, was that for Feb., 1809. The new journal was projected as a Tory answer to the Whig *Edinburgh Review*, edited by Francis Jeffrey. See pp. 215–216.

[7] Longman had an interest in the *Edinburgh Review* from its inception in 1802, but sold out to Constable in 1807. These rights were bought back in 1814; in 1826, when Constable failed, Longman took over the journal (Harold Cox and J. E. Chandler, *The House of Longman, 1724–1924* [London: Longmans, Green, 1925], pp. 17, 20).

sure, the public may not fare much the better for exchanging one imbecile dictator for another; but, from all I hear of Gifford, I cannot think him so depraved a coxcomb as Mr. Jeffray: and anybody will admit that there must always lie a presumption in favor of a set of rascally Englishmen opposed to a set of rascally Scotchmen: on this ground I myself propose subscribing to the Quarterly Rev.—By the way, I must mention that this hound Jeffray has—in a review of Cromek's 'Reliques of Burns' in the last No. which I saw at Liverpool —renewed his scurrilous trash about Mr. Wordsworth:—this must have been written about the time he was correspondg. with Mr. Coleridge. At the time I read this, I could not help hoping that Mr. Wilson would at length cease to encourage such a work; and I should think that, if he were reminded that he might see it on his visits to Liverpool and elsewhere at the public libraries, he would; particularly if it were added that he may in London supply himself with any numbers (to prevent his set being imperfect) in 2 or 3 years *after* their publication at the real value—viz. 6d. per pound.—There is a 3rd. competitor—viz. 'The London Review'; [8] of which the 1st. No. has appeared: but I understand that it has not given satisfaction;—some young men in Liverpool informed me that the language was 'cursed low.' In the mean time the 3 rival powers make equal pretensions; all the way down Fleet St. and the Strand you see them lying side by side; and, whereas heretofore the Edinb. Rev. used openly to insult all the other reviews by advertising itself in a simple annunciation of a single line—whilst they were mean enough to present themselves sneaking with their bill of fare in their hands, now—in answer to 'The Edinburgh Review is this day arrived'—you see 'The Quarterly Review is this day published': This last circumstance has given me such an opinion of the *blood* (to use the game term) of the Quarterly that, if for no other reason, I think I must have it.

I shall now resume my Diary; premising however that—not having had time to read over my last letter—I have no guess whether it reads into entertaining gossip or into something surprisingly dull: however, if you will have the candor to say that is not to be endured if you find it so, I will endeavour to mend in my next attempt.—

N.B. XXXXXXXXXXXXXXX

(As I wrote these words, it struck 2 o'clock—which reminded me

[8] This *London Review,* edited by Richard Cumberland, survived only from Feb. through Nov., 1809.

that it was time to go to bed;—I am now writing in a coffee-house on Tuesday afternoon—March 7th;—having been all yesterday so much engaged in a long chace—and a very successful one—after books (one day's delay in which would have lost 2 works of Ld. Brooke's which I never before heard of etc.) and also in my walk to Baldwin's (the printers) [9]—that I had not time to add a line. My delay has luckily enabled me to add that just before I left home I received by a messenger fm. Northumberland St. your last (i.e. 3rd.) letter: [10]—I shall make all of the corrections this evening; for to-morrow morning will be as soon as I shall be able to get the 1st. two sheets of the four received on Saturday out of the printer's hands; since, when I went yesterday, I found that the compositor—who is employed on the pamphlet—was (according to established practice) celebrating the orgies of St. Monday.—I have put some uncouth marks at the head of this division—to attract your notice—for fear that you might not make the full tour of my letter, but content yourself with short incursions here and there: however I must petition to be read through; because I have no means of specially directing your attention to those latitudes of my letter where something may be found; and I write now in too great a hurry (to save the post) to be able to write with much order.—I shall write on till 5 o'clock.—I must, now I recollect it, apologize for paying for my letters:—but really I could not with any pleasure tax you for letters of mere table-talk.) Here procedes my Diary:

Saturday night—February 25th. I left off with saying that—'being so near to Drury-lane, I determined to look at the ruins.'—Accordingly I went; and first I took my stand at the corner of Brydges St.: on this side—and on this side only—the walls were standing; except that about 10 or 14 feet had fallen along the whole course of the tops—everywhere but in one place where a solitary piece of the wall—some yards in breadth—remained entire; and, having been shaded on one half by the smoke, it looked like a *round* turret springing out of an immense ruin; for, by the obscure light produced between a dim clouded moonlight and the light of lamps, the whole was like an ancient ruin—the sky seen through its windows having a very fine effect; and, from the uncertainty of the light, the turret (which was really very high, as you may recollect) seemed almost in the clouds.—On this side however

---

[9] C. and R. Baldwin, on New Bridge Street.

[10] None of these seems to have survived.

no fire was to be seen; and therefore, as I had heard that parts of the Theater were still burning, I went round to the Drury-lane side: here there was a very fine spectacle:—that, which on the other side (i.e. the outside) had seemed a tower from the effect of shading,—on this side had changed it's whole shape and appearance: it was now the pinnacle of a temple: at the base of this pinnacle, shot out a large tabular ledge like an *altar* supported by all kinds of fantastic imagery formed by the wreaths of smoke that might be interpreted into animals &c.— On the altar was a fire—the largest mass that now remained: it was feeding and licking—at times—up to the edges of the altar; and above, round some wood-work I suppose, another fire was coiling itself like a large snake up almost to the uttermost summit of the pinnacle.— Immense fogs of smoke, that were rising continually from the vast area of the Theater, served to shroud the unsightliness of the ruins:—the fire, which was on the altar that surmounted the whole, had a very sublime effect—seeming to be literally up in the clouds and carousing and exulting over the whole desolation.—A great multitude of people was gathered on all sides of the Theater—but especially on the Drury-lane side: they were silent beyond what I thought possible in so large a crowd.—I was ready to fall asleep even whilst gazing; and therefore I went away in a short time to the only coffee-house where I was *certain* of getting [*torn:* ? a bed] that at Charing Cross;—which however, from former experience, I knew to be a most miserable abode [*torn*] immediately went to bed: but love or money could gain nothing more than a choice between 2 rooms communicating [*torn:* ? other;—I] chose the innermost as being freer from intrusion, though the worst, and a truly Cimmerian hole it was:—through the window, blackened by accumulations of at least a century, I could discover that—to those who were so happy as to be in the street—the moon had begun to shine; and I was just thinking how miserable I was, when I fell asleep— (Since this evening, the ruins have all fallen or been gradually pulled down—excepting one part about as high as a moderately-sized house.) —Sunday, Feb. 26th.—The morning I spent in reading the papers for 3 or 4 days back: I read with particular attention the debate on Ld. H. Petty's motion; and was surprised to find not one sentence to the purpose except something which Mr. Canning said about the non-competence of military men to make articles contracting for *civil* arrangements—and Gen. Ferguson's disclamation of the whole Convention, by which he trampled upon the mean insolence of a Mr.

Somebody [11] who spoke immediately before him and had insinuated an insult to the whole people of England by saying 'that for his part—what so many able military men had approved, he could not presume to censure.'—Dined at the hassan Coffee-House: there I met with a young man—an old coffee-house acquaintance—who had taken great interest all last summer in the Spanish affairs:—he gave me a long account of a severe fever (the Scarlatina) which had come on about the opening of the campaign in Spain: after the delirium had gone, his memory did not return for some weeks; so that, by the time he recovered his faculties, the English Army had returned home; and a whole campaign had been fought.—Some of his friends had been there, and come home well.—He had dined a few days before with a part of the English Staff Officers:—they all agreed that Sir J. Moore had met his death by being where he ought not; i.e. as I understood him, by exposing his person more than military etiquette authorized him:—but whether that was not the very thing which in such a war and in such circumstances as those at Corunna he was summoned to do, they forgot to ask—He was fond of parade, they said; but much beloved by the soldiers;—and no complaints were stirring in the army against *him,* I found;—the complaints were *from* him—but against *whom,* I could not learn:—I suppose the Commissariat:—After dinner, I walked in search of lodgings; but, finding none which complied with all the conditions I had thought of as *sine qua non* of an eligible abode for the whole business I had in London—and disliking the prospects of changing in a week, I did not take any this evening; but, recollecting that the New Hummums (at which I had never been) might be on a different plan from the Old H, I went there, and not only procured a bed, but found a remarkably pleasant coffee room (at the Old H. there is none) where I spent the evening:—a person in the room described the fine spectacle of the roof falling in at Drury Lane:—he saw the Apollo fall fm. his pedestal; and could have counted the strings on his harp by the light.—I forgot to mention that the young man at dinner mentioned that he was near Westminster Abbey at the time of the fire:—he went out upon the roof of the house, and could distinguish what o'clock it was by the Abbey clock better than in the brightest daylight.—Indeed, everybody is full of stories to illustrate the power of this fire which seems to have searched

---

[11] Capt. Joseph Sidney Yorke, representing St. Germains (St. Germans, Cornwall).

every corner in London by it's light:—almost everybody, when first
coming out into the street, thought it must be at his next door neighbour's.—There being no wind, there was (during the extreme agony
of the fire at the time the roof fell in) a mass of fire—seemingly motionless resting itself upon the four walls—equal in magnitude to the
whole building:—and this poised upon a building which—seen from
almost any part of London—overtops all Westminster and Marybone
by a full story.—Here I am obliged to leave off—we have no news
to-day; but the last reports (which I copy fm. this morning's *Times*
are that the three frigates chaced under the batteries near Rochefort—
are destroyed;—mails have also been received fm. Heligoland up to
the 28th. ult. which state that a revolution has taken place in the
politics of Russia—so far at least as respects Austria:—and finally
we have daily strengthenings of the reports of war between Austria and
France.—God bless you all! my dear Madam, at Grasmere, and believe me, most affectionately yours,

Thos. de Q.

[*Address:*] Miss Wordsworth / Grasmere / Near Kendal / Westmoreland /
    Free—Single Sheet / Tuesday, March 7th.
[*Postmark:*] MAR 7 1809

12. *To Dorothy Wordsworth*

Ms. Dove Cottage. Unpub. Qtd. Eaton, pp. 155, 174, 176, 177.

82, Gt. Titchfield St.—Saturday, March 11th. [1809]

My dear Madam,

 Having some distrust of the Ambleside post, I will (before I answer
your last letter) put down all that I have sent and all that I have
received up to this day—Sat. March 11th.—About Wednesday or
Thursday (March 1st. & 2nd.) I wrote my *first* letter:—on the Sunday followg. (March 5th.) I began a *second* letter which I concluded
and sent off on last Tuesday—March 7th.:—this present letter is my
third.—The list of my *receivings* stands thus:—on Sat. last (March
4th) I received 2 double letters:—on Tuesday (March 7th.) 1 single
letter:—These, I believe, I acknowledged in my last letter.—Since
then—I have received 4 single letters—viz. 2 containing the winding-
up of the pamphlet on Thursday (the 9th.)—and 2 yesterday—

(one dated Monday morng. before you walk to Rydale—the other dated Tuesday—being your long and kind answer to my first letter).[1]—One suggestion about the sending of letters I will here make (though, as it must have occurred to you, no doubt there may be some reason against it)—viz.—A letter, put into the post on Wednesday night in London and directed to Miss Crossthwaite's—Keswick, will (it is clear) reach Grasmere by Sat. night; because the Courier of Wednesday which is at G. on Sat., comes by that route:—whereas, if sent by Kendal, it would not be at Rydale until *Sunday* night—(since if I recollect the post leaves K. on Friday before the mail comes in)—and therefore most probably at Grasmere not before *Monday*.—As to the comparative *safety* of the 2 conveyances, I mention one fact in addition to the many told by Mr. Scambler[2] &c. which may tend to put the matter in it's proper light.—When I was in Liverpool, I found that I had wronged the carrier in supposing that he had lost my letter containing the 5£. note:—*that* had been duly received; but the answer to it—acknowledging the receipt (which of course came by Kendal)—was never received at Grasmere. Luckily, it contained nothing of importance—except the names of 4 subscribers to The Friend—and some hints for it's management (which however, coming fm. the Editor of a News-paper, *might* have been very valuable).—I will add here—as it may be important, until the pamphlet is published, that my letters should reach you as soon as possible—that, whenever you feel disposed to walk to Rydale on a Friday night (which is, I think, the early post-night), you will be *sure* to find a letter from me; as I shall *always* put a letter into the post on Monday or on Tuesday night: and I take it for granted that a letter, which leaves London on either of those nights, will be at Rydale on Friday night.—I had no difficulty at all in readg. your letter about the furniture &c.—The plan you propose, I think, is much the best;[3] and I should have proposed it myself, if I had not hated

---

Letter 12:

[1] For the last two letters see *MY,* I, 263–264 (misdated March 26 for March 6) and *MY,* I, 259–263 (misdated Feb. 28 for March 7).

[2] The local apothecary-surgeon.

[3] This letter seems not to have survived. Dorothy had apparently suggested that in furnishing Dove Cottage for De Quincey she get help from John Kelsall of Manchester, his father's former clerk, now acting as De Quincey's banker.

that any Manchester kind of people should have to say that they had 'corresponded' with Mrs. or Miss Wordsworth:—However, if it must be, it must: and among Manchester people the Kelsalls are by no means the worst.—I must mention however, for your guidance in writing, that Mr. Kelsall is not a *shop-keeper* but a rich *merchant;* and, though very humble *out* of his ware-house, *within* it he supports —to the utmost—the right of a merchant to take precedency of a shop-keeper, and has sometimes complained to me very pathetically of ladies of my mother's acquaintance who have sent orders to him addressed as to a retail vendor of cloth.—On the whole, if you have no objection, I should think it would be best to write to *Mrs.* K. If you write to Mr. K., you will receive the followg. answer:—

Miss D. Wordsworth,

Your esteemed favor of the 15th. was duly received;—in reply to which I have sent you as per underneath:—

1 piece of calico—6 ells wide—at 3d. per yd.

1 do.—do. &c. which please acknowledge per return of post: and in so doing shall greatly oblige

Yr. Obt. Jno. Kelsall.

P.S. I wrote Mr. Q. 3 weeks ago—which he has never acknowledged: —when you write him, please beg him to write me as soon as possible; and in so doing shall greatly oblige

Yr. Mt. Obt. Jno. Kelsall.

On the other hand, Mrs. K. is cruelly *orthodox* in her religious opinions; indeed quite Moorish,—I mean to say, *Hannah Morish*— in her way of thinkg.—but perhaps, as one need not be heterodox in writing about calico, that may be no objection: and she will certainly send a very sensible letter containing all the knowledge of the subject—which she will get fm. her husband—untechnicalized.—To Mrs. Kelsall—the best way of directing is—No. 7. Faulkner St., Manchester:—otherwise, simply Mr. John Kelsall, Merchant, Manchester: —and it will go to the Warehouse.

Here I break off to say that I have this moment received fm. Northumberland St. a letter fm. Mr. Wordsworth containing the supplementary intercalation beginng.—'*In Madrid, in Ferrol, in Cor-*

unna.' [4]—In answer to it, I will now say what I was going to have said concerning the other corrections received before:—viz. *that they are all in time;* for, being anxious about the exact reading of the imperfect sentence mentioned in my last (viz. 'and in fullest confidence that the surest means to render operative the knowledge already possessed, *or* to increase the stock of knowledge' *a.b.c.d.*), I have not suffered the printer to strike off any sheets *finally* since I came to London—excepting that which was in his hands (containing the sentence about the Mineral Spring—which I came in time to expunge before it had been finally struck off);—particularly as I found that, from the number of *cases* (I do not *yet* know the technical name) they could go on printing *proofs* without waiting for those already printed to be struck off—and without occupying the *press.*—However, even this has gone on rather slowly;—chiefly on account of Mrs. Clarke; whose Memoirs &c. are now pleaded at every press in London as an apology for neglecting all other business.[5]—The whole of this latter part—especially the part about the incompetence of ordinary Statesmen to deal with indefinite things—seems to me more beautiful than anything I ever read in prose.—One thing I grieve for—that the work ends with a *quotation;* which to me destroys the feeling of a full choral peroration: [6]—however, as being only a *first* part, it did not perhaps demand such a close.—With respect to the printing, nothing can be more correct: [7]—they have attended very closely to all the corrections of any consequence;—and, accordingly in 96 pp. finally struck off, which I got some days ago at the press, I cannot detect a single error:— In the 1st. editions of Edmund Burke's pamphlets, which are now lying by me, there are many.—

To go on about the cottage,—I beg that you will draw upon Mr. Kelsall for any money which you want; if you like that mode:—

[4] See Dicey, p. 158.

[5] Mrs. Clarke's own *Memoirs* were indeed printed, although not then published; the *Times* for April 12 reports that 10,000 copies were burned after a substantial settlement was made upon the fair author. Printers were also busy on at least six other "memoirs" of her which appeared in 1809, and on numerous satires and attacks upon or defenses of Colonel Wardle and the Duke.

[6] Wordsworth persisted in ending with two quotations: from Petrarch in Latin, and out of "respect to the English reader," from Milton.

[7] Contrast this with Letter 16.

otherwise, I will send it.—And in all parts give directions as you would choose it to be. There are only 2 things which I have any special affection for in furniture—viz. the colors of *pink or white* in bed-rooms;—and only one which I specially hate—viz. *stuff* in bed-hangings;—which I mention not as things worth attention; but that, if your choice should be evenly balanced between something that is and something that is not *stuff,* there may be a motive to decide you.—I was never thoroughly reconciled to my bed-room in Oxford: because the bed was hung with a tawdry yellow stuff or something of that kind.—

---

a.b.c.d. I have given the *substance* of the clause for fear my last letter should be lost:—but, the M.S. being still in the printer's hands, I cannot give the exact words. About the book-shelves—would it not be as well to have them (i.e. those not already made) made of mahogany—or of some *native* wood?—Deal is risen to a price never heard of before: in illustration of its rise, the master of the house in Northumberland St.—who is a master-builder—told me that the other day he paid (for the use of a great house he is finishing in Piccadilly) 18 guineas—or thereabouts—for what—before the closing of the Baltic ports—cost 43 shillings.—Mahogany has not risen at all;—and might afterwards be made into a book-case.—My Irish friend also in the coach mentioned that the Catholic college in Donegal —which was to have been built this winter—is delayed until a peace with Russia—on no other account. I have a multitude of things to say:—But no time just now or paper.—On Thursday night I sent you down an Eveng. paper (The Statesman)—which I hope you received: —I sent it not on acct. of the Debates—but of Saragossa:[8] I had not seen anything; but I heard in all the streets a glorious shout fm. the News-men—'*Saragossa!*—2nd. Edition!'—I meant to have sent a message to my dear friend Johnny: but cannot find room.—I have just heard fm. my sister that she has a letter fm. my brother—dated Feb. 19th. fm. on board the Superb off Gottenburgh:—he was in

---

[8] Saragossa was to Spanish apologists a symbol of the country's will to fight, for the city successfully resisted French attacks by Marshall Lefebvre from June 15 to Aug. 15, 1808, and held out against a new assault from Dec. 20 to Feb. 20, 1809, for the last month carrying on a bitter house-to-house defense within the city itself. Wordsworth wrote a sonnet, "Hail, Zaragoza! If with unwet eye" (*Poetical Works,* III, 132).

hourly expectation of his exchange arriving: and we have since seen that the Superb is on her way home. God bless you, dear Madam!— yours most affectionately. Thos. de Quincey.—

[*Across back in another hand, probably Dorothy's*:]

> B. cases
> Carpet
> Portraits &c.
> Post-Tuesday.

[*Address:*] Miss Wordsworth / Grasmere / near Kendal / Westmoreland
Free / Single sheet / *Sat. March 11th.*

[*Postmark:*] MAR 11 1809

13. *To Dorothy Wordsworth*

Ms. Dove Cottage. Unpub.

Tuesday, March 14th. [1809]—82. Gt. Titchfield St.
Dear Madam,

I am so very busy to-day—searching for errors in the proofs—that I should not have written, but to keep my promise of meeting you in Rydale on Friday night (if you walk that way) with a letter: for I think that, if I failed on the very first Friday after that promise was made, you would have no faith in it for the future.—

Yesterday morning I received your letter of Friday afternoon: and I cannot help fearing from it that my last letter but one (i.e. my *second*) may have been lost; for, as you intended to walk to Ambleside on that evening, you would most probably stay there till the post came in; and would therefore not close your letter until you knew whether there was any letter from me (since you would expect to find in it (as indeed there was) a question in it—repeated in my last—about the pamphlet):—I conclude therefore that you did receive no letter from me on that evening:—and yet my letter—having been delivered by *myself* to the post on Tuesday night (i.e. this day week)—ought to have been at Ambleside on Friday night.—If this letter has been lost I shall be very sorry; because I put into it all which had any chance of amusing you of what I had met with up to the date at which it closed (though I doubted much of it's succeeding): and, if it should be so, shall be happy to entertain three attorneys, at my proper cost, to draw up a petition—remonstrance—or anything else which may obtain a regular post.—In your answer will [you] be so good as to write for me a list of the persons to whom I must send the pamphlet *as from the author?*—Don Padilla, a gentleman in the suite of the Spanish Ambassador, has promised to convey it to Don Pedro; I applied to him through Bohn, the German bookseller (who is a very respectable man) to whom I explained the nature and objects of the work; adding that, if Don Padilla would engage to deliver it, I would send it by him: otherwise, I would send it myself by a porter to Don Pedro's door.—He returned for answer that he would be happy to communicate anything of the tendency I had described; and would engage for it's getting into the right hands.—I shall therefore enclose it to him accompanied with a Latin note to the Ambassador—containing a very summary analysis of the work—and the reasons for sending it to him: unless Mr. Wordsworth disapproves of this plan. Something of this kind would, I should think, be more in the form of Castilian courtesy, than if it were sent in a blank cover.

I have put down the alterations which I have made on my own discretion in the pamphlet; that, if any of them (or all of them) should be disapproved, I may receive the corrections in time at any rate to be inserted as *errata;*—and there is a possibility that the plan of printing proofs and then going on to others without waiting for the first to be finally struck off may be carried on to such an extent that I may receive the corrections in time for the text:—1st. For—'that the power, *that* would attend it'—I wrote *which.* 2nd.—For 'Riddance, mere riddance—safety, mere safety, are objects far too *re*fined'—I wrote '*de*fined,' (I do not doubt that I am right in this correction:—but on referring to the M. S., I see that it there stands—as in the proof— refined.) 3rd.—'The Parliament has therefore persisted *to withold'*— I wrote *'in witholding'* (this seeming to me the English idiom; yet in Burke's ('54 Acts of Impeachment against Fox'—p. 72. I see 'persisting to assert'; so that I am perhaps wrong, as it could scarcely be an oversight in both places:—yet it sounds awkward to my ears.) 4th. —For—'lay in this; that *this* army was made an instrument of injustice, and was dishonored,' &c.—I wrote—'lay in this; that *the English* army was made' etc. (this alteration I made for the sake of euphony; but, on reading the whole paragraph over, it seems to me to improve the emphasis of the passage, from a feeling of the opposition between what is *English* and *dishonor.*) 5th. For,—'by the act of *making* this *avowal* of incompetence to the man himself'—I wrote—'by the act of *announcing* this *presumption* of *his* incompetence to the man himself—'[1] (some alteration here seemed necessary; since, as it stood, the *incompetence* seemed to be the minister's—not Sir H.D.'s[2] incompetence: and, when I was making the alteration, it occurred to me that *presumption* was a better word than anything expressg. simply *a belief in his incompetence* or a *declaration* of it; as it seems to involve 1st. that the minister intimated his persuasion of Sir H.D.'s incompetence so strongly as even to *take it for a thing granted*—and which was notorious even to the worthy Bart.—2nd. that he did so *on no ground and previously to all proof*—which, as they have since assigned—as a shelter to themselves for having appointed Sir H.D.— their confidence in his abilities grounded upon the singular talent displayed by him in issuing 1500 rusty muskets to the Spaniards, makes their inconsistency more flagrant).—I have here noted down the slightest alteration which I have made (and which I should have hesitated in making but for Mr. Wordsworth's permission in his last letter); that you may not find anything unaccounted for, when you come to read the pamphlet;—and may see, by my keeping a list of them, (what however I am sure you would otherwise give me credit for) that I have not made the minutest change hastily or without a rigid trial of it's effect both in the particular member of the sentence in which it stood and in the whole paragraph of which that sentence was a part.—All this would be more properly addressed to Mr. Wordsworth than to yourself:—however I send everything—grave and gay —to you, as being the Grasmere Secretary for foreign affairs.

On Thursday evening, as I mentioned in my last letter, *2nd.* editions of the evening papers were printed on the strength of news reflecting a great 'victory gained by Palafox'[3] at Saragossa communicated by the

Letter 13:

[1] See Dicey, pp. 144, 113, 155, 142, 151–152.

[2] Sir Hew Dalrymple signed the Convention of Cintra on Aug. 30, 1808, eight days after he took over command of the English forces in Portugal from Sir Harry Burrard, who the day before had taken over from Sir Arthur Wellesley. Dalrymple had been governor of Gibraltar, in which post he had given some assistance to the Spanish insurgents in Andalusia.

[3] José de Palafox y Melzi (1780–1847) was popular leader in Saragossa. Wordsworth wrote a sonnet, "Ah! where is Palafox? Nor tongue nor pen" (*Poetical Works*, III, 135).

Spanish Ambassador:—the next evening (which was a singular circumstance) I saw a 2nd. edition even on the *Sun* (the ministers'
official paper) advertised at their office by a great sheet of paper hung
at the door announcing the surrender of Saragossa on the strength of
reports in the non-official French papers (I could not help marveling
at the meanness of this paper—whose regular duty it is to create the
taking of a corvette from the enemy into a trophy of ministerial
wisdom and energy—thus hanging out a line for a few odd six-pences
by giving currency and sanction to a mere report—which was sure at
any rate of being heard quite soon enough:—I hope however that his
masters have chastised him for it.)—This seemed to me such totally
insufficient ground for crediting it, that I did not choose to mention
it in my letter. Nevertheless yesterday I found (for today I have
not been out) that all the papers *do* credit it; yet *why* I confess I cannot see. They say; that their chief reason for believing it—is not the
assertion of the Dutch papers *professing* to copy fm. French papers
merely—but that assertion taken jointly with the *previous probability*
that Saragossa would surrender about the time stated;—now I not only
cannot guess from what they collect this *previous probability*:—but
also, if I could see any such probability, cannot tell why *that* should
not be as good a reason for supposing that it would create fabrications
in the French papers—more especially in *Dutch* papers—since at this
time, it appears that no impositions which can be practiced, are more
than enough to quicken the Dutch into the military zeal that their
task-master is levying upon them. Moreover, it seems impossible to
explain how minor French papers should receive such important news
sooner than the Government (who cannot be supposed willing to
withold any gratifying news *at this time* even for a single hour); and
no less difficult is it to explain by what bill of oblivion and amnesty
the reports of any FRENCH paper—official or not official—have acquired a title to be received with the credit given to the papers of
other nations only on the *attestations* of their governments.—Not
having seen the papers to-day, I do not know whether Mr. Percival's
motion [4] has been agreed to or not—or whether the House has again

---

[4] Spencer Perceval, then Chancellor of the Exchequer, on March 9 moved
that Col. Wardle's motion asking for the Duke of York's removal as
Commander-in-Chief be amended to read (according to the *Times*) that
the House found "no just ground to charge his R.H. with personal corruption or criminal connivance" but regretted that "a connection could ever

adjourned (which, I believe, it was generally expected they would). What a miserable wretch this Percival appears!—A foolish reprobate is to become 'a bright example *of easy virtue*' (as he phrases it) on a motion of the House of Commons!!—and they gain a confidence that he will become so chiefly from a letter of his [5]—which many of themselves have treated as a high breach of their privileges!!—and this is the hopeful set of youths whom one of their own members the other day styled 'the combined wisdom and talent of England'!!!—If they declare that the D. of Y. has been guilty of no malpractices in the exercise of his office,—I cannot imagine what business the H. of C. has with his virtues and their brightness.—

Last night I saw a person extensively acquainted in the City.—He tells me that the City, who are still breathing vengeance for the insolent answer to their last address,[6] are now lying couchant—waiting for the issue of the debates—and meaning, if the D. of Y. is not at least (on Mr. Bank's motion) [7] displaced, to address in a style

---

have existed" which exposed him to calumny, and hoped that in the future he would "be guided by the bright example of those eminent virtues which have uniformly distinguished his Majesty's life."

[5] The Duke of York addressed a letter to the House of Commons on Feb. 23 denying any guilt in the discharge of his official duties, regretting "that a connection should have existed" which exposed his character to animadversion, and asking not to be condemned without a just trial. Whig member Samuel Whitbread protested that the letter struck at the privileges of the House by stating that it had examined evidence which it ought not to have considered.

[6] On Oct. 12, 1808, the London Common Council addressed the King on the Convention of Cintra, petitioning immediate inquiry "into this dishonourable and unprecedented transaction" for the "discovery and punishment" of "misconduct and incapacity." The King's reply rebuked them with a reminder that it was "inconsistent with the principles of British jurisprudence, to pronounce judgment without previous investigation," and unnecessary for him to be petitioned to inquire into "a transaction, which disappointed the hopes and expectations of the nation." Wordsworth defended the Council's action vigorously in his pamphlet (Dicey, pp. 101–106).

[7] Henry Bankes on March 10 moved to amend Perceval's motion to the effect that, although there was no ground for charging the Duke of York with personal connivance, corrupt practices prevailed and, in the best interest of the service, he should be removed from his post as Commander-in-Chief. His motion failed 199 to 294, and on March 17 Perceval's motion carried 278 to 196; but the next day the Duke resigned.

which has not been seen since the days of Charles Stuart the elder—
and which will make it impossible for the ministry in their retort to be
more than *even* with them in severity.—Here I must break off:—I
will endeavour to make my next letter more amusing; though it is
somewhat difficult to be so just now:—'there being, at present' (as
Mr. Dickie justly observes in the Courier of last night) [8] 'a great want
of entertainment for the public.'—I must again defer my message to
dear John.[9]—With kind love and respects to all at Grasmere, I
remain, dear Madam, most affectionately yours, Thos. de Q.

[*Address:*]   Miss Wordsworth / Grasmere / Near   Kendal / Westmoreland
          Single sheet / Free / Tuesday, March 14
[*Postmark:*] MAR 14 1809

14. *To Dorothy Wordsworth*

Ms. Dove Cottage. Unpub. Qtd. Eaton, pp. 155, 174.

          Tuesday, March 21st. [1809]—82. Gt. Titchfield St.
My dear Madam,
  I am in the greatest hurry (expecting the Devil every moment);
and therefore do not know how long I shall be able to write on.—
First of all, I must mention that I have this morning received your
long and most welcome letter of Friday afternoon; and, at the same
time, the Oxford letter which you were so kind as to forward. This
last put it in my power to give you *an* answer (though not *the* answer
you meant) to one part of your letter—viz. that which concerned
the subscribers' names:—you asked, I conclude, for the 4 Liverpool
[*torn:* ? names] which unfortunately (having been obliged, on the
night I left Lpool, to break [*torn:* ? an engage]ment I had made with
the Newspaper Editor to whom those names were communicated) I
cannot send, until I have. written for them—which I will do, the
very first moment that I have any leisure.—In the Oxford letter,
however, are given the names of 7 subscribers—which, though not

---

[8] This observation comes from an advertisement of T. Dickie, Bookseller,
who was just opening rooms and planning to offer lectures (*Courier*, March
13).
[9] See Letter 17.

given fully, I write down here as sufficiently accurate to insure the
work reaching them safely:

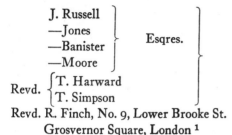

J. Russell
—Jones
—Banister   Esqres.
—Moore

Revd. {T. Harward
       {T. Simpson

Revd. R. Finch, No. 9, Lower Brooke St.
Grosvernor Square, London [1]

All at Worcester College,
Oxford [*inserted here, inverted:*] (I hope Miss
Hutchinson is not unwell,
that she returns so unex-
pectedly to Grasmere? Most
probably her return is connected with '*The Friend.*'
Pray, give my kind respects
to her.—)

When this Oxford letter was written, the prospectus had not been
received in Oxford; or at least had not been circulated: indeed, I
fear that Miller [2] has not come up to college this term; and that the
prospectuses may have been sent, and may now be lying unopened in
his rooms: I shall therefore immediately write to his brother-in-law,
requesting him to distribute them.—On this subject I may add that—
some days ago—my sister informed me that Shepherd—a Bristol bookseller—said he had received a *great many* names:—this was the term,
I think: but what is the import of a *great many* remains to be seen.—I
have obtained about a ½ dozen prosp. from Mr. Stewart [3]—and
hope to do something before I leave Town: but at present I have not

---

Letter 14:
[1] These names appear in this order and incompleteness in the original
list of subscribers to Coleridge's *Friend*. De Quincey himself is third on
the Coleridge list, down for five copies, and his mother for two more
(*Lake Poets*, pp. 451, 459–460, .463).
[2] Probably John Miller of Worcester College, whose name appears on
the list of subscribers to the *Friend* and who was probably the friend
"named Millar" whom Woodhouse says offered to try for Honors if
De Quincey would (*De Quincey and His Friends*, ed. James Hogg [London,
1895], p. 99), for he achieved Class I honors in the Easter term of 1808.
[3] Daniel Stuart, joint proprietor of the *Courier*, was a friend of Coleridge's
and was giving him some financial support for the projected *Friend*.

had time or opportunities to do more than to send 2 or 3 a cruising on proper stations; and I did not think it just to Mr. Coleridge to seem always *prepared,* even when I had an opportunity, like a hawker of lottery bills.—The whole harvest of Oxford and Cambridge remains yet to be reaped;—and in all places I have no doubt that there are (as I have been *assured* that there are in Liverpool) numbers waiting to see the first—what shall I say? I must not say *number* again—the first *part.*—I mentioned, I think,—as we were parting at Rydale—that Mr. Kelsall is a subscriber.—I shall write directly for those names which my mother may have [*torn*]

I have not written to you since last Tuesday (this day week): the reason is, be [*torn:* ? because I] have been more than usually busy;—the *Appendix* A [4] which I got about that time from the [*torn:* ? printer] it was quite necessary shou[*torn*] remodeled since the appearance of an official Report of the Board of Inquiry's proceedings and, as this required nothing but an attentive examination of this Report, I was sure that Mr. Wordsworth would wish that I should do it myself without consulting him rather than not have it done at all:—accordingly, as Mr. Stewart sent up to me—soon after I wrote last—2 reports (1 official—1 demi-official) of the proceedings, I took the liberty of detaining them to search for the documents which I wanted–and also to verify some quotations–and to examine whether other passages (which I suspected, should have been marked as quotations) were so or not.—Mr. Stewart added 3 other pamphlets— all to be forwarded to Grasmere:—I shall [send] them to-morrow or the *next day at farthest* (directed *to Mr. Cookson,*[5] Kendal—for Mr. Wordsworth &c.)—Another thing which has made [me] more busy than I should else have been is that latterly—a new compositor having been set to work upon the pamphlet—the proofs are filled with such monstrous errors (whole passages left out—and words substituted

---

[4] Appendix A undertakes to "lay before the reader an outline" of the proceedings of the Board of Inquiry which investigated the Convention of Cintra in ten public sessions at Chelsea Hospital from Nov. 14 to Dec. 14 and concluded that no further military proceedings were necessary "because however some of us may differ in our sentiments respecting the fitness of the convention . . . it is our unanimous declaration that unquestionable zeal and firmness appear throughout to have been exhibited by" Dalrymple, Burrard, and Wellesley.

[5] Thomas Cookson, of Kendal, was a convenient friend of the Wordsworths.

which leave a *kind* of meaning &c.) that I am now obliged to insist
on having a *second* proof before they are laid aside to be struck off.—
    The day I wrote last to you, I was altogether incredulous about
the fall of poor Saragossa; but on the very next day arrived the
sorrowful confirmation of it's surrender in that execrable bulletin!—
On the passage relating to Saragossa I have, in consequence [*top of
last page, containing about 9 lines, torn off*] thought of surrender-
ing—Saragossa!—She also, the wasted and twice [*torn*]ity, has borne
witness–in her glorious martyrdom–to the efficacy of these passions.
[*torn*] has pledged herself to the same self-devotion, The Multitudes
of Men, who were [*torn*]ed in the fields of Baylen [6]—!—or something to that purpose. But this, on consideration, seemed improper on
2 accounts;—1st. that it was to do a grievous injustice to Saragossa
—to make only an incidental and bye-the-bye commemoration of her
great struggle; and 2ndly. that, as the pamphlet could not be supposed
to have been written since that news was received, it looked too much
like an artifice to make [*seal, torn*] thing. Therefore, on the whole,
I have thought it right to do as follows:—[*torn*] a foot-note, as from
a friend of the author's employed to correct the press errors [*torn: ?
saying*] that, whilst that sheet was passing through the press, the
33rd. bulletin had been received—containing an account of the enemy's
having possessed himself of the ruins of Saragossa;—that, in a pamphlet adverting perpetually to passing occurences, it seemed necessary
to notice this,—that it's date might be established:—but that, from
the distance of the author it was impossible to do [*torn*] without oc-
casioning a very serious delay:—that, finally, this was the less necessary as the friend of the author was well assured that he would wish
to make no other change than to declare, in a more full and solemn
tribute to Saragossa, that all which had been here prophesied of her
she had faithfully ratified: and that, for the truth of this assertion,
the reader—if unwarily he had adopted the *conclusions* of the French
—was referred with the greatest confidence to the statements made
even by that base enemy upon which those conclusions professed to be
grounded. [*Probably 9 lines missing, back of top of last page.*] I
believe that I always promise to mend in my next letter: however mend
I really will in my next of all, which I shall put into the post *with-*

---

[6] On July 19, 1808, the French General Dupont had been forced to surrender 20,000 men at Baylen. This significant Spanish victory caused the
French to retreat northward, abandoning for then the siege of Saragossa.

out fail on Saturday night.—Dear little Totty![7] I am very sorry for him! and hope anxiously that your next letter will give a better account of him. To my very dear friend John I shall send a long message either in my next letter to you—or inclosed in the parcel of books; and, as that is (I believe) unlawful, I shall place it within an unopened leaf of *Decius's* pamphlet [8]—that, if curious eyes should examine, they may not see it. God bless you! and all at Grasmere, my dear Madam.—Your affectionate friend, Thos. de Q.

[*Address:*]   Miss Wordsworth / Grasmere / Near Kendal / Westmoreland / Free / Single Sheet / Tuesday, March 21st.
[*Postmark:*] MAR 21 1809

15. *To Dorothy Wordsworth*

Ms. Dove Cottage. Unpub. Qtd. Eaton, pp. 156, 174.

[London]
Saturday evening, March 25th. [1809]

My dear Madam,

It is so nearly post-time that I can do no more than write a few lines to keep my promise. I am always in a hurry, you will say I am afraid: but the truth is, that I really have been in one long hurry for these last 10 days: for it is impossible to guess at the strictness of the scrutiny which it is necessary to make in order to be *sure* that there are no errors in the proofs. When Mr. Wordsworth,—who, remembering of course his own words, could instantly detect the errors,—looked over the proofs himself; I did not think it necessary for me to be so vigilant in my inquisition: but now I scarcely ever fell satisfied, until I have collated the proof 3 or 4 times with the *M.S.* to be sure that nothing is left out—added—or altered;—and then afterwards (which is far the most fatiguing part of the labor) inspected it *verbatim et literatim*—to see that the words—when ascertained to be the true words—are truely spelt. In this last office—as the labor is not lightened by *understanding* a word of what

---

[7] Thomas Wordsworth, born June 15, 1806.

[8] One of the books De Quincey was sending for Stuart—probably *Observations on the American Treaty, in eleven letters. First published in "The Sun" under the signature of Decius* (London, 1808).

I am going over—it is difficult to think how often one may read a word mis-spelt without knowing it to be so.—Some days ago, I discovered that, in one proof, *Saragossa* was spelt *Sargossa;* and yet this proof I had gone over at least 15 times without discovering that it was so.—This instance of one's proneness to modify any word, though misspelt, into the word which one is anticipating—added to the daily instances of extreme carelessness of the compositor—makes me now fearful of letting any part be printed off, until I have seen a *3rd.* proof: I rose before from *one* to *two;* and, I believe, the compositor thinks that I shall soon after want a dozen. As a specimen of his ludicrous blunders—he printed, soon after I first came to Town— From the *Swedish* democracies to the *depositions* of Imperial Rome &c.—and made the city of London call the Convention 'this *unprescribed* transaction.' [1]—I wish however they were all as gross and palpable as these.

I find, on looking back, that I have been pronouncing an encomium upon my own diligence and fidelity in my task. But I meant it only as an excuse for not writing a longer letter (which however I shall certainly write on or before next Tuesday).

The proof, in which the *first* mention is made of Saragossa (viz. 'Saragossa! she also has given her bond,' &c.) and which I spoke of in my last letter, I have kept up to this day—in the hopes that I might receive some directions about it from you (as I conclude that you would hear of the fate of Saragossa this day last week): but— nothing having arrived—I am afraid that I shall find it necessary to let it be struck off, with my note annexed, to-day; since they have lately been very urgent at the press to strike off at least 4 proofs (viz. *N.O.P.Q.*) to release the types.—*M.* which was the last proof that Mr. Wordsworth saw (the one containing the *mineral spring* allusion) has been struck off a fortnight or more.

I have not received anything since your last letter—viz. that which I received on Tuesday last—and acknowledged in my letter of that day.—This, I mention, that, if you should have sent anything, you may have the information of it's not having reached me as soon as possible.

I put into the post on Tuesday night (after I had written my

Letter 15:

[1] The correct readings were "Swiss Democracies to the Despotisms of Imperial Rome" and "unprecedented transaction" (Dicey, pp. 103, 101).

letter) an *Inquisitor* of that night; because I had learned, to my
great mortification, that there is a district office in Lombard St. for
receiving *newspapers;* and that consequently the 2, which I (being
near Lombard St.) had myself put into the *letter* office the night
before, would probably not reach you: if that should be the case, you
may conclude that it is not the postman's fault but mine.—The papers
were—the *Examiner* of Sunday—and the *Statesman* of Monday
night:—The *Statesman,* from what I have seen of it, is so villainous
a paper—that I owe you an apology for sending it [at] all: But my
reason for sendg. it has been that the office of that paper is in Fleet
St. through which I pass frequently about post-time to the Press which
is near Black-Friars Bridge, and, being an unflourishing paper, the
office hangs out a summary of the contents; so that I do not know
generally, till I pass it, whether there is any news.—To-day I have not
been out:—yesterday, the only news was that Mr. Wynne's motion of
Thursday night for committing Gen. Clavering was agreed to Nem.
Con.[2] Pray tell me how dear little *Totts* is:—and tell me everything
that you have leisure to tell me about my two dear friends *John* and
Dorothy. Has Dorothy come home with Miss Hutchinson?[3]—Everything will be interesting that relates to them.—John will think me
very forgetful of my promise: but I will certainly write to him in the
parcel (which, I am sorry to say, cannot go till Monday:—it will be
sent, on that day, by the coach to Mr. Cookson at Kendal.) Believe
me, dear Madam, most affectionately yours, Thos. de Quincey.—
[*Across folded back:*] If you have not lost my letters, you will see—
in 2 of them—a question about the right readg. of a passage which
I have not room here to repeat.—That passage being in Proof *R,*
your answer may yet come in time.
[*Inserted, inverted above salutation:*] I *believe* that I have made out,
in Mr. Wordsworth's note (contained in your last letter) where the
addition—'In Madrid—Ferrol'[4]—&c. is to come in: but will you
have the kindness to repeat it—that, if I *should* have made a mistake,
it may be corrected?

---

[2] *Nemine Contradicente* (no one opposing). General Clavering was committed for perjury in testimony intended to discredit Mrs. Clarke and defend the Duke of York.

[3] Wordsworth's daughter Dorothy continued visiting at Penrith (*SH*, p.
15).

[4] Dicey, p. 158. See *MY*, I, 274.

[*Address:*]   Miss Wordsworth / Grasmere / Near Kendal / Westmoreland /
Free / Single Sheet / Saturday, March 25th.
[*Stamped:*]   More to pay
[*Postmark:*]   MAR 25 1809

16. *To Dorothy Wordsworth*

Ms. Dove Cottage. Unpub. Qtd. Eaton, pp. 156–157, 169.

82, Gt. Titchfield St.—Tuesday, March 28th. [1809]
My dear Madam,

Having none of this smooth–silky–paper left on Saturday last, I was obliged to abridge my letter (by spreading it) in order to get over the ground in time: but to-day, though no less busy than then, I hope to be able to crowd a little more into my letter; having so fine a course to run over.—I should not have written at all to-day (but that I fear lest you might take a walk to Rydale on Friday night—and have the trouble of sending to Ambleside for nothing); since to-morrow I shall send, by the mail, Mr. Stewart's books directed *to Miss Crossthwaite's, Keswick;* and shall then inclose a longer letter which I hope to have time to write this evening. Having twice deferred sending the books after I had fixed the time, I am afraid I shall scarcely be relied upon this 3rd. time; but indeed you need not fear walking down to Town end on Saturday night; for the books will certainly be there; i.e. if the carriers are punctual, and if the carriage of books from Penrith to Keswick is as regular as that of letters.—I have kept them beyond the time fixed for sending them in my last, chiefly that I might transcribe the Armistice & Convention from authorised copies (which is a work of some time); and it occured to me that, if I sent the parcel off even on Monday night, it would not—being directed to Mr. Cookson—most likely reach Ambleside till Friday night—and Grasmere therefore not much earlier (if at all) than if sent on Wednesday night to Miss Crossthwaite's.—The parcel will contain Mr. Stewart's books—which are 6 in number (I believe, I said 5 before; but, on looking at them again, I find I was wrong); viz. 2 Reports of the proceedings of the Bd. of Inquiry;—3 Letters to Don Francisco Rigueline (commander of the 3rd. division of Blake's Army), who died of his wounds received at Espinosa;—the letters of Decius;—Mr. Leckie's books;—and the *'Exposure &c.'* by

Cevallos.[1]—All these come from Mr. Stewart.—I shall add, for dear
Johnny, a dozen pictures which I bought for him last night;—and the
portraits &c. if I have before then an opportunity of learning which are
really authorized portraits: for they all profess to be so; and yet they
are very little like each other:—of Sir J. Moore, in particular, there
are several which have no shadow of resemblance to each other; and,
as the printseller in the Strand—of whom I bought Johnny's pictures
—told me last night, there is yet no 'super-extra official' likeness of him.
—If I am not able to ascertain this point in my perambulations of to-
day, I shall send them with the 14 copies of the pamphlet.—I shall be
able to send then a portrait of *Palafox* also (which I was very glad to
see in a Sunday newspaper advertised as now engraving from a picture
in possession of an officer in this country).—Mr. Vaughan's pamphlet [2]
I have not yet seen; but I conclude that it must be a respectable work;
because, in the dispatches of Ld. Castlereigh to different English
Officers (laid before the house) it is alluded to as an authority:—I
shall be much obliged to you for it's character, when you have read
it; since, if it is well done, it will be a book to put into a library.—
There is an account (I believe *two*) of the battle of Corunna: if I
hear that it is or *they for 2* anything more than a transferal of the
Gazette, I will send it.—On Sunday night we had a mail from Gotten-
burg:—it confirms the former account of the insurrection in the Swedish provinces; with the addition of the king's having been suspended
and imprisoned by a synchronous insurrection in Stockholm headed by
his uncle the duke of Sudermania.—Two proclamations have been
issued by the insurgents—both so temperate, that it seems impossible
to deny the request (contained in one of them) to suspend all censure
of their conduct;—more especially as, from the accounts of all the
Swedish refugees in this country, the extreme wretchedness of Sweden
did absolutely demand some change of measures with respect to Russia
and Denmark; and as there is so great apparent forbearance and spirit
of moderation in the *manner* in which this revolution has been ef-

---

Letter 16:

[1] Pedro Cevallos, *An Exposure of the Arts and Machinations which led
to the Usurpation of the Crown of Spain, and of the means pursued by
Bonaparte to carry his views into effect,* translated from the Spanish. . . .
Revised and edited by John Joseph Stockdale (London, 1808).

[2] Charles Richard Vaughan, *Narrative of the Siege of Zaragoza* (London, 1809).

fected.—This, if you received a paper on Thursday night, will be old news to you: but I add it, as knowing it to be probable that you will not.—I did not myself know of the news until after post time last night; or I should have sent you a paper. Our only other news of yesterday is that a requisition has been presented to the Ld. Mayor, and another to the High Bailiff of Westminster, for a meeting to consider of the late business in Parliament. The last has been admitted, and a meeting summoned ;—the former is returned for revision ; the *shape* of it, it seems, not being sufficiently *tangible:* one would have thought that they had had enough of *tangible shapes* for one season in the H. of Commons and in the Courier.—This puts me in mind of Cobbett, who (in his last week's No.)[3] has given the Courier and Mr. Curwen [4] especial praise. Indeed, Mr. Curwen has done himself infinite service by his conduct in this affair; all the weekly papers (excepting one—The Phoenix [5]—an infamous hireling of the D. of Y.'s) having singled him out for particular and formal thanks; and the weekly papers are incomparably the best indexes to the popular feeling from the class of shop-keepers downwards.—I am in some doubt whether or not to send you a copy of the pamphlet—so far as it is now printed off—in the parcel of to-morrow :—I have read it three times over, and detected only one error of the press—viz. an insertion of a word (added, I suppose, in the margin) in a wrong part of the line: but, at the same time it must be mentioned that in the *punctuation* all my care (before the time I arrived in town) has been wholly thrown away; the stupid compositor having attended to my alterations, or not, *ad libitum;* and thus, in many places, made the punctuation farther from what I designed it for (viz. a representation of the logical divisions—and a gamut of the proportions and symmetry of the different members—of each sentence) than if he had followed his ordinary guide —viz. his own blind feeling of propriety; which blind feeling (I told

---

[3] William Cobbett, in his *Weekly Political Register.*

[4] John C. Curwen, Whig member for Carlisle, was active in denouncing corruption. De Quincey probably mentioned him because he was an acquaintance of the Wordsworths; years later Wordsworth's son John married Curwen's granddaughter Isabella. In a letter which crossed this one the poet asked De Quincey to send Curwen a copy of the pamphlet (*MY,* I, 271).

[5] F. W. Blagdon's Sunday paper, in 1809 called the *Phoenix, Patriot and Albion,* was probably subsidized by the Treasury. See A. Aspinall, *Politics and the Press, ca. 1780–1850* (London, 1949), pp. 86–87, 407–408.

him, for his edification) was not, as he flattered himself, a rude natural
dictation from the demands of the case; but a dictation from the the
[*sic*] artificial and conventional demands grounded at first on pure ca-
price arising out of a non-perception of the possibilities of a logical equi-
libration of sentences;—that, in short, it was nothing more than an abstraction from all which he had read; put to the test generally by his
eye; and now and then perhaps by his voice.—In consequence of this solemn remonstrance (which, I believe, he took for an imprecation) I have
now even the first proofs pretty accurate in this point:—but up to
page 96 inclusively, none of the errors are imputable to me.—Ld.
Cockrane,[6] you will have seen, is come home again: the passage, therefore, relating to him—must, I conclude, be altered.—*R*, containing the
passage about which I doubt—viz. '*that* (it is) *the best and surest
way to render operative that knowledge which is already possessed,*
(or) *to increase the stock of knowledge*'—has not yet gone farther
than the 2nd. proof:—so that I may still receive the alteration if it is
not right as here printed.—I have not *yet* (viz. Tuesday, after the
delivery of the letters) received anything from you since this day last
week, when I had your letter.—However, I dare say, something will
come to-morrow or Thursday; and (if there does) not the least delay
will have been occasioned at the press by this long pause on your part;
for (partly in consequence of neither Mr. Stewart's nor the pressmen's having discovered a line of the *interlineary corrections* until I
come to Town) there was a good deal of time spent in getting the
press to rights—which added to the different Monthly publications (of
which this printer prints a great many) and to Mrs. Clarke's memoirs,
so delayed the printing for the 1st. fortnight that I shall not receive a
1st. proof of the *last part of the M.S. which can be printed before the
whole arrives* until to-morrow morning.—Do not be surprised at not
hearing fm. Mrs. K[elsall].—She has written a long story to me,
which I will inclose in the parcel to-morrow.—Believe me, dear
Madam, your most affectionate friend, T. de Q.
[*Across folded back:*] I wrote to you on Saturday; but was obliged to
trust my letter to a child.—I shall at all events find time to write

---

[6] Captain Thomas Cochrane, later tenth Earl of Dundonald, had just
returned from extraordinary success at harassing the French with the
frigate *Impérieuse*. The advisability of combining British sea and land
power in a peninsular war was one of Wordsworth's points in the pamphlet.

something to-night for the parcel; and will endeavour to write something that may amuse even dear little Tottles.—

[*Inserted, inverted before salutation:*] I expressed some doubt in one
of my last letters, as to the place of the addition:—This is *how* I have
arranged it (to borrow dear Dorothy's phrase).—Directly after *'and
hope has inwardly accompanied me to the end'*—I have placed *'In
Madrid:—in Ferrol:'* all along to the *end* of the addition. Then, in a
new parag. I resume *'Whilst I was writing the earlier part of this
tract'* up to *'feed and uphold'* the bright consum. *flower* [7]—where the
press will stop.

[*Address:*] Miss Wordsworth / Grasmere / near Kendal / Westmoreland /
Free / Single sheet / Tuesday, March 28th. /

[*Postmark:*] MAR 28 1809

17. *To John Wordsworth*

Ms. Dove Cottage. Unpub. Sent in box of pictures and books.

At London—on Tuesday night [Mar. 28, 1809]
My very dear Johnny,

This is not the real letter of all that I am to write to you; for that
letter will be printed; but this is in writing hand; and therefore your
aunt will be so kind as to read it to you. The reason why I do not send
you the printed letter yet—is this; that I suppose you cannot read very
fast yet; because I have only been gone from Allan Bank 36 days; and
scarcely anybody can learn to read fast in 36 days. Therefore, if you
can only read very slow, it would not be a pleasure to you—but a pain
—to have to read all that I have to tell you; and I should like my letter
not to be a pain to you, but a pleasure; and then it will be a pleasure
to me to write it.—There is one more reason too why I do not send the
printed letter now; and that is—that I am so busy now that I should
scarcely be able to get time enough to print it; for it takes a great deal
more time to print than it does to write. But in 15 or 20 days more I
shall have plenty of time; and then perhaps you will be able to read it
faster than you could now.

As I am writing about printing and reading, and as you want to

---

[7] Dicey, pp. 158, 190.

know everything that can be known both about printing and about
reading—I shall tell you now one thing that I have found out about
printing since I went from Allan Bank. I go very often to talk to a
man who lives at a house where they print books: this man's name is
Overseer-of-the-Press: (perhaps this is not his real name; for I remember that when he writes letters to me, he says his name is George
Westray;) but every body calls him so however. When I get to the
house where this man lives, I go first into a very dark passage, then
I come to a stair-case which goes round and round and keeps growing
darker and darker till at last it is so very dark that they are obliged
to have a candle burning there all day long, even in the very middle of
the day. When I am at the top of this stair-case, then I push against
a door which opens and then shuts again of it's ownself—as soon as I
have gone in—without my touching it. I go through this door; and
then I get into a large room full of men all printing; then I go into
another room still bigger where there are more men printing; and, in
one corner of this room, a little wooden house is built with one window
to it and one door—the least little place you ever saw; there is only
room for about 2 men to sit down in it. In this house Overseer-of-the-
Press lives almost all day; only he does not have his breakfast or his
dinner there. I can always see through the little window, whether he
is there or not; very often he is not there; but whether he is there or
not, I almost always see a boy sitting with a book that is about as big
as you (only he is a little older than you, for I asked him how old he
was; and he told me seven years old). This boy is always reading the
book, or spelling to himself; and, whenever Mr. Overseer is there, I
find Mr. Overseer helping him and teaching him to read. So one day
I said—'Well, Edward, you read very well for a boy that is only seven
years old' (Edward is his name)—'I suppose you will soon begin to
be a printer'—Edward only laughed; but Mr. Overseer, who heard
what I had said to him told me—oh! yes! that he should make a
printer of him *directly*. 'Well, but Mr. Overseer,' I said, 'how can that
be?—It will take as long to learn how to print as to learn how to read;
and Edward has been more than a year learning how to read;—so he
will be a year at least learning how to print;—and then that won't be
directly.' Then Mr. Overseer said—'Oh no! it won't take a year—or
half a year—or a quarter of a year—or anything like it;—it won't
take more than 2 or 3 days to learn how to print.' 'But then will he
be able to print as well as all these men that are here in 2 or 3 days?'

I said:—'No'—Overseer said, 'not quite so well as them:—but he will
be able to print by himself, without anybody to stand by him and tell
him what to do, in 2 or 3 days: and then he will be able to teach himself all the rest—and he will grow a better printer every day—so that,
in a few weeks, he will be as good a printer as any man that is here.'—
When I heard this, I was very glad; and I determined to tell you;
because I was sure that you would keep thinking that there were 2
hard things which one must learn before one can print books;—first to
learn to *read,* which is one hard thing; and then to learn to *print,*
which is another hard thing.—But now you need not think that any
longer; for I am sure that everything, that Mr. Overseer says about
printing, is true; and he says that it is very easy; and besides I have
looked at the men to see how they print; and I am sure that it is very
easy: it is the easiest thing you ever saw. So, as soon as ever you can
read, then you will have no more trouble but a very little; and you
may be a printer directly.

Now that I have said enough about printing I will tell you what I
think about the little mouse that comes under the parlour fire-place. I
do not think that it is a fairy; and I think that you will find in a little
time that it is only a mouse: for you thought that it was a fairy, because you could not see the hole where it came in at; but most likely
that was because the ashes covered it up. Maybe, you will say—
'What *for* don't I think that it is a fairy?'—The reason is this:—I have
read in many books about fairies—to know what they are, and how
powerful they are, and where they live:—but, though no book (that *I*
have seen) can tell where fairies are gone to and where they are now,
all books agree that they never come into houses except in the night-
time when everybody is asleep; and they do not seem to be over-fond
of houses at any time—even at night. They are far fonder of mountains
and green fields.—But I do not know *all* that is written in books about
fairies and geniuses and magicians: there is a great deal more to be
known about them than I know: and the way to know it is to read
books:—So I am determined to get more books, and to read them, and
to learn all that wise men have said about them; and then perhaps I
shall be able to tell you what is the really truth about a great many
things that you have asked me.

I have another thing to tell you:—it is about a new kind of carriage
that I saw last week. First I will tell you how I came to see it; and
then I will tell you what it was like.—Last Friday was the very finest

day that has been since I saw you; though there have been a great many
fine days in London; but Friday was the finest of them all;—the sun
shone all day long; and, though it was only spring, yet it looked like
summer. So, as it was such a very fine day, I determined that I would
go somewhere where I might see the grass and the flowers and the
trees; and about 12 o'clock I set off and walked to the very end of
London, where there is a great park which is called Hyde Park (most
likely you know what a Park is; but, if you do not your aunt will tell
you). I went into this park, and I saw in it hundreds and hundreds of
soldiers marching up and down and learning to fight, and hundreds and
thousands of men and women and children—walking and running and
riding and playing; and many of the children were riding in little carriages that were drawn by maidens: all the carriages almost were
pretty; but there was one that was the prettiest of all: it was so pretty
that I went up to look at it; and then I found that there were six boys
and girls sitting in the inside; and yet one boy was able to draw it
and sometimes to run with it, though it was not down hill. I thought
this very strange, because your carriage is hard to pull when only you
and Sissy are in it—except when it is going down hill; so I looked at
it a long time to see how it was made; and at last I found out.—I
cannot tell you very well, until I see you, what it was that made it so
much easier to pull: but I will draw here something like a picture of
it:—

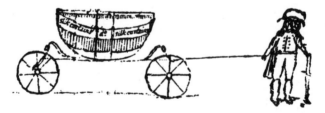

the boy, who is drawing it, (you see) is turning round to look at me:
only there is not room for me; else I ought to be drawn just before
him—asking him who made the carriage.—The children are all hid by
the silk curtains: those strokes below the curtains are meant for rails
made of *cane* wood not thicker than your little finger: these cane rails
in wet weather, or when it is cold, are covered up with curtains of
leather that are buttoned on the outside: above the silk curtains there
are posts, like little bed posts, that hold up a top like the top of a

bed: and between this top and the silk curtains there are other curtains
that may be drawn in cold weather or when you please: (but they are
generally undrawn in fine weather;) and so may the silk curtains, if
you choose: so, you see, the whole of the carriage may be shut up with
curtains, so that not even the wind can get in; or it may all be wide
open, as is best in summer; or only half open, which is better for
spring.—When I had looked at this carriage all over, I determined
that I would get one just like it for you and Sissy—before I come
back to Grasmere:—either I shall get it here or at Liverpool [1] (which
is another great town).—I forgot to tell you that the carriage is not
held up by wood, but by straps made of leather called *springs;* and that
is one reason why it is so easy to pull.—I really believe that little
Thomas could pull it, if only Catherine was in it.

There is another thing which I must tell you; and then I believe I
must leave off.—The great play-house, that was burnt down, had begun
to burn before I came to London (as your aunt told you, I dare say).
—Last week, when I had been more than 30 days in London, I went
past it; and it had not done burning then. A great many fire-engines
were spouting out water upon it. (A fire engine is a great large box,
as big as a waggon, full of water—with a pump that can shoot out
water almost as far as from Allan Bank to the school:—it is carried
on wheels—and pulled by horses sometimes—and sometimes by men
and boys.)—There was a great smoke coming out of the play-house
that went up to the clouds; and the people, that lived round about it,
were afraid that if a great wind should come—it would carry sparks
of fire that might get amongst the shavings in their timber-yards—and
perhaps burn down many and many a house more.—So they kept
engines always there trying to put the fire out; but, when I saw it last,
they had not put it out; and maybe they have not put it out yet.

My dear Johnny! I shall be glad indeed to see you again; and I am
sure, when I do, that I shall find you quite as good as when I left you
—and a great deal better scholar: but I would rather see you not a bit
better scholar than find you at all less good than you were in the
winter: for it would be a great grief to me, if you should learn any
bad words from the boys at school: but I am sure that you will not;
because your mother told me that you promised her that you never

Letter 17:
 [1] Dorothy Wordsworth negatived this generous idea in her letter of April
5 (*MY,* I, 281).

would.—So I hope that you and Sissy [2] and I shall have many long walks and rides and many happy days at Town-end [3] all next Summer: for I have learnt a great many things that you will like to learn also; and I shall have many stories to tell you, when I come back.

When your aunt writes to me, you know, you can ask her to tell me anything that you want me to know about Town-end and the snow-drops and crocuses—or about the carriage—or anything else.

If you please, give my love to your mother and your father and god-father and to your aunt and your aunt Sarah: and, if you see Sissy before I come home again, you must give my love to her.

I have sent you a few pictures—which I hope you will like. There is one that is meant for angels or geniuses—I do not know which.—

I must here leave off writing; or else the parcel will be too late to go; and then it will not be at Grasmere till Tuesday night instead of Saturday night.—So, good bye, my dear Johnny! and remember that I am and always shall be, with the greatest love to you, your friend,

Thomas de Quincey

18. *To Dorothy Wordsworth*

Ms. Dove Cottage. Unpub. Sent in box of pictures and books.

[London]
Wednesday afternoon, March 29th. [1809]

My dear Madam,

I was so much occupied last night that it was not until after 12 o'clock at night that I could begin my letter to Johnny; and I was not able to finish it till this morning.—I have therefore no time left but for a few lines.

The pictures are not such, I am afraid, as will be very interesting to Johnny:—I looked over a very large collection of port-folios on Monday night; but it was a very bad collection: there being neither battles

---

[2] Nickname for young Dorothy, John's sister.

[3] Dove Cottage was in the southern part of Grasmere known as Town End, and itself seems to have been so called (see *Unpublished Letters of Thomas De Quincey and Elizabeth Barrett Browning*, ed. S. Musgrove, Auckland [New Zealand] Univ. Coll. Bull., No. 44 [1954], p. 1).

nor storms—nor bright-colored pictures of any kind amongst them.—
Such as seemed the best, however, I selected.—The caricature I bought
at a shop where I had received a civility, and therefore thought it
necessary to buy something:—I thought it would do to cut into pictures
for Totts.—The head of Milton, I told the man who sold me the
prints, I thought he ought to give me for having taken a dozen of his
pictures; and, on consideration, he declared that it was his opinion
also; and so I got it.

Mr. Stewart has called here this morning: and is this moment gone
away. He came to ask about the pamphlet—and to give me a message
to Mr. Wordsworth.—He says that he *advises by all means* the remainder of the copy should be sent up [1]—so as to have the pamphlet
published on Monday or Tuesday next but one: if this is done, he is
decidedly of opinion that it will come out under greater advantages—
in point of time—than it could have done, if published *at any other
time whatsoever:* his reason for thinking so—is that the present en-
grossment of the public mind by the Duke of Y's affair—will naturally
have gone off a good deal by that time;—that the house and others,
who will be then coming up after the Easter recess, will have their
minds a little dejaded;—and finally that there are a number of papers
on Spanish affairs now before the house, and a number of motions on
those affairs, which will begin to come before it just at that time.—
Not to mention that, after April and May, the whole hay-making time
for pamphlets is over; unless they have fairly made themselves known
before the latter end of May; and accordingly no pamphlets are
published after that time.—

I was very glad to hear him say this:—because it was the very thing
which I had thought—for the reasons here given and also for this
general reason, viz. that it would have been a disadvantage to have
appeared in the throng of the pamphlets on this subject, as it would
be more readily presumed that it was a few hasty strictures put together
on the instant call of the occasion for the purpose of being *out in time.*
This cannot now be thought. The change in the title would indeed

---

Letter 18:
[1] Daniel Stuart had published the first part of Wordsworth's tract in the
Courier, and he continued to act as the poet's man of business in publishing the pamphlet. The "remainder of the copy" had already been sent and
arrived the next day (see beginning of Letter 19).

alone have secured it a better chance for immediate circulation:—but, if it had appeared at or before the time of Ld. H. Petty's motion [2] (which was an intercalation in the midst of the D.Y's affair), it would certainly have been overlooked at the moment from the immeasurable absorption of the London mind in that affair; and then, afterwards when they began to take breath and look round them, they would be [sic] have been told that it was an old pamphlet.—

I write in the utmost hurry; having to send off the parcel to the mail-coach office;—and not knowing it all [sic] from what Inn the Carlisle mail goes;—so that I am afraid of being too late; for it is past 4 o'clock.—

I shall write at length on Saturday without fail—The Paris papers of last night mention that Palafox is *not* dead but recovered from his sickness.

I remain, my dear Madam, with best respects and love to all at Grasmere,

ever your most affectionate friend,
Thos. de Quincey.

[*Across folded back:*] The letters to the Spanish General—you will find cut open & torn:—but it was sent to me in that state.—

[*Address:*] Miss Wordsworth

19. To Dorothy Wordsworth

Ms. Dove Cottage. Unpub. Qtd. Eaton, p. 157.

82, Gt. Titchfield St.
Saturday, April 1st.—1809.

My dear Madam,

I received the 4 letters sent off on Sunday from Grasmere—on Thursday morning; and yesterday I received Mr. Wordsworth's letter of Tuesday [1]—containing some corrections &c.—I meant to have written to-day to Mr. Wordsworth to complain a little of the very great injustice which he has done me in what relates to Saragossa:—how it is

---

[2] See Letter 10, note 4.

Letter 19:

[1] One of the four Sunday letters is *MY,* I, 266–272 (misdated March 27 for March 26); the Tuesday letter is *MY,* I 272–274.

possible that the purport of my note should have been so entirely mistaken, I cannot guess: if my letter be not yet destroyed,[2] it will surely shew that my note said the very *contrary* (not *rhetorically* the contrary, but *logically*) of what Mr. Wordsworth has supposed it to say.— Indeed, so complete is the misapprehension of the substance and object of my note, that—if no other reason, than the one grounded on that misapprehension, had been given for canceling the sheet—I should have thought it right to wait for further directions: particularly as the delay, occasioned by the canceling, is very serious: but, as this reason is given merely as an accessory one to an other (though that other does not *seem* to say more than that the accounting to the reader for the retaining of the prophecy after the accomplishment of the prophecy— would be introduced *as well* in an advertisement as in a note on that prophecy:—but it does not say that it would be *better* there) ; I have thought it right (after considering every expedient suggested by the printer for avoiding a complete cancel of *P* (which contained the note —and had unfortunately been struck off) and the breaking up of *Q-R-S-T-U* (all of which had been composed; but not struck off) which will fling us back several days) not to lose time but to have the sheet canceled immediately ; and it is accordingly returned to the printer for that purpose. I cannot say that I ever did anything with so much reluctance in my life ; being convinced that 2 objects of some importance were gained by my note; both of which must now be lost, or gained very imperfectly.—But I was a great deal more hurt that it should be thought possible that I could have held (and expressed in print) such an opinion as (in some way or other utterly inexplicable to me) I am supposed to have held and expressed about Saragossa. However on this subject I will write to Mr. Wordsworth on Tuesday: and will also send you a copy of the canceled sheet—that you may see what I really did say of Saragossa.

The parcel was sent off on Wednesday night: but everything went wrong about it :—3 of the pictures were unfortunately left out :—1 of them the caricature for dear little Totts; and 1 the Angels for Johnny :—but I was in the greatest hurry ; fearing that the mail-

[2] Curiously enough, part of that letter (Letter 14) is missing, although sufficient remains to substantiate what De Quincey here says, as does a partial draft of his Note in the Cornell Lib. Wordsworth Coll. (No. 2804, fol. 41).

coaches might load several hours before they set off; and it was then 5 o'clock:—Mrs. Kelsall's letters were also left out;—the substance of which I will give on Tuesday.—Lastly the porter, who was sent with the parcel—and particularly directed to seek out the *Carlisle Mail,* brought back a paper from a coach-office by which it appeared that he had delivered it [to] the office of a Carlisle coach *not* a mail; and thus, I fear, you will not receive it until Tuesday evening. And (as this coach, by the printed bill he brought back, goes a circuitous route through Liverpool) the chances of it's being lost are something more, I suppose, than by the Mail.—The ink made so faint a mark on the strong brown paper, that I put half a dozen or more directions on it—to give some of them a chance of being read.—I directed it to Miss Crossthwaite—Keswick. [*Inverted*] I wish Johnny had been with me; for there is a *whale* to be seen nr. Blackfriars Bridge.[3]

What follows—between these and the next double lines—relates to the pamphlet.—The M.S. being sent to the printer, I quote & refer from memory.—1st.—It is said, in speaking of the English Troops, that they were *broken* at *Corunna*—in *Egypt*—and *elsewhere.*—Now 1st., with respect to Corunna,—allusion is here made, I conclude, to some private account of that battle, no authentic account having (as far as I remember) hinted at anything more than a *check* in an attack on a village:—but would it be right to rest such a position on an unacknowledged report; particularly as the pamphlet will naturally have among it's readers, many who were present in that battle and who, therefore, if it be a mistatement will instantly detect it?—Secondly, as to Egypt,—there were in that expedition, 3 actions fought in all (Sir R. Wilson's capture of the convoy in the Desert having been effected, I think, without bloodshed); of which I suppose the last (i.e. that called by Gen. Raynier—the battle of the Pyramids) to be the 1 here alluded to: but, if my recollection of the circumstances of that action be accurate, the Scotch Regiment—which was penetrated by the French Cavalry—was scarcely broken; and if it was—and that should be thought equivalent to *vanquished,* still (if I remember) it restored

---

[3] The whale had been killed in the Thames at Sea Reach and was exhibited on a barge between Blackfriars and London Bridge. The *Times* for March 31 protested that "The *stench* was intolerable."

itself as *technically* as it was defeated—viz. by *rallying* into groupes—
and taking advantage of the embarrassment of the French who found
themselves unable to act from the *ruins* amongst which the Scotch
Reg. had been posted.—If this be so, it will vitiate the illustration:
since he, who pleads for the supremacy of the military art over any
other reliances of an army, will say—"No:—the fact is this:—that,
whereas by the help of this art we did at the beginning of the storm
hold by 2 anchors, afterwards 1 of our anchors drove; and we rode it
out at single anchor."—However on this point I am not sure; and
besides most readers will suspect their memories in relation to an
expedition of 9 years back; so that, if it should be incorrect, it will not
signify so much. But with respect to Corunna,—as that is fresh in
everybody's recollection, it will be necessary to be strictly correct; and
therefore I should have consulted the official account and the 2
pamphlets on that battle before I parted with the M.S.; but that
yesterday when I carried that sheet to the printers being Good Friday,
no shops were open:—however, I will examine these documents before
I suffer the proof to be struck off.—I will examine also the Egypt
question.[4]

IInd.—In the latter part of the answer to those who think that National Independence is of no value to the peasant &c. something, to
this effect, occurs:—'the range of *his* intellectual notice is compara-
tively narrow: no selfish or antipatriotic interests control the force:'
here—i.e. at the word *force*—this clause of the sentence stops:—
Thinking that something must have been omitted here, I have supplied something to this purpose:—controls the force *of those nobler
sympathies and antipathies which he has in right of his country.* This
I put in—to gain room for the real insertion, if I should receive it in
time:—if not, and mine shd. differ materially fm. the real one, it can
be put into the errata.[5]—I made this insertion very unwillingly; being

---

[4] Ultimately the reference to Corunna was omitted. See Dicey, p. 181;
below, p. 138; and *MY*, I, 286.

[5] The passage reads: "For he is in his person attached, by stronger roots,
to the soil of which he is the growth: his intellectual notices are generally
confined within narrower bounds: in him no partial or antipatriotic interests
counteract the force of those nobler sympathies and antipathies which he
has in right of his Country" (Dicey, p. 169).

miserable in making any discretional alterations since the canceled note (as I never could have a fuller warrant from my judgement than I had in making that addition); but something seemed necessary.

III. In a part of the M.S. sent up to London before I arrived, it is written—*"at least from the animating efforts of the Peninsula."*—Is this right?—animat*ed* has a more obvious sense, but it has been printed animat*ing*.—[6]

I grieve for sweet little Catherine. Pray do not omit to let me know how she goes on.[7] I am very glad to hear of Tott's recovery; but, as to his *growing handsome,* I think Totts has reason to complain, for I always thought he was very handsome before.— —I have explained to the printer that no further delay will arise on the part of the author, and have been promised that the utmost expedition shall be used to get the work out (if possible) by Monday after Easter: I will take care that they shall not wait for me. So I hope that it will be out then.—I am very glad to tell you that I have succeeded in finding the 11th. vol. of the State Trials (the whole of what is wanting in your copy). This makes the work worth 20 guineas or more:—copies, not in nearly such good order as yours, are never sold for less than 21£ and of course for considerably more, if in good preservation.—The reason I suppose to be that this work has not been superseded by any better of the kind; and that, having been published in Nos. it is rare to find it complete. I mention all this, that you may know that it is worth putting out of harm's way.[8] Believe me, my dear Madam, your very affectionate friend.

Thos. de Q.—

[*Across folded back:*] Last night I read with great pleasure, the Decree for giving no quarter to the French Troops (under particular

---

[6] Dicey, p. 109.

[7] Some members of the Wordsworth family had measles, and Dorothy had pronounced Catharine "grievously reduced" but not yet broken out (*MY,* I, 272).

[8] Probably *A Complete Collection of State-Trials, and Proceedings for High Treason, and other crimes and misdemeanors . . . To which is prefixed a new preface, by Francis Hargrave,* 11 vols. (London, 1776–1781). This set was still in Wordsworth's library at the time of its sale in 1859. De Quincey was unlucky that in 1809 *Cobbett's Complete Collection of State Trials* began to appear, depreciating his find.

limitations).[9] Everything proves that the military force of the French in Spain is settling into an even balance with the *present* Spanish force. How easy would it be for the English to make it kick the beam in a fortnight!—Sir A.[rthur] W.[ellesley] has vacated his seat; and re-signed his office;—so that it is supposed he is going out with 60,000 men to Portugal.—But, as ministers are apparently induced to this measure only by a breeze of fair rumors—what reliance can there be on their steadily standing to it?—

[*Inserted inverted above salutation:*] Mr. Wordsworth says that the passage about knowledge is *'as I wrote it'*: but I wrote it 2 ways, I think: so that I am almost at a loss to know which way is meant:—however—I think I said that I thought this readg. the most likely to be the true one: viz.—'and in full confidence that to render operative the knowledge already possessed *is* the surest way to increase the stock of knowledge.'—*So* therefore it will be printed off.

[*Address:*] Miss Wordsworth / Grasmere / near Kendal / Westmoreland / Free / *Single* sheet / *Saturday, April 1st.*
[*Postmark:*] APR 1 1809

20. *To Dorothy Wordsworth*

Ms. Dove Cottage. Unpub. Qtd. Eaton, p. 157.

Wednesday, April 5th. [1809] 82, Gt. T. St.
My dear Madam,—I was yesterday so busy that I had resolved to write a few lines only to meet you on Friday night: but I was obliged to give up even that, in consequence of Mr. Stewart's calling and taking away a good deal of my time.—I am sorry for this; because I have a presentiment that you will be at Rydale on Friday night. Tell me, if I prophecy truly. I think so—partly because you were *not* there last Friday—and partly because I conjecture that you have very fine weather just at present.— —On Monday morning I received *both* the letters relating to the note on Sir J. Moore;[1] which shall be done as

---

[9] The Supreme Junta issued a decree, dated Seville, Feb. 7, 1809, de-claring "That no quarter shall be given to any French soldier, officer or general, who may be made prisoner in any town or district, in which acts contrary to the laws of war have been committed by the enemy."
Letter 20:
[1] Only one of these letters seems to have survived (*MY*, I, 274–279). See above, p. 72.

well as I can do it and as the time and the want of official documents will permit.— —The note on the Saragossa Bulletin, as Mr. Wordsworth does not think it material, I shall not put even into the Appendix. —For Gen. Ferguson I have (to borrow Mallet's phrase to Garrick) *'found a niche'* [2] where he will be seen by everybody:—I think he might justly complain (considering the subject of the work)—if he were placed at the back-door of the Appendix; where most people will not look, as supposing that nothing will be found there but musty treaties and state papers &c.—On this account, and because Mr. Wordsworth seemed to regret that he had not mentioned him in the body of the work, I have put him into a footnote (which was indeed, in mere *justice* to Gen. F., called for—supposing that Mr. Wordsworth had not wished to mention him with *praise*). I hope this will be approved of.—About Egypt I was wrong:—Mr. Stewart told me that he heard an officer of Moore's own brigade—say that brigade or one regiment of it, was in a good deal of confusion: about Corunna, as far as I can learn, I am right: no English reg. appears to have been broken or nearly broken; so that, unless I hear something further, I shall conclude that I am to expunge the word *Corunna.* (However I shall make more inquiries to-night.)—The note upon Charles IInd's. parliaments I have not placed at the foot of the page, but in the Appendix:—it seemed to me quite *digressional* enough to warrant (or even require) this.—I don't know whether there is such a word as digressional: but I wanted it: and this leads me to say that I have been lately in the habit of coining words a good deal; being in too great a hurry generally to summon the real word; and, I am afraid, they may not always be intelligible. *Dejaded* I recollect: but that I suppose the context wd. explain.—Ghenghis—Genghis—or Ghenghiz Khan or Khân (for this person has a multitude of aliases), I fear, you will not recognize when you see him in the pamphlet:—but you must not suppose it is spelt, as you will see, by *accident:* it is in the very latest fashion of the *Asiatic Researches* which I examined, in order to sport the most learned and *ineffable* orthography.[3]— —Should the Title-Page

---

[2] To a passage in the pamphlet which reproaches the "whole body" of British generals in Portugal for approving the Convention, appears the note: "From this number, however, must be excepted the gallant and patriotic General Ferguson. For that officer has had the virtue publicly and in the most emphatic manner, upon two occasions, to reprobate the whole transaction" (Dicey, p. 143 *n.*).

[3] Chengiz (Dicey, p. 112).

say—by *William Wordsworth*—simply—or with the addition of—
Author of 'The Lyrical Ballads' and of other 'Poems'—?— —There
is still a conditional promise of some work to follow this in the passage
—'On some future occasion (if what has been said meets with attention)' &c.—This, I conclude, was meant to remain, as no direction
is given for erasing it.— —When I said that *Q. R. S. T. U.* must be
broken up, I used the printer's word to me: but I found, from Mr.
Stewart yesterday and also from the printer on further quentiong.,
that this meant no more than that this must be *dislocated* to fill up the
chasm made by the removal of the note; and not that the whole must
be *verbatim* decomposed. The former process takes up a deal of time;
but not so much of course as the last; or nearly so.—This is Easter
week with us; and everybody is idle on Monday; most people on
Tuesday; and a great many all the week. So that, I am sorry to say,
the pamphlet has languished since Saturday: however to-day, if the
men can be made to attend, the overseer promises that it shall begin to
advance again by forced marches. If therefore you do not receive a
letter from me on Tuesday next, you may conclude that it is because I
am haunted by—or haunting—Mr. Baldwin's fiends: for, if I give
them half an hour's respite they are ready to make that an excuse for
going off to some other work.—If the pamphlet is out (as I am
promised) by Monday next,—any questions, which I may have asked
above, will most likely be with you but a little before the pamphlet
itself: however, as a printer *may* break his word, the answers might as
well be sent (if you have an opportunity)—particularly what relates to
the title-page, as that will be done last.— —I sent (or rather, ordered
to be sent) a *Times* of Monday morning last:—did you receive it?—I
called at the office of the *Times;* and they were all sold; so that I was
obliged to leave an order with a newsman to get one and send it off for
me.—I sent it on account of the speeches at the Common Hall; [4] and
that you might have the pleasure of knowing, as soon as possible, the
humiliation and punishment of this infamous tool of the ministry—the
ld. Mayor—in being obliged to propose a vote of censure on himself,

---

[4] The *Times* for April 3 reported the meeting of the City at which a long
series of resolutions were presented, denouncing corruption, praising Colonel Wardle and his supporters (especially Alderman Combe, the one City
member who voted to address for the Duke's removal), censuring three
who did not, and censuring the Mayor. The Mayor first refused to admit
that resolution, but finally offered it himself.

which was carried by acclamation.—I passed by the Mansion House
on Monday about 2 o'clock:—the ld. mayor was to go in a short time
(I found from the immense multitudes of people collected) to Christ
Church:—I waited therefore to see how he would be received; and I
am happy to say that, from the moment he made his appearance [*torn:
? until*] Alderman Combe came out, there was a universal roar of
groans—hisses—hootings &c fm. man, woman, and child—which might
be heard, I hope, almost to Downing St.—The stratagem, by which
he hoped to have outmanoeuvred the popular party, was this: 1st. he
returned the requisition as not quadrating with his notion of a *tangible*
requisition; 2ndly. when they brought it back shaped to his own prescription, *he took time to consider of it:* 3rdly. he took so much time,
that—when he agreed to grant a common hall—it was too late to
appoint Thursday: and therefore, the next day being Good Friday, he
appointed Saturday. Now the meaning of this was as follows:—All the
respectable people in the city (in the money phrase)—i.e. all the people
who have country-houses and can afford to lose a day, go out of Town
—for the Easter Holidays—on Thursday night:—this is so general,
that it has become a test of *gentility* not to be found in London on
Saturday—that being the only *open* day (as they call it) in the whole
series of the holidays.—On Saturday therefore it was hoped that there
would be a very thin attendance: but fortunately bills were stuck up
every-where on Thursday to warn the merchants &c. and they all made
a point of attending—in such numbers as have been rarely known.—
And the issue was accordingly.—I mention these facts (which were
told to me by an acquaintance in the city) that you may rejoice the
more in the triumph which has been gained.

I hope I write legibly: but I have not time to see.—If dear Johnny
had been with me, he would have seen a fine show on Monday—with
all the state carriages and beautiful horses with gay trappings.—I think
I must send him a description of it.—Did he get my letter?—Everything abt. the parcel being done in a hurry, I am not sure that even
that was put in: but, as I did not find it lying out, I suppose it was.

Again I recollect Mrs. K's letters; but I have not room to say more
about them than that their drift is to recommend that the carpets &c.
shd. be made under her inspection at Manchester.—I have not answered her letter yet; but I shall tomorrow, if possible, to say that it
must be done as you think best. But I will give you her letter more at

length on Sat. if possible—if not on Sunday.—For the present—farewell, my dear Madam, and believe me ever your most affectionate
friend, Thos. de Quincey.—

[*Across folded back:*] I hope to get Johnny some better pictures for
the next parcel. The clock strikes 5.—"I can no more!" as the tragedy
men say.

[*Inserted, inverted above salutation:*] Everybody in London is readg.
Miss H. More's '*Coelebs in search of a Wife*'—She has got 1000
guineas for it!!!!!!! 'O tempora! oh &c' The Carpet, I hope, will be
with you in a few days.

[*Address:*] For Miss Wordsworth / Grasmere / To care of Miss Cross-
thwaite / Keswick / Cumberland /
Free / *Single sheet* / *Wednesday, April 5th.*
[*Postmark:*] APR 5 1809

21. *To William Wordsworth*

Ms. Dove Cottage. Unpub. Qtd. Eaton, pp. 157, 163, 179.

[London]
Saturday afternoon—April 15th. [1809]

My dear Sir,

I must first congratulate you on the good news from Gallicia. I never
was more rejoiced than at hearing so total and peremptory a refutation
of Sir J.[ohn] M[oore]'s and D. Baird's calumnies against the Spaniards as that given in the affair at Vigo; [1] which besides it's value as
demonstrative of the spirit in that part of Spain (and the South and
West need no vouchers for *their* spirit), seems very important for
itself; as the deduction of 1300 men from a force previously incompetent to keep the country down—must put the French into a condition
of great danger in the North.—The news was in London by Wednesday last; but I did not see it till Thursday evening after post-time: I
then procured from a waiter of a coffee-house the *Times* of Thursday
morning—both for this news—and for an account given in it of Sir R.

Letter *21:*
[1] On March 27 the British frigates *Lively* and *Venus,* with the aid of
Spanish patriots, captured the French garrison at Vigo.

Wilson's corps in Portugal.[2] I sent it off last night. Fresh news had then arrived in Town from Portugal; but, as it rested on the authority of a private letter only—and was *bad* news, I did not send any paper: indeed, seeing it only in the *Statesman,* I hoped it was not true; but afterwards seeing it in the *Courier,* I was obliged to suppose it of some authority. This news was that the French had entered *Oporto;* and that Gen. Victor has beaten Cuesta in Estramadura. The circumstances added by the Courier respecting the capture of Oporto—viz. that the Portuguese had 1st. put to death all those who were indisposed to resist—and then afterwards surrendered the city without an effort at resistance—seems utterly incredible: and indeed the whole account given in the Second Edit. of the Courier is nothing more than an abridgement of the private letter in the Statesman—written by some coward or other in Lisbon, hearing of course nothing but rumors—and panic-struck for his own person and property.—I have heard nothing more to-day: if I find anything, I shall send a paper.—I sent a *Times* last Monday night—containing an account of the rising of the people in Portugal against Gen. Friere &c.[3]—

It being now nearly 5 o'clock,—I must report as briefly as possible about the pamphlet.—But first I ought to mention that I received your letter—written on your return to Grasmere [4]—last Monday morning. —The passage in your former letter about Saragossa—which I referred to in my letter to Miss Wordsworth—was this: 'Besides, you will see, by what is now sent, that—so far from thinking that Saragossa has broken her bond—in my estimation she has discharged it to the letter.' —This seemed to me at that time urged as in contradiction to some opinion which I had expressed: and, therefore, knowing how entirely my *thoughts* (and, as far as I remembered, *words*) had gone along with what you have said,—I felt (and expressed, I dare say) some surprise and sense of injustice; but, I hope, nothing more; I mean, nothing which could lead you to think seriously that I felt any soreness or unkindly feelings of any kind which could make me ready to imagine "new matter for misconception" in your letter on this subject: I am

---

[2] Sir Robert Wilson, in command of the Lusitanian legion recruited in England from Portuguese refugees, was successful in harassing actions against the French in northern Portugal.

[3] General Bernadim Freire de Andrade was killed by the people at Braga for supposedly treasonous agreements with the French.

[4] *MY,* I, 284–286.

sure that I felt in perfect charity—even before I had written what
would set right what I then thought your mistake on this subject
[*scratched through:* and until then I felt rather uneasy, and more so
perhaps from having unconsciously swallowed I suppose a pretty large
quantity.—] I have so much to say—which I must say, if possible—
that I must quit this subject; only begging you to excuse anything
which may have been improper in my mode of expressing my feelings;
and to believe that my love and veneration for all at Grasmere are far
too great for it to be possible that I should 'let the sun go down' upon
any feelings of petty vexation or anger in any case: but in the present
I did not in my thoughts accuse you of more than having read my
letter too hastily to see *what* alteration it was that I proposed respecting Saragossa—and then very naturally classed me with the multitudes
who are dupes of the French Bulletins. But I am now perfectly sure
that it was *I* who misapprehended *you*.—The pamphlet, I am very
sorry to say, is not yet finished: what is the cause of the delay, I cannot learn. Mr. Stewart, whom I saw on some day this week (I forget
which), promised me to call on Mr. Baldwin, as he was going that
way: but they have gone on no better since: there remains at least a
whole sheet of which I have not yet seen a proof; and the whole of
the Appendix (about 3 half-sheets).—Yesterday night, they promised
to send me the 2nd. proof of X; in which, as usual, they failed:—the
whole will go up to about *A2;* and the latter part of the Appendix—
the compositor told me last night, he could not possibly want till
Monday morning: (this latter part I have kept back until the last
minute—to add anything which the publication of further papers might
furnish: and have accordingly got an important passage from Sir J.
Moore's last despatch.)—I fear therefore that it is vain to hope that
the pamphlet can be ready for publication before Wednesday night
next.—They have such innumerable demands on *immediate* attention
at this press in the shape of *bills* &c. that they hold no promises sacred
if anything of this kind interferes.—I think to-night, if I find at the
press that they have not done [*torn:* ? what] they promised to do last
night, to call on Mr. Baldwin—whom I have already seen once; and
who then assured me that his 'best endeavours' &c should be used to
get it done as soon as possible: but this it is impossible to believe from
the pace at which they have advanced since—Easter Week, however,
accounts for some part of the delay; as most of the workmen made a
jubilee week of it—seldom staying but a few hours of the day—and

many of them none at all.—I write without any order, it being now considerably past 5 o'clock:—and I am quite out of spirits at having to make such a bad report to you: the moment it is out, I will send it; if on Wednesday night—by Miss Crossthwaite; if on any other night—by the Ambleside post.

I have never written once since I received your last letter: that is I have missed *twice:* it happened that on both Sat. and Tuesday night last I was very busy: and, having nothing pleasant to communicate about the pamphlet, I felt reluctant to write at all.—I have besides been very unwell since Good Friday: on that day, our weather changed entirely and most abruptly to extreme cold—so cold that on Easter Monday or Tuesday it snowed more than once in light showers: this brought on all my old rheumatic pains about my head and face: so that I have had only one uninterrupted night of rest since then: and, being obliged to put cotton soaked in laudanum into my mouth at times to allay the pains which run round the whole circuit of my teeth, I have at times unavoidably swallowed a good deal—which has much disturbed my head.—However, I am now getting daily better; though the weather is still cold, though fine.

I feel as if I had been guilty of a crime in not writing to Miss Wordsworth for so long a time: but I will endeavour to make atonement by a more amusing letter, than my late ones can have been, next Tuesday night.—I remain, dear Sir, with the greatest respect, your affectionate friend. Thos. de Quincey.—

[*Address:*] William Wordsworth, Esqr. / Grasmere / near Kendal / West-
     moreland / Free / Single sheet / Saturday, April 15th.
[*Postmark:*] APR 15 1809

22. *To Dorothy Wordsworth*

Ms. Dove Cottage. Unpub. Qtd. Eaton, pp. 158, 160.

       Tuesday night, April 25th. [1809]—82, Gt. T. St.
My dear Madam,

Two evils are come upon me: shortness of time—and roughness of paper; for, finding all my paper exhausted, I have been obliged to send out for some; and this chalky kind, upon which it is a manual labor to write, has been sent me:—First of the pamphlet:—it is not yet finished: never has it advanced so slowly as last week:—I can scarcely guess what you will think about it: but the case is simply this; last week, out of the six days, the man attended *two;* and must then undoubtedly have been drunk from the absurd blunders and omissions which he made:—and they *will* not (they say, *can* not) put any other compositor to the work.—Perhaps you do not know the extent to which it it [*sic*] will reach;—it will go up (i.e. the *body* of the work) to page 192;—the Appendix cannot make less than 3 half-sheets; i.e. the whole will go up to page 216: one whole half-sheet of the body—i.e. from page 184 to 192—still remains which I have not seen; though I learn from the overseer that it is nearly composed.—Last night, when I was at the press, I found that the compositor had never appeared the whole day:—this morning, however, I conclude from a message which I had from the press that he is there.—This is the whole state of the "existing circumstances:"—that is, there are 4 entire half-sheets for me to see.—

—I am truly sorry that I cannot make my anxiety for the early appearing of the work *manifest* itself more in the progress of the printing: but, after the representations and remonstrances which I have made, I cannot think of any plan for quickening the progress—but that of taking it out of Mr. Baldwin's hands; which is perhaps not a thing that can be done; and, at any rate,—as it is so nearly finished,—seems not to be an eligible plan now.—In the meantime, though I do not suppose that Mr. Stewart would hazard any representation of the affair without first satisfying himself as to the real cause of the delay, I yet collect from a note which I received from him on Saturday—that he has either guessed—or been told at the press—that it is the multitude of my corrections which causes it:—and indeed they are so ready to make this excuse even to me, who have the means of contradicting it in the dates of my receipts and sendings, &c. that I cannot but suppose that, if he has ever inquired about it at the press, they will to *him*— for their own credit—have imputed the whole delay to this cause. I must therefore say—that, though I have been very rigid in exacting from the compositor a minute attention to all my punctuation &c. (and am glad to think that I have; because thus, without any time having been really lost, an accuracy has been gained which might have been some compensation if time *had* been lost),—yet no part of the copy has ever been given to him without having been first pointed with so much deliberation that I have not, in half a dozen instances, made any changes *after* it has been composed:—where he neglected it—and disturbed the sense—I did of course restore what I had put before:— but in general, ever since I gave him warning that I *should* restore it, he has been remarkably attentive to this point;—and his errors have been of a more serious kind—very often omissions of whole sentences &c.—and therefore, as I told them at the press, if I have troubled them with numerous corrections—it is because they have troubled me with numerous blunders.—But you will be weary of this subject; and therefore I leave it.

I did not mean that my hasty note of Friday night should have been a substitute for my usual Saturday's letter:—but on Saturday afternoon I found myself at Cornhill about 4 o'clock—with only a hour to write in—no place to write in but a noisy coffee-room—and wearied with a long toil through the streets of London on business: I therefore [*torn:* ? contented my]self with sendg. you the official report of the affair [*torn*]—and of the Debates in H. of Lords—in the *Times* [*torn:* ? of] Sat. morning.—Since then we have had an account (which probably you will have seen) that the campaign opened on the part of Austria on the 10th. of this month—by an irruption into Bavaria on which the King of Bavaria and his court quitted Munich:— we had also on Sunday a report, by letter from Rotterdam, that the Emperor of Russia has been dethroned:—this account was so generally disbelieved that only one Sunday paper made it an article of their summaries: but yesterday other accounts from Heligoland, to the same purport, have given it some credit with the respectable papers.—Has the Courier given you the decree of the Junta respecting Saragossa? If not, I I [*sic—next page*] will search for it at some newsman's office and send it.—After Marshall Beresford's proclamation,[1] one cannot think that the people of Oporto have behaved as the Spaniards would have behaved in the same circumstances: but still the fact that the French appeared before Oporto on the 25th, and did not enter it till the 29th. proves that some resistance must have been made; and that therefore the English papers are not justified in their account of that affair.—Perhaps by next Saturday, or before it, I may have to send you an account of a battle in Portugal:—if anything depends upon

---

Letter 22:

[1] The English General William Beresford had just exhorted the Portuguese people on the occasion of his appointment as Commander-in-Chief of the Portuguese forces.

promptitude, what can be thought of the present ministry—when Papers of Saturday tell us that on Thursday last Sir A.[rthur] W.[ellesley]'s expedition passed Plymouth with a fair wind for Lisbon?—[*sentence obliterated*].

My dear Madam! I must complain that I have not been rejoiced by the cheering sight of a Grasmere letter since—when shall I say?—I believe, since Mr. Wordsworth's letter.—I fear that I shall not leave room for a direction if I go on: therefore pardon my dulness: and believe me, dear Madam, with kindest respects to all at Grasmere, your affectionate friend, Thos. de Quincey.—

[*Inserted inverted before salutation:*] Within an hour after my letter of Friday was written,—a gentleman came into the coffee-room where I was dining,—and informed us that Ld. C. was not killed: [2]—I thought this very probable at first; guessing that, from his eagerness in quest of danger, the news-makers would be sure to create some such rumor.—

[*Inserted inverted between salutation and body:*] Would not Mrs. Wordsworth or Miss Hutchinson honor me by lightening your labor in writing to me?

[*Address:*] Miss Wordsworth / Grasmere / near Kendal / Westmoreland / Single sheet / Free / Tuesday, April 25th.
[*Postmark:*] APR 25 1809

23. *To Dorothy Wordsworth*

Ms. Dove Cottage. Unpub. Qtd. Eaton, p. 150.

Saturday—April 29th. [1809]—82, Gt. Titchfield St.
My dear Madam,

I write a few lines (for I have literally not a whole sheet of paper to write on—and nobody in the house but a little girl, who may be wanted to open the door, to send for one)—to say that, though the pamphlet is not finished, it will now go on without stopping; as they promised on Thursday to put a new workman to it as [of] yesterday: I have not indeed received a half-sheet this morning, as they assured me I should: but I cannot doubt that I shall find at least one ready for me

---

[2] Apparently in a letter of April 21, which has not come to light, De Quincey had passed on a rumor that Lord Cochrane had been killed.

at the press—to which I am just going. It will advance regularly, of course, under this new workman: and therefore on Wednesday I should hope it will be published.—Notwithstanding the blame having been all along thrown upon the compositor's drunkeness at the press, —I have learnt a circumstance which makes me doubt this much:—I found, from an advertisement in the paper, that Mr. Baldwin is at this time completing a work which has been in his hands for many years— viz. An Abridgement of the Philosophical Transactions: on question- ing the overseer about it, he told me that they were now making the very greatest exertions to get this work out which had been in a sleep- ing state for some years; so that one set of men sate up all night to get it done in time: this work is Mr. B's own property; and therefore I cannot but suspect, as the time of this advertisement (which was an offer of the work on advantageous terms to the booksellers—in con- sequence of the acceptance of which terms this activity began) tallies about with the time when the pamphlet began to be neglected—that the Irish compositor has very likely been as regularly as before at the press —(only removed into another room where I could not see him):— this is my suspicion; and I shall this evening state it to Mr. Baldwin. —At any rate it appears to me that Mr. B. must be a *rascal;* because it can never be meant, on making an agreement with a printer, that the execution of it shall be subject to the caprices of a compositor.—In excuse for not putting on a new workman, they told me for sometime that any compositor in the house would give them warning—if put to *finish* work which he had not begun: this, at any rate, appears to be false from their promise on Thursday night—Yesterday I was not at the press: [*struck through:* for the first time for many weeks] but the reason was—that they told me that, with the corrections of former sheets returned (which had been lying by in the hands of the overseer), the compositor could not do more than get one half sheet ready by eight o'clock last night or early this morning.— —Amongst the portraits &c. there will be a picture for Johnny—which, I hope, will give great satisfaction; it is nothing less than "London Church" in its glory. Pray tell me some news about him and dear Sissy. Dear loves! I think of them perpetually, and have their sweet faces always coming up before me: most glad shall I be to see them again.

It may seem odd to you, my dear Madam, that I make excuses for shortness of time &c.: but the truth is—that I never can write a letter before hand with any pleasure: and therefore, if I have not leisure allowed me just at that time when it suits the post—and when both suit my inclinations I find it difficult to write at all. Of late also the vexations of the Press have accumulated upon me so much that I am obliged to turn away from the subject to maintain any tolerable spirits in this dull atmosphere.—But yet, after all, if my epistolary labors—since I left Grasmere—were all collected together; surely there would be enough to astonish all those who have ever known me before: I really believe that the collective labors of my whole life in that line, before that time, would not make above *as* thick a 4to. vol. as what I have written in that time to yourself.—Therefore, in excuse for me; you must recollect that I am held between two forces—my hatred of letter writing generically—and my love for communication, by any mode or channel, with Grasmere.—Everybody in London is on tiptoe for news from Portugal: it will be very singular if, as seems now probable, another battle should be fought at Vimiera or Roleia [1] —the situation and relations of the two armies being just inverted.— Some apprehensions are entertained; for ministers have now almost a certainty that *Victor* from the East and *Soult* from the North will so concert their movements as gradually to converge before they attack the Eng. army; they will thus have, on any calculation, at least from 60– to 70,000; to meet which the ministry have deliberately—knowing all these probabilities—and at the very moment when they were torturing their brains for excuses for errors of *the same kind* in Spain, sent out reinforcements which, *if they are in time,* will make us 30,000!!!!!! Have you seen any of the *private* accounts of Lord Cochrane's exploit in Basque Roads?—They show, I think, that Ld. Gambier is far too much engrossed by *religion*—and (as Admiral Harvey says) by *"psalm-singing"* to have any leisure for *justice* when it interferes with his personal dislikes.[2]—The *Orders in Council* were on Thursday

---

Letter 23:

[1] An engagement at Roliça (Roleia) preceded the battle of Vimeiro (Vimiera), Wellesley's partial victory which led to the Convention of Cintra.

[2] Captain Cochrane was in charge of an attack by fire ships on the French fleet in the Basque Roads which resulted in the destruction of four ships, reported on April 23 as a "Glorious Naval Exploit." Cochrane maintained, however, that if he had enjoyed the full coöperation of Admiral Gambier, who commanded the Channel fleet, all the French vessels could have been destroyed. Gambier, who had a reputation as a strict Methodist, both deplored the use of fire ships as inhumane and was irked that the

rescinded;[3] and Ld. Castlereagh has been pronounced innocent by a small majority in the H. of C. on the ground that he contented himself with manifesting an intention to commit a crime: but that he lost the opportunity of executing his intention:[4]—This is all our news— up to *last night*.

[*Across folded back:*] I shall certainly begin to brighten up soon into a most entertaining correspondent. But I shall not give notice again.— Will not Ned Wilson[5] think himself aggrieved by transferring the commission for the shelves to an other person? If they were made of any native wood—(as cherry-tree, for example)—would not N.W.— be able to make them?—Believe me, my dear Madam, ever your most affectionate friend. Thos. de Quincey.

[*Inserted inverted before salutation:*] If you have any commissions of any kind to be executed in London, pray send them to me: if you want any articles for presents &c.—they can be packed up in my book packing-cases.

[*Address:*]   Miss Wordsworth / Grasmere / Near Kendal / Westmoreland / Free / Single sheet / *Saturday, April 29th.*
[*Postmark:*] APR 29 1809

---

junior Cochrane had been sent out by the Admiralty on this mission. Cochrane, who sat in the House of Commons, opposed a vote of thanks to Gambier; the admiral demanded a hearing by court-martial, whereupon officialdom closed ranks and cleared him.

[3] The "Orders in Council," a British paper blockade of France and her possessions, were not finally revoked until June 23, 1812—too late to stop the War of 1812 with the United States. Revocation was, however, officially promised by David Erskine, envoy to the United States, on April 19, 1809, to take effect on June 10; and President Madison accordingly proclaimed renewal of trade with Britain the same day, only to withdraw his proclamation on August 10 after the British Ambassador's action was declared to have been unauthorized.

[4] Castlereagh had tried to get his friend Lord Clancarty a seat in Parliament in return for the disposal of a writership (or clerkship) in the East India Company—patronage which had come to Castlereagh indirectly from his former position as President of the Board of Control. The negotiations, however, fell through. Castlereagh admitted the circumstances, but denied that he had erred intentionally. The April 25 resolution condemning him lost 167 to 216.

[5] Grasmere carpenter at work on Dove Cottage.

24. *To Dorothy Wordsworth*

Ms. Dove Cottage. Unpub. Qtd. Eaton, p. 161.

Moor St. [London]-Tuesday night, May 9th. [1809]
My dear Madam,

I was unwilling to let a third opportunity pass by me (though I knew I should not be able to write much) ; and therefore I carried out with me a sheet of smooth paper—that I might stop at the first place where I found time, and write a few lines.—I shall however write again to-night—and shall send it to-morrow evening to Keswick; so that you will be sure to have one letter at least from me this week, if you shd. not go to Rydale.

Our calamitous news will no doubt have reached you long before this letter :—I should not have sent it, I believe, if I had been in time; as such news would come soon enough, whenever it came:—but, though 2nd. edits. of the papers had (I found been published) by 5 o'clock, I did not hear it till it would have been too late to get up to Lombard St. in time.—I never was more dejected by any public event that I recollect:—it seems to make such a hopelessness, from some cause or other, in any efforts of Austria—that, thinking herself strong enough to act offensively, she should be then overthrown within 10 days of the commencement of hostilities.—As to the battle itself, —I cannot say that, taking it in the French account, it seems to have been so productive and conclusive a one as our papers represent it— calling it—'the total destruction of Austria' &c.—There have been since this news of Sat. night, other reports of advantages gained by the Austrians, but I am afraid there is no truth in them.[1]

I have received, since I wrote last, 3 letters from Grasmere ;[2] for which I am very much obliged to you and Miss Hutchinson.—Yesterday I had the last; viz. Miss Hutchinsons: it happened that I had written a note on Sat. night to Mr. Stuart—and had proposed to accompany him on Monday to Mr. Baldwin's; to which he had

---

Letter 24:

[1] The advance of the Austrians, launched on April 9, came to its first major defeat at Eckmühl on April 22. Archduke Charles was able, however, to withdraw across the Danube, and the other wing of the Austrian army checked the French.

[2] *MY*, I, 292–296, 298–300.

agreed:—so that the whole affair of the cancel was settled between us there. That was the first time we had met at Mr. Baldwin's; for we had both been separately several times before: but as the pamphlet was going on at the old pace and as I found fm. Mr. Stuart's note of Sat. night that they persisted in making one set of excuses to me and another to him (telling him that it was all my fault)—I proposed to him that we should go together to confront the different persons concerned.—On our road thither however I found from Mr. Stuart that they did not accuse me of keeping back the copy—or, at least, that they did not make that their ordinary charge—but of making too many corrections (of which I spoke formerly).—Not to trouble you however with these feuds,—the whole state of our conference with Mr. Baldwin—and the whole state of the pamphlet:—up to Friday night I had got only the 1st. half sheet of the Appendix—which carries us to the end of the *Armistice:*—the 2nd. half-sheet will be nearly filled with the Convention;—and the 3rd., I suppose, will be just filled with my note on Sir J. M.'s letters—which, for several reasons, I thought it best to place as a postscript:—this closes the work.—At our solemn meeting of yesterday,—Mr. Baldwin promised to put 2 hands upon it; and then gave us hope that the last proof (i.e. the Title-page and Advertisement) should be in my hands on Wednesday—that is to-morrow—and that the pamphlet should be in Longman's hands for publication on Thursday.—I am just come from the press; and find that there are really 2 hands now upon it; and that the 2nd. half-sheet will be with me to-night.—The cancel [3] has luckily been so contrived by a fortunate spare leaf which they calculate on having at the end (a thing which I do not perfectly comprehend;— but, as Mr. B. & S. understood the possibility very well, no doubt it is all right) that only one half of that half-sheet will be lost.—I was not sorry about the cancel;—because it prevented all this wretched delay, at which you will have been so much vexed, from being entirely

---

[3] On May 5 (*MY*, I, 298) Wordsworth had asked that the sheet be canceled which contained the statement that the Convention generals had "brought upon themselves the *unremovable contempt and hatred* of their countrymen," and that the reading be changed to the "unalterable sentence already passed on them." This was done, as De Quincey says; but some of the uncanceled sheets were circulated, and the original form still stands in the texts of W. A. Knight (*Prose Works*, London, 1896), and of Dicey (p. 98); Grosart (*Prose Works*, pp. 104 f.) has "the sentence passed upon them by the voice of their countrymen" (see above, pp. 82–83).

flung away:—though, as to the libellousness of the passage, I would willingly have insured the passage on the chance of the thing: though perhaps they would give a commander-in-chief large damages.—Mr. St. was inclined to think that the passage, under the indefiniteness of the law of libels, would be thought actionable:—though it is certain that he was of a different opinion some weeks since: for a particular circumstance makes me recollect that I asked him about the passage when I came up to Town.—I doubted about the classicality of *un*removeable, thinking that it should be *ir*removeable; and having therefore had my attention drawn to the passage—by taking a note of it to consult Johnson at a shop: I recollected that this was a passage of which at the time he wrote it Mr. Wordsworth doubted; and therefore, when Mr. St. was once mentioning to me that he had not yet got any fair copy after *L,* he said that he would read them all over to see if there was anything libellous: and that reminded me to mention this passage as perhaps being so in Mr. Wordsworth's opinion:—but he answered 'oh! I don't see anything in *that.*' However I did not think proper to claim my due praise yesterday; because, I knew, from his then opinion of the passage, that he must have forgotten all about it.—The change, sent by Mr. Wordsworth, was adopted—only leaving out the word *already* which, Mr. St. observed, had occurred just before.—I proposed a slight amendment as it then seemed to me;—but I did not press it because Mr. St. was satisfied with what stood (i.e. with some slight alteration which I now forget)—and would have thought it captious in me to object;—but I did not entirely like it: however, I shall perhaps think differently when I read the whole passage—In walking with Mr. St. along the Strand yesterday—we overtook Mrs. Morgan and her sister.[4] I knew them slightly—and therefore told Mrs. M. all I knew about Mr. Coleridge concerning whom she questioned me very anxiously.

I cannot think how I have contrived, writing only about business, to tell you so little in a whole sheet:—But, as somebody says, I had not time to write a shorter letter. I have passed a miserable week all last week—nearly the whole of every night lying awake with a raging tooth-ache.—But that would not have prevented me from writing, if I could have told you *then* anything satisfactory about

---

[4] John Morgan, his wife, and her sister, Charlotte Brent, were old Bristol friends of Coleridge now settled in London. He several times lodged with them in Berners Street and in Portland Place, Hammersmith.

the pamphlet.—In the mean time, I do not know how far I may have
been misrepresented to you about this business.—Mr. St. would not,
I am sure, intentionally misrepresent; but not knowing much abt.
me—he may have some difficulty in disbelieving all that they may
have told him at the press:—as I told him yesterday, they serve him
as ill as me; for when I shewed them (as I did regularly) his notes
to me—they all denied that they had laid the blame on me; though I
have no doubt they did.—Therefore I do not know *how* much reason
I have to complain of Mr. St.:—I am sure that I have *some*.
[*Across folded back:*] I will send off the pamphlets the moment they
are done:—God bless you! my dear Madam. Your's most affectionately, Thos. de Q. Pray thank Miss Hutchinson for her kindness in
writing: [5] your letters [*torn: ? brought*] me my only pleasures last
week—

[*Address:*]   Miss Wordsworth / Grasmere / near Kendal / Westmoreland /
Free / Single sheet / Tuesday, May 9th.
[*Postmark:*] MAY 9 1809

25. *To Dorothy Wordsworth*

Ms. Dove Cottage. Unpub. Qtd. Eaton, p. 172.

[*Printed:*] #A long letter–wondrously dull!—being all in defence
of myself:—therefore do not honor it by reading it before the 3
Couriers; or you will be disappointed.

82, Gt. Titchfield St.
[May 10, 1809]

My dear Madam,—We have now here the most beautiful weather
imaginable; the heat is just a pleasant summer heat. It came upon us,
sometime in the middle of last week, as suddenly as the cold weather
that intervened between my first coming to London—(when it was
perfect spring)—and our present summer: on May day, I was up
very early in the morning; and thought I had never seen such a 1st.
of May;—it was a complete rainy December day: and on the day
following we had a hail-storm—rain, thunder and lightning. *Now,*
within this day or two, fires have everywhere disappeared;—every

---

[5] Sara Hutchinson added a postscript to William's letter of May 5 (*MY*,
I, 299–300).

third man has his waistcoat unbuttoned;—and umbrellas have fallen 30 per cent.—When you hear of my being up early in the morning, you will perhaps marvel; or ask what is meant by 'very early': but really I have, in many places before now, had a *character* for getting up early; and, whenever I get into the habit, I always continue in it for a long time: this morning, for instance, I was up before 7; and that I mention not as my *chef-d'oeuvre,* but as a mean ratio of the different times: the misfortune was, at Grasmere, that I never got into the habit; or else, no doubt, I should have continued in it.—I thanked you in my letter of last night (for I am now writing on Wednesday morning) for your letters; and I must thank you again. I am very proud to have had so many in so short a time.—I got the first yesterday week: I received that morning a note from Mr. Stuart— mentioning that *he* had also had a letter from Mr. Wordsworth [1]— and begging me to make a point of seeing Mr. Baldwin himself: accordingly that day I called, but found unfortunately that I was a minute too late; Mr. St. having himself been there immediately before and gone out with Mr. Baldwin: I saw his brother however—The next day happened what I said, in my last letter, I thought I had some reason to complain of Mr. Stuart for:—To explain it—I must first mention that though I found on Monday last that they never had directly accused me of keeping back any part of the copy, yet in some way or other Mr. St. must have had some obscure thought of this kind— as his notes shew; though, on Monday, he said that he did not mean to insinuate this. (The true state of the case was this:—the last sentence of the *body* of the pamphlet had been given to the printer on Easter Tuesday—most of it before: but the final part beginning at —"feed and uphold the bright consummate flower" [2]—having been sent on a sheet containing a letter to me—and having besides a Latin quotation in it which was not written quite distinctly enough to prevent the printer fm. making blunders—and being, in a manner, matted into the preface (which, from the alterations and insertions since sent, it was necessary should be written out fair)—for all these

Letter 25:

   [1] Probably Wordsworth's letter of April 26 (*MY,* I, 288–289), requesting Stuart to use his exertions "to procure the immediate finishing of the work."

   [2] Dicey, p. 190. Part of De Quincey's transcription is in the Cornell Lib. Wordsworth Coll., No. 2804, fols. 56–57.

reasons I thought it better to write all this over again; and had accordingly kept back—until Easter Tuesday—so much as I have said
for that purpose, well knowing that, at the rate they were then going
on at, they did not want it. And, in reality, the half sheet, closing
with this part, was not composed until last Saturday night but one—
April 29th.—Secondly; the notes, which are 6 in number and stand
first in the Appendix, had been kept back one or two days longer—I
cannot be positive as to the *day*, because it was not a rememberable
day like Easter Tuesday, but it was in the same *week* certainly;
and the reason that they had been kept back at all—was because the
notes E and F related to the addresses of the Italian Deputies to
Bonaparte which it was necessary to find, that the exact words might
be quoted; and I had some difficulty in doing that—as I had first to
make out, by following back a chain of connexions in my memory,
about what time it was that we read this address at Grasmere; and,
when I had settled that, had to search for it; and then, not being able
to find at the newsman's any but morning papers (which had not
given it), had at last to consult the file at the Courier office.—These
notes however they had, as I have said, sometime in Easter week:
and they were not composed until last Friday night, May 5th.—
Thirdly—the Armistice and Convention I had not given them at all—
for this reason; Mr. Baldwin prints 2 papers at the same house where
the pamphlet is printed (the St. James Chronicle and some other):
this Mr. St. had himself reminded me of; and therefore, at the time
I gave the notes, I said to the over-seer that their own papers would
be as good a copy as any other (for the alters. which I had taken fm.
the Report of the Board of Inquiry—beginning at—"The words
'a ses frais' to be omitted." [3] &c.—on second thoughts, it appeared
to me needless to print): to this he agreed; only doubted whether, in
a 3 day paper, they might not have been abridged:—this I did not
think likely, considering how much attention they had attracted; and,
on a reference to the clerk of the office, it was found that they were

---

[3] *The Proceedings upon the Inquiry (held at Chelsea) related to the
Armistice and Convention Concluded in Portugal, in August 1808* printed
as item 60 in its Appendix a list of the revisions and qualifications which
the lieutenant-generals made to the first draft of the Convention. Apparently this list, which begins, "Article 3d. The words *à ses frais* to be
omitted," De Quincey once intended to put in the Appendix of Wordsworth's pamphlet.

not abridged:—therefore it was agreed that they should be printed
from their copy. But on Wednesday morning last I received a note
fm. the overseer—saying that, as they had no copy of their papers but
one—and that, being last year's paper, bound up,—the office would
not allow it to be used by a compositor:—I went out therefore, and—
within an hour and a half of receiving the note,—I had procured a
copy of the A. & C. which I took to them. But having occasion to return to the press in the afternoon, I found that Mr. Stewart [*sic*]
had just sent a note inclosing copies also. And thus it plainly appeared
that, on Mr. Stuart's visit on the day before, somebody had made this
excuse for their tardiness—that I had not yet furnished them with
copies of the A. & C.—and that Mr. St. had done me the honor to
believe them and to suppose that I grudged that two-penny expense.
I did not feel inclined to vindicate myself on this point to Mr. Stuart;
but I mentioned it and made it clear to Mr. Baldwin, in Mr. St.'s
presence on Monday by reading the overseer's note which I kept for
the purpose.—No time however, it appeared, had been lost; as they had
a full page and a half of my note on Sir J. M's letters to go on with
—in the 2 hours or thereabouts that it took to make the communication to me and to get the copies: and it appeared afterwards, from
that sheet's not having been produced till Friday night (and little
more of it than a single page that was not filled with the *notes*
previous to the A. & C.) that they could not have set up to the end
of the notes on Wednesday morning when they got the A. & C.—
though if the 2 hours had been lost, it wd. have been their own fault.
—Fourthly and *lastly* (to end this long story which I did not mean
to have extended to this length—but which I entreat you to read,
as it [is] the last time I shall torment you about it)—my note on Sir
J. M's letters had—all but a little to keep them from stopping—been
kept back purposely; and I had told everybody, concerned in the
work, *why* it was kept back; 1st. because, the correspondence having
been published piecemeal, it was possible that every day might produce something new (and accordingly but 3 or 4 days ago there appeared another letter of Sir J. M's to Mr. Frere though, as it happened, of no consequence); and 2ndly. that I might square the
dimensions of the note to the space which should be left (which was
one reason for placing that note last); i.e. that, if by retrenching
anything of no great importance or abridging any part of the note, it
might be hindered fm. running over unnecessarily into another half-

sheet,—I might have an opportunity of making those alterations.—
But then they were all told that this was to be understood as being
in subordination to the main object of getting on as fast as possible;
and that they were to have the note any day when they would say
that it would be of use to have it.—All this long account I have sent
you—not as thinking that you would readily [readily *added*] believe
that the pamphlet had been delayed [delayed *sub. for* neglected] thro'
my means; but because, as Mr. St. has so little interest in ascertaining
with whom the delay has really been, and as it is plain that—in one
instance at least—he had trusted to their representations of the case,—
I cannot know how much misrepresentation you may have had to
disbelieve for me. Indeed they often talk to me very gravely, when I
am expostulating with them, of the delays made in sending the copy;
and, when I ask them what they mean, it comes out that they are talking about the delay after I first came to Town (occasioned by the
insertion).—I have unfortunately too given some color to their statements by really keeping back those parts which I have mentioned for
the reasons that I have mentioned;—it not being necessary for them
to add that they never asked for those parts—and did not want them.
—After all, as Mr. St. now says they do not charge me with with-
holding the copy (tho' that seems implied in his notes)—I am bewildered about the whole matter; and therefore will say no more
about it than that I have here put down all that I believe is necessary to put you in possession of the real facts; as I should be much
grieved if you should suppose that I—knowing, as I did, how important it was that the pamphlet shd. appear as soon as possible—
would have made any delay—or have permitted any as far as I had
the power to prevent it—God bless you, my dear Madam, most
affectionately yours, T.Q.
[*Inserted inverted on top of second page:*] I will acknowledge Miss
Hutchinson's goodness in writing—in a day or two.
[*Cross written:*] The note to Mr. Jeffray I will very gladly write [4]
—and shall put my name to it—that it may not be possible for any
body to suppose that Mr. Wordsworth has ever honored him and his
dull malice with any notice.

[*Address:*] Miss Wordsworth / To the care of Miss Crossthwaite / Keswick
          / Cumberland / Free / Single sheet / Wednesday, May 10th.
[*Postmark:*] MAY 10 1809

[4] See p. 216.

26. *To Dorothy Wordsworth*

Ms. Dove Cottage. Pub. in part, Eaton, pp. 167–169, 164.

[*Printed:*] See the end of my letter for *Glorious News!!*—82, Gt. Titchfield St.—Friday night

May 12th. [-13th, 1809]

My dear Madam,—I date *Friday* night; because it is really so; but, being after post-time, this letter will not go till to-morrow.—First; as to public news:—Our accounts to-day are much more chearful; that is, speaking only of our morning's news; for if our news of this evening be true, it is more than chearful. This morning there arrived in London Dutch papers—of as late a date as the day before yesterday (May 10th.): they are so far to be considered good news— that they bring no confirmation of the rumors in the Dutch papers of the 7th. of the Archduke John's having been cut off in a movement towards the Tyrol—and that they make it very probable that on the 19th. of April the Austrians won a battle in Poland.[1]—About 8 o'clock this evening, as I came up Fleet St. from the press, I found that fresh news had arrived fm. the Continent; though I do not know by what channel. I copy fm. the Statesman the substance:—"Second Edition:—We understand that intelligence has been received of the Austrians having taken Warsaw, after the battle of the 19th. on the frontiers of Poland.—It is stated also that there have been two actions in Italy; one on the Piava, after which the French retreated: they were attacked a second time by the Archduke John; and defeated with the loss of 6000 men."—This news I should not mention, but that I found the ministers' official paper—the Sun—had also printed a 2nd. edit.—It strengthens the probabilities of the Austrians having had some successes in Poland at any rate; and still further discredits the

---

Letter 26:

[1] Archduke John defeated Napoleon's inexperienced stepson Eugène de Beauharnais, at Sacile on April 16, but after Archduke Charles' reverses in the north John retreated and was defeated at Raab in Hungary on June 14. The Archduke Ferdinand forced General Poniatowski to evacuate Warsaw on April 23, but he himself had to withdraw after Russia declared war on Austria on May 5. Napoleon entered Vienna on May 12; and, although he suffered his first defeat at Aspern on May 21–22, he recovered to win on July 5–6 the hard-fought battle of Wagram, which put the Austrians out of the war again.

rumors about ye. A. D. John.—There was also received to-day the
Prague Gazette; giving the Austrian account of the battles up to the
22nd.;—the tone of which makes it probable that the French bulletins
have in this instance gone beyond their usual limits in exaggerating.
It admits advantages of the French; and claims other advantages for
the Austrians; but does not anywhere speak in the tone of men defeated
to the extent stated by the French. Indeed Bonaparte's own proclamation—telling them he will be at Vienna in a *month* (why not in 10
days?)—proves *that,* I think.—But here in London everybody is so
besotted with admiration of Bonaparte and "the talents" of French
Generals—that no one thinks of detecting contradictions &c. in French
accounts. Yesterday, none of the papers could see any reason for
suspecting the credibility of a French account which, in one paragraph,
described the Austrians as universally panic-struck and scarcely making
any resistance—and, in the next but one after, spoke with spite against
them for defending Ratisbon so desperately—and fighting from house
to house. All the papers that I saw—were "afraid that there was too
much truth in it's statements" &c.—Oh! that Bonaparte had these
fellows!—And then they think to make amends by scribling away
now and then some vile stuff about 'our inveterate foe!'—'the disturber
of civilized society!' 'the merciless adversary!'—'the murderer of
the Duc d'Enghien!' [2]—and, by way of climax insinuating that he has
no great respect for the law of nations.—How the Courier talks,
I do not know, as I seldom see it; but, as a farmer told my Liverpool
acquaintance that his paper was "grown too Foxy by half for him"—
so, the Courier was always too Canningly by half for me; and lately
I hear everywhere that it is too Castlereaghy by half. I am sure
that it has given great disgust by the defence which I hear that it
has made for Ld. Castlereagh—representing his attempt to purchase
a seat with a writership as nothing more than the ordinary borough
traffic. On this account I was quite sorry to recollect that the *Courier*
stands in the 1st. page of the Preface; scarcely any paper, among
the rational ones, having (I am sure) less the reputation of being an
impartial paper. The *Times* seems to me the only really impartial
paper; and, for ability, certainly ranks (in the public estimation here)
far beyond all the rest:—wisdom it may not have much more than
the others; but I must say that—for a barrister's address in manag-

[2] Louis, Duc d'Enghien, last of the house of Condé, was executed in 1804
after a perfunctory trial at the order of Napoleon.

ing an argument, neatness of language &c.—I see nothing near it
among the Daily papers.—However the acknowledgement to the
Courier perhaps could not perhaps [*sic*] have been avoided; though,
for the interests of the pamphlet, it is to be regretted.—This leads
me to the subject of the pamphlet. (I will only add first—to conclude the summary of the news—that Despatches were received to-
day from Sir. A.[rthur] W.[ellesley] up to the 25th. of April—
who had begun his march for Oporto;—where, by the way, you may
have seen, in the private letter of a captain of a trading vessel, that
the French did not enter without very great resistance.)—

[*Printed:*] Concerning the Pamphlet.—Chapter the last

At length the pamphlet has climbed up to the top of the hill; and
has now only to roll down a little way further to the end of it's
journey:—which means that last night at about 5 min. after 9 o'clock
(for I must fix the date of so interesting an event)—a devil knocked
at the door with the last half-sheet: this I returned to them to-day
corrected; and on going again after dinner obtained from them the
2 canceled pages and a *revise* (i.e. a 2nd. proof) of the last half-
sheet but one:—they promise to do to-morrow what follows;—to
print and correct the preface and title-page; to correct the last half-
sheet; and to strike off at least one fair copy of all which is not yet
struck off—in time for me to send it off to you by the mail: which
I hope they will do; as I shall be very sorry to lose 3 days by not
sending it off on a Saturday night.—The remainder with the other
things, I shall send off on Tuesday night.—If I find that this is not
likely to be accomplished, I think at present of sending off—at least
up to the end of the body of the pamphlet; so much having, I know,
been all struck off; as I have had the fair copies to read in order to
collect the Errata:—of which, I *believe* there is but *one* in that part
superintended by me: I say *believe;* for I am not sure that some
readings which I have given as my best guesses, are the true ones:
in particular you will smile to hear that the *famous* sentence (as I
may now call it)—about knowledge.[3]—I was obliged to have printed
off upon guess:—I had indeed two answers about this sentence; but
both ambiguous ones. Mr. Wordsworth said that I had guessed

---

[3] See Letters 11, 15, 16, and 19; *MY*, I, 267; Dicey, p. 131.

rightly;—but, as I said in my answer, I guessed 2 ways; and, though I remember saying that I thought one the most probable, I forget which that one was; for, by thinking them over very often, I have alternately thought each the most probable—Then came your answer. But alas! it was like the old answer of the Oracle—'I say that Rome the Epirot conquer shall';—so maliciously enigmatical that I was obliged to end, as I began, with pure guessing; and have now only to hope that I may have guessed under a happy star.—Another passage about animat*ing* efforts of the Peninsula I sent a quere respecting;[4] but suppose that I put it into some corner of my letter where you overlooked it, as I did not receive even an *oracular* answer about this.

11 O'clock, Saturday morning.

Thus far I wrote last night; meaning to keep the space below for answering some of your late letters; particularly the long one which I received on Thursday by Mr. Jamieson[5]—for which I cannot say how much I am obliged to you: I received it under circumstances that made it doubly interesting—in the evening, and at a time when I did not expect it. Mr. J. I have not yet seen; as I was out when he called. But I must defer this for the present—having just this moment received Mr. Wordsworth's letter of Wednesday night.[6]—As it is probable that, from the work to be done at the Press to-day, I may not have another opportunity of writing before 5 o'clock—I will here answer it as far as I can.—I shall go first to the Courier Office; and shall there propose that, *if Mr. Stuart is not quite sure that there is nothing libellous in the Pamphlet,* the publication may be delayed till Tuesday;—that, in the course of this night and to-morrow, I should finally read through the whole pamphlet—marking every passage about which there can be a doubt; and then on Monday morning, giving the whole collection of passages so marked to Mr. Stuart for his decision upon them;—which, as they cannot certainly be very numerous, he can give in an hour:—all that remains to be done at the press—viz. making the last corrections in the Appendix and printing the New title-page and the advertisement—will go on, in the meantime, without any delay; and thus, at the

---

* See Letter 19; Dicey, p. 109.
* *MY,* I, 300–304.
* *MY,* I, 309–311.

utmost, only one day will be lost. But I rather think *now* (as they have not kept their promise with me this morning—to send down a boy by 8 o'clock) that they will not have finished even the *revises* before late this evening; and then there are the 500 copies of the 3 last half-sheets and of the Title &c. to strike off; which perhaps could not be done till Monday (and other customary forms of calling over the copies &c. to go through); so that, on the whole, even one day may not be lost.—I say, IF Mr. St. is not quite sure; because I think it likely that he will by this time have read through the whole, as he received the fair copies up to the end of the body of the work last Monday for that purpose.—The *'insidiously or ignorantly employed'* &c. passage—I had altered myself according to Mr. Wordsworth's direction;[7] clumsily enough, I fear; but not so as by any torture, I think, to be racked into a libel.—However, I will ask Mr. St. about it. I still intend to send off a copy of the pamphlet—so far as it is finished—to-night; if the whole should not be finished in time to send you the proper title &c.—I wish it had occurred to me to do this before; as it might have been of use to Mr. Wordsworth in composing.—3 o'clock. My dear Madam,—I have just been to the Courier Office:—I have great joy in telling you that, as I sate with Mr. Stuart, a messenger came in and told him that the Austrian Bulletin had just arrived;—and that all is true:—the Arch-duke John [*printed:* has . . . Generals] has defeated the French; and taken six thousand PRISONERS;—with bevies of Generals!—Oh! Jubilate!—

[*Across folded back:*] The plan I proposed to Mr. Stuart has been adopted;—Mr. St. does not think that the passages referred to by Mr. Wordsworth, can be thought libels: my alteration, he is sure, is not. And nothing he is of opinion would be thought libellous that was short of positive defamation or charge of some specific notoriously unlawful act—on any of the men concerned excepting Sir A.W.—Therefore there is no hope of Newgate. However—all shall be

---

[7] Wordsworth had said that the King's reproof of the London Council's petition was "a sophism insidiously or ignorantly employed." De Quincey moderated it to "a sophism, which, if our anxiety to interpret favourably words sanctioned by the First Magistrate—makes us unwilling to think it a deliberate artifice meant for the delusion of the people, must however (on the most charitable comment) be pronounced an evidence of no little heedlessness and self-delusion on the part of those who framed it" (Dicey, p. 105).

carefully read through:—I have a world of things to say. Pray send on Friday night to meet the post: i.e. send with confidence that letter &c. will be [*seal*] me. God bless you, my dear Madam. Yours— T. de Q.

[*Address:*] Miss Wordsworth / Grasmere / near Kendal / Westmoreland / Free / Single sheet To be forwarded by the first person going to Grasmere. / *Sat. May 13th.*

[*Postmark:*] MAY 13 1809

27. *To William Wordsworth*

Ms. Dove Cottage. Unpub. Qtd. Eaton, p. 164.

82, Gt. Titchf. St.—Tuesday evening—[May 16, 1809]
My dear Sir,

Having promised to write, I write; but, as it is now not far off 5 o'clock, I must write in a very hurried manner.—I will put down journal-wise the progress of the pamphlet.

Saturday last:—was able to get nothing more at the press than the title-page and advertisement:—they were correcting—at 8 in the evening—the 1st. half sheet of the Appendix.

Sunday.—Read over the whole pamphlet; and extracted all the passages (about *eight,* I think) which I thought could be suspected to be libellous.

Monday:—called on Mr. St., by appointment, at 1 o'clock; found him out; but left my paper:—called at 3; found that he had returned: and had weighed all my extracts. He thought not one of these libellous;—but—strange to say!—thought one which I had not suspected so much as to think it worth extracting—a libel.—This was the passage—'that the British army *swarms* with those who are incompetent—' is plain &c.[1] He was sure it was libellous; and thought government would be happy to have an opportunity of avenging themselves under the masque of standing up for the army.—I was sure it was *not* a libel;—1st. because it charges them only gravely—with what others do daily sneeringly—want of judgement: 2ndly. *whom* does it charge?—only those particularly who were thus charged through-

Letter 27:

[1] Dicey, p. 151.

outꞌthe work;—and whom to charge thus—is involved in every sentence of the work.—But Mr. Stuart said, it was a libel on the whole
body of the Army; and to say anything against a body—was more
libellous than to say it against an individual.—This I could not believe. Mr. St. said that to say of the profession of the law that most
of it's members were rascals of necessity—would be a libel:—Well
but, I said, we any of us say every-day (if we choose) of the medical
tribe—that they are all Assassins; and that is not necessarily a joke.—
But however a libel it was, Mr. St. was sure.—I proposed that we
should ask a barrister: because, since (except the Cintra men &c.)
it does not entitle any man to determine whether he is among the
excluded—or the *included* (—for *swarms* certainly might allow that
some, and many, were competent), I was very reluctant that it should
be canceled.—But Mr. St. said such a reference could only delay us
still more;—and therefore I, in the extremest affliction, said that—if
he were *sure* it was a libel—of course it must be canceled.—We then
walked away together to the Press—to direct about it:—as we went
along, Mr. St. told me the news from Spain in the morning papers—
all very favorable,—the most important part was an intercepted letter
from *Kellermann* in Asturias[?] to *Soult* at Oporto—describing himself as in a very embarrassed situation—which had been published by
Marshall Beresford;—he also mentioned a report—'on the authority
of a letter' fm. Hamburgh to a great merchant in London—of the
Arch-duke Charles's having defeated Bonaparte with the loss of 50,000
killed–wounded, & prisoners:—Mr. St. being very incredulous in general about such reports—I was very glad to find that he thought it
worth telling (The above news still continues to obtain some credit;—
I have seen no paper to-day; and therefore do not know whether on
any fresh grounds: 2nd. editions of the Statesman and Sun were
printed last night in consequence of it:—but I sent a *Pilot* to you in
preference; as guessing from their summaries, that they give it as
official news, when I knew that, at least yesterday morning, there was
no further authority for it than what I have mentioned.—There is
also—yesterday and to-day—a strong report of Oporto's having surrendered to the English army.) [2] I had scarcely time to see whether
the Pilot gave the Spanish news;—I suppose and hope it did.)—We
arrived at the Press;—Mr. Baldwin was summoned; each party
d[*torn:* ? drew out]t his forces;—Mr. Baldwin joined me; and I

---

[2] On May 12 the English drove the French from Oporto.

obtained [*torn*] over Mr. Stuart.—I did not triumph; but I could no [*seal; torn*]—I told Mr. St. on Sat. that I believed in reply to Bonaparte—viz. that the '*mystery*' of generalship was a '*craft*'—might be said also of what is termed *a knowledge of the world*—or *a knowledge of business.* The half-sheet was therefore NOT not canceled;—for Mr. Baldwin was peremptory in his opinion that nobody could appear as prosecutor in the first place;—and 2ndly. that no libel could be made out if any man could claim to be the object of it.—

Got from the press the revises of the two 1st. half-sheets of the Appendix:—corrected them;—found them done so inaccurately that I was obliged to insist on seeing them once again: as a specimen—they had introduced a *not* in the followg. place—'Done and concluded *not* the year and day above-mentioned.'—Took them back.

Tuesday (to-day.)—Got the last proofs of the 2 1st. half-sheets;—corrected them at the press;—left them for press:—this was an hour and a half ago:—there remains now only the last half-sheet and the advertisement—to be *corrected.* This, they say, cannot be finished till to-morrow morning.—Then it will be published.—

I am obliged to conclude: I remain, my dear sir, with kindest love and respects to the ladies,

Yours most respectfully and affectionately,

T. de Q.

[*Address:*] William Wordsworth Esqre. / Grasmere / near Kendal / Westmoreland / Free / *Single* sheet / *May 16th. Tuesday* /
[*Postmark:*] MAY 16 1809

28. *To Dorothy Wordsworth* (?)

Ms. Dove Cottage. Unpub. Qtd. Eaton, pp. 150, 165.

[London]
Wednesday afternoon—almost
4 o'clock.
Indeed it's now striking. [May 17, 1809]

My dear Madam,

I continue the journal:—

Tuesday evening:—The people at Mr. Baldwin's had told me that there would be a page to spare; and supposed that Mr. Longman would like to fill it with his advertisements:—This I did not at all relish:—but, as I did not know how far it was deemed the privilege of a publisher to do so, I went to Longman's: they recollected that Mr. Wordsworth had desired that it might not be done in his Poems; and therefore: on the whole, it was agreed that the leaf should be left blank.—

Wednesday morning: at 12 o'clock I went to the Press; and fortunately; for they had just finished correcting—being 2 hours earlier than they had calculated: —(I mentioned, in my letter of last night, that the last half-sheet of the Appendix—and the Title-Advertisement &c. remained to be *corrected;* by which I meant—*corrected by the compositor;* for *my* corrections had been made on Thursday night last when I received the last half-sheet—and on Saturday when I received the Title &c.)—Mr. Westray was fortunately going to dinner; I took possession therefore of his little wooden tabernacle; set at nought the ravings of the devils without;—and steadily persevered in correcting;—a little before 3, just as I had gone—for the last time—over last half-sheet—title-page—advertisement—table of Errata—Mr. W. returned:—I extort a promise from him that 4 copies shall be struck off—with my final corrections—in time to be sent off by the mail to-night; am to be at the press again by ½ past 5 to have them sent off;—solemnly restore the pen into the inkstand;—issue from the tabernacle in a paroxysm of joy—meaning to have embraced the devil, if I had met him on the stairs—and sally homewards to announce the great event.

My note on Sir J.[ohn] M[oore]'s letters—I have regularly forgotten to say anything about:—What I say now—will most likely not be in time to anticipate an apology for what you will dislike in it (as the pamphlet will doubtless have precedency of a letter); so I may as well defer *that,* until I have more time:—only, in general, I must say—1st. That I wrote under a sense of constraint;—making a point to prepare the course of what I was saying to receive nearly all of Mr. Wordsworth's thoughts on these letters—and sometimes his words;—and 2ndly.—that—in some places where Mr. Baldwin and Mr. Stuart thought yesterday (as I forgot to mention in my letter of last night); that what I had said was too harsh though not libellous —I wrote under a further constraint—from wishing to size the pas-

sages substituted to the vacancies made by the passages withdrawn;
as that considerably lessens the delay.—I have corrected some passages—before page 97—in the table of Errata on guess; my editorship
having begun at that page; so that I had no MS. to consult for this
early part.—I have dated the advertisement, according to the booksellers' practice for pamphlets, two days later than the day of delivery
to the publisher—viz. May 20th. and have altered *my* date in the
postscript to the Postscript to the Appendix—(so as to tally with
this)—from April 20th. to May 18th. that I might lie with consistency.—The putting a date to the Advertisement I had thought
of before; and, before mentioning it, it was strongly recommended
by Mr. Stuart who observed that, else, the Advertisement fixes the
date of the commencement—but not of the end—of the work.—

There remains, to be *printed off fair,* the Title &c. and some part
of the Appendix: making the corrections will take (Mr. Westray
thought) till after 5 o'clock;—and then it takes an hour to print
off 250 sheets; therefore 2 hours to print off 500:—consequently, if
there are only the title &c. and last half-sheet of the Appendix to
print off,—those, with the 2 canceled pages, will make a sheet and
a half; that is, will take 3 hours printing off: but if the 2 *first* half-
sheets of the Appendix are not printed off yet, then there is another
2 hours' work;—so that, after ½ past 5 this evening, the work remaining will be at least a 3 hours' work—at the most, a 5 hours'
work: but in either case, will (I hope) be done to-night;—and, at
any rate, before noon to-morrow Mr. Longman will be sending them
abroad: so that (as I saw—in coming through Long Acre—"His
Excellency" Ld. W's [1] travelling trunks—Spanish beds &c. exposed at
the trunk-maker's)—it may be in time for him to carry out a copy to
his "excellent" brother—to regale him in Portugal.—I begged of Mr.
Westray to strike off only 4; because he told me that they must be
done in haste; and therefore could not be done so carefully as at
the regular striking off.—And, as I must at any rate send another
parcel with the pictures &c., it wd. be better to send them off *then*
perfectly correct—than *now* less correct: and, in the mean time,
I thought that 4 would enable you to send copies where you would

Letter 28:
[1] Richard, Marquis Wellesley, brother of General Arthur Wellesley, was
going as ambassador extraordinary to Seville.

be most anxious to send them early.—The remaining 10, with everything else, will be with you (through *Keswick*) on Tuesday night
next.—I hope that my dear Johnny will not be up when you receive
this parcel; or he will be disappointed at not finding his pictures in
it: but, in the hurry in which we shall probably be to get off the
parcel, it would not be possible to pack up pictures—so as not to
spoil them—particularly in a press-room: and the press is full two
miles from me.—This puts me in mind that I have two miles to
walk; and it is now past 5 o'clock. You perhaps do not know how
long I am in filling a sheet of paper: for I have really been an hour
over this.—I have not heard any news to-day; but I have seen no
paper.—Last night, as I was going to P. Noster-Row, I saw 2nd.
editions advertised of the Sun and Pilot: but Mr. Westray tells me it
is nothing more than an account fm. Admiral Cochrane of his having
blocked up the French squadron from L'Orient—3 sail of the line—
in the Saints;—where he means to attack them by land and sea,
when Gen. Beckwith arrives.—Monday, we had rainy weather; but
warm.—Now we have full and perfect summer going on again. I
long to be at Grasmere. God bless you! my dear Madam, and believe
me your most affectionate friend,

Thos. de Quincey.

[*No address; probably this letter went with the parcel of four pamphlets.*]

29. *To Sara Hutchinson*

Ms. Dove Cottage. Unpub. Qtd. Eaton, p. 166. De Quincey says in his letter of
May 24 that he did not send this letter. It is not postmarked.

82, Gt. Titchfield St. [May 20, 1809]

My dear Madam,

I write chiefly to acount to you for not sending the parcel, as I
promised, to-night; and I address myself to you; as not wishing any
longer to delay my acknowledgements to you for your goodness in
writing to me.

The 4 copies, which I sent off on Wednesday night last, I hope
that you will have this evening (Saturday, May 20th.); but I have
some doubts about it: for, as I was closing my letter, the clock struck,
and, as I thought, *five;* but, when I came downstairs, I found that

it was *six:* it takes 3 quarters of an hour, within a minute or two, of
very quick walking to go from my part of Titchfield St. to the press;
so that, when I got there, it was nearly seven o'clock: and, after
the clock strikes *seven,* they take nothing in at the mail-coach offices:
however we were not above a quarter of a mile from one of the inns
at which the Carlisle mail touches;—Mr. Westray, who is a zealous
friend of mine, had got everything ready;—he is very expert at making
up parcels; and the little boy, whom he has with him, being a very
fleet runner (as he told me); was sent off with it in 2 minutes after
I got there; so that, on the whole, I hope it was sent off that night.
But, unfortunately, I dated it and my letter wrong—Wednesday,
*18*th. Mr. Westray had led me into this error in the morning; and I
did not discover it until I went into a coffee-house where I took up a
paper that set my chronology right.—I was very sorry for this; as
knowing that the people at the office might avail themselves of it to
keep it back a day, if it should suit their convenience better; since
it would not appear whether the mistake lay in the *Wednesday,* or
the *18*th.[1]—The little boy however assured me, the next morning,
that he was in time; and that it would go that night.—

On Wednesday night I looked over the last half-sheet &c. and
found that even in the few corrections which I had made in the morning, they had contrived to make a mistake. I had substituted for
my own description of Blake's army [2] Sir J.[ohn] M[oore]'s; viz. was
'mere peasantry' etc.—and the compositor had done his best to make
nonsense of it by inserting a comma between the *was* and the *mere.*
The Title-page also might have been mended (which, I must [have]
mentioned, was arranged by a triumvirate of Mr. Baldwin—the compositor—and myself: it is on the whole admired by all three; and each
admires especially his own share in it: I, for instance, greatly admire
the words—'*The Convention of Cintra*' which were by my direction
reduced to their present size from letters of an inch long almost; which
thus stood foremost in the page; and would, I doubt not, have injured
the pamphlet: Mr. Baldwin piques himself, with less reason I think,
on the distribution of the first words: and the compositor in vain
tries to hide his vanity on a particular dash and semi-colon which, he

---

Letter 29:
    [1] The letter is dated only "Wednesday afternoon."
    [2] Joaquín Blake, a Spanish general of Irish extraction, then in command
of the forces of Galicia.

says, belong to him). I had a fair excuse for expelling the motto from Horace (which I cannot say that I admire at all) ; [3] as it would have made room—for more symmetry in the title page:—but however so conscientious was I that I had it inserted, as you see, since it had been sent.—On Thursday morning I went to the press to get the mistake corrected;—for they told me on Wednesday night—that Mr. Stuart had requested that they would not strike it off until they had given him notice:—but, notwithstanding, they *had* struck every copy off—before breakfast; thus making it impossible for Mr. Stuart to make any use of the notice:—but, I believe, there was nothing approaching to a libel in it.—I said—'Well, then, now it's gone to Longmans': Oh! no—it would take till Monday to *dry*. At this I fell into despair; and instantly went to Longman's:—there I saw Mr. Orme; [4] he promised me that, if 50 for immediate distribution could be sent up, they should be stitched up and circulated in 2 hours:—accordingly by 6 that evening (Thursday last) 50 were sent up—to be [*torn:* ? dried] by the fire.—and—

Here the bell is going about—I do not mean this to stand for a letter;—only for an apology for the parcel: which how I cannot send it to-night I will say on Monday night.

I remain, my dear Madam, affectionately and respectfully yours,
Thos. de Quincey.

I did not see Mr. Jamieson till last night at 11 o'clock:—when he got home: he found them all gone to bed; and so returned and staid all-night at my rooms.—

[*Address:*] Miss Hutchinson / Grasmere / near Kendal / Westmoreland / *Free / Single sheet / Sat. night, May 20th.*

30. *To Dorothy Wordsworth*

Ms. Dove Cottage. Unpub. Qtd. Eaton, pp. 177-178.

82, Gt. Titchfield St.—Wednesy. May 24th. [1809]
My dear Madam,—I hope that, as you have received what would be

---

[3] Qui didicit patriae quid debeat; . . .
Quod sit conscripti, quod judicis officium; quae
Partes in bellum missi ducis (*Ars Poetica*, 312, 314-315).
[4] Cosmo Orme, who became a partner in the house of Longman in 1804.

the most important part of the parcel, you will not have been greatly disappointed at not receiving the remainder when I promised. But first, I ought to hope that you *did* receive the parcel (containing 4 copies of the pamphlet) at the right time. I sent them off *this day* week (to-day is *Wednesday*); but, as usual, I was within a minute or two of being too late: for, as I was about to close my letter, the clock struck something:—I thought *five* (as, I believe, I mentioned):—but it proved to be *six,* when I got down stairs; and after *seven* nothing is received at the mail-coach offices; so that, in the space of one hour, I had to walk to the Press (which,—so much of the road lying through crowded parts of the town—takes ¾ of an hour within a few minutes of very fast walking)—and after that to make up and send off the parcel: however everything being ready on my arrival at the press—and Mr. Westray offering the services of a little boy, a fleet runner, to take it—I believe it reached the office in time (one of the offices being in Lad lane within a quarter of a mile); at least the little boy assured me it did. But unfortunately I had dated it wrong—Wednesday, May *18*th.—instead of *17*th. and this, I am afraid, would put it in the power of the office people to keep it back a day,—if it should be inconvenient to them to send it that night:—as nobody could tell whether the mistake lay in the *Wednesday* or the *18*th. It was Mr. Westray who had led me into the mistake in the morning; and I did not discover that I was wrong until I went into a coffee-house—and there a newspaper set my chronology right.

The parcel that was to have been sent on Sat. night has not yet gone; indeed I have never sent anything—letter, parcel, or newspaper—since last Wednesday night. I *wrote* a letter, on Sat. night, to Miss Hutchinson; and had sealed it and given it to a child to carry to the office: but the delay in putting on the bonnet &c. giving me time for second thoughts, I called for it back again. The reason was—that I did not feel sure but Miss Hutchinson might think it taking a liberty to pay the postage; and, on the other hand, it was so drearily dull (being all filled with explanations about the pamphlet—the parcel &c.) that I could not reconcile myself to putting her to the expense of it.—I take some praise to myself for this; for it is a doleful thing to look at—a long letter that has taken some hours' writing; and that no one is ever to read. Yesterday I should have written; but that—as I felt sure of being able to send the parcel to-night—I had so distributed my time that, when I found I most probably should *not* be able to send it, it was too late to write.—What it is that delays the sewing up and publishing of the pamphlet, I cannot tell; for I have not yet been able to see Mr. Stuart—who told me that he would take all the business upon himself—nor Mr. Orme since Thursday last.—On Wednesday night (i.e. this day week) they told me at the press—that they were not to strike off the 500 copies until they had given Mr. Stuart notice that the last half-sheet was ready to be struck off:—this, I suppose, was to give him an opportunity of seeing whether there was anything libellous in it:—I concluded therefore that they would wait until they heard from Mr. Stuart: but the next morning, on going to the press with a correction or two of errors made by the compositor in his *third* revisal of the half-sheet—I found that they had contented themselves with giving Mr. St. notice—without allowing him time to make any use of it; for the whole 500 copies were struck off on Thursday morning before breakfast. (I mention this to account for the errors of the last half-sheet. The principal mistake was in inserting Sir J.[ohn] M[oore]'s description of Blake's army—which I had substituted for my own—*'was mere peasantry'*—in which he had done his best to make it unintelligible by placing a *comma* between the *was* and the *mere*. I mention this—as one of a thousand instances of the carelessness of the compositors; for I had written the corrections with the utmost legibility; and Mr. Westray had particularly cautioned him in this instance—as this was the last proof that I was to see before it went to press.)—'Well, come now,' I said to Mr. Dillon, 'make the best amends you can for your long delay by getting it into Longman's hands as soon as possible: when will it be dry?'—'Why, about Monday, I suppose.'—'Monday' !!!!—I said—and instantly went to Paternoster Row, to know if this could be true; for I was in absolute despair; having understood that it would be *published* the same day it was printed. Here I saw Mr. Orme:—he told me that if 50 could be sent up that day, they should be dried at the fire and sewed in 2 hours: —I went therefore back to the Press: and they promised that 50 should be sent up:—as soon as they could collect and arrange them. At 6 o'clock that night accordingly 50 were sent up; and all that I have been able to learn since then is that *"they are not yet out."*—I called yesterday on Mr. Stuart and afterwards in P. Noster Row: Mr. St. was not in;—and at Longman's I could see only some of the young men—who said that they knew only that it was not published.—It may be that Mr. Stuart does not mean Longman to publish it; but this did not occur to me till last night;—for though (when I was once mentioning to Mr. Stuart that I had been to Longman's to request that they would *advertise* it in the usual way) he seemed to think that I was interfering with his business—and said that there was no occasion for Longman to advertise—(and accordingly I told Longmans afterward that Mr. St. would take that upon himself)—yet I had no doubt that, as Longman's name stands in the title-page, *he* was to publish— i.e. distribute it; and therefore, in directing the 50 copies to be sent up, I had no thought of interfering with what Mr. Stuart might think *his* province; but was thinking solely of the interests of the pamphlet; as 50 might have answered the demand as well as 500 during the time which it required to get the other 450 ready.—However, as I have never seen Mr. Stuart since I may have seemed by this step to be a second time encroaching on his privileges and have filled up the measure of my perfidies in his account.—However I do not mean to in [*torn:* ? interfere] again further than to let Mr. Stuart know how the matter stands with the pamphlet viz. that several persons, who have applied for it in the course of the last 4 days to [*torn:?* the] booksellers in Piccadilly–to Baldwin–and to Longman, have not been able to procure a copy—though the printing of it finally closed at 9 o'clock on *Thursday* —*morning, May 18th.*—and it is now *Wednesday, May 24th.*— —

My brother is at length arrived in England; very much broken down by 6 years of hardships—and 18 months' imprisonment with bad food &c. among the Danes:—I was sauntering home on Thursday night last through Greek St.—thinking of a passage I had been reading at a bookseller's where I had been sitting in the neighbourhood—when, by accident, my way was stopped by 2 men—whom I, from having my thoughts occupied should not have noticed;—but, in our efforts to get past each other, I got planted directly opposite to one of them who stared a moment and then cried out—in a voice that shook all Soho— Mr. [de *scratched out* [1]] Quincey, I am very happy to see you!—The

---

Letter 30:
[1] A remarkable example of scrupulosity on De Quincey's part. John Kelsall had been his father's clerk; and, since the elder Thomas did not use the "de," it is likely that in an outburst of surprise Kelsall would have said simply "Quincey."

voice made me know that it was Mr. Kelsall—the husband of your Manchester correspondent—to whom my brother had written as being the most stationary person known to him; and who had accordingly immediately come up to London to meet him.—The other person was a relation of his—who had never been in London: Mr. Kelsall had himself been there only once before; and they were in high dispute about which way St. Pauls lay from Greek St. at the time I met them; and, before telling me anything about my brother, they appealed to me to decide this question.—I thought this a very singular accident—i.e. my meeting, after they had been in Town only 5 days, the 2 men who of all others out of a million most wanted to meet me (for they remembered no more of my address than that it was *Titchfield St.* which is nearly half a mile long)—and meeting them too not in the Strand– Fleet St.-Holborn-&c. where everybody goes—but in an obscure— 10th. rate street such as Greek St.—It is mentioned, in some of the lives of Dr. Johnson, that he and some other Litchfield person walked about London for 40 years I think (or more)—and never met;—though both perpetually out when not ill. My stay in London is a little lengthened on my brother's account;—but I shall leave it, I believe, on Sunday or Monday night next for Clifton—where I shall stay until my mother goes to Westhay—which will be in 2 or 3 weeks;—about the 17th. of June, I believe.—Whenever therefore, after the receipt of this, you have the kindness to let me hear from Grasmere,—direct, if you please, to No. 8, Dowry Parade—Clifton, near Bristol.—The paper relating to the Seville Decree abt. Saragossa—and to Ld. Cochrane—will be in the parcel;—for, if I sent them by the post, you would be sure there were some great news on the 1st. sight of them; and would be disappointed.—Talking of *News* puts me in mind—that last night 2nd. editions of the evening papers informed us—that a schooner has brought the intelligence that *Oporto* is in possession of the English army: but the particulars could not be sent;—as no vessel has been able to cross the bar of Oporto.

[*Across folded back:*]—Pray do not scruple to say all the ill you think of my Postscript; for I have no parental feelings about it; though I did it as well as, under the circumstances, I could [*torn*]—God bless you, my dear Madam! Most affectionately yours, Thos. de Quincey. [*Inserted inverted above salutation:*] Mr. Jamieson I never saw until last Friday night—about 11 o'clock: when he got to his lodgings—he found every body gone to bed; and so he returned here—and staid all night.

[*Address:*]   Miss Wordsworth—Grasmere / to the care of Miss Crossthwaite / Keswick / Cumberland /
Free / *Single* sheet / *Wednesday, May 24th*
[*Postmark:*] MAY 24 1809

31. *To Dorothy Wordsworth*

Ms. Dove Cottage. Pub. in part, Eaton, pp. 170, 171, 172–173, 175, 179–182.

[London]
Thursday night—May 25th [-27th]—1809.
My dear Madam,

This is the last letter most probably that I shall address to you from London; and therefore it shall be a long one: and on that account I begin it on Thursday night, though it is not to go until Saturday.— The news of this day makes it a day to be remembered: what it is, you will have seen no doubt before you get this letter.—The Park and Tower guns announced it to London this morning; but I did not hear them; and my first informants were the horns of the newsmen and the ribbons in their hats—passing my window as I sate at breakfast.— In my way to the news-world—the Strand—I called upon walking Stewart [1] who told me he believed that Soult's rear-guard had been cut off;—next I called upon my barber Mr. Strachan—a very great politician—and one of my great authorities, when I want the latest news; he told me Soult and 18000 men were prisoners. Well, thought I, it mends; by the time I reach the Strand, it will be something very grand.—However, when I got to Catherine St., I saw hung out—at the Inquisitor Office—"Dreadful News from Germany!—Entrance of Bonaparte into Vienna—! *Defeat* of the French in Portugal!"— This word *Defeat* did not sound quite so well; as it did not promise their capture.—Thence I went to the Courier Office; where, after a

---

Letter 31:

[1] John Stewart (1749–1822), known as "Walking Stewart" from his feats of pedestrian travel, was also a prolific writer of rambling, eccentric philosophical works. De Quincey described him in two papers: in the *London Magazine* for Sept., 1823, and *Tait's Magazine* for Oct., 1840 (M, III, 93–117).

conversation about the pamphlet, Mr. Stewart spoke to me about the news; of which he said (and really I think, after reading the Gazette, that he was right) that he saw nothing in it to fire the guns about [2]— though *any* success against this Soult must be very pleasing—as retaliation for his half-triumph over the English army in having pursued them to Corunna—and still more for his execrable treatment of the people of Oporto.—I, in my turn, told him that I saw nothing so very 'Dreadful' in Bonaparte's having entered Vienna; and could not guess why everybody in London—and especially the newspapers—had been for some weeks anticipating this event with so much more alarm than they expressed at his entering *Ratisbon*—or any other place whatever. For, unless the Austrian government had conferred importance upon his threat of taking Vienna—by shewing anxiety to defend it—what more is Vienna than a mile-stone to shew how many miles he has marched into Germany? But the public, it is easy to see, have no other reason for thinking it important—than 1st. because it is a celebrated capital; and 2nd. because the taking possession of it was announced by Bonaparte as a *threat;*—and so, they think, it must be something very prodigious and alarming;—though what it is, they never asked themselves.—To return to the Peninsular news—I am very much rejoiced that the armies of the Supreme People have again drifted the 'tyger-monkey' nation (as Walking Stewart calls them); though I am sorry that Sir A.W. should be carrying away the glory: but I am much more delighted to see this evening—in a letter from Gilbraltar—what (for fear that, not being printed in a conspicuous part of the Courier, it may escape your notice)—I here put in characters such as you must see, if you honor this page by looking at it (which, as you cannot be yet tired, I conclude you will);—viz. that

[*Printed:*] THE CORTES IS TO BE ASSEMBLED IMMEDIATELY!!

The present Junta at Seville, I conclude from the style of their measures, cannot be the same with that which fled from Madrid at Bonaparte's approach:—but, if they were, I should think that by this act they might have a chance of saving themselves from "eternal perdition":—for, without it, I think there could have been no redemption for them.—For my part, if I had been a Spaniard,—I should perhaps

---

[2] The guns were fired upon receipt of Wellesley's despatch that Soult had retired from Oporto in "the utmost confusion" with "very large" losses. The French general, however, extricated himself through sacrifice of much of his equipment, and retired to Spain with most of his army intact.

have decided that my first duty was to shoot Bonaparte;—but I should certainly have thought it my second to shoot the Supreme Junta: who seem to me—the more I think—and read or hear of the facts—to have been the most imbecile wretches—and most to have fallen short of their duty—and most to have squandered the means they had—of any persons, in such a situation, mentioned in history.—But these wretches are not to be spoken of with any temper;—and therefore, having settled the era of my letter by shewing that it began to be written on the same day when we in London heard that the French were flying 'in the utmost confusion' from one kingdom—and taking possession of the capital of another—I here quit the business of the nation—and the world for my own.

I have in vain endeavoured, my dear Madam, to awaken some interest in you about my successes in book-hunting: first, I think, I told you how I had bought Lord Brooke's other works (viz. his Posthumous Poems: —and his '5 years of King James: or the State of England &c. and the relation it had to other provinces'—a prose work) ; [3] next, I think, I told you how I had made your State Trials worth more than 20 guineas by finding the 11th. vol:—and, I dare say, many other triumphs I must have recorded: But still 'no applause ensued;'—not an atom of sympathy did I receive;—else you should have heard further how I had bought Spenser's own edition of the Faery Queene;—how I had nearly made up a set of Milton's Prose works in his own corrected editions (which will enable the Grasmere Press to issue a better edition of Milton's whole works than has yet been given) ; how this very evening I met with Mr. Wordsworth's 'Descriptive Sketches' [4] —among the Alps—which, for so many years, I have sought in vain ;— how, if Mr. Heber [5] by the strength of his purse had not prevented me,

---

[3] Sir Fulke Greville, first Lord Brooke, *The Remains of Sir Fulk Grevill; Lord Brooke; being Poems of Monarchy and Religion* (1670). *The Five Years of King James; or, the Condition of the State of England, and the Relation it had to other Provinces* (1643) is now thought to have been wrongly attributed to Fulke Greville.

[4] In 1814 Wordsworth wrote De Quincey telling him that "after a persevering search" they had found a copy of *DS* for use in the 1815 edition, so that he need not "persist in the kind search" he had offered (*MY*, II, 628). One wonders if this 1809 find was more real than De Quincey's other "triumphs."

[5] Richard Heber (1773–1833), a famous book collector.

I *should have* bought a book * [6] with Milton's M.S. notes on the margin;—how I have a chance of buying &c.—all which, 'with many things of worthy memory, now shall die in oblivion.'—However about Ld. Brooke's works I do suppose that Mr. Wordsworth will be glad; —because I have never heard him mention these 2 works of his—which are much rarer than the small Folio (that which contains Alaham &c.) —and which to me seem (at least the Posthumous Poems) very interesting indeed. They are grave moralizing poems—on Government— Religion &c.—I have got also the work on Episcopacy by the other Lord Brooke (not *Fulke Greville*—but *Robert*) [7] mentioned with so much honor by Milton in his Areopagitica!—

About making presents—what I meant—was—that 1st. *everything* is to be had in London;—and 2ndly. that most things may, by looking about, be had cheaper.—To prove the 1st. point—I need only mention that, when I first came up to London, there was stuck up (at the lower end of the street in which I live) a bill advertising *'Artificial Ears'*: —at first I thought—on reading no more of it than this—that this was some banter on gentlemen who had been so unfortunate as to forfeit theirs to the law;—but afterwards I found that it was seriously an offer to furnish delicate people with false ears for every-day use—especially in cold weather; the real ears to be brought out only on Gala days and grand occasions.—As to the 2nd. point—much of the apparent cheapness is no doubt imposition;—but still, where there is so much competition, there must (I should think) be something real in it;—as most trades, I should think, could afford (if they chose) to reduce the price of their wares considerably by contenting themselves with a more moderate profit.—One trade, I am sure, could:—for I have experimentally learned lately that for 20 guineas laid out in a proper way you may buy as many books as at shops would cost 70 or 80 guineas at the least. But perhaps the other trades do not take such exorbitant

---

* The Book was "Les Delices de la Suisse."

[6] The only *Les Délices de la Suisse* I have found is that by Abraham Ruchat in 1730. *A Catalogue of Heber's Collection of Early English Poetry,* ed. J. P. Collier (London, 1834), contains item 1527 with Milton marginalia: "Dante L'Amoroso Convivio, 1529—Rime et Prose di Giovanni delle Casa, 1563. Sonetti di Benedetto Varchi, 1555."
[7] Robert Greville, second Lord Brooke, *A Discourse opening the nature of that Episcopacie which is exercised in England* (1641, enlarged 1642).

profits.—However, as you would not commission me to buy presents,
—I have ventured to buy one myself—as my offering to Allan Bank;
and I hope most heartily that it will prove a fortunate one. It is a
patent *Smoke-Dispenser;* which I have long meditated to buy; and,
since the pamphlet is published, I have had leisure to inquire about it.
I did not go at all 'greenly' to work about it: for, after I had made
inquiries elsewhere, I asked the man of whom I bought it—how many
possible causes there were in his opinion, for a chimney's smoking;
because then I should be able to tell whether his specific would cure
my patient:—whereupon he entered upon a very elaborate nosology—
and therapeutics—of chimnies; and, before he had gone very far, he
got to class the 5th.—subdivision the 1st.—*'Standing under a hill!'*
'My dear Friend!'—I said—'that's the very thing:—but will your
Smoke-dispenser cure it?'—And then he assured me most solemnly,
and upon the honor of a Patentee, that it would;—and, more than this,
that it would cure *every* disease in chimnies—except one—viz. the 3rd.
Species of the Genus—*'Original Mal-formation'*—namely too great
narrowness of draught.—Upon this assurance I have ventured to buy
one by way of trial; and shall send it off to-morrow or the next day;
for, if unfortunately it should fail at Allan Bank, it may do for a
present to somebody in Rydale—where, they told me at the post, every
house smokes. But I hope it will not fail; for I should be very happy
if, through my means, your long trouble and vexation from this cause
should have an end. And I shall then think that I have made you
amends for the long delay in sending the carpet; which, I am very
sorry to acknowledge, has been entirely owing to me; not intentionally,
you will believe; but, in my hurry, I had directed that all the things
directed to Manchester should be sent off—forgetting that the carpet
was not among them; and accordingly I have since learned from Mr.
Kelsall that the books &c. have arrived at Manchester, but no carpet;
that having been left with the servant, as I have since recollected, to
be sold or not (as I should direct him) to the person who had offered
to purchase the rest of the furniture.—I hope now however that it will
be with you soon; though, to make it worth sending, it goes by the
boat.—

Saturday, May 27th. in the morning.
I begin to write this morning in the intervals of breakfast. Yesterday I
had no opportunity of writing until the evening—when I felt more in

a humor for reading; and therefore did not attempt to write.—I was at Longman's last night; and I had at length the pleasure of finding that the pamphlet was in a course of delivery; Mr. Orme has promised to send me up the remaining 10 copies for you this morning; and I have just received from Mr. Baldwin 4 copies which I had directed to be put into a cover—that they might be a little dressed to go to the Spanish and Portuguese Ambassadors:—I shall send one to Admiral Apodaga; but none, unless Mr. Wordsworth directs it, to Don P. Cevallos; for I am sure, from the conversations which Bohn the German bookseller reports to me as passing between himself and Don Padilla and other members of the legation, that Cevallos and his suite are not sound;—indeed, *I* did not like what I saw of his pamphlet; [8]—and, whilst Apodaga has been very actively employed in purchasing horse-accoutrements &c. and everything which the Spaniards want, Cevallos has done nothing; and is going back, *it is said,* to Spain—no doubt, to run away to S. America at the first approach of danger; for in his suite are chiefly *Rio de la Plata* Spaniards; and they make no secret of having sent thither all the property which they had in Spain—as being confident in Bonaparte's ultimate triumph.— —Pray, speaking of Cevallos's pamphlet, did you read a letter of Charles IV to his son?—I think, connected with such infantine feebleness,—I never read of so much cool iniquity as there seems to be in this detestable old man. And he prates about virtue and patriotism; and seems verily to believe himself a Patriot King!—"Everything," says he, "must be done *for* the people; and nothing *from* them." [9]—I said that I would say no more about the affairs of Europe; but really, being here reminded of them, I cannot forbear asking you—Don't you think this *Schill* [10] an excellent fellow?—And the noble Tyrolese! Though I sent you with so much gladness the account of the Archduke John's victory (both on account of it's real individual importance —and also because a victory of a regular army was likely, I thought,

---

[8] See above, pp. 110, 121–122.

[9] Southey quotes this passage from Charles IV's letter to his son Ferdinand VII as "Every thing ought to be done for the people, and nothing by the people" (*History of the Peninsular War* [1823–1832], I, 225).

[10] Ferdinand Baptista von Schill, a Prussian major who on April 28 led his regiment in a revolt against the French. He had slight success, however, and lost his life on May 31 in a battle which crushed his small force. Wordsworth wrote on him the sonnet, "Brave Schill! by death delivered, take thy flight" (*Poetical Works*, III, 133).

to do so much good by breaking down the belief in the *peculiar*
strength of the French (as it's *effect*) and by implying (as its *cause*)
some improvements of system in the Austrians)—yet I felt more delight a great deal in the triumphs of peasantry—for themselves. And
—even as to their consequences—I cannot help hoping that, at this
time—they may have the glory, by occupying the Italian army, to
secure a fair field to the insurrections in the North and in Hungary—
to the great Austrian army in Bohemia—and the victorious army in
Poland (for *victorious* they must have been to a great extent;—for you
will have seen that Prince Poniatowsky confesses, in his report of the
battle of April 19th.,[11] to as great a loss on the part of the French
and Poles &c. as the French confessed to in the battle of Jena) : and
thus Bonaparte's progress may be his peril.—At any rate this miscreant,
who is telling Europe that 'the first duty of the people is to obey their
governors'—(in the same breath, by the way, with which he approves
of some Austrian deputation for reviling their Emperor's policy), will
find the peasantry in two parts of Europe a thorn in his side at the
moment when their opposition has the best chance of being effectual.—
—But, to return to the pamphlet,—I shall send you two out of the 4
covered copies; as perhaps you may have some present of ceremony to
make; and might wish to have them look a little *'genteel'* (as Mr.
Westray says) without having the means of getting them done.—I
conclude that you would understand how the cancelled sheets were to
be managed in the 4 unsewed copies which I sent at first:—I should
have mentioned it in my last letter but ladies are so clever, that I
should have thought it presumptuous to send you any directions in this
affair.—The pamphlet has been priced, by Longmen [*sic*], 5s.; I
said to Mr. Orme that that seemed to me rather a high price—comparing it with other pamphlets of nearly the same size (though, to be
sure *'The Siege of Saragossa'*—which is only 3 sheets—is 2s. 6d. in
price) ; but he said that, as only 500 had been printed, less than 5s.
would not clear the expenses—even if all were sold; 750, he said,
ought to have been printed—to have made anything by it: however I
said heroically that Mr. Wordsworth would be satisfied, in this case,

---

[11] The *Times* for May 26 reports: "General Prince Poniatowski has published an account of the battle of Raszyn, of the 19th of last month, according to which the loss of the Poles, French and Saxons amounted to 450
killed, 900 wounded, and 32 taken prisoners."

to clear his expenses; for I thought that we were entitled to a boast at
any rate; and it would not be believed so readily—coming *after* the
loss as *before* it.—This is the worst side of the prospect;—viz. that, if
all sell, there will only just be a reimbursement; and that thus, so far
as this edition is concerned, Mr. Wordsworth will have given all his
labor and thought to a rascally public for nothing. But then, on the
other side, Mr. Orme justly observed that—if this edition all sold and
a second was called for—there might then be 750 or 1000 printed; and
2ndly.—as consolation if a second edition were *not* called for—he said
that they usually calculated that, out of 20 pamphlets on political subjects, *one* would clear it's expenses; thus hinting that, if Mr. Wordsworth dies, he dies in company with the glorious army of pamphleteers.
—One *serious* consolation however I learned:—viz. that a pamphlet
published before the 4th. of June, is considered to have it's fair chance;
—before that day, Mr. Orme said, it was as well as at any time excepting at the beginning of the Session of Parliament—which is much the
best time, he says:—however then the advantage must be like that of
the Strand over bye streets to a tradesman; viz. that the opportunities
of selling are more; but then there are more competitors.—At present
—I do not think that there are any pamphlets that are at all read;—
'there is nothing *stirring*'—as Mr. O. says—in London; and in London a bookseller is one's only authority on this subject; since one can
never have a sufficient *induction,* as the experimentalists say, upon
which to ground a report of what is generally read in such a large place
—from one's own personal knowledge: at Clifton &c. my sister informs
me that they are all languishing over *Marmion* [12] and simpering over
Coelebs in search of a wife (which I see is now in a 7th. or 8th. edition!): [13]—'the red plague rid them!' Indeed the book prospect seems
growing cloudier and cloudier:—the other day I was in the Chapter
coffee-house:—I had seen in a shop window, a No. of the British Critic
which, in it's list of articles reviewed, mentioned Mr. Wordsworth's
Poems:—recollecting that this Review had had the sense to hold some-

---

[12] Sir Walter Scott's poem, *Marmion, a Tale of Flodden Field,* was published in 1808.

[13] Hannah More's novel, *Coelebs in Search of a Wife: Comprehending
Observations on Domestic Habits and Manners, Religion, and Morals,* pub-
lished in Dec., 1808, went through twelve editions in 1809. (See below,
Letters 33 and 35.)

thing of a respectful tone in speaking of the Lyrical Ballads, I felt a wish to see how far it had dared to preserve it's consistency [14] in defiance of the tone set by the Edinburgh Review; and therefore, as I did not choose to encourage such trash by buying it, I went to the Chapter where all the reviews may be seen gratis. The *review* is contained, I think, in the February No.;—however I called for all the Nos. for this year; and ran over everything that promised any interest. —With respect to the review of Mr. Wordsworth;—it is contained in the space of a single page;—and is so utterly despicable as to make it impossible for any one to give it the honor of any public notice; and for this I am very sorry; for I propose, in order to escape the construction which may be put on giving Jeffray a separate and peculiar notice, to collect a few of the most flagrant misrepresentations in the other principal reviews—and thus put Jeffray to greater torment by shewing that he is not recognized as having any special claims even to infamy.[15]—I cannot express to you how disgusting an employment it was to turn over the pages of this senseless review—and to see that, in the very same number in which the vilest trash, written by milliners, about Miss Seraphinas—and Lord Fredericks,—is thought worthy to be gravely and solemnly analyzed—and quoted—and commented upon —only a few lines from the Happy Warrior are extracted from Mr. Wordsworth's Poems—and the whole dismissed by the conceited wretch, who—without being able to write a line of sense or grammar —has undertaken to *review* them (as they call it), with an intimation that really the author must reform before he can hope to appease the *severity* of *critics!!*—Miserable puppy! that thou were but of importance enough to justify a man in destroying thee!—Job says— 'Would that mine enemy had written a book!'—meaning, I suppose, that he would have reviewed him:—but *I* say—'Would that he had reviewed a book with common sense!'—that there might be an argument for crucifying him.—And in this same review (I think in the very same No.) is a highly panegyrical account of a wretched satire

---

[14] A quite favorable review of the *Lyrical Ballads,* probably written by Wordsworth's friend Francis Wrangham, appeared in the Oct., 1799, *British Critic* (XIV, 364–369). The journal's review of *Poems in Two Volumes* in March, 1809 (XXXIII, 298–299) was of a different character: "Such flimsy, puerile thoughts, expressed in such feeble and halting verse, we have seldom seen."

[15] See end of Letter 25.

partly leveled at Mr. Wordsworth and Mr. Coleridge—called 'English Bards and Scotch Reviewers': from the virulence of this book towards Mr. Southey and Mr. Wordsworth, I suspect (and for other reasons) that it is written by Peter Bayley [16]—in revenge for Mr. Southey's having exposed him in the Annual Review: he treats Walter Scott with some harshness—but for the silliest reasons possible; and more for having prostituted his *'genius'* than for a want of genius:—but his idols are *Rogers* and *Campbell* whom he speaks of as *neglected* bards: it has a truly mock-heroic effect—when, after a solemn invocation to some unknown geniuses and a long preparation made for their appearance, in strut Messrs. R. and C.—I read this Satire some weeks—or perhaps months—ago: but it is so deplorably dull and silly that I never thought of mentioning it before.—The other Satire, called The Simpliciad,[17] I have not yet read; because I have had no opportunity of borrowing it.

You will find, in the parcel, 2 primers—which are for Totts: Johnny of course would think such a present an affront;—and Catherine, besides that she is far off wanting them yet—sweet little love!—, is to be taught by nobody but *me:* this promise Mrs. Wordsworth once made me; and therefore I shall think it an act of the highest perfidy, if anybody should attempt to insinuate any learning into Catherine—or to hint at primers—to the prejudice of my exclusive privilege.—I hope my sweet pupil, that is to be, goes on well; though you have not said lately. Whether you will make use of these things for teaching the letters—I do not know—nor whether Totts will approve of learning his letters from them; but I thought he would like the pictures at any rate; and therefore selected the gayest I could find.—Johnny's pictures —will I hope some of them please him;—I mean the St. Pauls—which I called *'in its glory'*—since it shews more of itself than ever anybody has seen of the real St. Pauls; and the 'Lord's Prayer &c.'—of which, that you may be prepared with a connected tale about it; I shall write

[16] See above, p. 39. The first poem in Bayley's *Poems* was "An Apology for Writing," a satire in heroic couplets enough suggestive of *English Bards and Scotch Reviewers* to explain De Quincey's attributing Byron's anonymous poem to Bayley.

[17] *The Simpliciad; a Satirico-didactic Poem, containing Hints for the Scholars of the New School* . . . (London, 1808) was dedicated to Wordsworth, Southey, and Coleridge. Wordsworth believed it to be by Richard Mant (*LY,* I, 510).

a few hints outside my letter.—The slate is for Johnny also:—the pencil is of French chalk;—which is said to be better than slate pencil; and, for drawing, I suppose it is; and therefore I have sent 2 more in a separate paper.—All the loose pictures, excepting the Portraits and St. Pauls, I bought in a large lot at an auction where I was buying books;—hoping that there might be something in it that would do:— but,—though there was a great number in the lot, I could find none tolerable for Johnny but those which I have sent.—When I go down to Bristol, I hope to do better; as my sisters will be able to select a great deal better than I can—who do not know where to look for them;—and there will be as good an opportunity there as here.— There are however now sent, I hope, what will prevent Johnny from feeling any disappointment.—Of Sir J.[ohn] M.[oore] and D.[avid] B.[aird] I have sent no pictures;—hearing that the best are in some magazine or other;—and of both there have been several pictures, so wide of all resemblance to each other, that I should be at a loss to know which to send.—Of Sir J.M. in particular there is a profile which is that of a very mean-looking fop;—and 2 or 3 front faces which repre- sent him as a decent-headed manly-looking Englishman. Sir D. B's face has, in all the likenesses (though otherwise differing much), some- thing very repulsive and cynical in it. But, supposing that you care but little about either of them, I have sent you a picture of Miss Taylor [18] instead—which you may feel a little curiosity about; and it is esteemed a very good likeness.—As to Mrs. Clarke, I have sent the best I could learn to have any likeness: it is certainly not the most pleasing of them: and, after all, my means of information on this point have been so few (as every print-seller of course knows nothing of any print which he has no interest in himself) and the few opinions I have heard have been so contradictory—that I send this with but a very slight presumption in its favor—viz. that it is the one which has now taken the place of most of the others;—but then the reason may be that some of the others were much dearer—being more highly finished:—but, as none of the dearer ones were front faces—but only exhibitions of Mrs. Clarke's figure on a sofa (with very little even of the profile of her face discoverable) I have thought it best on the whole to send you this.

---

[18] Probably Mary Ann Taylor, sister-in-law of Mrs. Clarke, who was questioned before the House of Commons, and attracted so much public interest that a subscription was taken up for her benefit and had collected over £2,300 by early May.

—The head of Palafox is not a *proof*—which I should, in *his* case, have sent—if I could have discovered any the least difference between what was shown to me as a proof and the one I send;—but, as I could *not*—and the proof was double the price of this, I thought it an imposition.—Talking of portraits,—I must mention that, a few days after I gave you an account of a picture which I had seen of Sir A. Wellesley, an East Indian—a Mr. Duncan—with whom I was dining in a coffee-house—assured me I was wrong about the character of his face; for that it is a very fine one.—It appeared that I had seen only the worst picture of him—viz. one in which he is a standing by a horse rearing;—but even this; I must acknowledge, since it has been lowered (in consequence of the late news from Portugal), would not, I now see, justify my account of it. But the East Indian spoke from knowledge of his person; and referred me to a picture which I have since seen, and which certainly represents a very pleasing looking man. But however, be his face what it may, he is still (as I told Mr. D.) a villain; though all his villainy will soon be forgotten here, if he takes Gen. Soult prisoner.—I do this justice to Sir Arthur's 'physiognomy' as they say: but I really thought it what I described to you before; and the reason was that the picture was very high up in the window —when I first saw it (so that I could but just discover his name at the bottom of it); and I have lately discovered—to my great mortification and surprise—that I am very near-sighted.—I never had any reason to suspect this until the last day of my being at Grasmere; when Mrs. Wordsworth, after taking a deal of pains to direct me, could not make me see Johnny and his schoolfellows in the fields near the church. But the other day, in shewing my Manchester acquaintances about London, I was quite thunderstruck to find that, when we were standing in Guild-hall under the statue of Alderman Beckford, they could both *read* with the greatest ease an inscription where I could but just dimly perceive that there *was* an inscription;—and even, going back many yards to a distance at which I had lost sight even of the obscure haze made by the letters, they could still read it fluently. Afterwards I had a many [*sic*] proofs that my sight for slight differences at a distance must be very defective;—but gross differences—as in woods and mountains &c—I seem to see as well as others. They both comforted me a little by saying that near-sightedness is considered a proof of the strength and durability of the sight.

I have been writing on for a long time—hoping that this morning's post would bring me a letter from you—and that I should be obliged to leave off to read it and answer it. But, alas! the post has gone by some hours ago—for it is now 3 o'clock;—and therefore until Monday I cannot at earliest hear from you.—(I shall not go on to-morrow, as I purposed;—not until Wednesday, I think.)—This silence rather alarms me; as I half-collect from it that, in something or other, I have omitted or *committed* something with respect to the pamphlet—which you disapprove of, but do not like to pain me by saying so.—I extracted into a regular methodised index all the corrections sent in the letters; and therefore think I can hardly have made any mistake there.—It must therefore be in the Postscript—which certainly might have been done much better as to the arrangement &c. but I was satisfied that, in a part which so few would look at, there was the *matter* of the argument collected;—and I shall be quite content, if you think that. I do not however mean, by being satisfied, that I did not attempt to arrange it as well as I could.[19] But I wrote it, as I mentioned, under great constraint;—and under one oppression, which I did not mention to you—3 months' solitariness through the whole of my evenings; for the only acquaintances, which I have in London (I mean who are sufficiently intimate to permit me to visit them on the only terms which could make it not a pain—that is, when I like and without dressing), are—and have been the whole time—in the country; and the tribes of coffee-house acquaintances, whom I make at dinner,—some of them ask me to their houses; but I never, except in [a single *scratched* out] two instances, accepted their invitations; because that would oblige me to tell them my name; which I have never at any time felt ready to do to any coffee-house acquaintance;—and *now* it would be particularly injudicious; as it would expose me to visits from hundreds of loungers at the lakes—who might learn at Ambleside &c. that an acquaintance of theirs lived near the eccentric Mr. Wordsworth; and thus Town-end would be all 'the rage' for a season.—For this reason, excepting 2 evenings or 3 (I forget which) spent at an Oratorio and a concert, every night since I left Grasmere has been spent in utter solitude;—which I have tried to relieve as much as possible by varying the times and places of my walks: but, after all, it is a doleful burthen; and it

---

[19] Actually, the note seems to have pleased. Wordsworth pronounced it "very well done" (*MY*, I, 311), and Coleridge "much admired" it (to Stuart, June 13 [*STC*, III, 214]).

is only, when in tolerable chearfulness and spirits that I can gain a glimpse of the real effect of what I wrote.—I have certainly seen a good deal that might be mended in it since it was printed;—and once I thought that the whole had too much the air of a barrister's pleading —from the artificial construction of the argument—it's divisions and subdivisions &c. But still, as I could not see where it was wrong in *substance*—and as it certainly contains all the extracts from the letters which I could have used as answers—or have noticed as things *to be* answered,—I felt not much regret for not having made more alterations; since it seemed to want them only in the *manner* and not the matter; and the *manner* seemed of so little importance in that part of the work.

Here I must close, that I may have time to make up my parcel—and write to Miss Hutchinson. I intended to have *begun* to answer your letters in this letter: but I must defer it for the present: only, in answer to your account of the outrages at *Nabs-scar*,[20] I just say how sorry I am—for your sakes who have known it so long—that such wicked devastation should be going on.—I have been amongst the trees myself; and have several times walked under them with Mr. Wordsworth from Rydale; and therefore shall miss their beauty (even on the lower road, one shall miss that—I think): but you will miss more, to whom they have been objects of love for so long a time. I heartily pray that Mr. North may be compelled by some accident, great or small, to deliver the country from his presence; where, by all that I ever heard of him, he seems to live only to annoy and give pain.

God bless you, my dear Madam!

Your most affectionate friend,

Thos. de Quincey.

I shall send a copy to Sir. G. Beaumont this evening.

[*Across back:*] I send 2 Nos. of the Evening Mail—1 containing *one* of the private letters on Ld. Cochrane's affair:—the other the Decree

---

[20] Dorothy had written De Quincey (*MY*, I, 302–303) of a disastrous dispute between Mr. North, who had recently bought Rydal Mount, and Lady Fleming of Rydal Hall. He claimed the right to lop trees on unenclosed ground adjacent to his land; she denied that right and exercised her manorial privilege of felling the trees, in order to prevent him from lopping them—with the result that Nab Scar was denuded. In 1813 North sold Rydal Mount to Lady Fleming, and she rented it to Wordsworth (*MY*, I, 531).

about Saragossa.—Both will be found on the first pages of the 2
papers.—Will you have the goodness to keep these papers? as they
form part of a series—which I took at first—on account of news &c.
which might make alterations in the Pamphlet necessary—: and which
I now continue to take, as thinking that—in any future edition of this
pamphlet and for other purposes—it may be very useful to have a
regular series of journals at Grasmere.

[*No address; probably enclosed in parcel.*]

32. *To Mary and William Wordsworth*

Ms. Dove Cottage. Unpub.

Nothing but a long letter!!
which I mention on the outside
to prevent disappointment.

> 82, Gt. Titchfield St.—
> Wednesday morning, May 31st. [1809]

My dear Madam,

Mr. Jameson has just been here to tell me that he sets out on his
return to Ambleside to-morrow morning; and that he will carry anything for me to Grasmere; and therefore, though I did not mean to
have written until Saturday (fearing that I should scarcely be able to
write at all fully), I will at any rate use this opportunity to send you
the 'letter to Major Cartwright' [1]—and to write a few lines now—
before I am obliged to go out—and as many as I can between the time
of returning home and Mr. Jameson's calling for the letter.—Indeed
I proposed to Mr. J. to send it up to him at 10 o'clock to-night to the
inn; but, as there may be some danger of it's not reaching him in that
way—and as he will himself pass through this street about 5 or 6
o'clock, I think at present of giving it to him then—if I have can [*sic*]
be back before that time.

On Saturday night last, as you would learn from the date, I sent off
the parcel containing 10 copies of the pamphlet—Johnny's pictures &c.

Letter 32:

[1] *A Letter Addressed to John Cartwright, Esq.* . . . *on the Subject of
Parliamentary Reform* by the Earl of Selkirk [Thomas Douglas] (London,
1809).

—The porter, who took it, had very circumstantial and plain directions
given to him—viz. that he was first to go to the Carlisle mail office
and ask if they would promise to forward it that night (which, as it
was nearly 7 o'clock before I could get it sent off, I feared they would
not) ; if they would not, then he was to seek out the next earliest coach
on that road and leave it with them.—Accordingly on Sunday morning
he called with a ticket from the Saracen's head coach office purport-
ing that the parcel was left there to be forwarded by the next coach;
and I rested satisfied therefore that, at some time on Sunday at any
rate, the parcel would be on it's journey. This morning however I
learn from Mr. J. that he is going by a coach from this same inn;
and that the reason, why he did not go this morning, is because the
Penrith coach goes only twice a week—viz. on *Tuesdays* and *Thurs-
days:* and thus I have the mortification to find that the unfortunate
parcel lay no doubt at the coach office until yesterday morning; and
therefore will not be at Grasmere until Saturday night.—It was indeed
an unfortunate parcel; for, through my own miscalculation, it was not
ready to be packed up till some time after 6 o'clock;—and after it had
been once entirely packed up, I recollected that dear little Tott's Alpha-
bets had been left out:—they were not, to be sure, of so much importance; as any other picture would have contented him;—but still I
did not like *always* to be making blunders (though the blunder about
the last parcel was owing to the office) ;—and therefore, being sure that
I then was too late for the mail, I unpacked it.—I recollected also,
after it had gone, that I had placed Johnny's slate where it would certainly be broken. But I will bring him another when I come myself.—
On Monday I received the first letter sent after the receipt of the
pamphlets:—and, on Tuesday (i.e. yesterday), I had the very great
pleasure of receiving that written jointly by Mr. Wordsworth and
yourself.[2]—To the first letter—I was ready to say—as is said to the
angel of the church of Laodicea in the Revelations—'I know thy
words that they are neither cold nor hot; I would thou wert cold or
hot:'—but this second is so kind that I should think myself abundantly
recompensed for 50 times the trouble I have had in the present case.
Indeed I cannot sufficiently thank you for your goodness in suggesting
that letter: for, though the first said undoubtedly all that I had any
right to expect—supposing that it was interpreted literally, yet—since

[2] *MY,* I, 311–313, 316–318.

there are expressions of satisfaction out of mere courtesy for any *in-tentions* of service—I should not have had the pleasure, but for your last letter, of thinking that you were really satisfied; which I now have; and am a thousand-fold repaid.

To speak now of the *Errata*,[3] I went on Monday to Longman's; and asked if it could not be so managed—as that they should be printed on a slip of paper and pasted on below the present list: one of the house (I think, *Rees*)[4] told me it might: and therefore I went to Baldwin's in the evening; and desired that the list, which I would send them up on the next morning, might be printed as soon as they should receive it: this was agreed to; and I returned home meaning to make out the list immediately.—But, in my way, a difficulty occurred to me such as, I guess, you will hardly think of: it was concerning the motto from Ld. Bacon.—This, I was sure, I could not have mis-copied from the edition I consulted:—and yet this edition, I knew, was re-puted the best; indeed so much the best—that, whereas the *Folio* edit. of Mallet [5] in 4 vols. may be had for 4 guineas, this—from which I quoted—namely the one in 5 vol.4to.—1778—was offered to me, by the bookseller who owned it, for *12* guineas,—though unbound.—That the passage stood as I quoted it—(viz. '*zeal* or love')—in *this* edition, I could not doubt; having taken such great care in transcribing it:—however, to satisfy myself fully, I took the shop in my way home:—and accordingly, on examining the passage, so it was:—it stands at page 135 of the 3rd. vol.[6]—Here I am unfortunately called off by 2 letters; one of them from my mother on a very interesting affair—an account of which I will endeavour to give you this evening:—at any rate I will close my account of the mysterious *erratum;*—but, for the

---

[3] Wordsworth had sent, by Sara Hutchinson, a list of twelve *errata*, which De Quincey wanted to add to his own printed list of eight items. See pp. 238–239, and J. E. Wells, "The Story of Wordsworth's 'Cintra,'" *SP*, XVIII (Jan., 1921), 72–76.

[4] Owen Rees, partner of the Longman house.

[5] *The Works of Francis Bacon . . . To which is prefixed a New Life of the Author, by Mr. Mallet,* 4 vols. (London, 1740). This edition gives the passage in question as "a character of hate or love" ("An Advertisement touching the Controversies of the Church of *England*," Vol. IV, p. 460).

[6] *The Works of Francis Bacon,* 5 vols. (London, 1778, reissue of 1765 edi-tion). The disputed quote stands as De Quincey says, "zeal or love" (III, 135).

present, my mother's letter makes it necessary for me to go out immediately.[7]
Half past 2 o'clock.

My dear Madam,—I am come back again;—but I shall have to go out once more at least: in the mean time, I will write on as far as I can.—That the word in Bacon—was *zeal* and not *hate,* in that edition which I have mentioned, I did not even at first feel any doubt about: —but still the question was—Mallet's reading *hate*—which of the two was right:—this could be ascertained, of course, only by consulting some 3rd. edition;—and how to find such 3rd. edition—was part of my difficulty on my way home. For, as Mr. Wordsworth had not sent me the extract from Grasmere, I had before—in searching for an authentic edition to quote from—learnt how very scarce any copies of Bacon's works were in booksellers' shops; having had a fortnight's chace or thereabouts, before I found even a *single* copy; and I had purposely sought for the edit. of 1778—as knowing that it was undoubtedly better than Mallet's in one point—viz. that it contained *more* than Mallet's (as particularly a collection of Bacon's letters published first by Dr. Birch)[8]—and that it was otherwise *reputed* better in whatsoever it differed from Mallett's [*sic*]—so as to be called emphatically *the* authentic edition.—In the shops therefore I knew I had but little chance of meeting with any but Dr. Shaw's *Abridgement;* [9]—to public libraries I have no access, but at the British Museum—where I can gain admittance, even by means of an officer there who is one of my coffee-house friends, only at certain times;—and, as I mentioned in my last letter, all my acquaintances are out of town that

---

[7] His mother's letter concerned the mysterious return of De Quincey's younger brother Richard ("Pink"), who had run away to sea in 1803 and had a series of remarkable adventures, ending in the Battle of Copenhagen, where he had been captured by the Danes. He was just back, after eighteen months in prison, and was behaving peculiarly in keeping his distance from the family.

[8] *Letters, Speeches, Charges, Advices, &c. of Francis Bacon . . . Now first published by Thomas Birch* (London, 1763).

[9] *The Philosophical Works of Francis Bacon, Methodized, and made English from the Originals with occasional Notes,* ed. by Peter Shaw (London, 1733). It is curious that De Quincey should have found Bacon so rare, since editions of his works had been published in 1802, 1803, and 1807.

I recollect anything about.—And thus, strange as it may seem with one's ordinary feeling about London—that *there* everything may be had,—and perhaps with Bacon really in many a house in this very street,—yet such are the difficulties to a person having access only to the booksellers' shops (and even there only of course after having pre-concerted some excuse for the errand)—that—if I were to send out one man to collect *Bacons*—and another to collect *Kangaroos*—I verily believe the Kangaroo man would be the most successful.—I am afraid that you may think I am saying this—to make it appear that my trouble is very great:—but indeed that is not my meaning;—and, in reality,—where I know the bookseller—there is no trouble at all:—as I pass most of the great shops in my walks every day:—and, when I do not, the trouble is nothing more than searching in their catalogues for some book which I want—as an excuse for giving them the trouble of look-ing for the book.—My reason for mentioning it is this—that, as there has been so much delay already about the pamphlet, I resolved some time ago—always to send you at the time (whilst I remembered the particulars) an account of how the delay arose;—since I found that else you might have uncontradicted accounts from Mr. Stuart of the delay being due to me.—And, in this case, there *is* a delay in printing the errata until I shall succeed in finding that particular edition in 4 Folio vols. from which I suppose that Mr. Wordsworth quotes and some 3rd. edition to verify it. For (on the one hand) the more the substitu-tion of *hate* for *zeal* would add to the pertinence of the motto—so much the more would be the clamor if it should not be the real word used by Bacon, in the case of it's being found not to be so by any re-viewer &c.;—and yet (on the other hand)—if *hate* should be the word —then it would be a deplorable thing to omit the most important blunder in the list.—All the opportunities I have yet had—I have made use of;—that is, during part of yesterday:—and, in the morning, I wrote a note to Mr. Stuart [10]—explaining the affair—and begging him, if he should happen to have Mallett's Bacon, to ascertain the point. But I have not yet got his answer:—This mention of Mr. Stuart puts me in mind—that my note to him was partly in answer to one I had from him on Monday night—telling me that, having heard at Longman's that I had had 20 copies of the pamphlet, he conjectured

[10] For what appears to be a partial draft of this note, see *Unpublished Letters of Thomas De Quincey and Elizabeth Barrett Browning*, ed. S. Musgrove, Auckland (New Zealand) Univ. Coll. Bull. No. 44 (1954), p. 1.

that I had sent Mr. Wordsworth the number he wanted—and that
therefore he was to consider a direction given to himself to send 10—
as cancelled:—I said, in my answer, that I had sent 14 according to a
direction sent to me at the beginning of March; [11] and therefore supposed that, in consequence of it's having been sent so long ago, Mr.
Wordsworth had forgotten it.—Am I right in this?—or must we
send 10 more?—

In what I have said above, one word will perhaps surprise you—
viz. where I say that I *suppose* Mr. Wordsworth to quote from Mallett's edition:—I say this; because it has since occurred to me as possible (though not very likely) that Mr. Wordsworth quotes from the
M.S. extract made by Mr. Coleridge, or even from memory.—My
only reason for thinking this (over and above the strangeness that by
an error of the press 2 different editions should give 2 different words
—unlike each other to the eye, and yet both making sense)—is, that
Mr. Wordsworth said that the reason why he did not send me the
extract was that he did not exactly know where to look for it;—but, as
a general direction to me, he said that it would be found in a Treatise
on Church Government:—now this direction, I found, was not quite
accurate;—since it is in a treatise *'touching the Controversies of the
Church of England'*: and the same inaccuracy, which perplexed *me* a
little in finding it (there being 2 or 3 treatises upon Church affairs),
may also have made it difficult for *him* to find it;—so that he might
rely upon his memory.—But, on reconsideration, I do not think this
likely; as the word *zeal* making sense would naturally suggest a
mistrust, if he had no other authority than his recollection of it.—
Finally, with respect to the appositeness of the passage,—*as it now
stands,*—I should think that the first words—*'bitter* and earnest
writings'—would make it a justificatory motto—even without *hate,*
though that would doubtless make it better:—but, for my own part,
I had an objection to it on account of the word *'Christian',* which
restricts the allowance of hatred and *'bitter* writing' &c. to those, of
whom Ld. Bacon is speaking in that treatise, viz. to *polemical theo-
logians.* But then I did not think myself at liberty to reject it on that
account—as Mr. Wordsworth had desired me to insert it. Indeed I
bore a still greater spite to the Latin motto in the title page;—which
seemed to me but little pertinent to the work of it's first scale;—but,

---

[11] On March 6 (*MY,* I, 263, misdated March 26).

afterwards when it had been so much enlarged—and *that,* which was at first primary, had been made secondary—not pertinent at all; not to mention that, besides the great crime of being in Latin, no motto—however pertinent it had been—could give weight and sanction that was from *Horace,* I should think;—and therefore I made a point of suppressing his name.

With respect to all the other errata,—I have not had time yet to see which are due to me, and which to the M.S.; but in general, I [*struck out:* believe that more belong to the last:] believe that one half may be mine; and so we must 'forget and forgive.' By *we,* I mean Miss Wordsworth–Miss Hutchinson–and myself: for, I think that but very little was in your handwriting; and, I believe, that there is less ambiguity in it than in the occasional writing of the other ladies. However, all parties shall have justice done them: and therefore—to begin with myself—I acknowledge, with shame and contrition, that the ellipsis in 'calenture *of fancy*' [12]—is *my* blunder entirely: no lawyer could make out an alibi for these two words—which are written, I lament to say, with the utmost legibility and precision. But then, that Miss Hutchinson may not triumph over me, I must add that the other blunder of the 1st. rate class—viz. abus*es* for abus*ers* is *not* mine; and, as well as I recollect, it is in *her* hand-writing.

To Mr. Wordsworth.—Dear Sir,

One thing, before I conclude, I must add;—viz. that from my mode of telling the story [13] about the supposed libel on the army you have misunderstood me to mean that Mr. Stuart's objection to that passage was overruled by *me:* but, so far from that, *my* arguments were all before Mr. Stuart at the Courier Office; and it was fully agreed upon *there* that the leaf should be canceled:—what it was that induced Mr. Stuart afterwards *voluntarily* to withdraw his desire on this subject,—he only knows, as he did not say;—I suppose it was *Mr. Baldwin's* preemptory and unhesitating decision that the passage was not libellous: but *my* reasons it could not be; both because I only re-stated to Mr. Baldwin what I had before said without effect to Mr. Stuart himself; and because we were at issue upon this question—whether a passage, leveled at any whole *class* of men so large as the army, could be libelous (and therefore, if we could have agreed whether this passage were libellous if said of an individual, there would still have been

---

[12] Dicey, p. 187.
[13] See Letter 27.

a further question between us) ; which to me appeared a monstrous supposition—in support of which Mr. Stuart did not allege a single precedent—and in refutation of which Mr. Baldwin did allege a precedent from his own experience at the time of the American war.— However, with respect to our experience in this question, I and Mr. Stuart are pretty nearly equal;—for I was *never* prosecuted for a libel; and Mr. Stuart told me that he had only *once* been prosecuted; and that was for a libel on the duke of Portland's valet—when he was editor of the Morning Post [14]—not written by himself, I do not mean, but by some servant in the office. And, in questions of libels, I do not see that a man can claim any sound experience—unless it has been brought to a *decision* in a court of justice; and *decisions* are open to all the world; though all the world may not have so much interest in attending to them as newspaper editors. But that seems to be the only advantage they can fairly claim;—excepting that, amongst *manifest* and *indubitable* libels, they can judge which are most likely to be prosecuted—and which to be overlooked. Thus, Mr. Stuart cited the case of the editor of the Independent Whig—who was prosecuted and cast, after many libels of ministers had been overlooked, for a libel on *Juries,* as being a good basis for a *popular* prosecution. But then surely common sagacity would have suggested this to any man as a thing likely to happen?—But the question between us was not—concerning an avowed libel—whether it would be prosecuted; but concerning a passage supposed to be doubtful—whether it *were* a libel or not.—And on this question supposing even that Mr. Stuart *had* had any experience more than what was open to me, he had himself weakened it's authority—by telling me that, for any thing he knew, he himself wrote a libel once a week in the Courier,—And, if length of life be singly supposed to give more *experience* (in the *full* meaning) upon *any* question, then Mr. Baldwin has had more than either of us; for I am sure he looks a great deal older ;—and he has been editor of 2 papers— viz. 'The St. James' Chronicle'—and 'Baldwin's Journal'—time out of mind, I believe: and *he* thought decidedly, as I did; and his arguments, I suppose, it was that induced Mr. Stuart—I ought not to have said *voluntarily to withdraw*—but not to repeat his desire that it might be canceled to Mr. Baldwin: it was not of course my part, after I had given an opinion so decidedly upon it, to become the champion of Mr.

---

[14] Stuart had been joint proprietor of the *Morning Post* from 1788 to 1803.

Stuart's opposite opinion:—but it rested with Mr. Stuart to have had it canceled by saying a single word, if he had chosen to do so.—I have made a very long statement of all this affair;—but all, which was important to have said about it, is this; that the leaf's not being canceled was not owing to me; since, after saying before Mr. Stuart at Mr. Baldwin's only what I said to Mr. St. before at the office,—I sate silent, and had no share in the decision: that was what I meant by the words 'voluntarily withdrawing his desire'—viz. that it was not done on my re-urging him to withdraw it—when at the place of decision.

All this, about the supposed libel, I had addressed, my dear Madam, to you:—but, thinking you would be wearied of such a long dull letter, I have now addressed it to Mr. Wordsworth; to whom I thought it necessary to say something about it, as I am anxious to be acquitted on this point—on which I really am not at all in fault.—I hope to be at Grasmere at any rate in a month;—the 'interesting affair,' concerning which I promised some information, relates to my brother; and it is too long to be crowded into the little time I have for telling it.—Our letters happen both to speak so nearly in the same words of Catherine [15]—that together with the blunder about the parcel, you would almost suppose *my* last letter to have been written *after* receiving yours, —if I had not explained the matter to you.—I conclude that the parcel will be in Penrith to-morrow morning (*Thursday*), and therefore it will most likely be at Keswick that or the next day: but, if it should by any accident be delayed, Mr. Jameson has promised to get it on to Grasmere. Is Johnny ready for his *printed* letter?—For Town end [16] &c. I owe you infinite thanks for your kindness in taking all the trouble off my hands; which I was going to have said that I *feared* I had never expressed—but that, if I have not, you would be sure that I felt them.—I am greatly gratified by Mr. Wordsworth's and your approbation of the note:—and cannot help smiling at the 'flattering unction' which Mr. Wordsworth has been so kind as to lay to my vanity on the matter of *punctuation*. With respect to Sir J. M. I am truly sorry that it has not gall enough in it; because really I thought so too;—and had made it much more severe at the first, but, afterwards—

[15] Mary had written on May 26: "I hope you will find Catherine (your little Pupil, as I often call her) much improved" (*MY,* I, 318). Cf. De Quincey's letter of May 27 (Letter 31, p. 185).

[16] Refers to Mary's work in getting Dove Cottage ready for him.

partly on Mr. Stuart's earnest advice to deal gently with him—partly from observing that all parties were disposed to defend *him,* whoever else was given up (in compliment to the Duke of York, Mr. Stuart says, whose favorite Sir J. M. was)—and still more from thinking that I had used language which could not be reconciled with Mr. Wordsworth's direction to treat him respectfully—I altered several parts of it.—In saying that I was partly influenced by the clamor for Sir J.M. —I mean that I thought myself bound so far to concede to it as not to urge anything against Sir J. M. further than it might be necessary to do it in order to justify the Spaniards: because else, I might have been needlessly creating enemies to the pamphlet in any of those who might chance to look at the note—by offending at once the different parties— and the mere *John Bulls*—who would not permit any harsh words of a *'hero',* as Mr. Wordsworth had reminded me.—Mr. Kelsall, for instance, is a complete specimen of that class: he has no notion but Sir J. M. and Sir A. W. are both great heroes;—and he looked rather wonderingly and suspiciously upon me, when I told him that I had been editing a pamphlet in which Sir A.W. was treated by no means as a great man:—however I satisfied him by an assurance that it was not meant that Sir A.W. would not *beat* Marshall Soult whenever and wherever he met him; and still less was it meant that an English army would not beat a French one everywhere and always. "Oh! that makes a difference!" he said;—and accordingly I found that so great was his curiosity to see the pamphlet—that, though not a bookman, he took a journey to Paternoster row the night before he left London— to get one; and he begged so hard that tho' they had not then fixed the price, they let him have one—on his assurance that he was my friend. This I learned to-day in a letter from himself: and I hope he may thus serve the pamphlet in Manchester—by circulating it.—Concerning Mr. Frere I am still more sorry;—as I had fully resolved, at the time I mentioned his letters to Miss Wordsworth, to have made use of them:—but, as some real injudiciousness seemed to have been proved against him—(though not of a kind to affect any opinion given concerning the Spaniards) and as it seemed to be making a party matter of it to play off Mr. Canning's *Frere* [17] against the Grenville's *Moore*

---

[17] John Hookham Frere—better known for his contribution to the *Anti-Jacobin,* his Whistlecraft papers, and his translations of Aristophanes than for his diplomacy—was English ambassador to the Central Junta from Oct., 1808, until mid-1809. With enthusiastic confidence in the Spanish will

—and as Mr. Billsborough [18] told me that he was of the same college with *Frere* (Trinity) and that he had there and ever since held the character of a very rash and injudicious man—I thought upon the whole that, the object being neither to criminate Sir J. M. nor to defend Mr. Frere—but to defend the Spaniards, more upon the whole would be gained to that end by making so much concession to the party noise about Mr. F. as to say nothing about him: and therefore the passage about him, which came at the close near to the mention of La Romana,[19] was left out.—But yet I am sorry that it was; both as Mr. Wordsworth wishes it in; and as I all along thought just what he has said—that the opposition had behaved with the greatest meanness and malice to Mr. Frere.—I am sorry also that I said nothing about Sir D. Baird; those letters are more unjust to the Spaniards in one instance (about Blake) than Sir J. M's—because he wrote with an official statement of Capt. Pasley's [20] before him, which Sir J. M.

---

to resist he had injudiciously and persistently attempted to meddle with Sir John Moore's movements, and was blamed in some quarters for the defeat at Corunna (Coruña). The affair took on a political coloring because the ministry did not like Moore, and had appointed him only at the insistence of the Duke of York. In fact, the ridiculous change of command twice on the field of Vimeiro, which led to the Convention of Cintra, had been the result of the government's determination to have in Portugal two officers senior to, if less competent than, Moore, in order to keep him out of command. On Feb. 24, 1809, Mr. Ponsonby moved in Commons an inquiry into the government's conduct of the campaign in Spain, asserting Frere's incompetence. Canning, the foreign minister, upheld his appointee. On April 21 Earl Grey made a similar motion in the Lords, strongly supported by Lord Grenville. Wordsworth wished De Quincey had "contrived to say something handsome" about Frere (*MY*, I, 316), not because the poet supported the government, but because he saw the envoy as a fellow believer in the Spanish people, and the general as their calumniator.

[18] Probably Dewhurst Billborrow, who matriculated at Trinity College, Cambridge, in 1792, the year Frere took his B.A. Frere, however, was at Caius College.

[19] Pedro Caro y Sureda, third Marquis of Romana, a colorful Spanish general.

[20] Charles William Pasley, later general and a distinguished army engineer, after a reconnoitering mission to the headquarters of Blake, the Spanish general, reported to Baird on Nov. 17, 1808: "The very severe actions they fought with the best troops of France, show how formidable the Spaniards may become"; but Blake's army had just been dispersed, and Pasley also added, "if officers are allowed to abandon their regiments with

had not, and which must have told him that he was telling an infamous falsehood.—But, Sir D.B's letters not having been referred to at all, I did not then think it right to turn aside to say anything about him—I must here close to go out.—Do not suppose that by having 20 pamphlets from Longman's, I am making presents of the *10* left:—that number was mentioned by me at random—when in a hurry; but I know of nobody to whom I shall want any to send to—except to the Span. and Port. Ambassadors—Editor of the Times—and Ld. Lonsdale—the rest, if I find on looking back through your letters that no others are named, will be returned.—God bless you, my dear Madam! and believe me most affectionately and respectfully

your friend and servant, Thos. de Quincey.

8 o'clock—Wednesday night.

My dear Madam,

I went out, among other purposes, to get a copy of Ld. Selkirk's letter:[21]—the last new pamphlet, I found, was 'An account of the Supreme Junta';—which I bought at a venture, thinking it must contain something interesting—being on such a subject; and, from the little I have been able to see of it, it seems really interesting. I hope it will be so; at any rate, it will serve to give so much more bulk to the parcel as may hinder Mr. J. from forgetting that he has one in his pocket.

I have not been where news is to be heard to-day; so do not know if there be any.

Mr. Jameson has been here, I find, whilst I was out; so that I must endeavour to meet him at Snow Hill; and must therefore now close finally. What a reform has taken place, to be sure, in my letter-writing habits!

I had almost forgotten to mention that I send you a copy of the

---

impunity, when opposed to the enemy, under any pretext whatever, the cause of Spain is altogether hopeless" ([Theodore Hook], *The Life of General, the Right Honorable Sir David Baird* [London, 1832], II, 439). De Quincey became acquainted with Pasley in 1809: see Letter 33.

[21] See Letter 32, note 1. De Quincey's eagerness to send this pamphlet to Wordsworth is an interesting forerunner of their conservative political activity in 1818; for Selkirk's thesis is that, although he had formerly believed in Parliamentary reform, he no longer does after having witnessed the operation of more nearly free suffrage in the United States.

Times of yesterday on account of the German's paper about Schill.[22]
What a pity that he does not tell more!—When he does, I will send
him.—Is not there not something very ludicrous in the preamble of Ld.
Erskine's Bill?—with his lawyer's *whereas-es?* [23]

Again, dear Madam, God bless you! and farewell.

Yours respectfully—Thos. de Quincey.

Stewart the traveller [24] showed me some American pamphlets—and,
among them, one containing copies of documents suppressed by the
American Government in *their* account of the negociations with France
on the neutral rights' question—from which it appears that, whilst the
Americans were bullying us in England, Gen. Armstrong [25] was submitting to the utmost insolence from Bonaparte's ministers.—He says
himself, in answer to one copy of instructions sent him from home, that
he is well aware of the irreconciliability of Bonaparte's edicts with the
neutral rights; but that every minister of Bonaparte's had declared that
he dared not communicate Gen. A's remonstrances to Bonap.—from
the violence of his temper and his brutal modes of expressing it.

[*Address:*] Mrs. Wordsworth / Grasmere / Westmoreland

[22] See Letter 31, note 10. The *Times* for May 30 published a letter signed
L.T.T., which praised Schill and enlisted English support for *der neuen
Zeitgeist* in Germany.

[23] Lord Thomas Erskine on May 15 moved the second reading of a bill
to prevent "malicious and wanton cruelty to animals," with a Preamble
which began, "Whereas it has pleased Almighty God to subdue to the
dominion, use and comfort of man . . . ; and whereas the abuse of that
dominion. . . ." The Preamble was printed in an article on the bill which
appeared in the *Times* for May 30, adjacent to the letter on Schill.

[24] See Letter 31, note 1.

[25] John Armstrong, U.S. Minister to France, 1804–1810.

CHAPTER THREE

✍ ESTRANGEMENT

All the time De Quincey was laboring in London, the women of Wordsworth's household were preparing Dove Cottage for his return. How he must have savored the pronoun when Sara wrote, "your Orchard . . . is the most beautiful spot upon earth." Dorothy kept him informed on the progress of carpets, calico bedcurtains, and deal bookcases—he would have preferred mahogany, but the prudent Dorothy thought it extravagant. By August 1 she could report, "your house is quite ready, or rather it will be so in two or three days." For some time before that he had been half-expected in Grasmere, with especial eagerness by the children: little Tommy lisped his name, and John was learning "Chevy Chase" to recite to him. He was also supposed, according to Dorothy, to accompany Wordsworth and Wilson on a trip to Ireland.[1]

For all that, he characteristically delayed, remaining in London until the beginning of July. First he was held up by a bizarre episode concerning his brother Richard, who was just back from a lurid career at sea and refused to meet his family, so that his mother thought he must be an impostor. Then De Quincey dawdled another three weeks in deepest dejection at the thought of packing his books, before he finally got himself off to Wrington for a visit with his family in their new home, Westhay. There he found his mother indulging in her favorite pastime of remodeling another house, so that they all played musical chairs from one room to another ahead of the decorators. Despite this inconvenience, Thomas stayed on, suffering from an eye infection which terrified him with thoughts of approaching blindness, then feeling trapped in a round of "visiting debts," and at last remaining to be with his sailor brother, who had finally come home. On September 30 he wrote that he expected to be in Grasmere almost as soon as his letter; but on October 18, when he actually sent the letter, he had got only as far as Bristol. He probably did go on to Grasmere within a few days, for on November 18 Dorothy said that he had been there five weeks.

Was De Quincey's delay in moving into his new-furbished cottage symptomatic of some sense of grievance, foreshadowing the bitterness that was to come amid the "sweet solitudes" of Westmorland? The general assumption of the London correspondence had been that he would fly to Grasmere. On May 10 Wordsworth himself hoped that De Quincey would "soon" be back. The fact that Dorothy was reduced toward the end of June to begging, "do write, if but three lines, to tell us how you are," [2] may suggest some pique; but there were, as we have seen, other sufficient reasons to explain De Quincey's tardiness. As the Wordsworth circle was coming to realize, however, reasons were hardly necessary to account for his procrastination. Coleridge wrote to his wife in 1810, "between ourselves, he is as great a *To-morrower* to the full as your poor Husband." [3] Furthermore, letters on both sides, if somewhat less frequent, continued cordial. De Quincey still tried to entertain, as with vignettes of the "Holy Hannah" menage near Westhay; he was fiercely loyal to Coleridge's then appearing *Friend;* and he even paid a pilgrimage to Alfoxden to report on the condition of the Wordsworths' former home. No letter from William in the period has survived, but Dorothy wrote chattily reminding De Quincey to bring tea and silver spoons (which he apparently forgot) ; and Mary, visiting at Elleray, added a note to Wilson's letter in September: "All has been in readiness for you, and every one of us wishing to see you for a long, long time" (*MY*, I, 341).

The pamphlet episode undoubtedly left its scars: the kindness of the women may even have been in part self-consciously conpensatory. Limitations and deficiencies had been recognized on both sides; more care was being taken by both parties. But care is a gravel that wears down friendships. Nevertheless, De Quincey returned ostensibly on the old footing, almost as "one of the family," able to move right in. For when he arrived the "readiness" at Dove Cottage did not extend to a housekeeper and, as Dorothy put it, "he grew tired of that plan and lately has been wholly with us." [4] More than a month he stayed at Allan Bank, before Charles Lloyd's cook, Mary Dawson, arrived and proudly took over as housekeeper for the "far learn'd" young man. Mary had been a former servant of the Wordsworths, and had been elevated by Dorothy's selection; thus she was another link with the Allan Bank family, although, as it proved, an unreliable one.

The relationship into which De Quincey settled down at Grasmere was partly independent and partly symbiotic. He might have come to the Lakes even if there had been no Wordsworth: as he wrote, "from my earliest days, it was not extravagant to say that I had hungered and thirsted" for mountains. Although he was "the poorest of naturalists" —probably his nearsightedness had something to do with that—he read the mysterious hieroglyphics of nature in "innumerable solitary roamings." [5] He confessed also to a "nympholepsy" for the Lake Country, and sought to claim a sort of kinship with the region because his native Lancashire at least sent the tongue of Furness up toward the Lakes. But later he wrote simply, "the direct object of my own residence at the lakes was the society of Mr. Wordsworth." This seems to have been understood at the time, for Dorothy told him bluntly about the possibility of their having to give up Allan Bank: *"you* will be left in the lurch, for if we quit this house there is no prospect but of our quitting *Grasmere."* [6]

To her friend Jane Marshall, however, Dorothy was equally frank about the reciprocal advantages of having De Quincey at Dove Cottage: "we have now almost a home still, at the old and dearest spot of all." Before De Quincey arrived, as they were to do later in his absences, the Wordsworths made free with his cottage. And when he showed up with nine or ten chests of books and nineteen or more on the road, Dorothy understandably thought, "it is a great pleasure to us all to have access to such a library, and will be a solid advantage to my Brother." Coleridge, especially, exploited this advantage, sometimes having as many as 500 of De Quincey's books at Allan Bank.[7]

Reciprocity, of course, suited De Quincey exactly; he was glad his cottage was "useful," as he was generally anxious to please and willing to serve. Mary wrote, "Dorothy told me that I might, upon your return, receive a supply of Cash from you, you having been unable to procure for them at Manchester the full change for a bill." Instead of paying all the Dove Cottage furnishing bills through his own banker, he appears to have paid some through Richard Wordsworth, probably advancing the cash at Grasmere. In March 1810 he was writing to ask Charles Lloyd to perform a commission for Dorothy in Kendal; in August he was offering to make purchases for the Wordsworths in Liverpool. In November he was apparently holding the fort at Grasmere while the family were at Elleray, having fled from a fever. They relayed through him messages about butter, their dirty linen, and even their servant's finances: "Pray ask Sarah if she wants money. If she does, be so good as to let her have 5 or 10 shillings, or whatever she may want." [8]

De Quincey also threw himself into the social life of the Wordsworth circle, becoming especially friendly with another early, but apostate, disciple of Coleridge, the unbalanced Charles Lloyd; and with another youthful admirer of Wordsworth, the versatile John Wilson. Since 1807 he had known Lloyd, whose sister was married to Wordsworth's brother Christopher, but who was not a favorite with the Wordsworths. The connection between the young men became "close and intimate," [9] so much so that in 1818, when Lloyd escaped from an insane asylum, he came to De Quincey. Wilson, whom De Quincey had met at Allan Bank in 1808, invited him, at Wordsworth's suggestion, to join an unrealized expedition to Spain the next year. After De Quincey settled at the Lakes the two men saw a great deal of each other, and De Quincey became fond of the athletic and hearty Wilson, who in size would have made nearly two of him. Wilson and the Wordsworths were to participate in a gala Christmas Day housewarming of Dove Cottage— Dorothy wrote in happy anticipation, "We shall dine in the parlour below stairs." [10] The Christmas festivities, however, were shifted to Wilson's home at Elleray, where the Wordsworths and the Cooksons from Kendal made such a crowd that De Quincey had to sleep in Bowness with his host— setting a pattern for subsequent rambles on which they often shared the same room. In 1813 De Quincey lent Wilson £200 he could ill afford, and in after years received substantial favors in return. Although De Quincey later showed a strange undercurrent of antagonism to Wilson, he also came to think of him as a colleague in pioneer appreciation of and disillusionment with Wordsworth, and spoke of him as his "only close male friend." [11]

On the other hand, De Quincey was never close to Southey —there was something "a little too freezing" in his reserve. But neither was Wordsworth at this time intimate with his Derwent neighbor. De Quincey was at least on friendly terms.[12]

Understandably eager to introduce his family into this circle, the first summer after he moved into Dove Cottage De Quincey went to Westhay with the intention of bringing back his mother and sisters. They did not come then, but in the summer of 1811 paid a visit epitomized by Sara's remark: "This afternoon another *route* at Mr de Qu's." [13] The Wordsworths did the honors nobly. They invited the De Quinceys to tea in their new Grasmere home, the Rectory; they came to Dove Cottage to tea; and Dorothy and

Sara even "went to Ewedale" with the visitors to drink tea. Perhaps the poet sounds constrained: "The Misses de Quincey have just called, and I must walk with them to the Waterfall at Ghyll-side"—but what he *must* do he did gallantly. Mary De Quincey brought the Wordsworths two birch trees, and William himself responded with roots of *Osmunda regalis* on the day of their departure. So warm was this reception that after her return home Mary wrote to her brother begging to be remembered "most affectionately" to the Wordsworths. Such cordiality, of course, speaks eloquently of De Quincey's status for the first year or so of his residence in Grasmere. It is summarized in his easy use of "we" for himself and the Wordsworths in a letter of May 31, 1811, to Southey: "We received the Gazette last night and were a little disappointed by it: Wordsworth indeed was greatly mortified." [14]

On De Quincey's first New Year's Eve in Dove Cottage he put on an exhibition of fireworks for all the children of the vale. Sara declared "Mr de Quincey's House was like a fair." Thus he acted his enjoyed role of favorite with the Wordsworth children. Besides sending Johnny pictures from London, he had promised to bring him a cap and offered to teach him how to swim, sail a kite, walk on stilts, and—with the aid of his brother Richard—sail a boat. Later he undertook to teach him Latin. He was also fond of "dear Sissy" and "little Totts," to whom undoubtedly went the "Childers Carridge" for which Edward Wilson charged De Quincey six shillings in 1809.[15] In the summer of 1810 he stood as godparent, along with John Wilson, to the last of Wordsworth's children, William Junior. But he claimed as his own the child who was the youngest when he came into the Wordsworth orbit—Catharine, born on September 8, 1808. She seemed to him "an impersonation of the dawn and the spirit of infancy." Cathy was quite different in appearance from the other children, and the family thought her a bit odd-looking; Wordsworth called her his little "Chinese maiden." But De Quincey, as Sara reported, thought "Kate *beautiful*," [16] and Mary promised that the

child's education would be left to him. His character with
the young Wordsworths is charmingly suggested by a letter
Mary wrote to him in August, 1810, when he was at Westhay: "all . . . will be delighted at your return. John was
in extacies when I read him from your letter [apparently
lost] that his artillery was not forgotten. D.[orothy] talks
for ever about her Doll. C.[atharine] went through every
room in the cottage the other day to seek you, she even pulled
off the counterpane to see if you were in bed." [17]

The Wordsworths seemed to welcome and respect De
Quincey's love for their children, although they came to
doubt its practical reliability. When his favorite Catharine
died in June 1813, Dorothy felt he ought to know at once,
and wrote "you must bear the sad tidings . . . I wish you
had been here to follow your Darling to her Grave." Six
months later when Thomas Wordsworth failed to survive
the measles, William wrote to De Quincey the same night,
"Pray come to us as soon as you can," and concluded, "Most
tenderly and truly, with heavy sorrow for you, my dear
friend." [18] This curious expression of a father's sorrow for
a friend's loss at the death of one of his children may reflect
Wordsworth's memories of De Quincey's reaction when
Cathy died. For William and De Quincey were both in London then, and had commiserated with each other. Wordsworth apparently came with Crabb Robinson to inform De
Quincey, found that Dorothy had already given him the
news, then came back that night to talk. Robinson reported
that De Quincey "burst into tears on seeing Wordsworth and
seemed to be more affected than the father." [19]

This scene points up a temperamental difference which
was a cause of friction between the two men: De Quincey
was so much more effusive, Wordsworth so much more
practical. Wordsworth grieved for Cathy, but he had learned
the duty of resignation, that "the Gods approve / The depth,
and not the tumult, of the soul." He probably reflected that
she was a cripple, that had she recovered from the convulsions that caused her death she would—as Dorothy believed
—not "have retained the Faculties of her Mind," and con-

sidered that a wise Providence had ordained her death.[20]
De Quincey's tears were doubtless sincere, but one suspects
a touch of perhaps unconscious dramatization. Here was
the area in which he was fully accepted, his nearest approach
to the center of the Wordsworth circle, and he made the
most of it. He got off a letter to Dorothy immediately,
begging more details. The next day he began a long letter of
tender memories of Catharine and "happy hours" passed
with her—and bitter memories of Mary Dawson's unkind-
ness to the child. Then after he had Dorothy's more circumstantial account, he carefully wrote on June 21 an even more
impassioned outpouring of grief, rising to "Oh that I could
have died for her or with her!" Wordsworth probably re-
acted to this outburst in somewhat the same way that Robinson did to De Quincey's conversation—certainly on the
same subject—when they dined together on June 17: "his
sensibility, which I have no doubt is genuine, is in danger of
being mistaken for a puling and womanly weakness." [21]

The genuineness of De Quincey's sensibility is not necessarily impugned by the curious fact that this emotional letter
of June 21 exists in a complete draft, a partial draft, and
the sent version—but the circumstance implies some artistic
control. The mere existence of a draft is not remarkable:
De Quincey sometimes felt it necessary to belabor a rough
draft of so simple a thing as a note to Charles Lloyd about
ordering silver spoons. Three documents, however, suggest
his special eagerness to say just the right thing. Since the
complete draft is closer to the final letter than is the partial
draft, it appears that the latter was written first and
abandoned midway—probably because De Quincey caught
himself going into a personal digression that was off key.
Since he discarded the sheet and began again, he probably
thought of himself as writing a fair copy; and the complete
draft is relatively clean. Still it would not do. He copied it
over, making small changes—largely stylistic—and leaving
out a request that Mary Dawson be instructed to get mourning if she had not done so.

Little Catharine was really the perigee of De Quincey's

Wordsworthian orbit, and her short life almost coincident with the period of vital relationship. After her death De Quincey "returned hastily to Grasmere," and "every night, for more than two months running" stretched himself upon her grave. He conjured up her image from foxgloves and ferns, and generally indulged in such a luxurious "self-surrender to passion" that he became ill. Whether we credit De Quincey's diagnosis of his malady as "nympholepsy," or the modern speculation that he had poliomyelitis,[22] the whole affair shows pathetically his need for uncritical love, and for close identification with the world of the Wordsworths.

Although in this history of sacrificial service and studied intimacy the most prominent actors seems to have been women and children of the household, De Quincey also had significant contact with Wordsworth himself. In "May or June of 1810," for instance, he invited the poet to meet the French traveler, M. Simond—probably typical of the hospitality of his early years at Grasmere. He was still giving Wordsworth books. The poet's copy of James Burgh's *Political Disquisitions* is inscribed, "From Thomas De Quincey to William Wordsworth, Grasmere, Friday, June 22—1810." The familiarity of this traffic in books is amusingly suggested by Wordsworth's rueful remark to Crabb Robinson years later: "two Vols. of my Carendon had fallen into the Opium eaters hands they were however I believe a present from him so I have not much reason to complain in this case." [23] There was also traffic in talk and ideas, as on the nights the two men walked up Dunmail Raise to meet the carrier from Keswick. One such night, when Wordsworth rose in disappointment after having listened with ear to the ground for the sound of the carrier's wheels, his eye was caught by a bright star hung over Helvellyn. On the spot he gave De Quincey a discourse on the psychological fact of the acute perceptivity of the senses at the moment of relaxation after a tense effort.[24] Understandably De Quincey later boasted of having walked with the poet "both in the night and the day," and proudly claimed "daily nay hourly intercourse with William Wordsworth—the sublimest intellect and the most majestic, even if far from the most active, since the days of Milton." [25]

As De Quincey settled into his Grasmere routine, intimacy between the neighbors persisted; but there began to develop more awareness of temperamental differences, and of the younger man's dissatisfaction with the disciple's role. Although the poet moved on May 1, 1813, to Rydal Mount, which was to be his home for the rest of his life, he was still only something over two miles from Dove Cottage. De Quincey mentions a jaunt with Wordsworth through Legberthwaite Vale in 1813, and an undated "fine summer day" when he, Wordsworth, and Southey were "walking together." Indeed, if we can take "many years" at all literally, De Quincey long continued to have discussions with Wordsworth on matters of poetry and nature. For he records telling the poet of a miraculous transformation of the scene from above Scor Crag when he happened to view it at four o'clock on a summer afternoon, as he had not chanced to do "for many years." [26] Since, however, Wordsworth deflated him by declaring that he had repeatedly witnessed the same misty transfiguration, this anecdote presents a picture of De Quincey trying to meet Wordsworth on his own ground and being more or less snubbed as a novice.

That sort of belittling happened, and De Quincey resented it, just as he had some of the poet's peremptory behavior over the *Convention of Cintra*. An interesting ambivalence in this relationship shows in James Hogg's story of the appearance of an unusual display of northern lights in the fall of 1814 when he was visiting Wordsworth at Rydal Mount, along with Wilson, Lloyd, De Quincey, and other "literary gentlemen." Hogg says he essayed the pleasantry that the manifestation was "in honour of the meeting of the poets," and would never forgive Wordsworth for taking De Quincey aside to ask, "Poets? poets? What does the fellow mean? Where are they?" But he adds, "I have always some hopes that De Quincey was *leeing,* for I did not myself hear Wordsworth utter the words." [27] Hogg pictures De Quincey as the intimate of Wordsworth: the poet had his arm and took him aside for a personal remark. Yet Hoggs thinks De Quincey may have been lying maliciously. Even if he was not, he was at least betraying a confidence and showing Wordsworth in a bad light. Wilson printed the story in *Noctes Ambrosianae* and, according to John Gibson Lockhart, "Wordsworth took mighty offense at that matter." Of course De Quincey might not have told the anecdote until later, but he invited Hogg and Wilson to dine with him at Grasmere on September 22, 1814, and probably they all laughed at Wordsworth over a glass.[28]

Something in Wordsworth—De Quincey called it pride —seemed to hold the disciple off. De Quincey was made to feel in little ways that he did not "belong" even yet. He was galled, for instance, at Wordsworth's refusal to repeat to him something he had just told Southey about Lloyd, on the grounds that it was "not quite proper to be communicated except to *near friends of the family"*:

This to me! O ye gods!—to me, who knew by many a hundred conversations how disagreeable Wordsworth was both to Charles Lloyd and to his wife; whilst, on the other hand—not by words only, but by deeds, and by the most delicate acts of confidential favour—I knew that Mr. Wilson (Professor Wilson) and myself had been selected as friends in cases which were not so much as named to Wordsworth. The arrogance of Wordsworth was well illustrated in this case of the Lloyds (M, II, 389).

The same kind of refusal to accept him as an initiate showed in Wordsworth's more generally irksome tendency to arrogate to himself and his family, it seemed to De Quincey, the sole prerogative of intelligent comment on nature and the picturesque. When others essayed opinions "he did not even appear to listen; but, as if what they said on such a theme must be childish prattle, turned away with an air of perfect indifference; began talking, perhaps, with another person on another subject." The image is ludicrous: De Quincey, who fancied himself a "doctor seraphicus . . . upon quillets of logic," fine-spinning some theory such as the relation between the picturesque and the characteristic, until the bored poet could stand it no longer. If De Quincey indeed constructed the conversational fairylands which Christopher North put in his mouth in *Noctes Ambrosianae,* one can hardly blame Wordsworth. On the other hand, it is not surprising that De Quincey found such treatment "difficult to bear." He took his revenge later by writing: "Never describe Wordsworth as equal in pride to Lucifer: no; but, if you have occasion to write a life of Lucifer, set down that by possibility, in respect to pride, he might be some type of Wordsworth." [29]

In the same disgruntled vein De Quincey in his last years recalled to J. R. Findley that he had offered Wordsworth an account of the "origin and character of the language of the Lake district" for the early version of the poet's *Guide through the District of the Lakes* (published in 1810 as an introduction to Joseph Wilkinson's *Select Views of Cumberland, Westmoreland and Lancashire*), but "Wordsworth, who never liked to be obliged to anybody for anything, declined it in his usual haughty and discourteous manner." [30]

What especially irritated De Quincey about the poet's pontifical behavior was that he had no redress; if De Quincey protested, or sought to enter into any justification for his own conduct, he would be met with, "I will have nothing to do with fending and proving." [31] Now De Quincey delighted in nothing so much as the exercise of "fending and proving." One of the temperamental and intellectual differences between the two men was that in a certain sense De Quincey lived the life of the mind, which fed on distinctions, and Wordsworth the life of the spirit, which was nourished by certainties. De Quincey was rather like Peacock's Mr. Flosky—a caricature of Coleridge—in that he delighted in things that could not be made clear. Wordsworth was by comparison much more direct and, in an elemental manner, simple. His blacks and whites bothered De Quincey, and De Quincey's shifting grays annoyed him.

These temperamental cross-purposes showed up also in

certain differences in taste. Wordsworth had by then outgrown his Gothic period; De Quincey never left his behind.
The disciple, with his dreamy, feminine orientation toward
sentimental "horror" tales, could not appreciate the bluffer,
more masculine tastes of his master. He was shocked that
Wordsworth should laugh at Mrs. Radcliffe's *The Italian*
and not comprehend Schiller's *Wallenstein,* but delight in
Smollett, Fielding, and Le Sage, whom De Quincey found
"so disgusting by their moral scenery and the whole stage
of vicious society in which they keep the reader moving."
And he was hurt when he took to the poet Harriett Lee's
"splendid" story "The German's Tale," expecting him to
admire the "unrivaled" narration, only to be told "coldly
enough, that it left an uncomfortable impression of a woman
as being too clever." [32]

Thus the curious chemistry of this relationship was becoming more obvious. Between the two men there was at
least as much repulsion as attraction. The poet had his own
world into which the younger man could not enter very far
without being a disrupting influence, and that was not to be
tolerated. It is not strange that De Quincey wrote, "never
after the first year or so from my first introduction had I
felt much possibility of drawing the bonds of friendship
tight with a man of Wordsworth's nature." [33] Still, although
the bonds could not be drawn tight, they were real, and
De Quincey says he determined to "rest contentedly" with
what he had, expecting no more.

Whatever intimations Wordsworth may have had of the
younger man's dissatisfaction, early in 1815 he was still
speaking of De Quincey as his friend, and attempting to
make use of his intelligent discipleship. He wrote to Daniel
Stuart, "at the wish of Mr. De Quincey . . . a friend of
mine," asking that room be found in the *Courier* for a
series of letters by De Quincey on the "stupidities, the ignorance, and the dishonesties of *The Edinburgh Review,*"
and assuring him that "the Letters will be a credit to any
Publication, for Mr De. Q. is a *remarkably* able man." [34]
These attacks on Jeffrey, however, have a long and mysterious history that sketches a wry microcosm of the world

of De Quincey and the Wordsworths. Dorothy had first suggested such a defense of Wordsworth to De Quincey back in May, 1809, and he had avidly agreed, proposing by May 27 to include stupidities of other reviewers of Wordsworth, so that Jeffrey might not have the satisfaction of being singled out (p. 158). Crabb Robinson records that on February 4, 1814, De Quincey told him he was going to publish "in the *Courier* the attack on Jeffrey for his treatment of Wordsworth." By March, 1815, according to Dorothy, the "proof" was "actually in the hands of the Editor," and De Quincey's mother wrote on September 9, 1815, asking whether his "Papers" had appeared in the *Courier*.[35] They did not appear, and in 1818 De Quincey informed Wordsworth that he was still "finishing that course of Letters" which he had begun in February, 1815, but put aside because the public interest was dominated by Napoleon's escape (Letter 51). The letters were never finished, but undoubtedly parts of them were later incorporated in articles on Wordsworth, as for example the ridicule of Jeffrey's comment on "There was a boy." [36] The uncompleted project stands as a symbol of the De Quincey-Wordsworth relationship, betokening his too often futile desire to be of service, and their too often impatient desire to use his real abilities.

Appropriately, therefore, Crabb Robinson called De Quincey, when he met him in London in February, 1814, "a disciple and admirer" of Wordsworth, who talked of him "with the zeal and intelligence of a well-instructed pupil." [37] For the relationship still remained uneasily what it had been in Manchester Grammar School days—master and disciple. The principals knew each other much better, but even that operated as a bar to closer association. Although, as we have seen, De Quincey wrote later that he had recognized that this could never be a close friendship between equals, he probably never quite accepted that fact —and therein lay the difficulty. Certainly he was disciple in residence, and that was no mean thing. He continued to cherish the notion that there was something unique about his position: "Except, therefore, with the Lloyds, or occasionally with Thomas Wilkinson the Quaker, or very rarely with Southey, Wordsworth had no intercourse at all beyond the limits of Grasmere; and in that valley I was myself, for some years, his sole visiting friend." [38] A revealing passage deleted from his autobiography makes a contorted effort to prove that he was actually closer to Wordsworth than was Coleridge:

During much of this period I was more intimately connected with this great man than any other person, not being a member of his family, can pretend to have been. Coleridge even I need not except, for Coleridge might almost come within the case I have allowed for of being a member of the family. . . . Were it otherwise, and if Coleridge were viewed as a stranger, in that case I should have the advantage even of *him*: for I was ahead of him by several years in the mere duration of my connexion with Wordsworth: and in another point I had a still greater advantage over Coleridge, which was—that I made use of my time without willingly losing any part of it. . . . Whereas Coleridge passed much of the day in bed: at night he was always immersed in books: and either by day or by night he rarely walked. [39]

The validity of this analysis is, of course, suspect; but the feeling behind it is important. The ultimate bitterness owed much to De Quincey's disillusioned sense of Wordsworth's ingratitude for unique and peculiar services of discipleship and friendship.

An inevitable process of realignment in the Wordsworth-De Quincey relationship began with his initial arrival at Grasmere, when the Wordsworths found him an "insignificant"-appearing little man addicted to leaving his greatcoat behind, and he got the first intimation that, as he put it later, "Men of extraordinary genius and force of mind are far better as objects for distant admiration than as daily companions." [40] The *Convention of Cintra* episode wrought further adjustment, and De Quincey's settling in Dove Cottage seemed to establish a *status quo* of friendly, if not frictionless, relationship. By 1816, however, all personal relations between the two seemed to have been broken off. What happened? As in the affairs of nations, there was a

gradual worsening of relations and a final "incident." The
incident in this case was De Quincey's liaison with Margaret
Simpson, the daughter of a local farmer. But there is much
more to the story. There were misunderstandings and hard
feelings, and there was the purple specter of laudanum.

Years later De Quincey blamed Wordsworth's alienation
from him on the influence of "female prejudices." Certainly
the first definite rumbling in the Grasmere Elysium came
from the women, and it came long before Peggy Simpson
entered the picture. By December, 1811, Sara Hutchinson seems to have been sharply antagonistic toward De
Quincey.[41] The immediate provocation was that the new
master of Dove Cottage had laid sacrilegious hands upon
the shrine:

What do you say to de Q's having polled the Ash Tree & cut down
the hedge all round the orchard—every Holly, Heckberry, Hazel, &
every twig that skreened it—& all for the sake of the Apple trees that
he may have a few more Apples. . . . D.[orothy] is so hurt and angry
that she can never speak to him more: & truly it was a most unfeeling
thing when he knew how much store they set by that orchard (*SH,*
pp. 36 f.).

This dastardly deed released upon De Quincey's head other
disapprobation. Sara went on later in the same letter,
"Quincey . . . is very fond of her [Cathy] but yet does
not like to be plagued with her when he feels anything like
a duty which he had engaged to teach her to read &c, towards her—but he will contrive some how or other to shake
this off for he lives only for himself and his Books. He
used to talk of escorting Mary into Wales but I do not believe that she will have his company."

What a change is this! From being a "good tempered
amiable creature" and "one of the family," De Quincey is
persona non grata. Dorothy will not speak to him, Mary
will not accept his company, and Sara rather contemptu-
ously refers to him as "Quince" and "Peter." The storm in
the apple orchard of course subsided, and Dorothy did see
De Quincey again, although she was apparently angry
enough to refuse to come down when he called soon after

the mutilation. She still seemed cool on the following April 23 when she forwarded to William, already arrived in London, a letter which De Quincey had written from there giving a delightful analysis of coach services for the benefit of the poet's journey: "As this letter contains little more than information, to you now useless, I should not think it worth sending, but as it is written so plain I can write across, and perhaps it may save you the trouble of enquiring after the writer." [42] Yet, interestingly, she assumes that Wordsworth might inquire after De Quincey.

Sara's charge that De Quincey lived only for himself must, however, have reflected an abiding opinion. It is otherwise difficult to understand Dorothy's attitude in February of 1813. She wrote with a half-humorous sarcasm of De Quincey's performance as John's teacher:

He now goes to Mr. de Quincey for a *nominal hour* every day to learn Latin upon a plan of Mr. de Quincey's own 'by which a Boy of the most moderate abilities may be made a good latin scholar in six weeks!!!!' This said nominal hour now generally is included in the space of twenty minutes; either the scholar learns with such uncommon rapidity that more time is unnecessary, or the Master tires. Which of these conjectures is the more probable I leave you to guess (*MY*, II, 549–550).

But there is neither humor nor understanding in her report: "Mary Dawson talks in private to us of leaving Mr. de Quincey. . . . She is tired of Mr. de Q's meanness and greediness." It is surprising enough to see Dorothy repeating Molly Dawson's complaint without a murmur of objection, for meanness and greediness were not qualities of De Quincey's, and he had certainly been more than generous to the Wordsworths. Her attitude probably stems from hard feelings over the use of De Quincey's home. The Wordsworths apparently continued to regard Dove Cottage almost as a guest house; as late as 1817 when De Quincey took his bride there Dorothy wrote pettishly, "they . . . are now spending their honeymoon in our cottage." [43] De Quincey had always assured the Wordsworths that they were welcome to use the house when, as often happened, he was in London or Westhay. Molly, however, was telling them something different, as he explained years later in a helpless little essay which has been given the title of "Gradual Estrangement from Wordsworth." There, ironically, he accuses *her* of being "selfish and mean," and suiting her own importance and convenience by claiming that the "master" had given orders which made it possible for her to be spared the trouble of unwanted guests.

In his apologia De Quincey put all the blame on Molly, protested the futility of trying to combat the acceptance of her tales by friends who should have known him better, and even declared: "I began to despise a little some of those who had been silly and undiscerning enough to accredit such representations; and one of them especially, who, though liberally endowed with sunshiny temper and sweetness of disposition, was perhaps a person weak intellectually beyond the ordinary standards of female weakness" [44]—probably Mary. But undoubtedly there was another explanation —money. De Quincey's small fortune had almost disappeared. As early as June 8, 1811, he apologized to his brother for having to expect the return of a two-pound loan, "but my present income is so limited that every shilling is important to me." In 1818 he wrote to his mother, "the last penny of my fortune was gone in 1815." [45] Apparently he did not let his Lake friends know just how low his finances were; it was in May, 1813, that he generously lent Wilson £200. De Quincey did not indeed pretend to be a man of wealth: when Butterlip How was put up for sale, and Mary reported that Molly Dawson was sure he would buy it, he replied that the house was "far above" his powers (Letter 36). The Wordsworths, however, probably continued to think of him as a man of means, judging quite naturally by his books and the "scarlet Cloaks and silk Pelisses" which so impressed Sara when the De Quincey ladies came to visit. He, on the other hand, conscious of his vanishing capital, probably suggested economies to Molly which were misunderstood and translated into greed, meanness, and inhospitality.

As the Wordsworth women came to have a lower opinion of De Quincey's character, they had, naturally, less patience with his faults. Dorothy's wonted goodness is missing in an acid summary of April, 1815:

Mr de Quincey, notwithstanding his learning and his talents, can do
nothing; he is eaten up by the spirit of procrastination; but if once
in two or three years he actually does make an effort, he is so slow a
labourer that no one who knows him would wish to appoint him to it;
if it might not as well be 3 months in hand as three hours; though in
itself but the work of one sitting for another person (*MY*, II, 665).

Nor does there seem much kindness in the remark a month
earlier when De Quincey had just returned from a visit to
Westhay and brought news of Hannah More's approval
of *The Excursion:* "As usual Peter is very entertaining,
now that he is fresh." [46] Obviously she found him sometimes wearing. Sara, in November of the same year, is even
more uncharitable:

Quince has gone off to Edinburgh at last with Mr Wilson who was in
the neighborhood about a fortnight . . . he was tolerably steady
though Quince was often tipsey & in one of his fits has lost his gold
Watch val: 60 Gs which was given him (being his Uncles) as being
according to his own [words] *'the very properest person'* to take care
o[f i]t. We believe that he will marry Peggy S[impson] after all—
He doses himself with Opium & drinks like a f[ish]—and tries in all
other things to be as great a [*torn*] legs as Mr Wilson (*SH*, p. 88).

How objective Sara's reporting was is hard to determine.
De Quincey was not wont to drink like a fish, but he may
have been dosing himself with laudanum, a solution of al-
cohol and opium. The Wordsworths had at least suspected
his opium-eating for more than a year. When Mary and
William went to visit him during an illness in October, 1814,
Mary recognized the symptoms she had seen too much in
Coleridge. Irritation is patent in her report to Dorothy:
"Mr S [Scambler, the apothecary?] says he has a
diar[rhea], such a one no doubt as C's—and from the same

cause, so I hinted not very darkly to him." De Quincey
later "confessed" that "the Paradise of Opium-eaters" had
first been laid open to him in 1804, when he visited the
seraphic druggist of Oxford Street to obtain a remedy for
facial neuralgia, and that he used the drug intermittently
and luxuriously for about ten years thereafter.[47] All of the
examples which he gives of his opium "debauches," however, occurred in London and among strangers; probably
he did not mention these exploits to his friends and family.
Even Coleridge, who might have been considered a privi-
leged initiate, seems to have had no more than suspicions;
and in 1809 De Quincey disingenuously wrote to William
of the disturbing effect of having "unavoidably" swallowed
laudanum from soaked cotton pads he was holding in his
mouth to allay a toothache. His dissipation must, however,
have been difficult to hide after 1813, when he became "a
regular and confirmed" opium-eater out of the necessity to
assuage "a most apalling irritation of the stomach." [48] In
the next two years—from a chain reaction of bad health
and bad spirits over the interrelated problems of his
financial difficulties, his connection with Peggy Simpson, and
his relationship with the Wordsworths—he raised his daily
consumption to 8,000 drops of laudanum.

The Wordsworths viewed De Quincey's addiction with
regret, condemnation, and even mockery. How soon they
could do more than hint "not very darkly," is uncertain,
but at least by 1816 De Quincey had abandoned all attempt
at dissimulation. On September 22 he wrote to Crabb Robinson apologizing for appointing 1:15 as an hour of meeting at Ambleside, because his "opium diet" prevented him
from rousing himself early.[49] Since to tell Robinson anything was to tell Wordsworth, the cat was clearly out of the
bag at Rydal Mount. Dorothy wrote sadly in 1817: "he is
utterly changed in appearance, and takes largely of opium."
In 1821 when De Quincey returned a publicized opium-
eater, however, Sara recorded sarcastically, "He tells Miss
W. that he had entirely left off opium before he came
hither, but has been obliged to have recourse to it again;

'as he has *no Shoes* to walk in & without exercise he is obliged to take it'—I suppose it is *easier* to send to the Druggists than to the Shoe Makers." William did not take the matter so lightly. Crabb Robinson noted on September 5, 1816: "I had read a bad account of him from Wordsworth, whom he has not seen for a long time. It appears that he has taken to opium, and, like Coleridge, seriously injured his health." [50]

The comparison with Coleridge was no doubt significant in the Wordsworth thinking. They had had experiences with one opium-eater—heart-breaking, irritating experiences. They had struggled through the *Friend,* suffered Coleridge's disruptive habits and the drain upon Sara Hutchinson, and they had given up. Coleridge put down in his notebook: "W.[ordsworth] authorized M.[ontagu] to tell me, he had no Hope of me!" [51] Wordsworth denied giving any such authorization; he merely intended to prevent misunderstandings by warning Basil Montagu what kind of a house guest he was taking to London. Still, the sentiment was accurate enough, and it was undoubtedly Coleridge's realization of that fact rather than Montagu's ineptness which brought an unpleasant rupture between the two poets that had been patched up but never really healed. All that, the Wordsworths did not want to go through again. Probably, on the other side of the coin, De Quincey's reaction was also conditioned by the comparison of himself to Coleridge, which was encouraged by renewed contacts in London.

De Quincey went to London in April, 1812, with the intention of mending his fortunes through the Law, and entered himself on June 12 at the Middle Temple. Since his notion of keeping a term was "masticating for three days in the Hall" (Letter 37), he never got very far in the legal profession. Keeping terms, however, sent him to London several times, where he frequently saw Coleridge; he mentions occasions in June, 1812, and July and August, 1813. It was most natural for Coleridge, still sore over his sense of Wordsworth's treachery, to talk of his grievances to

De Quincey. How strong the younger man's common feeling was then can only be speculated upon, but later he was
much aware of the parallel. Wordsworth was

a man so diffused amongst innumerable objects of equal attraction that
he had no cells left in his heart for strong individual attachments. I
was not singular in this feeling. Professor Wilson had become estranged from him: Coleridge, one of his earliest friends, had become
estranged: no one person could be deemed fervently his friend (M,
III, 202).

Perhaps Coleridge expressed to De Quincey feelings like
those recorded in his notebook: "It is not in nature to love
those, who after my whole manhood's service of faithful
self-sacrificing Friendship have wantonly stripped me of
all my comfort and all my hopes—and to hate them is not
in *my* nature. What remains!—to do them all the good, I
can; but with a blank heart!" [52] Surely this resembles the
note that De Quincey was to strike—distorting surprise at
the ingratitude which seemed to allow sacrifical friendship
so little weight.

For a time, however, De Quincey probably felt a gratifying superiority in his own capacity to walk gently among
the quirks of genius and "rest contented" with Wordsworth
as he found him. Alienation of others only enhanced his
position. There is a hint of gossipy complacency in his telling Crabb Robinson in February, 1815, that Wilson was
estranged from Wordsworth because the poet was offended
at Wilson's plagiarism and, "This pains Wilson, who has,
besides, peculiarities in his manners, etc., which W does
not spare." [53] The implication was that Wordsworth was a
difficult man but that he managed to keep on good terms
with him. But as Coleridge and Wilson were, so was De
Quincey to become. What temperamental differences and
opium addiction had begun, a woman finished.

Margaret Simpson was, according to Dorothy Wordsworth, "a stupid, heavy girl, and was reckoned a Dunce at
Grasmere School"; according to De Quincey, "a lovely
young woman" with "arms like Aurora's, and . . . smiles

like Hebe's." Some allowance should be made for prejudice on both sides. If we can judge by her daughters, Peggy must have been an attractive woman—perhaps large, at least in relation to De Quincey. She was, of course, not educated, and she was naïve enough to accept *The Vicar of Wakefield* as a factual narrative;[54] but she was hardly stupid. She proved capable of writing in 1824 an intelligent, if not grammatical, letter to De Quincey's publisher J. A. Hessey, and in 1832 a rather eloquent letter to the solicitors who were pressing to foreclose on her family home.[55] She was the daughter of John Simpson, who farmed his own land (making him what Westmorland called a " 'Statesman") and whose rugged radicalism later caused De Quincey some embarrassment. The Simpsons lived in the Nab, a diamond-paned cottage built in 1702, by Rydal Water under Nab Scar—just a pleasant walk from Dove Cottage.

At the Nab De Quincey found something he did not find at Rydal Mount. William was surrounded by women—in Crabb Robinson's phrase, "happy in *three wives*." De Quincey may have felt, at least subconsciously, some of the agonized jealousy which Coleridge poured out in his notebook: "O the vision of this Saturday morning—of the Bed —O cruel! is he not beloved, adored by two—& two such Beings—and must I not be beloved *near* him except as a satellite?"[56] At the Nab De Quincey was no satellite, and Peggy was kind. On November 16, 1816, "William Penson, illegitimate son of Margaret Simpson, Nab" was baptised in the Grasmere church—named for De Quincey's brother and his mother's family.[57]

The beginnings of the affair are vague, but at least by March, 1813, De Quincey had established some sort of relations with the Nab.[58] By the fall of 1814 his visits kept him late, as Wilson discovered when he walked over to Dove Cottage one night: "De Quincey was at the *Nab*, and when he returned about three o'clock, found me asleep in his bed."[59] That Christmas De Quincey begged Wilson to come to meet a party, including the Simpsons. The draft of his letter is eloquent:

My dear Friend,
         promised   will
   I have ~~engaged~~ for you that you ~~are to~~ meet a party (viz. young
                                    and others
Mrs. Jackson, Miss Huddlestone,—the family from the Nab etc.) on
Christmas eve; that is to say, to-morrow night—Saturday, Dec. 24th.
Now therefore, I conjure you, do not bring me your sponsor into
discredit, ~~by not appearing. If ever you~~ nor disappoint the company
(who are all anxious to see you), by not appearing. ~~You your you wish
to do me the greatest favor that you can~~ So may a just ~~go~~ God prosper
                        schemes
you in your Law ~~designs~~—as you attend to this request.
   This note will be delivered to you by young J. Simpson, who ~~has b~~
is kind enough to ride over on purpose.
                               Most affectionately yours,
                               Thos. de Quincey.
   Come to dinner, if you can; but, at any rate, *come*.[60]

"The family from the Nab" is not given special prominence
in the request, but it is "young J. Simpson" who rides over
on purpose, and one suspects that the "greatest favor"
Wilson could do would be to lend his social prestige to the
Simpsons. De Quincey must already have been thinking of
marrying Peggy.

At first, it appears, he tried to keep his relations with
Peggy secret. He wrote to his mother in 1818: "I had long
been attached to a young woman, and had visited her; for
some time this was undiscovered; but when it was discovered, I felt myself as much bound in honour as I was inclined by affection to marry her." [61] A curious passage in an
unpublished section of De Quincey's essay "William Wordsworth" suggests that he had some difficulty keeping his
secret from the Wordsworths. He had just described his
embarrassment at accidentally overhearing a quarrel between William and Dorothy in which Dorothy exclaimed,
"Oh ~~Brother~~ William I will walk by myself." He goes on
to say: "strange it is that in after [*torn*] years from that
time at least, I found myself in the same situation almost
every night: [*torn*] time almost a hatred for Wordsworth

as though a malicious purpose had possessed him: [*torn*]
possible unless he had corresponded with fairies, that he
should then know ~~of my~~ anything [*torn*] He could not: it
was impossible: I am sure it was: And yet oh Heavens! it
makes / it drove me crazy then, it drives me crazy now." [62]
What was it that Wordsworth could not then know without
supernatural assistance that would drive De Quincey crazy
in retrospect? It could have been his visiting Peggy. Wordsworth's malicious purpose may have been to continue to
accompany De Quincey on nights when he would have preferred to walk by himself—to an assignation. Possibly the
poet was trying to save De Quincey from an injudicious
alliance.

For certainly the Wordsworths looked upon the affair
in that light. It was perfectly understandable that they
should have. De Quincey's mother protested; Crabb Robinson referred to an "unfortunate transaction"; and Mary
Lamb wrote simply, "what a blunder the poor man made
when he took up his dwelling among the mountains." [63]
De Quincey expected such a reaction, or he would not have
tried to keep his visits to the Nab secret. When the discovery was made, probably he sought to win the approval
of the Wordsworths, even as he sought to get the social
acceptance of Wilson. When Dorothy wrote in 1817, "He
utter'd in raptures of the beauty, the good sense, the simplicity, the 'angelic sweetness' of Miss Sympson," she was
obviously referring to earlier ecstasies. Sara's remark in
November, 1815, "We believe that he will marry Peggy
S. after all," [64] implies "in spite of all we can do." He
came with his raptures, and they poured cold water—possibly even wrote to his mother. For Mrs. De Quincey awk-
wardly brought herself to remonstrate in September, 1815:

It seemed to come from high authority that you were about to marry,
and nothing short of an oracular Voice could have made us listen to
the tale, considering your want of means to meet the demands of a
family. . . . I cannot help begging you to let me know your designs,
and also to consider well before you trust the mere impulse of feeling,
if, as I have but just now heard, the sober judgment of your Friends

cannot approve the step. I can abate much of what the world demands
in marriage, but I know there are congruities which are indispensable
to *you* (*Memorials,* II, 109 f.).

After the pleasant visit of the De Quinceys in Grasmere in
1811, the Wordsworths may have felt close enough to use
the "high authority" which gave the mother word of her
son's actions contrary to the "sober judgment" of his
friends.

It has been suggested that part of the reason for the
Wordsworths' disapproval of Peggy was their expectation
that De Quincey would marry Dorothy.[65] The idea is tan-
talizing, but backed by little evidence. As early as 1809,
when Peggy was but thirteen, De Quincey's sister Jane
thought that he had some romantic interest in the Lakes.
She offered to help him furnish his cottage, "But ought not
that beautiful and wild-hearted girl to be consulted? She
certainly must have taste, and is the best judge of what
will please herself." Dorothy was consulted, and she might
well be described as "wild-hearted"—De Quincey said "she
was the very wildest (in the sense of the most natural)
person I have ever known." [66] But it is questionable whether
she could be described as "beautiful"; and she was then in
her thirty-eighth year, nearly thirteen years older than
De Quincey. Young Jane would scarcely have thought of
her as a "girl." Probably Jane knew nothing about the
matter, but merely assumed in feminine fashion that her
brother would not be furnishing a cottage to live in alone,
and conjured up an appropriate partner. De Quincey's
picture of Dorothy—although, of course, it was written
much later and may not be valid for his earlier feelings—
is not at all lover-like. He manages to give a generally favorable description, and at the same time to point out that
she often bore an "air of embarrassment, and even of self-
conflict," and that she stammered, and appeared "ungrace-
ful." Almost in so many words he says that she had no sex
appeal. He several times speaks affectionately of Dorothy,
but the tone is brotherly. He even takes refuge in numbers,
lumping himself with Wilson—"two hearts at least, that

loved and admired you in your fervid prime," he wrote in 1839, changing it to "knew and admired" in his revised *Selections*.[67]

Still, it may be worth noting that in his 1839 essay looking back on 1807, he remembered Dorothy as then "somewhere about twenty-eight years old," instead of her actual thirty-five—much more plausibly within reach of his twenty-two years. One might also be suspicious of the emphasis which De Quincey put on the blessedness and voluntary character of Dorothy's maidenhood: "Miss Wordsworth had several offers; amongst them, to my knowledge, one from Hazlitt; all of them she rejected decisively. And she did right." And one might imagine a sour-grapes note in Dorothy's comment on *Waverley*, early in 1815: "as usual the love is sickening." [68] We remember that in 1808 she had drawn an intimate sketch for Catherine Clarkson:

Mr. De Quincey, whom you would love dearly, as I am sure I do, is beside me . . . he is loving, gentle, and happy. . . . His person is *unfortunately* diminutive, but there is a sweetness in his looks, especially about the eyes, which soon overcomes the oddness of your first feeling at the sight of so very little a man. John sleeps with him and is passionately fond of him (*MY*, I, 255 f.).

A "Freudian" analysis of that passage could produce some startling, and possibly entirely unwarranted explanations of why Dorothy was so much concerned about De Quincey's *unfortunate* diminutiveness and ended with thoughts of his sleeping companion. There does seem to be an excessive violence, which may reflect subterranean jealousy, in the disturbed comment she sent to Catherine on his marriage:

Mr de Quincey is married; and I fear I may add he is ruined. By degrees he withdrew himself from all society except that of the Sympsons of the Nab (that pretty house between Rydal and Grasmere). At the up-rouzing of the Bats and the Owls he regularly went thither —and the consequence was that Peggy Sympson, the eldest Daughter of the house presented him with a son ten weeks ago. . . . This is in truth a melancholy story! . . . I predict that all these witcheries are ere this removed, and the fireside already dull. . . . As for him I am sorry for him (*MY*, II, 778 f.).

As for Peggy, one gathers that Dorothy was not sorry for her! It is remotely possible that the Wordsworths, perhaps at a subliminal level, viewed Peggy as a rival; but there were more obvious reasons, as his mother's letter set forth, why such a social and intellectual melange should strain relations between Dove Cottage and Rydal Mount. Dorothy's passion is probably from her great disappointment at the mess De Quincey seemed to be making of his life—this promising young admirer of William's poetry, from whom she had expected so much.

It was bad enough that Peggy was below De Quincey in the "indispensable" congruities of status and education. She may even have been his servant! In October, 1813, Mary Wordsworth wrote Sara indignantly and cryptically: "We have strange domestic news—Mary D. expects her confinement next month! Q has got a new servant—but I will not enter into the wonderful events of Grasmere—disgraceful to be sure they are." Mary Dawson's confinement was probably one of the "disgraceful" events, since she was apparently unmarried.[69] What else was exercising Mary is not clear, but De Quincey's "new servant" seems suspect. By 1818 Barbara Lewthwaite was in that situation, and she may have taken Molly Dawson's place at once. Introducing so young a girl as Barbara into a bachelor's house would perhaps have met with Mrs. Wordsworth's disapprobation. Peggy Simpson, however, was herself only seventeen; and an acrimonious attack on De Quincey in the *John Bull Magazine*'s "The Humbugs of the Age" series states flatly that the beautiful *Electra* whom the Opium-Eater celebrated in his *Confessions* "was his servant maid long before he married her, and had often made his bed before she ascended it." [70] Seventeen years after the lampoon De Quincey answered it in a *Tait's* essays which has been editorially entitled "Story of a Libel with Thoughts on Dueling." He was, however, vague about the exact nature of the insult which excited him, declaring only that the author must have known his opinions, for he had "often spoken with horror of those who could marry persons in a condition which obliged them to obedience." The implication seems to be that he would not have done anything so much against his principles; but the meaning could be that he was all the more susceptible to attack because of his loudly announced convictions. Anyway, the notion persisted, whether from *John Bull* or other sources, for in 1854 gossip in Westmorland reported that De Quincey married his housekeeper.[71] It is perhaps significant, also, that De Quincey, in his description of setting up his establishment in Grasmere, emphasized that the daughter of a very respectable farmer applied to be his servant, for in the district service was not considered to be degrading.[72] Thus maybe Peggy did make De Quincey's bed. The point is unimportant except as it struck Mary Wordsworth and therefore, as he firmly believed, depreciated his stock at Rydal Mount. In such matters believing has the effect of making it so.

Just how soon the real rupture came, and which party precipitated it, is not certain. In the fall of 1814 De Quincey apparently wrote from London offering to search for a copy of *Descriptive Sketches,* and probably also to see the new edition of Wordsworth's poems through the press. For Wordsworth sent back a hasty note saying that they had found a copy of the *Sketches* and could go on with the printing under the superintendence of Dorothy.[73] A letter of February, 1815, however, shows appreciation of De Quincey's critical assistance:

I wished you had mentioned *why* you desired the *rough* Copies of the Preface to be kept, as your request has led me to apprehend that something therein might have appeared to you as better or more clearly expressed—than in the after draught; and I should have been glad to reinstate accordingly. Pray write to us (*MY,* II, 629).

This letter closes warmly, "I remain affectionately and faithfully yours." In June Dorothy was taking little Willy "to Mr de Quinceys"; and even in November, when Sara was so scornful of his tipsy condition, there was apparently continued contact. In early April, 1816, however, Wordsworth wrote to R. P. Gillies, "Mr. De Quincey has taken a fit of Solitude; I have scarcely seen him since Mr. Wilson left us." By September Crabb Robinson reported that De

Quincey had not seen Wordsworth "for a long time"; and his diary makes it clear that the two were avoiding each other childishly: "Wordsworth conducted me over the fell and left me near De Quincey's house . . . De Quincey accompanied me on the mountain road to Rydal Mount, and left me at the gate of Wordsworth's garden terrace." By this time, of course, Peggy was some seven or eight months pregnant, and De Quincey, "very much an invalid . . . very dirty and even squalid," [74] holed up in despair.

According to Robinson, De Quincey had "broken off" with the Wordsworths, but they still had enough charitable feelings to urge that the visitor accept the Opium-Eater's offer to act as guide on a walk because it would be *"beneficial* to himself." Robinson's summary of the situation is revealing:

He spoke about himself and his situation with a frankness that I am far from disliking. 'Tis his misfortune, perhaps, that he has taken some disgust with the Wordsworths and has broken off all attentions with them. This, I suspect, arose from an attachment he has formed for a girl, the daughter of a statesman, one Simpson. Mrs. Wordsworth has expressed her disapprobation of the connection, and I expect has affronted him. . . . De Quincey still praises Wordsworth's poetry, but he speaks with no kindness of the man.[75]

Clearly the break with the Wordsworths did not come after De Quincey's marriage and because the ladies refused to visit his farm-girl wife, as Robinson's later *Reminiscences* seem to assume. It did not even wait until Peggy's pregnancy forced the issue. Although what Wordsworth called in early 1816 a "fit of Solitude" may be explained partly by the opium-eater's seclusion and partly by the lover's preoccupation, any noticeable absenteeism from Rydal Mount certainly indicated some breach. Perhaps it might be fair to say, not that the Wordsworths had been unfriendly, but that they had strained the privileges of friendship by expressing too freely their disapproval of Margaret. Such conduct almost any lover would interpret as interference, hostility, and sheer obstinate refusal to perceive the goddess in the stone.

Perhaps his friends' efforts to laugh him out of what they thought was a ridiculous infatuation was behind De Quincey's remark to Woodhouse in 1821: "Nothing causes a greater rankling in the heart, than to find that you have laid open its finer feelings and have got laughed at for your pains—the revulsion is dreadful." [76] An interesting passage in an unpublished open letter to William Tait on Wordsworth, written in 1838, probably bears on this frustrating effort:

a man of great intellectual power had disputed with me for years on questions lying within the direct reach of logic; and neither of us, however wide our difference, had ever outstepped the limits of good temper or been tempted to do so. But once my voice trembled with anger toward this man, and I received an impression of disgust towards him from which after a lapse of five-and-twenty years I have not yet recovered, because he could not see the loveliness of a fair face now laid low in the dust—and was callous or indifferent to an angelic sweetness in that face and an innocence as if fresh from Paradise which struck my own eyes with awe as well as love. I may say that I perfectly hated him for his blindness. [77]

Was Wordsworth the callous man, and Peggy's the face of "angelic sweetness"? Dorothy said De Quincey raved over " 'the angelic sweetness' of Miss Sympson." It is perhaps relevant also that in his "Recollections of Charles Lamb," likewise written in 1838—the year after Margaret's death —De Quincey remarked: "I hold it to be very doubtful, also, whether Wordsworth's judgment in the human face —its features and its expression—be altogether sound, and in conformity to the highest standards of art." [78] "Five-and-twenty years" seems too much like a round number to be taken literally; still it is possible that as early as 1813 De Quincey sounded out Wordsworth on Margaret's charms and realized what he was up against.

All his efforts failed, and by 1816 things were out of his control—Peggy's condition was obvious. He did not know what to do. Considering his financial condition and Peggy's status, the marriage would have been difficult at best; now it seemed impossible, and yet it seemed more imperative.

He really loved Peggy, and he was in a most awkward
situation. Naturally he blamed someone else. The Wordsworths had, he felt, betrayed and deserted him; they should
have been understanding and helpful, instead of critical and
obstructive. He rehearsed and magnified the obligations
which they owed him. Had he not given himself in sacrificial
friendship? Now he looked for some small sacrifice in return. When a friend has fallen in a ditch, you do not lecture him on his carelessness and leave him for fear of
getting mud on yourself. So reasoned De Quincey. He later
stated his case plainly in a section of his essay on Wordsworth which he cut from his collected works:

I imagine a case such as this which follows:—The case of a man who,
for many years, has connected himself closely with the domestic griefs
and joys of another, over and above his primary service of giving to
him the strength and the encouragement of a profound literary
sympathy, at a time of universal scowling from the world; suppose
this man to fall into a situation in which, from want of natural connections and from his state of insulation in life, it might be most
important to his feelings that some support should be lent to him by a
family having a known place and acceptance, and what may be called
a root in the country, by means of connections, descent, and long
settlement. To look for this, might be a most humble demand on the
part of one who had testified his devotion in the way supposed. To
miss it might—but enough. I murmur not; complaint is weak at all
times; and the hour is passed irrevocably, and by many a year, in
which an act of friendship so natural, and costing so little, (in both
senses so priceless,) could have been availing. The ear is deaf that
should have been solaced by the sound of welcome (*Lit. Rem.,* I, 297).

Most of the blame De Quincey apparently laid on Mary.
Robinson suspected that it was she who had expressed disapprobation and affronted De Quincey, and his contempt
for one of "sunshiny temper" but "weak intellectually"
probably fits Mary better than any other of Wordsworth's
"three wives." In his essay De Quincey excused William:
"I have learned to know that, wheresoever female prejudices are concerned, *there* it will be a trial more than
Herculean, of a man's wisdom, if he can walk with an

even step, and swerve neither to the right nor the left." [79]

Wordsworth was in a difficult position. He could hardly condone illicit sexual relations—De Quincey himself admitted in his article on the Green tragedy [80] that even by easy-going mountain standards there was a stigma on illegitimate children. Wordsworth was now a freeholder and since 1813 Stamp Distributor—a man of position and family: he had a daughter not so much younger than Peggy. But, could he in his attitude toward De Quincey forget Annette Vallon and his own illegitimate daughter? If De Quincey knew about that episode, the situation was even more awkward—and De Quincey may have, for it was no secret among the family, and De Quincey made a point of writing that William's intellectual passions "rested upon a basis of preternatural animal sensibility diffused through *all* the animal passions (or appetites)." [81] That italicized *all* is eloquent. If De Quincey did indeed know, he exercised admirable restraint in his essays on the poet, under the circumstances. Since he blamed "female prejudices," and since when relations were finally re-established overtures seem to have been made through Wordsworth, it is possible that William made some gestures toward broad-mindedness. When Robinson first arrived at Grasmere he wrote: "I understand, too, though Wordsworth was reserved on the subject, he has entangled himself in an unfortunate *acquaintance* with a woman." Robinson's letter to William on De Quincey's "sore state" of mind is disingenuous: "I had no doubt before I heard it avowed that the estrangement I so much regretted proceeded from resentmt at imagined comments on an unfortunate transaction." For Robinson's *Diary* suggests some reality to those "imagined comments": "He [De Quincey] asked me whether Wordsworth had spoken on the subject, which I denied and was forced to utter an untruth, that I might not violate confidence—I hope the most excuseable of falsehoods." If Wordsworth was somewhat "reserved" in his condemnation, that was hardly enough—De Quincey still indicted him to Robinson as "incapable of friendship out of his own family." [82]

The same charge is implied with dignified bitterness in a

letter of De Quincey's, probably written in 1816 or 1817, presuming to introduce a stranger to Wordsworth on the strength of having been at one time "honored" by the poet's "good opinion." First he wrote "friendship," and scratched it out. That friendship which the boy's first ornate letter had begged, and which the poet promptly insisted could only grow of its own accord, De Quincey now denied had ever really flourished.

33. *To Dorothy Wordsworth*

Ms. Dove Cottage. Unpub. Qtd. Eaton, pp. 175, 178; Edward Sackville-West,
A Flame in Sunlight (*London: Cassell, 1936), p. 89.*

Wrington near Bristol—Friday, July 7th. [-8th, 1809]
My dear Madam,

I arrived here last Monday night from London; and found your *two*
letters lying here—(the first dated "Sunday June 3rd. or 4th.";—the
second "about the 25th. June") : [1]—In the midst of my pleasure in
reading them, I was greatly pained and made many self-reproaches for
not having written to you for so long a time; though, under the circumstances of my London life during the latter part of it, I really found
it impossible to write or read with much pleasure, though I was not at
all ill: but this is a long story; and I must leave it till I return to
Grasmere, as it would be no amusement to you to have it engrossing a
whole letter. It will be sufficient to say—that first of all I staid in
London on my brother's account who was ill and did not wish, until
somewhat recovered, to see my mother and sisters; and my mother had
many communications to make to him and about him—which, for some
time, passed through my hands;—and afterwards, when his departure
from London to the sea-side set me at liberty from this cause of delay,
I found myself with 2 or 3 hundred books &c, which I had collected,
to pack up: here began my own delay;—for I am so miserable at the
thoughts of anything of this kind—that I keep putting it off from day
to day—sometimes, as in this case, for weeks together, and am wretched
the whole time.—This was very foolish certainly; and so I think now,
when I look back and see that 3 weeks were spent in resolving and
breaking resolutions;—but I always went to bed with the firmest intention to do the books the next day; and wrote twice to Bristol to tell
them that I was comng.—However, though I could not (ridiculous
as it may seem) help falling into the deepest dejection from the toil
that I had to go through, I wrote during that time one letter addressed
to yourself—which I fear that you have not received,[2] as your last

---

Letter 33:

[1] The first seems to have been lost; for the second see *MY,* I, 329–331.
[2] This letter seems not to have come to light.

letter does not notice it; but as you have dated this last letter *Thursday about June 25th.*—whereas the 25th. fell on a Sunday, there may be so much mistake in the date that it may have been written before mine could have reached you; for my sisters cannot recollect on what day your letter arrived; and I cannot recollect on what day my last was written:—only I remember that it was written on a *Wednesday*—because it was directed to Miss Crossthwaite's:—this letter was the only one which I have written since the one to Mrs. Wordsworth sent by Mr. Jameson: it contained nothing of [much *scratched out*] any interest—excepting an opinion of an English surgeon, who had lately come from Gallicia, on the state of the French army in that province —which I think you would have noticed, if you had received it;—some words about the canceled sheet;—a message to John and Dorothy about a magical gift that I shall bring with me for them &c.— —Tuesday and Wednesday were taken up by visitors,—particularly an old schoolfellow; and yesterday I was too unwell from drinking the bad cyder of this country, to be able to write in the evening which I had reserved for that purpose. I was at Longman's—inquiring about the pamphlet—this day week; and I was told that, up to that day, there had been sold in all 170 copies; that is, about 10 a day; for it was printed, I think on the 17th. of May; and not fairly published, I believe, for a fortnight or more afterwards:—this seemed to me a pretty tolerable sale for a 5s. book at the beginning; and I could not help expecting that a second edition might be called for; and that then something might be made of it in a money way—to make Mr. Wordsworth amends for so much trouble and anxiety spent upon it; indeed I sometimes hope (particularly from it's good reception, as I hear, among the army) that it may become *the rage*—and produce some thousand pounds: I shall be rejoiced to go to London again on this errand;—'Welcome, ye Devils!'—I shall say—'Hail, ye Proof Sheets!' —and I will take care that no more *'Calenture of Fancy'* [3] errors shall appear: but, by the bye, this error was not the one I laid to Miss Hutchinson's charge; for it was *my own;*—the words, of Fancy being (as I recollect mentioning) written *'with the most provoking legibility'* in the M.S. so that I could not have missed seeing them, if I had looked for them:—but I trusted in this passage, I suppose, to the compositor's not omitting anything; and read the proof over with my eye and not with my mind.—The Table of additional Errata, I forgot

---

[3] See Letter 32, note 12.

to mention, was *not* printed; as Mr. Stuart wrote to me, begging that
I would not print them; though the delay would not have been much.
—I have this moment (I am now writing on *Saturday* morning) received the *Times* of Thursday: it contains the 20th. Bulletin of the
French Army; and, being dated June *20th.* shews that the main Army
have been obliged to continue inactive for one entire month. What a
chastisement they must have received in the battles of the 22nd. and
23rd. of May! [4]—I never felt so anxious about the news as I have done
for this last month; Europe seems to be in such a perfect *agony* ever
since the great battle. Indeed this seems to be felt everywhere—the
anxiety for the issue of the next battle appearing to suspend all other
anxieties. But I cannot see why the loss of the next battle on the part
of the *Austrians,* should be more decisive of the whole war than the
loss of the first at Eckmuhl; though, to the *French,* the loss of another
battle (I should think) *would be* decisive of the war.—With all my
present interest in the German war, however, I have leisure to rejoice
greatly in the prospects of Spain; and greatly indeed I did rejoice two
days ago in Capt. McKinley's 2 letters in the Gazette [5]—containing
the account of Ney's defeat by Carrera at St. Payo. What infamous
liars and fools every despatch from Spain proves our English upper
officers to have been!—I wonder what Baird says to these accounts.—
What a pleasant and *significant* sound it is also to hear again of a
Captain General of Arragon! [6]—*Romana* I absolutely adore; what an
unconquerable mind he must have to live out such storms as he has
done; rising again always in a few days after he seems to have sunk
utterly [7]—and after the French have proclaimed his total ruin. And to
think of this man having been sneered at by such a poor miserable
'white-livered runagate' as David Baird!
I have been here, as I mentioned, since Monday night; and every day
since then has been rainy and cold:—to-day it has ceased raining with
a full December rain. This is very vexatious to me; as we have so

---

[4] Probably refers to Napoleon's defeat in the battle of Aspern (May
21–22).

[5] Captain McKinley, of the frigate *Lively,* announced the Spanish victory
of June 7 at St. Payo.

[6] General Blake, after a modest victory at Alcañiz on May 23, had been
appointed Captain-General of Aragon, Catalonia, Valencia, and Murcia.

[7] On May 18 Romana's army was dispersed and he forced to flee in a
Spanish ship; six days later he was again in command of a force in southern
Galicia.

beautiful a country all about us;—at the back of my mother's house
(which will be very pretty, when finished) a beautiful wood 4 miles
long; and on every side quiet Somersetshire lanes with the most luxuri-
ant hedges;—and endless downs on the tops of the hills. I have often
regreted, since I left Grasmere, that I had not my beloved friend John
with me; but never so much as here; for besides the beautiful woods
and fields, we have here, on a visit to my mother, two little girls—9
and 7 years old—who are very amiable and would make excellent play-
fellows for him; and my youngest brother is within 3 miles of us and
is over almost every day. There is another great recommendation at
this time—viz. a little white pony, the most elegant and gentle little
creature that ever was seen: he is so exquisitely graceful that last summer at Sidmouth every body used to collect to admire him—and those,
who would be thought knowing, used to tell the gazers that he was an
Arab (though my mother bought him in Cheshire where he was born);
and so gentle and easy in his paces that I am planning to bring him to
Grasmere—to carry Miss Hutchinson: if I can manage this, he will
be the darling of John and Dorothy—and being very spirited with all
his gentleness, will serve admirably for them to learn to ride upon. At
present he is ridden by nobody but my brother—whom he carries over
the downs to and from Brockley Coombe; but if I can prevail on my
brother to exchange him for a larger horse (which, if he has not a very
great affection for him, he will be glad to do—for the glory of riding a
larger horse), I shall certainly beg him of my mother and send him to
Grasmere.

   We are within a mile of the Miss Mores; and, as I have received
a civil message from Holy Hannah (as Dr. Beddoes [8] called her)
through my sisters, I must go (I believe) and see them; th[*torn:*?
though I have] great aversion to the elder sisters from all that I
hear about them: [*torn:*?so] convinced are they of the incurable
Jacobinism of Mr. Wordsworth and Mr. Coleridge—that none of
them but Hannah, I am told, will suffer you to say a word about
them: but for Mr. Southey they have all a little kindness—enough to
make them wish him out of such corrupting society—'*he was such
a Strephon!*' they say, when they saw him in Bristol.—I shall write

----

[8] Dr. Thomas Beddoes (1760–1808), friend of Southey, Wordsworth, and
Coleridge, had his "Pneumatic Institute" at Clifton, near the house of Hannah
More and her four sisters, Barley Wood, and Mrs. Quincey's new home,
Westhay.

you an account of what they are like: but I own, from many proofs that I have heard of their impious carelessness of all the poor people's feelings here in the mode of dispensing their *'charities'* as they call them, I do not expect to find them worth writing about.—By the way, at the house of a London acquaintance where I was dining about 10 days ago, I found *Coelebs:*—and, whilst my acquaintance was dressing for an evening party, I read about 40 pages in the 1st. vol: such trash I really never did read—except from the *Minerva Press*.[9] I could not have believed that even the reputation of H. M's godliness could have sold 9 editions (it is now, I believe, in the 10th). I could not find a sentence with any thought in it; and the grossest errors in propriety and good sense in every page.—The Quarterly Rev. is as miserable a thing, I think, as any of it's fellows: The Review of the Missionary Question—and of the Austrian State Papers—were the only Articles that seemed to me to have any merit in them.—The article about the 3 Sanscrit Grammars is a good lesson, I thought, on *'how to review any question without having got to the horn-book of the knowledge of it.'* [10]—This puts me in mind of the Sanscrit M.S. &c. which I will bring; and also—what, I believe, will give Mr. Coleridge pleasure—a work of *Giordano Bruno's; viz. De Monade Numero, et Figurâ: Item de Innumerabilibus, Immenso, et Infigu-*

[9] William Lane's Leadenhall Street publishing house issued, from 1790 to 1820 under the imprint of the Minerva Press, a flood of sentimental and gothic novels which floated the circulating libraries.

[10] De Quincey is writing about the first two numbers of the *Quarterly Review,* Feb. and May, 1809. Art. XVII, No. 1, entitled "Periodical Accounts Relative to the Baptist Missionary Society. Major Scott Waring—[Thomas] Twining, Vindication of the Hindoos, &c. &c.," is by Robert Southey, and is a defense of Christian missionary activity in India (Feb., pp. 193–226). Art. XVII, No. 2, entitled "Proclamation of the Archduke Charles to his Army— Declaration of War by the Emperor of Austria—Address of the Archduke to the German Nation, April 1809" (May, pp. 437–455) is probably by Sharon Turner and George Canning. Its deprecatory attitude toward Napoleon undoubtedly recommended it to De Quincey. Art V, No. 1, a review of (1) *A Grammar of the Sanskrita Language,* by Charles Wilkins (London, 1808); (2) *A Grammar of the Sungskrit Language, composed from the works of the most esteemed Grammarians . . . ,* by William Carey (Serampore, 1806); and (3) *Grammar of the Sanscrit Language,* by H. T. Colebrooke (London, 1805), is by the historian and pioneer in Anglo-Saxon studies, Sharon Turner. (Hill Shine and Helen C. Shine, *The Quarterly Review under Gifford: Identification of Contributors 1809–1824* [Chapel Hill, University of North Carolina Press, 1949], pp. 5, 7, 4.)

rabili; seu, de Mundo, et Universis, Libri Octo. Francofusti: 1591.—
655 pp.

I have read only the 2nd. No. of *The Friend* [11]—which I bought at
Clement's on Sat. June 24th. (the day fixed for the arrival of the
3rd.) ;—this was the last copy of the 2nd.; and the 1st. was then out
of print: for unluckily, when I had seen them a few days before, I had
no money in my pocket: and this 2nd. No. I had scarcely time to
read; for, having it in my pocket where I was reading Coelebs—as
Capt. Pasley happening to come in (who could not get the 2nd. No.)
I lent it to him; and had no opportunity of seeing him again.—There
are great Nos. of Subscribers in and about Bristol; not one of whom
had received even the 1st. No. at the time my sisters last inquired.—
They are all clamoring against Shepherd the bookseller here.

[*Across folded back:*] I have scarcely left myself room to thank you
for your most kind and interesting letters:—I was really cut to the
heart to think that whilst you were writing with so much goodness to
me, I must have seemed to be inattentive and remiss; but the truth is
that, besides [*torn:?* I have] been so much occupied with my brother
Richard's affairs, I could [*torn:?* not] help feeling that my letters
must generally have been rather wear [*torn:?*isome] ; but, as you have
been able to create them into something amusing and as I have now
plenty of leisure, I shall resume the old plan of writing—until I return to Grasmere (which will be in about 3 weeks, I believe.) I shall
write to dear Johnny next week: your anecdotes of him were very
interesting to me. My sweet love Dorothy had, I fear, by this time
forgotten [*torn:?* me a]s a friend; but you must keep me in her
memory, if you please, by g[*torn:?*iving m]y best love to her now
and then when a letter comes.

[*Inserted inverted above salutation:*] (WRINGTON NEAR BRISTOL)
God bless, you my dearest Madam!

    Most affectionately yours. Thos. de Quincey.

[*Address:*] Miss Wordsworth / Grasmere / near Kendal / Westmoreland /
        Single Sheet / Free
[*Stamp:*]   Wrington

---

[11] The first number of Coleridge's long-awaited periodical appeared on
June 1, 1809.

34. *To Dorothy Wordsworth*

Ms. Dove Cottage. Qtd. Eaton, p. 188.

Westhay near Wrington—Wednesday, August 16th. [1809]
My dearest Madam,—It has been a great pain to me for this last
month, that I have been unable—from two causes—to write to you
with any pleasure: one cause has been an inflammation in my eyes—
which I dare say had come on before I wrote to you last—as I remember to have found my eyes more pained than usual by writing that
letter: however I did not discover it until sometime after that, when
the increasing pain and dimness of my eyes made me very fearful
lest I might be going to lose my sight; and then, on examining my
eyes, I saw red streaks all over the white part: before I made this
discovery, I had unfortunately been contributing myself to confirm
the inflammation by bathing every day in a river near us; and after
this the dimness of sight increased so much that I became almost
certain that my sight was rapidly decaying; and at this thought, I was
more dejected than I ever was before in my life. What increased my
fear was that I remembered to have heard that many persons had
caught the *Ophthalmia* by sleeping at the Hummums in beds which
had been slept in by officers of the Egyptian expedition; and I had myself slept at the Hummums on the second night of my stay in London:
however I have since heard that the Ophthalmia comes on with acute
pain; and I had not more pain than usually attends an inflammation
from cold &c. My eyes are not yet nearly well; indeed I do not think
they will be, until they are braced up by Northern air: but they are
better, as you may guess by this small writing: however it is now
pretty early in the morning; and I do not know how long they may
continue to serve me through the rest of my letter; for this is the
first piece of writing (excepting a note of 3 or 4 lines) that I have
attempted from the day on which I wrote my last letter to you—
up to last Saturday evening when, being at Stowey, a very urgent
occasion obliged me to try my eyes in assisting Mr. Poole;[1] but I
found myself thoroughly wearied out by a page and a half.—I will
mention here, for the benefit of any persons you may know with in-
flamed or weak eyes, the prescription of the London oculists:—*Hot*

Letter 34:

[1] Thomas Poole, Nether Stowey tanner, and friend and patron of Coleridge.

water and vinegar to reduce the inflammation; and to strengthen the
eyes afterwards, hot water alone. The water must be as hot as it can
be borne. *Port wine and water* also is said to be very serviceable to
weak eyes.—Any other cause you will perhaps dispense with: however, to give you a notion of our situation here until very lately, I
must mention that when I first came here (Monday, July 2nd.)—we
had below stairs only one room habitable, besides the kitchen; and
in every other part of the house workmen of every class—stone-
masons, carpenters, painters, plaisterers, bell-hangers &c.; and even,
after the bed-rooms were finished, it was impossible to make use of
them in the day-time; for there being no front stairs yet erected—and
there being no road to the back stairs but through the hall which
the workmen used as a workshop, there was no getting up stairs without displacing all their benches &c. which was a complete ceremony
and process; and, being up, one was a complete prisoner—which did
not suit me at all:—since then we have migrated successively into a
parlour of a neighbouring farm-house;—into a green-house with no
floor;—into a room with a floor but no cieling;—into a closet 6 feet by
6;—and finally, after having been hunted round the house by the
painters and paperers, we have revolved into our original sitting-room
—with the library adjoining—completely finished. The effect of living in the house under these circumstances will be to get it finished in
one third the time that it would otherwise have taken. / On Saturday
night last—being at Mr. Poole's—Mr. Ward [2] brought in the 3rd.
No. of *the Friend* (there was none, by the bye, for *Mr. Poole*):
This No., I myself liked very much: but, as nobody else had read it
when I left Stowey, I do not know how it will be liked in general.—
At Stowey, as everywhere else, I heard complaints of the great
obscurity of the Friend; which complaint, for my part, I cannot well
understand: it certainly requires some *attention,* as I told them, to
follow the course of the thought; but I could not find anything that
was, as they said, unintelligible—if a man took pains to understand
it.—Mr. Coleridge alludes in this No., I suppose, to the Edinburgh
Review of a work of Belsham's: [3] it is rather singular that I had,

---

[2] Thomas Ward, Poole's partner and also a friend of Coleridge.

[3] Coleridge mentions a statement in an unnamed journal which launched
him on his essay "On the Communication of Truth and the Rightful Liberty
of the Press in Connection with it." De Quincey possibly refers to the review
of Vols. XI and XII of William Belsham's *History of Great Britain* (London,
1805) in the July, 1805, *Edinburgh Review* (VI, 421–428).

from recollection of that review, marked it down in a memorandum book—as noticeable for its extreme stupidity and extravagance—but an hour or two before the Friend arrived. My mother is the only person that I have seen who sincerely and *thoroughly* likes the Friend hereabouts: she has been used to read a great many old religious books —and is therefore not unwilling to give the necessary attention to the transitions—the train and bearing of the arguments &c. However she has seen only the *1st.* No. as yet, and that I was obliged to borrow from Mr. Cottle; [4] for not one No. has ever been sent to her though her name was down before any other in Bristol: I mention this, that Mr. Coleridge may know how ill he is served by either *Brown* [5] of Penrith, or *Shepherd* of Bristol: Shepherd says it is Brown's fault: but we are disposed to think it is Shepherd's—who seems to know and to care very little about the work: for about a fortnight ago my mother, being in Bristol, called at his shop—and was told that the work was *discontinued.* My mother sent out Prospectuses to the East Indies—and distributed them amongst her friends throughout the kingdom:—how many of these may have put down their names, I do not know; I imagine not many; for most of my mother's reading acquaintances are religious people; and in general very tolerable bigots: she put down, in Shepherd's subscription book, 1. her own name; 2. Major Penson's [6]—which may be sent to her also;—3. Miss Ann Kemp's—28, Richmond Place, Clifton near Bristol;—4. Mr. Burroughs's name, Mall, Clifton.—I have heard also great complaints of the *delay* in publishing—which seem to me still more unreasonable than the former complaint—especially when coming from the same persons who make that former complaint. But no one, it seems to me, has any right to complain that he does not receive a No. regularly once a week—so long as he is not required to pay a shilling once a week.—However the complaint has been made very often in my hearing—and sometimes very angrily by persons who (I afterwards found) *were not subscribers:* of this class is a member of the *Dulce domum* club at Stowey—who, when I was dining with the said club, came

---

[4] Joseph Cottle (1770–1853), Bristol bookseller, author, and early friend and publisher of Wordsworth, Coleridge, and Southey (see above, p. 25).

[5] John Brown, the young Penrith printer whom Coleridge set up to print the *Friend.*

[6] Major Thomas Penson, Mrs. Quincey's brother, who was in the East India Service. The subscription list does not carry Major Penson's name, but shows two copies for Mrs. de Quincey. The other names appear, but last on the list.

up to me and spoke thus:—'As to your friend Mr. Coleridge, Sir,—
this is what I have to say—that, if he goes on as he has done, he'll
damn himself; and so you tell him!'—This man looked very much like
a civil demon in face; they called him *Bryce*, I think; and I believe
he is a commissioner about the Property Tax appeals.— / Mr. Poole,
I found, had only very lately received the pamphlet from his bookseller; and for the last fortnight his whole time had been occupied
in writing petitions—memorials &c, and in making interest by every
avenue within his knowledge, to obtain the pardon of Robert Blake
—a young man of Stowey—aged 23—who was found guilty of forging
a 10 £ Bank of England note at the Winchester Summer assizes—
and left for execution on Sat. August 5th.—He had already obtained
a respite until next Saturday—to allow time for collecting evidence
of his insanity: evidence in plenty had been collected to prove his insanity *previously* to the commission of the forgery: but in Ld. Liverpool's communication of the respite—it is required that evidence shall
be given that he was mad *at the time* of committing it:—to prove
this, there are only the affidavits of 2 women at Portsmouth; for the
Undaunted frigate, on board which it was committed, has sailed to
Canada with her whole crew:—the whole of the evidence was laid
before Baron Graham at Bridgewater last Sunday:—he was to give
his determination upon it on Monday: but, as I left Stowey on Monday to obtain Hannah More's intercession with one of the Ministers
(which, if the judge's answer should be unfavorable, Mr. Poole did
not wish to leave untried), I have not yet heard the result:—if everything else fails, Mr. Poole has prepared a petition to the King: we
are all well convinced, from the evidence, that he is a lunatic; and are
therefore anxious to hear the end.—In consequence of this affair, he
had not had time to read more than about 60 pages: but what he had
read, he spoke of repeatedly with the highest admiration: he said
many times to me that he thought it the finest political work he ever
saw; and I saw many passages marked with a pencil which were just
those that I should have marked: I told him that, in my mind, he had
much the finest part to come.—I read the pamphlet up at [*torn*] and
all here were delighted with it. / On Friday last, when at Stowey, I
walked over to Alfox [*torn:*?ton [7] Mr.] Poole gave me a letter to

[7] William and Dorothy lived from July 14, 1797, to June 25, 1798, in Alfoxton or Alfoxden, a house in Somersetshire about four miles from Nether
Stowey, owned by the St. Albyn family.

Mr. St. Albyn; but, as he was not at home, the servants said they were not permitted to shew the house to strangers: so I saw nothing of the inside: but the outside I went all round and over:—that beautiful wood and glen—the park—the old paling—the deer—in short, everything out of doors—had no marks of change upon them; and, I dare say, were just as you left them: but an addition of 4 rooms had been made towards the sea to that end of the house which faces you as you come out of the carriage road in the wood: but this is not seen from the hills that front the house: *there* nothing new is seen about the house, except one tall chimney which *seemed* to me newer than the other two. I spent a delightful day at and about Alfoxton; and fortunately the day itself was very beautiful;—a very rare thing with us!—we have had here the rainiest summer I ever remember; and were quite surprised to hear that you had had a fine one. / I received your last letter this day week (i.e. Wednesday, August 9th): it is dated August 1st.; [8] so that I suppose it was not sent till some days after it was written.—The next morning, when I was preparing to answer it, a lady called who offered to carry me down to Burnham on the Bridgewater road; and, as I had long purposed to visit Stowey before I left the country, I thought it best to accept her offer: this is the reason that I have not acknowledged that letter before. You begin with reproaching yourself for not having written earlier: but I hope, my dear Madam, you do not suppose that I looked for a regular exchange of letters: I am very happy and proud whenever I hear from Grasmere; but I always receive your letters as favors, and not as debts; and shall therefore always continue writing, whether I hear from you in return or not;—i.e. when I can: for since I wrote last, I have been so much dispirited by the complaint in my eyes—and by the unpleasant disturbances from our situation as described above and from the noise of workmen, and the still louder noise of two little girls who were visiting us and playing all day long in the same room—that I have scarcely been able to read anything; and utterly indisposed and almost incapacitated for writing.—I have now nearly finished my letter; and I do not find my eyes at all the worse for it.—I am glad to hear that you have made the cottage useful; but I took it for granted that you and little Dorothy had settled there a long time ago, as you talked of doing.—My dear sweet Sissy!—I am truly sorry

---

[8] *MY*, I, 333–336.

to hear that she is grown *wayward:* but perhaps you said this of her, when she had just returned from a place where probably they made a little queen of her.—I am very much gratified by my faithful friend Johnny's continued remembrance of me: I cannot say how much I long to see my two darling friends again.—Johnny's letter I shall now print immediately:—I had thought of employing one of my sisters to print from my dictation:—but I hope that will be unnecessary now.—Johnny's hat shall not be forgotten.—What present would be acceptable to Hartley Coleridge?—I hope to be at Grasmere in about 17 days;—I am afraid that I must take London in my way. I shall not leave Westhay of 10 days. But I will write again in 4 days. [*Across folded back:*] My best love and respects to Mr. & Mrs. Wordsworth—Miss Hutchinson—& Mr. Coleridge.—Yesterday we had the news of the great victory gained by the English & Spanish armies.[9] Oh! If our Walcheren expedition [10] were but in Biscay!—to hold the ne[*torn:?*net into] which the Southern armies might drive the French force.—[*torn*] Austria, except as the scourge of France,—after the article relati[*torn*] Tyrol, I care nothing:—God bless you, my dear Madam! Your affectionate friend, Thos. de Quincey

[*Address:*] Miss Wordsworth / Grasmere / near *Kendal* / Westmoreland
        Free / Wednesday, August 16th. /
[*Stamp:*]   Wrington

35. *To Mary and John Wordsworth*

Ms. Dove Cottage. Pub. in part, Eaton, pp. 184–187, 149–150, 178.

To Mrs. Wordsworth Saturday, September 30th.
[-Oct. 18, 1809]—Westhay near Wrington

My dear Madam,

Within a day after you receive this letter perhaps, I shall be at Grasmere. You will wonder indeed why I have not been there long ago: much delay has, according to custom, been occasioned by my own intolerable procrastination—which, having made me miss opportunities

---

[9] The battle of Talavera, July 27–28.

[10] On July 28 a British expedition arrived off Walcheren Island in the mouth of the Scheldt, on an inept and fever-plagued attempt upon French shipping and arsenals in the Antwerp area, a futile effort finally given up on December 9.

which I had in one week of finishing matters of business and paying visiting debts that had accumulated during my residence here, has forced me to stay the next for that purpose; this next has brought with it fresh debts of its own—and so on. But however I should at any rate have staid much longer than I first talked of—in order to see my brother the sailor who did not come to us till yesterday three weeks— after an absence from home of more than seven years. His stay here has occasioned so much visiting &c. that I have never had one day since his arrival which I could call my own; and thus has rendered it impossible for me to write a letter long enough to travel 300 miles.— This neighbourhood has but small attractions for me in it's society: we know almost everybody round about us; but they are all wretched creatures in my opinion;—hostile to the Spaniards to a man—even to rancor; and all of them battening on the Edinburgh Review: I have accordingly tormented them to the utmost of my power—and have the satisfaction of thinking that I have given extreme pain to all the *refined* part of the community here. With respect to the Spaniards, my knowledge of the events of the two campaigns (which I have brought to as much accuracy as anybody can—who was not personally engaged in them) has put it in my power to gain an easy triumph in every conversation; and my hatred of the intolerable spirit of mis-representation and selfishness which appears in all that these men say of Spain—has so barbed my words, I hope, as to inflict no little misery upon many of them.—It would scarcely be believed that in respect to the battle of Talavera in particular—not even Wellesley's admission that the Spaniards 'did their duty'—nor my seventy-times repeated admonishment to them that in that battle we were *attacked* and that therefore it rested with the French to choose who should bear the brunt of the action (even in which choice private accounts say that the French were determined by *the nature of the ground*)—has had weight enough to make them forbear repeating that *there* we received a lesson to teach us how little the Spaniards are to be relied upon as allies; indeed that wicked calumny which was published in almost all the newspapers before the Gazette account contradicted it—viz. that the Spaniards had been drawn off by Cuesta [1] before the battle began

---

Letter 35:

[1] Gregorio García de la Cuesta, Captain-General of Castile, the aged and suspicious leader of the Spanish forces with whom Wellesley was trying to coöperate.

—shewed sufficiently what it was predetermined should be said of the Spanish—and how much lying was to be received—rather than that the nation should be called upon to renounce one tittle of it's selfishness in behalf of any nation but the worst.—Among others Mr. Cottle is a perfect zealot in his hatred of the Spaniards: the *expression* of it was first drawn out by my having lent him Mr. Wordsworth's pamphlet to read: or rather *that* had served to accumulate his bile; for the immediate occasion which called it out, I recollect, was his sister's having observed to me upon the battle of Talavera—'What a sad pity—that so much blood has been shed' &c., whereupon, I, instead of the expected assent, assumed a most Catonic severity—and told her that a far better thing for the English nation than the restoring to life all that had died would in my mind be the restoring a little of that spirit which taught the old Lord Talbot to say 'that he would not exchange his dead son for any living son in Christendom.' Mr. Cottle had kept the peace till now; but this he took for a defiance; and immediately there was a grand explosion of venom against the Spaniards and all who were so *'unchristian'* as to defend throat-cutting; however *they* had the worst of it; for nearly at the close of the debate I recollect Mr. C. said—'But really you're so furious, there's no talking with you.' The religious magazines, I believe, have all taken part against Spain; certainly that in which Wilberforce dictates ('The Christian Observer') [2] has most violently. Blessed fruits their 'Gospel knowledge' produces!!—

Sunday, October 8th. Westhay.—I was interrupted by a visitor; and have never found time to go on till now.—My trunks are packing up—and therefore I shall certainly go on Tuesday.—We have received the *Friend* regularly from No. 4 to 7 inclusively; and to-day we hope to have No. 8: I have understood, I believe, almost the whole; and have been much instructed by many parts: the only complaint we make here is—that, *besides* the intricacy and weight of the thought, there is some other cause that makes it difficult to read a series of passages as

[2] The *Christian Observer,* edited by Zachary Macaulay, was the organ of the evangelical and abolitionist views of the "Clapham Sect," of which the M.P. philanthropist William Wilberforce (1759–1833) was the most influential member. The *Observer* was lamenting "the supineness and indifference of the population both of Spain and Portugal, and the imbecility and improvidence of their governments" (June, 1809), VIII, 404.

'a fluency' (to quote Mr. Wordsworth)—or so at least to give them
the full effect of *Eloquence*. I have lent them where it was likely that
they could be understood; and have endeavoured to expound to Wrington understandings such passages as I imagined that I comprehended
myself;—but the *flattering* complaint is still made—that *"they are so
obscure"*. *Flattering* I call it; for, considering what manner of stuff
it must be that men idolatrous of Hannah More would call plain
and good, it sounds music to hear any one of my friends accused of
obscurity; and when I hear them say it is obscure, I am ready to cry
out with joy—'But do you really think so, my dear fellow? I hope
you're not flattering.'—As to Hannah More, having mentioned her
—I was going to describe her at length: but, besides that I do not
think you would be much interested in any thing relating to her, she
has described herself sufficiently in her books [3]—if you ever looked into
any of them: her conversation (for *that* she thinks her forte) is just
like them—aphoristic; epigramatic—nothing been thought to be said
well at Barley Wood but what is said pointedly;—full of trite quotations—hardly ever introduced to confirm or illustrate—or because they
might adequately convey the feeling—but as cold ornaments and
garnishings; or, when she does sometimes make a formal quotation in
proof of what she says, it is always—for fear of being thought 'a
learned lady'—ushered in with an affectation of doubt as to the author
—as 'I think, it is my lord Bacon who says'—&c. Then everything
must be *'improved;'* as, if Westhay stand on low ground—and Barley
Wood on a hill,—then "what a benevolent dispensation of *Providence*
it is that—when there were but two pieces of land to be sold in the
valley for so many years, *that* should have been put up for sale when
the old wanted to purchase which made it unnecessary to climb hills
for a walk—and on the other hand, when the young who could climb
hills wanted to purchase, *that* only should have been to be had which
made it necessary for them to take the exercise necessary for their
health before they could find any good walks." Moreover she is restless until every thought is brought into such a shape that she can
translate it into some of her received positions; and thus every avenue

---

[3] De Quincey later drew upon these experiences to describe Hannah More
in *Tait's Edinburgh Magazine* for Dec., 1833 (partially reprinted in D.
Masson, ed., *Collected Writings of Thomas De Quincey* [London, 1896];
omissions supplied by W. E. A. Axon in *Transactions of the Royal Society
of Literature*, Series II, Vol. 30 [1914], pp. 5–19).

is shut up against gaining or communicating anything in her company; since, if she finds that the case is desperate and that you will not permit what you say to be lopped down into some of her own previous thoughts, then she makes no further answer but by bowing her head.— On the whole, her house would be the very dullest place I ever was in (since generally everybody thinks it a duty to sit silent until he has some literary anecdote or formal sentiment to offer)—but for the endless succession of visitors (for one fortnight lately 3 families on an average a day from distant parts, as they told me)—and but that, as all the 5 sisters knew every body of any celebrity in the last age, I always draw one of them into an account of Louisa the lady of the hay-stack [4]—Edmund Burke—Garrick—Mrs. Montagu and her society [5]—Dr. Johnson &c.—To pass from the lady to her book—what would you guess that she had got by her last work *Coelebs?* She told me several weeks ago that within the 1st. 8 months from it's publication there had been published 14000 copies—at 12s. each—out of which she cleared 3s. a copy; making *there* a clear profit of 2100£.— A few days ago we heard that a 12th. edition had been called for!!— I am indignant at this; though I never got farther than 40 pages in the book: but is it not a disgrace to the nation?—I see, on looking back, that I have omitted the best thing that can be said of her—viz. that she is very courteous in her manners—as far as she can be so, not being benevolent;—but then I had also omitted the worst thing— viz. that she is, as you know, a horrid bigot—censorious—and greedy of flattery to any amount under cover of a frequent disclamation of all merit—and with all the forms and phrases of profound humility.

---

[4] Louisa was a deranged girl found living under a haystack in Burton parish, near Bristol, about 1781. Apparently she spent three years in the field, refusing to go into a house because *"Man* dwelt there." She spoke with a German accent, showed vestiges of a cultured origin, and was even suspected of being Mlle. La Freulin, an illegitimate daughter of Emperor Francis I of Austria. But she could not or would not reveal much of her past, and was finally committed to Guy's Hospital, where she died in 1801. The Misses More superintended a public fund for her benefit; and Hannah wrote a halfpenny tract, "Tale of Woe," to procure subscriptions, and had it translated into German in the hope of reaching her relatives (*Gentleman's Magazine,* March, 1801 [LXXI, 280]; Annette M. B. Meakin, *Hannah More* [London: Smith, Elder, 1911], pp. 152-154).

[5] Hannah More was intimate with Mrs. Elizabeth Montagu (1720-1800), "The Queen of the Blues," and acquainted with Mrs. Elizabeth Carter, Mrs. Hester Chapone, Mrs. Delaney, Mrs. Vesey, Mrs. Boscawen, Mrs. Thrale, and other members of the society she praised in her 1781 poem, "Bas Bleu."

—Monday, October 9th.—This afternoon we have received the Friend
—No. 8 (only *one* copy, by the way, tho' the cover says *two*). We
have all been greatly interested with it; and upon the whole I believe
it is liked better than any preceding one here:—we are not a little surprised, and very greatly delighted, to find that the Friend goes on so
regularly:—I wonder how the soi-disant metaphysicians of Edinburgh
have made their way through the philosophy of two or three numbers;
and how it is *generally* received. I forgot to extract before, for your
amusement, the following anticipation of it's reception from a letter
which was forwarded to me from Grasmere soon after I left London: it is a fair specimen of Oxford eloquence—coming from a
Master of Arts who is esteemed a clever man: 'He' (i.e. Mr. Coleridge) 'will have to repel equally the arrow of criticism—the dagger
of envy—the bludgeon of calumny—and the (broad-)—sword of
literary persecution.' I confess to have added the word *broad;* as it
seemed to me necessary to the climax—and the music; but the rest
is correct.—If you have seen Mr. Wilson [6] since I wrote to him, you
will have heard that I have consented to go to Spain: I promise myself
much benefit in many ways from this scheme; I am afraid however
that I cannot conveniently be ready in less than 4 weeks from this
time: however this can be settled when I get into Westmoreland—
Before I conclude, I must thank you for your goodness in writing—
tho' so short a letter [7]—from Elleray: I have been necessarily very
long in answering it; but Grasmere has not the less for that been in
all my thoughts—night and morning:—I must now conclude in order
to make room for my letter to Johnny. I shall be at Grasmere certainly
within a day or two after this letter; for I shall travel like a hur-
ricane, when once I set off; and that will be, I hope, to-morrow.—I
beg my kindest love to Miss Wordsworth and Miss Hutchinson—and
remain, my dear Madam, with the greatest affection and respect, your
faithful friend and servant, Thos. de Quincey.

[Letter to Johnny is printed.]

My dear Friend, ever since your Aunt Dorothy told me that you
could read, I have been intending to print a letter to you—both be-

---

[6] John Wilson, of Elleray, later to be "Christopher North" of *Blackwood's
Magazine* and professor of moral philosophy at the University of Edinburgh.
(See above, p. 207.) The Spanish tour did not materialize.
[7] *MY*, I, 341.

cause I promised that I would—and also because I thought that you would like it. But perhaps you will not like a very long one; therefore I shall make it only a middling sized one.

As soon as I come to live at Grasmere, I shall begin to teach you all the things which I know that I think you would like to know: one thing will be Swimming: another will be how to fly a kite: and another will be swinging: and another walking on Stilts. But the best thing of all will be how to sail a boat upon the lake—and to make the boat go which way you like—both when it has a sail and when it has not one. But it is not I that am to teach you this— but it is my Brother [8]—who is a sailor. He has promised to come and teach both you and me all about Ships and Boats—both how to sail them and how to make them: for he can make boats.

And besides teaching us these things, my Brother can tell us a great many stories that are really [sic]. For he has been sailing all round the world ever since the time when you were a little Baby as little as Catherine. He has been in cold Countries—where there is no daylight for many many weeks. He has been amongst great Forests where there were only Lions and Bears and Wolves—And up Rivers and Lakes where nobody lived—And amongst many nations of Black men and men that are the color of copper. He has also been past the country where Giants live: they are called Patagonians. He has been in Battles—and seen great Towns burning: And sometimes the men that he fought against caught him and put him in prison. Once he was in that Island where Robinson Crusoe and his man Friday lived: I dare say your Mother or your Aunt has told you about them.

One of the Stories that he told me is a short story: therefore I shall print it here. One fine [torn] night my Brother was sailing near Africa in an English ship that was called [torn]na: there were about one hundred more men with him in the Ship. Just as th[torn] was going down, they saw another Ship that was sailing towards them. Soon it came close to them, then the men in my Brother's Ship said Where do you come from?—The people in the other Ship said We come From Spain—We are Spaniards. So then because the Spaniards were not the Friends of the English at that time as they are now there was a Battle between these two Ships in the dark night. And the English Ship beat the Spanish Ship. Then the Captain of the English Ship said to my Brother and to some other men. You must go

---

[8] See Letter 6, note 1; Letter 32, note 7.

into that Spanish Ship and put Chains upon all the Spaniards that are
not dead and then make the Ship follow this Ship. So my Brother and
thirty other men went and did as the Captain told them to do. They
put chains upon the Spaniards and chained them down in a dark hole
in the Ship. And then they made the Spanish Ship follow the English
Ship. But soon after this there was a great Storm of wind and rain
and thunder and Lightening: And it lasted two whole days: And
there was a great Fog: And when the Storm and the Fog were gone
then my Brother and the other Englishmen that were in the Spanish
Ship looked out to see where the English Ship was: But they could
not see it anywhere. It was gone away Or maybe it had sunk to the
Bottom of the Sea whilst the storm had made it dark. So they were
obliged to sail by themselves. And every day all the men that were
chained kept trying to get loose. But there was one of them that never
tried to get loose. The reason was because he was very badly. So
when my Brother knew that he was badly then he unchained him and
gave him Physic and was very good to him. But all the other Spanish
men were still kept chained. So they kept trying more and more every
day to get loose. And at last one man got his chains off—and then
before any body knew it He helped all the rest to get their chains
off. Then they all came up out of the dark hole where they had been
chained. And at that time it was bright moonlight. And my brother
and a few other Englishmen were walking on the deck of the ship.
Then one man came behind my Brother and was going to knock him
down with a bar of iron. But then that Spanish Gentleman that my
Brother had unchained because he was badly jumped upon the other
Spaniard and took the Bar from him. So my Brother was neither
killed nor chained. But most of the other Englishmen were asleep in
bed. And they were all chained by the Spaniards.

My dear John   There is no more Room to print in. So I must tell
you the rest of the Story when I come to Grasmere which will be in
one day or two days more. I shall be very very glad to see you again.
Give my love to my dear Sissy if you please.

I am your most loving Friend

Thomas de Quincey.

[*Across folded back:*]

Wednesday morning, October 18th.—Bristol;

My dear Madam,

Such is my infirmity that I am still in Somersetshire. However I

have left Westhay; and I am now writing from Mr. Cottle's; so that
I shall certainly set off this evening. Indeed I am just now going to
[*torn:?* take] a place in the Birmingham mail; for I shall not go
through London: So that [*torn:?* it is not impossible] that I may be
at Grasmere before my letter. Most happy I shall [*torn*] God bless
you my dear Madam. Most affectionately yours. Thos. de Quincey

[*Address, printed:*] For / John Wordsworth / Allan Bank Grasmere / near
               Kendal / Westmoreland /
               Single Sheet / post paid
               [*Changed to*] to the care of Miss Crossthwaite Keswick
               near Penrith
[*Postmark:*]   Bristol, Cumberland. OCT 18 1809

36. *To Mary Wordsworth*

Ms. Dove Cottage. Unpub. Qtd. Sackville-West, p. 117; MY, p. 417.
[*Top 3/4 of first page and narrow strip out of second page missing. Begins,
apparently, as he takes up the letter again.*]

[Wrington]
Monday, August 27th.—1810

On [*torn*] last I received your letter of the 20th.[1] It was very welcome; and also very seasonable; for on the very day I received it I was
purposing to set to work and write you a long complaint for leaving
me so long without any account of my dear Catherine's progress. I am
very greatly obliged to you for your kindness in sparing me so much
of your time—and especially for writing so much at length about
Catherine. I hope that she will now advance rapidly (having cut her
last teeth) without haltings or relapses. But if she does not visibly
mend in her lameness, I should most strongly recommend one of Mr.
Cheser's steel instruments; which, being worn at so early an age,
will save her a world of trouble and confinement that she would
have to go through at a more advanced age, But I should hope, by
your account, that nothing more may be necessary than her steel
draughts and perhaps a little sea-bathing:—this last she can have next
year with great convenience, if you will let me bring her down here

Letter 36:
  [1] *MY*, I, 393–396.

on my next visit to this place. [*Gap of back of top page*] Indeed, I have been daily lamenting—since I came down [*torn*] did not prevail [*torn*]dren *this* year;—I would, in that case, have come round by Westhay in my road to London—[*reconstructed from bottoms of letters only:*] and have left any of them that came in the care of my sisters who would have been most faithful and delighted nurses. But however there is no use in talking of this, as it is now gone by. But next year I shall be a more importunate suitor for this favor;— as in addition to the pleasure of the journey and the novelty, there would be great store of amusement for them here—besides the special benefit to Catherine of sea-bathing.

My sisters do *not* come with me to Grasmere this year: besides other hindrances to this scheme at present they are looking for my brother the sailor to pay them a visit next month: his ship the Amethyst being obliged to come into port about that time for provisions. They have promised however to come with my mother for one month in the early part of next summer.

Our weather for the last ten days has been uninterruptedly fine and hot: indeed I do not remember ever to have seen more perfect and delightful summer days; and there is every sign of it's continuing. The second crops of hay were got in last week; and the wheat harvest is now beginning. The first crops of hay fall so short—that, in spite of the partial amends made by the second crops, it is *now* very dear (about 6£ a ton)—and, before winter, is expected to be very dear indeed. Horses, it is said, will then sell for old songs. However,—to balance this—the wheat harvest here promises to be a very fine one; and from the wheat counties—where, I believe, it is all got in by this time—there is the same report.—Walter Scott's last novel—*The Lady of the Lake*—is the grand subject of prate and chatter hereabouts. I have read it aloud here, to oblige my mother; and a more disgusting task I never had. I verily think that it is the completest magazine of all forms of the Falsetto in feeling and diction that now exists; and the notes, as usual, the most finished specimen of bookmaking (alias, *swindling*). I have given great offence to some of Walter's idolaters—by expressing these opinions with illustrations— and, in particular, by calling it a *novel* (which indeed it is—only a very dull one). Yesterday at a dinner-party I had a hornet's nest upon me for only observing that the true solution of Walter's notoriety was to be found in this—that, whereas heretofore if one would read

novels one must do it under the penalty thereunto annexed of being
accredited for feeble-mindedness and *missiness,* now (by favour of
W.S.) one might read a novel and have the credit of reading a poem.
—An excellent joke is—that all these good people think *'The Lady of
the Lake'* infinitely superior to *Marmion*—and that it is possible to
be even disgusted with the one and enamoured of the other; a still
better joke is that the difference is ascribed to the criticisms of Mr.
Jeffray.—'Oh! dear'—a lady said to me, 'the inferiority of Marmion
is infinite in my opinion—positively infinite.' 'Strange! Madam,' I
replied—(to her unspeakable horror)—'Strange! that such a difference should be 'Twixt Tweedle-dum and Tweedle-dee.'—Miss Wordsworth half desires me to write to her in her last letter: but this
last letter being dated from Cole-orton which she talked of leaving
about the 13th. of August—and no other address being given, I have
not known how to direct to her:—from your letter I now conclude
that she is visiting Mrs. Clarkson at Bury St. Edmonds.—I have
mentioned, in the accompanying letter [2] to Dorothy, that I shall be at
home some time in the course of next week:—I shall certainly be so
on some day of that week; but, as I cannot say positively on which,—
Dorothy may tell Mary Dawson [3] that she had better make no further
preparation than to have one of the beds ready.—I heard a very interesting account the other evening at Barley Wood, of Ge[*torn:
?*neral Whittingham [4] an English] his parents being greatly distressed
at the thought of his going into the army, he renounced his own plans
to please them—and entered into some mercantile connexions—on
some business or other he went to Spain, and had there made himself
master of the language about the time that the present war in Spain
broke out: just about the same time, his parents both died: he came
home—quitted his mercantile pursuits—went into the army—then got
leave to go out as a volunteer to Spain—and there, being recommended from Gibraltar, was instantly made a Colonel—and since

---

[2] These letters seem not to have survived.

[3] De Quincey's housekeeper.

[4] Sir Samuel Ford Whittingham (1772–1841), then Major-General in the
Spanish army. According to the *DNB,* De Quincey has somewhat telescoped
his career: he returned to England and was gazetted ensign in the British
army in 1803, went on a secret mission to the Peninsula in 1804–1805, and
served in South America in 1806–1807, then returned to Gibraltar in 1808,
volunteered to join Castaños' forces, and was made a colonel for his services
at Baylen.

then has risen rapidly to the rank of General; and, from his talents—
his thorough knowledge of the Spanish language and manners—his
having throughout shown himself a Spaniard in his thoughts—feelings and actions—even to the marrying a Spanish wife, he has now
gained the confidence of the Spaniards so entirely—that, upon a late
attempt to send him over to England to make some representations
to our government,—they would not let him go—a Spanish general
sending word to Mr. Wellesley that Gen. Whittingham 'was the
strongest link that united the two nations in Spain.'—From all the
private letters which the old ladies at Barley Wood get a sight of
through their friends in office,—it appears that he is daily rising in
reputation—and that a general impression has gone out amongst the
Spaniards who know him that he is destined to act some great part
among them—and to become one of their first-rate avengers.—A
Spaniard, who was at Barley Wood some weeks ago, made a diverting
speech about him: the old ladies asked him if Gen. Whittingham was
a fine-looking man: 'Oh!' he said with great enthusiasm, *'he is a
beautiful man of war'*—He is, it seems, at present unceasingly exert-
ing himself to keep the Spaniards from general actions.—I shall write
this evening to Mr. Kelsall, to apprise him of your having drawn
upon him.—His address is, as you have put it down,—Mr. Kelsall,
Manchester.—Perhaps it might be as well to add *Merchant*. My
mother's house is much improved of course—and the grounds still
more so, since I was here last—but at an expense enormously beyond
the estimate: from what I recollect—of the price asked for Butterlip
How, it will most probably be sold for one sixth of what Westhay
has cost; and then what a beautiful cottage might be built on it for
1000£—By the bye,—Butterlip How [5] is far above my powers, I am
afraid:—for no doubt the neighbourhood of the lake will weigh with
the bidders considerably.—Moreover, for my own part,—I should
prefer a situation not so public: Allan Bank, I think, is worth a
hundred of it. But I should prefer that place on the right hand side
of Ease-dale—close to the desolate valley—to any other place in or
about Grasmere. However, I wish I could buy it—and make a birth-
day present of it to Dorothy & Catherine. But I fear it will cost too
much for my purse.—I beg my kindest love to all my dear young

---

[5] Mary had written De Quincey that Butterlip How, a house in north
Grasmere, was advertised for sale and she feared it would fall into un-
congenial hands, but Mary Dawson was sure he would buy it (*MY*, I, 396).

friends—God bless them all! and am, my dear Madam, with the greatest affection and respect, ever your friend and servant, Thos. de Quincey.

[*Across folded back:*] I shall certainly leave Westhay this week: but, if you want anything that can be bought only in a great Town,—a letter addressed to the [*torn:*? care] of Mr. Wright, Bookseller, Castle St. Liverpool—will meet me t[*torn:*? here] also any letter addressed to the care of Mr. Cookson, Kendal will [*torn:*? meet] me there: as I promised to call on him in my [*torn:*? way b]ack.—

[*Address:*] *Monday, August 27th.*

    Mrs. Wordsworth / Grasmere / near Kendal / Westmoreland / [*torn:*? *Single* Shee]t / paid

[*Stamp:*] Wrington

37. *To William Wordsworth*

Ms. Dove Cottage. Unpub. Qtd., Eaton, pp. 198–199; Sackville-West, p. 128. Dorothy forwarded this letter to William, and wrote across it (MY, II, 488).

      82, Great Titchfield St.—Cavendish Square
        Thursday, April 16th.—1812.

My dear Sir,

 I may perhaps save you as much money as will buy a decent edition of Shakespeare by giving you some information respecting the coaches from Liverpool to London.—There are two heavy coaches—I don't know how many light ones—and a mail:—the mail, when I passed through Liverpool, was charging 5 £, the light coaches 4 £; and the two heavy ones 2 £ 12s. 6d.—a fellow passenger, indeed, from whom I learnt these rates, told me that he believed all the fares would soon be raised; but, if you should find this to be so, no doubt the proportions would still continue nearly the same. The heavy coaches start in the evening; one at 5 or ½ after 5, from the Talbot Inn in Water St. close to the Exchange (Water St. leads down from the Exchange end of Castle St. to the water side): this, I understand, is the quickest and *genteelest* of the two; but unfortunately I was too late for it; and was obliged to put up with the disgrace of going by the other which sets off at ½ past 6 in the evening from the Saracens Head in

Dale St.—The bad points about this coach are that it keeps you up two nights—is 12 hours longer on the road than the light coaches (it calls itself indeed *The Expedition;* but it is called, on the road, *Old Heavy*)—and finally, as I said before, that it is not a coach for a gentleman. But on this head I say as a Roman Emperor said to his son who reproached him for a certain tax by holding up a chamber-pot to his nose and asking him if that was a fit source of revenue to a Roman Emperor—Ah my son! but I find nothing offensive in the money which this yields me. True it is that I set off from Liverpool at ½ past six on Tuesday evening March 24th.—and was not landed in Piccadilly until the Thursday night following after the lamps were lighted; nonetheless I agreed with myself, as I was walking up Piccadilly, that two guineas (or upwards) was an affront that in such a case ought to be pocketed. For two guineas, I believe, is an under-calculation of what you may save by this coach; since, besides the difference of fare, they charged me nothing for luggage—and, from the irregularity of it's motions, no meals are prepared on the road except Breakfast; so that it rests with yourself to determine your own expenses in that article.—A further recommendation of this coach to *you,* I believe, will be that it carries you through Oxford; which the light coaches and the mail, I think, do not. However, as it stops only to change horses, only so much of the city is seen as the coach passes through.—Still I would not disguise that the coach is *infamously* blackguard; I do acknowledge that every man in it was ashamed of his vehicle;—accordingly one had been disappointed of a place in the light coaches;—another made it a constant rule that nothing could induce him to depart from—No! on that point he was inflexible, never to get into a heavy coach ever since he had (many years ago) by ac-cident got into one and discovered what sort of a conveyance it was; but most unfortunately, in this case, he found all the places in the mail engaged; and go that night he must;—a third had a mind to see what sort of a thing it was;—&c. &c.—Balancing all the pros and cons, however, I still think that so long as it continues at a decent blackguard price, this blackguard coach ought to have and shall have my patronage.

I called on Dr. Stoddart [1] the Monday after I arrived in London.

Letter 37:
[1] John Stoddart (1773–1856), later knighted for his services as Chief

He was very friendly and communicative; so that I got all the information that was necessary to me in forming a judgment on the Civil Law as a profession; indeed quite enough to make me anxious for no more,—I have now determined to enter at Gray's Inn;[2] and, as a preliminary, have written down to my College for an attested account of the number of terms which I kept at Oxford;—to expedite which, and for other purposes, I am now on the point of going down to Oxford. I shall be up again, of course, in time to keep the Easter term at Gray's Inn; which point is accomplished, as perhaps you know, by masticating for three days in the Hall of that honourable society.—In the mean time, if you should have leisure enough to give me the favor of a call, you will either find me at this place or hear where I am.

You will not, I presume, want lodgings for yourself whilst in London: otherwise I can recommend the rooms which I now occupy, as comfortable and tolerably respectable;—the family is a very decent and orderly one.

I remain, dear Sir, with kind respects to the ladies—and my best love to all the children,

Your faithful friend,
Thomas De Quincey.

Dr. Stoddart can give you Capt. Pasley's address, I believe:—Capt. P. is now in London, Dr. S. says,—on some business relating to improvements projected by him in the constitution of the Artillery Corps: his improvements, I believe, will be adopted, unless a quarrel with Lord Mulgrave about some breast works which P. wishes to obtain, should stand in the way.[3]

Poor *Sir* Humphrey Davy!—From anything that I know of him, I never could think very highly of him in any way; but verily I thought him above this: his ambition for himself was then, it seems, to be as great a man as Sir Richard Phillips; and for Mrs. Apreece, that she

---

Justice of Malta, then practicing in Doctor's Commons and writing leaders for the *Times*.

[2] He actually entered the Middle Temple on June 12, 1812 (Eaton, p. 199).

[3] See Letter 32, note 20. Pasley was then advocating a Lancasterian or monitorial system of self-instruction among the noncommissioned officers and men of the engineering corps, with the result that he was appointed by Lord Mulgrave, Master-General of the Ordnance, as director of a new school for field instruction at Chatham.

might not be obliged to yield the *pas* to Lady Branscomb—relic of Sir Jas. Branscomb, late keeper of the fortunate lottery office![4]

[*Address:*]   William Wordsworth Esqr. / to the care of Mr. Cookson, Merchant / Kendal / Westmoreland [*Forwarded:*] at Sir George Beaumont's Bart. / Grosvenor Square / London
[*Postmark:*] APR 18 1812

38. *To Dorothy Wordsworth*

Ms. Dove Cottage. Pub., Eaton, pp. 207–208.

[London]
[June 12, 1812]

My dearest Friend

Yesterday morning I received your letter [1] with its bitter tidings. Oh that I might have seen my darling's face once again! Oh what a heavy increase of affliction to me and to her parents is this! what a bitter pang that we might not see her blessed face again. I parted from her in chearfulness, and had no misgivings; but I cannot bear to think of this. My dear friend,—write to me as circumstantially as you can; it cannot add to your grief to do this; and it will be an inexpressible consolation to me. Particularly, her father and I wish to know where she is buried. Do not, my dear friend, omit anything that you remember.

I saw Mr. Wordsworth off on the Hereford Coach this day at 2 o'clock. He had deemed it best—with the advice of some friends—to write to Mr. Thomas Hutchinson to break the news to poor dear Mrs. W. He will write to you from Hindwell,[2] if possible, so as that

---

[4] On April 8 Davy, a celebrated chemist, had been knighted by the Prince Regent; three days later he married Mrs. Apreece, a wealthy widow. De Quincey wrote of him in *Tait's Magazine* for March, 1837, ascribing the dislike for him to Coleridge (M, III, 16–23). De Quincey's other examples of dubious knighthood are Sir Richard Phillips (1767–1840), founder of the *Monthly Magazine* and a radical publisher of cheap compendiums, and Sir James Branscomb, a proprietor of a chain of lottery ticket offices.
Letter 38:

[1] *MY*, II, 502–503.
[2] Mary Wordsworth was visiting her brother, Thomas Hutchinson, at Hindwell, in Radnor, Wales, when Catharine died on June 4.

you may receive his letter on Wednesday. He expects to be at Hind-well on Sunday morning.

God support Mrs. Wordsworth under her mighty affliction!

My dearest friends, God bless you! is the prayer of

Yours most affectionately

Thos. De Quincey

82, Great Titchfield St., Oxford St.

Friday, June 12th.—1812.

I will write again to-morrow.

39. *To Dorothy Wordsworth*

Ms. Dove Cottage. Pub. Eaton, pp. 208–210.

[London]

[June 13–15, 1812]

My dear Friend

After I parted with Mr. Wordsworth, I took a walk—and left my-self too little time to say all that I wished to you. But I told you all, I think, that you would be chiefly anxious to know; namely, that Mr. Wordsworth would be at Hindwell on Sunday, and would write to you immediately. His plan was, if he could gain Mrs. W's consent, to make short deviations here and there from the direct road; if not, to go directly home. By this time, poor afflicted mother! she has heard of her heart-breaking loss; God grant her fortitude, and make her capable of comfort.

Mr. Wordsworth called on me an hour or two after I received your letter; in the evening he was so kind as to come again, and sate some hours with me. We found some lightening to our anguish in comparing what has been with what might have been. As you have suggested, it is but too likely that if she had lived, it would have been to the perpetual sorrow of us all. But yet it remains true that we had a blessing of our lives amongst us, and that this blessing is taken away. Effectual comfort for this thought there can be none, until long years shall have made her sweet image and all the circumstances that now surround her in our recollections dim and indistinct. My greatest consolation is that she must have lived a most happy life; excepting that grievous sickness in the whooping-cough, she had no other trouble to disturb her happiness. Oh what a thought of comfort it is also that I was one of those who added to her happiness. What tender what happy hours we passed together! Many a time, when we were alone, she would put her sweet arms about my neck and kiss me with a transport that was even then quite affecting to me. Nobody can judge from her manner to me before others what love she shewed to me when we were playing or talking together alone. On the night when she slept with me in the winter, we lay awake all the middle of the night—and talked oh how tenderly together: When we fell asleep, she was lying in my arms; once or twice I awoke from the pressure of her dear body; but I could not find [it] in my heart to disturb her. Many times on that night—when she was murmuring out tender sounds of endearment, she would lock her little arms with such passionateness round my neck—as if she had known that it was to be the last night we were ever to pass together. Ah pretty pretty love, would God I might have seen thy face and kissed thy dear lips again!

Oh dear Friend—what a comfortable what a blessed faith is that of a true Christian, who believes that no more change will pass over us than may take away our frailties and impurities—of which she sweet innocent could have none—and is assured that he shall meet and know again the child *as* a child, and his beloved *as* his beloved!

Monday morning, June 15th.

What goes before was written on Saturday: but being interrupted soon after I wrote thus far, I was obliged to keep my letter to this day —there being no post yesterday. I have written almost illegibly, I see, —having bad pens, and no means of mending them; but I hope you will be able to make it out.

I intend leaving London on Saturday night next; I long to be with you, and have no doubt that I shall be at liberty by that day. I shall reach Liverpool at furthest in the course of Monday—and shall leave it either on Tuesday or Wednesday morning. If you should have any occasion to write to me,—a letter put into the Ambleside post by Sunday night—addressed to the care of Mr. Merritt [1] No. 60. Castle St.

Letter 39:

[1] Senior member of Merritt and Wright, booksellers. He had been a friend since De Quincey's boyhood days at Everton, visited him in the Lakes in 1814, and still provided a forwarding address in 1824 (see *Diary*, pp. 228–229; *Memorials*, II, 38).

Liverpool—will be sure to reach me. Let Mary Dawson know, if you please, how much I am obliged to her for her attentions to you at this time. I hope she has had good health whilst I have been away; but I am afraid her spirits must have been much dejected since the news I sent her from Liverpool. I was sorry that I could do so little to lighten her distress; but, as the case stood, it seemed to me that nothing could be done.

What follows is only for yourself.

I say that I am obliged to M.D.; and so I am: but indeed she owed everything that she could do and much more as a fitting expression of the sorrow and contrition which she ought to feel for the most unprovoked harshness of language and manner with which she used sometimes to speak to Catherine. But on this subject no doubt her conscience must have bitterly reproached her; and therefore I shall say nothing to her about it. I spoke to her frequently about the extreme unreasonableness of this behaviour; but, as her harshness was rather in the tone and manner of what she said than anything in the matter of it which I might cite and insist upon as a proof of what I charged her with, I had no other remedy than to take care that Catherine should not be left under her care; which she never was except in one or two instances when I could not prevent it.

Four days have now gone by since I received this heart-rending news; and my grief has been continually growing upon me, my mind being constantly employed in calling up before me the thousand incidents and little passages of merriment or tenderness in her life with which I was connected—and in retracing the whole history of our affection for each other. It was at all times a tender employment to me in solitude to go over her pretty sayings and actions; and much more so when I had been for some short time separated from her: but now it is moving to me almost beyond what I can bear to do this—when such a heart-breaking interest is reflected upon them by the thought that they were the sayings and actions of a child who was so soon to be taken from us.

On this day last week, then, this dear child was buried. I do not mourn that I was spared the agony of following her to the grave, though I would have given up years of life to have seen her again. One thing hurts me, when I think of this: I fear that the custom of the country would oblige you to let many idle gazers look at our darling's face after she was dead—who never gave her a look of love or interest whilst she was living. But you would not, I am sure, permit this—if it could be avoided: only that, from your own exceeding tenderness and benignity, perhaps you sometimes attribute too much depth of feeling to others. It must surely be affecting even to a stranger to think that some should have gazed upon her with no more emotion than the most unfeeling must have from the thought of an innocent child having departed to God, and that we three who doated so passionately upon her—her mother, her father, and I should have been allowed to see her face no more!—God bless you and comfort you, my dear Friends Most affectionately yours, Thomas De Quincy.

[*Address:*]   Miss Wordsworth / Grasmere / near Ambleside / Westmoreland
              Post paid
[*Postmark:*] JU 15 1812

40a. *To Dorothy Wordsworth*

Ms. Craig Papers. Pub. Japp, I, 167–170. This is apparently a draft of 40b, although it is relatively clean, showing few revisions. There is what appears to be another partial draft in the Dove Cottage collection. Its variants are shown between ⟨ ⟩ in this text.

[London]
Sunday evening, June 21st. [1812]

My dear Friend,

I thank you much for your long and most affecting letter [1] ⟨, which I received on Friday⟩. One passage troubled me greatly; I mean where you speak of our dear child's bodily sufferings; her father and I trusted that she had been insensible to ⟨all⟩ pain—that being generally the case, as I believe ⟨have believed⟩, in convulsions. But thank God! whatever were her sufferings, they were short in comparison of what she would have had in most other complaints; and now at least sweet love she is at rest and in peace. It being God's pleasure to recal [*sic*] his innocent creature to himself, perhaps in no other way could it have been done more mercifully to her; though to the bystanders for the time few could be more terrible to behold. How much more suffering would she have had in a common fever from cold; and what anguish to us

---

Letter 40a:
[1] This letter is apparently lost.

all ⟨,⟩ if she had called upon our names in delirium—and fancied that we would not come to her relief! This I remember witnessing at my father's bedside on the morning when he died: I was but a child ⟨of seven or eight years old⟩, and had seen too little of my father to have much love ⟨any deep affection⟩ for him; but I remember [having] been ⟨being⟩ greatly affected at ⟨agitated on⟩ hearing him moan out to my mother a few minutes before he died—Oh Eliza Eliza! ⟨Eliza—Eliza⟩ why will you never come and ⟨will you not⟩ help me to raise this ⟨great⟩ weight?

I was truly glad to find from your account of her funeral that those who attended ⟨was glad to find that those who attended at⟩ her funeral were in general such as would more or less unaffectedly partake in your ⟨feel an unaffected⟩ sorrow ⟨for her loss⟩. It has been an awful employment ⟨thought⟩ to me—the recollecting where I was and how occupied ⟨employed⟩ when this solemn scene was going on: at that time I must have been ⟨I must at that time have been walking⟩ in the streets of London; ⟨for, having just recovered from a sharp illness, I thought that after the heat of the day was declined, I would try⟩ [end of partial draft] tired, I remember, for I had just recovered from sickness—but chearful, and filled with pleasant thoughts. Ah! what a mortal revulsion of heart, if any sudden revelation [2] should have laid open to my sight what scene was passing in Grasmere vale! On the night of June 3rd.-4th. I remember, from a particular circumstance which happened in the room below me, that I lay awake all night long—in serious thought, but yet as chearful as if not a dream were troubling any one that I loved! As well as I recollect, I must have been closing my eyes in sleep just about the time that my blessed Kate was closing hers for ever! Oh that I might have died for her or with her! Willingly, my dear friend, I would have done this. I do not say it from any sudden burst of anguish, but as a feeling that I have ejaculated in truth and sincerity a thousand times since I heard of her death. If I had seen her in pain, I could have done anything for her; and reason it was that I should; for she was a blessing to *me,* and gave me many and many an hour of happy thoughts that I can never have again.

---

[2] Curiously, De Quincey told Woodhouse in 1821 that he had had a presentiment that ill fortune was overtaking Cathy when he heard a dog howl three times outside his door on the night before he received news of her death (*De Quincey and His Friends,* ed. James Hogg [London, 1895], pp. 86–87).

You tell me to think of her with tender chearfulness; but far from that, dear friend, my heart grows heavier and heavier every day. More and more of her words and looks and actions keep coming up before me; and there is nobody to whom I can speak about her. I have struggled with this dijection [*sic*] as much at I can; twice I have passed the evening with Mr. Coleridge; and I have every day attempted to study. But after all I find it more tolerable to me to let my thoughts take their natural course, than to put such constraint upon them. But let me not trouble you with complaints, who have sorrow enough to bear of your own and to witness in others.

Yesterday I heard from Mr. Wordsworth, and was grieved to hear of Mrs. Wordsworth's state of mind; but I knew that it could not be otherwise. She would have borne her loss better, I doubt not, if she had been on the spot: as it is, this great affliction would come upon her just when her mind would be busiest about thoughts of returning to her children. I think of her often with the greatest love and compassion.

This afternoon I was putting my clothes and books into the trunk; whilst I was about it, I remembered that it was the 21st. of June, and must therefore be exactly a quarter of a year since I left Grasmere; for I left it on Sunday, March 22nd. This day thirteen weeks therefore I saw Kate for the last time. The last words, which she said to me (except that perhaps she might call out some words of farewell in company with the rest who were present)—I think were these: the children were speaking to me altogether, and I was saying one thing to one and another to another; and she, who could not speak loud enough to overpower the other voices, had got up on to a chair; and putting her hand upon my mouth she said with her sweet importunateness of action and voice—Kinsey, Kinsey—what a-bring Katy from London? I believe she said it twice; and I remember that her mother noticed the earnestness and intelligence of her manner, and looked at me, and smiled. This was the last time that I heard her sweet voice distinctly; and I shall never hear one like it again! God bless you, my dear Friend!—Ever yours, T. de Quincey.

N.B.—Mary Dawson would surely suppose that, as a mark of respect to your family, I should wish her to get mourning at my expense:—if she has not done this, pray tell her that I particularly desire it may be done. I forgot to mention it before.

I shall leave London not earlier than Tuesday, not later than

Wednesday. I have been detained in a way that I could not prevent. How soon I get to Grasmere—will depend on the accidents of meeting conveyances etc. I trust I shall find you all well.

I wrote a second letter to you last Monday, June 15th.

40b. *To Dorothy Wordsworth*

Ms. Dove Cottage. Pub. in part, Eaton, pp. 211–212.

[London]
Sunday evening, June 21st. [1812]

My dear Friend

I thank you much for your long and most affecting letter. One passage in it troubled me greatly; I mean where you spoke of our dear child's bodily sufferings. Her father and I trusted that she had been insensible to pain—that being generally the case, I believe, in convulsions. But thank God! whatever were her sufferings, they were short in comparison of what she would have had in most other complaints; and now at least sweet love she is at rest and in peace. It being God's pleasure to recal [*sic*] his innocent creature to himself, perhaps in no other way could it have been done more mercifully to her, though to the bystanders for the time few could be more afflicting to behold. How much more suffering would she have had in a common fever from a cold; and what anguish to us all, if she had called upon our names in delirium—and fancied that we would not come to her relief! This I remember witnessing at my father's bedside on the morning when he died: I was but a child, and had seen too little of him to feel much at his death; but I was greatly affected at hearing him moan out to my mother a few minutes before he died—Oh Betty Betty! why will you never come and help me to raise this weight?

I was truly glad to find from your account of her funeral that those who attended were in general such as would unaffectedly partake (more or less) in your sorrow. It has been an awful employment to me —the recollecting where I was and how occupied when this solemn scene was going on. At that time I must have been in the streets of London; tired, I remember, for I had just recovered from sickness— but chearful, and filled with pleasant thoughts. Ah what a mortal revulsion of heart, if any sudden revelation could have laid open to my sight what scene was passing in Grasmere vale! On the night June 3-4—I remember, from a particular circumstance, that I lay awake all night long; in serious thought, but yet as chearful as if not a dream were troubling any one that I loved! I think I heard the clock strike *five:* if so I must have been closing my eyes in sleep just about the time that my blessed Kate was closing hers for ever! Oh that I could have died for her or with her! Willingly dear friend I would have done this. I do not say it from any momentary burst of grief, but as a feeling that I have ejaculated in truth and sincerity a thousand times since I heard of her death. If I had seen her in pain, I could have done anything for her; and reason it was that I should; for she was a blessing to *me,* and gave me many and many an hour of happy thoughts that I can never have again.

You tell me to think of her with tender chearfulness; but far from that dear friend my heart grows heavier and heavier every day. I have done what I could against this oppression of spirits; twice I have passed the evening with Mr. Coleridge; and I have often endeavoured to study. But after all I find it more tolerable to let my thoughts take their natural course, than to put such constraint upon them. But let me not trouble you with complaints who have sorrow enough of your own to bear—and to witness in others.

Yesterday I heard from Mr. Wordsworth, and was grieved to hear of Mrs. Wordsworth's state of mind; but I knew it could not be otherwise. She would have borne her loss better, I doubt not, if she had been on the spot: as it is, this affliction would be doubly poignant to her—coming upon her just when her mind would be busiest with images of a delightful return to Grasmere and meeting again with her children. I think of her with the greatest compassion and love.

This afternoon—whilst I was putting up my clothes and books into a trunk—I remembered that to-day was the 21st. of June—just a quarter of a year from the day on which I left Grasmere; for I left it on Sunday, March 22nd. On this day thirteen weeks therefore I saw Kate for the last time. The last words that she said to me (except that perhaps she might call out some words of farewell in company with the rest who were present)—I think were these: the children were speaking to me all at once, and I was saying one thing to one and another to another; and she, who could not speak loud enough to overpower the other voices, had got up on a chair by which I was standing; and putting her hand upon my mouth she said with a sweet importunateness of voice and gesture—Kinsey, Kinsey—what a-bring Katy from London? I believe she said it twice; and I remember that her mother noticed the earnestness of her manner, and looked at me, and smiled. This was the last time I am almost certain that I heard her sweet voice and saw her sweet countenance distinctly; and I shall never hear or see anything so delightful again. Oh if I had known that it was to be the last!

I shall leave London not earlier than Tuesday, nor later than Wednesday. I have been detained in a way that I could not prevent. How soon I reach Grasmere—will depend on the accidents of meeting conveyances &c. I trust I shall find you all well.

Remember me most kindly to Miss Hutchinson and to the children.

I wrote a second letter to you last Monday, June 15th.

[*Bottom of page, probably only close and signature, cut off.*]
[*Address:*] Miss Wordsworth / Grasmere / near Ambleside / Westmoreland
       Post Paid / June 22, 1812
[*Postmark:*] JU 22 1812

41. *To William Wordsworth*

Ms. Dove Cottage. Unpub. Qtd. Sackville-West, p. 105.

5 Northumberland St. Mary-le-bone
Saturday, July 3—1813

My dear Sir,

I am now in London for the Trinity Term, and shall not *at any rate* leave it until this day week. If you write therefore by the Wednesday's post,—I shall get your letter in time to transact any business for you, connected with your office, that may happen to be pending at this time. It has only just occurred to me that you do not know my address; and, for want of that knowledge, may possibly be missing at this time an opportunity of employing my services.

Between keeping the Easter and Trinity Terms I spent three weeks in Somersetshire. A few days before my arrival at Westhay, my mother had a violent bilious attack which began with a fit very much resembling an apoplectic one. The medical man, whom my sister sent for from Clifton, differed so much in opinion from our Wrington Apothecary—that I do not well know even yet what name to give it;—but,

from a recollection of former illnesses of hers, my sister is disposed to
think that it was only an unusually violent attack of her old bilious
complaint. She was removed, as soon as she could bear it, to Clifton;
and about a week ago she returned to Westhay considerably better, but
very nervous. I have promised to go down again to Westhay; so that
I shall not be at home quite as soon as I gave Mary Dawson some
reason to suppose I might. If I find my mother tolerably well recovered,—I shall stay about a fortnight in Somersetshire; and then
walk up to Liverpool through South and North Wales—and so home.

I spent last night with Mr. Coleridge and the ladies in Berners St.[1]
He seemed uneasy and out of spirits when anything was said to draw
his thoughts upon himself or his family; but as well able as usual to
abstract his mind from such thoughts; and, on the whole, I thought
pretty well in health as far as I could judge from his looks. I asked
him, at parting, if he could not contrive to go down to the North in a
few weeks; and I would join him on the road: but he only said that
he would take some opportunity of speaking to me on that subject.
Morgan is in the country on account of ill health.

I still keep my intention of going into Germany; but shall wait to
see what turn things take there. If the allies make peace with Bonaparte,—I shall for ever dismiss from my mind all concern for their
welfare. If they are content so to dishonor themselves—and are so
amorous of slavery,—God grant that they may have it in perfection for
themselves and their children!

I was told at the East India House on Thursday that I might have
an order on the Treasury to-day for my 100 guineas. But I fear that I
shall not be able to get it in time to send Mary Dawson anything by
this letter; indeed I do not know that she wants any money. But, if I
hear that she does, I shall in my next letter be well able to send it. I
beg my kind respects to the ladies—and my best love to the children;
and remain, my dear Sir, most faithfully and affectionately yours,
Thomas De Quincey.

If you see Southey, will you mention to him that I am offered by a
bookseller Dr. Francis Buchanan's Travels in the Mysore—3 vols.
4to. in *boards* (published at 6 guineas)—for 2 guineas and a half? It
is of the class of books, I believe, which he buys.

Letter 41:
[1] Mrs. John Morgan and her sister. See Letter 24, note 4.

I hope the Lloyds [2] are well; and beg my kind regards to them.

[*Across folded back:*] I wrote a note to Mrs. Wordsworth from London the day of my arrival from the North; and hope she received it.

[*Inserted, inverted above salutation:*] I have taken the liberty of paying for my letter; not feeling it right to send my messages to M.D. at your expense.

I began to write on a sudden thought very near to the post time; and find that I have only half a sheet of paper.

[*Address:*]   William Wordsworth Esqr. / Rydal Mount / near Ambleside / Westmoreland
    Paid
[*Postmark:*] JY 3 1813

42. *To Dorothy Wordsworth* (?)

Ms. Craig Papers. Pub. in part, Japp. I, 175–176. This is a much corrected draft.

Westhay
Friday August 6th.—1813

My dear Madam,

I will trouble you or Mrs. Wordsworth, when either of you happens to be in Grasmere, to let Mary Dawson know that I may possibly be at home on Saturday night August 14th.: before that day she need *certainly* not expect me; and I fear not even then: but, that I may not in any case appear to have come upon her by surprise, [*canceled:* (as perhaps she might suspect if I came home suddenly and without warning)] I think it as well to give her notice that my purpose hitherto has been to reach Grasmere about that day—and that I have not yet determined to renounced [*sic*] it. If I do not leave this place in time enough to be at home on the 14th., most probably I shall stay a fortnight longer.

---

[2] Charles Lloyd, who lived at Old Brathay near Ambleside, was a friend of Lamb, Coleridge, and Southey, and the author of some sentimental verse and *Edmund Oliver,* a satirical novel supposedly drawn in part from the career of Coleridge. The Wordsworths did not much like him but were at least neighborly because his sister Priscilla was married to Christopher, the poet's brother. Charles was subject to fits and delusions, and suffered a breakdown in 1813.

On Sunday last one of my sisters received a letter from my brother Richard—dated London. I believe you know that he is as restless as the sea; so you may guess our astonishment on hearing that he had only just left Westmoreland. [*The following sentence appears to have been canceled.*] If he had known of my being here, probably he would have communicated some tidings from Grasmere or it's neighbourhood; as it was, his letter told us only one solitary article in the shape of news which gave. In the way of news from Grasmere or it's neighbourhood his letter communicated nothing except a very short and indistinct mention of Mr. Lloyd's illness in July: this gave us all great concern: but we collect, from the wording of it, that he had recovered before my brother left the North. Grasmere can be considered a change of scene to Mr. Lloyd.—I trust that you will not scruple to make use of my house: even if I come as early as I talk of, there is (you know) room for us all.

I say above that I *fear* I shall not be in Grasmere by the 14th.; referring, by that expression, chiefly to the roses on my cottage— which, I grieve to think, will be—after that time—nearly extinct.

The other night Mrs. H. More lately from a *progress* among her people (if you think *that* any honour) made very minute inquiries respecting Mr. Lloyd's pursuits—habits—and tastes, told me that she had met the senior Mr. and Mrs. Lloyd at Mr. Galton's,[1] I think; and had a good deal of conversation with them.

[*A thin line through suggests De Q. canceled this paragraph.*] I have been twice in London since I saw you. On my last visit I saw a little of Coleridge: but during the latter part of my stay he would see nobody—not even Mrs. Morgan or her sister. He fancied that he had a fit of the gout coming on;—and one day Mrs. M. told me that he had flung a note from the top of stairs—to this effect—that the gout had already mounted to his stomach, and—if he were at all disturbed or agitated—would speedily attack the brain. It happened however on a night after this, when I had staid till past one o'clock with the two ladies, that they perceived a body of smoke turning the corner from Oxford St. into Berners St. accompanied with a strong smell of burn-

---

Letter 42:

[1] The elder Charles Lloyd was a Quaker philanthropist and gentleman scholar. This meeting could well have been in the home of Samuel Galton, Quaker gunmaker of Birmingham, whose family was related to the Lloyds and friendly with the Mores.

ing. C. was dressed and reading in his room; and, on Mrs. M's knocking at his door, he instantly came out and tripped down stairs with her as lightly as ever.

Give my love to the Wordsworths; and say, if you please, that I have written to them twice since I left the North. My first letter was to Mrs. W; my second to Wordsworth.[2] I was disappointed in having no answer to this last: but I suppose he did not want anything in London. [*Rest of sentence canceled*] and might have no opportunity of sending Southey's answer about the book within the time

We have company in the house; and I write in some hurry: else I have matter of one kind or another that might fill a long letter.

Begging you to excuse my brevity,—I remain, dear Madam

Your very faithful friend and servant,

Thomas De Quincey.

43. *To William Wordsworth*

Ms. Dove Cottage. Unpub.
[*Upper left corner torn off.*]

[?Grasmere]
[?1816–7]

gentleman, who delivers this note to you, is a gownsman of Cambridge. My know [*torn*] more than I could gain in an hour's conversation this afternoon; but in the course of [*torn*] intelligently on the subject of your Poems and so fervently acknowledged his own obliga [*torn*] that I could not but draw very favorable conclusions as to his character and abilities: [*torn*] when he asked me with some earnestness at parting whether from my knowledge of you [*torn*] that a stranger, who should present himself to your notice self-introduced, would be looked upon as having taken an unwarrantable liberty,—I did not hesitate to assure him that, in a case such as his, he would not: at the same time, finding that he would feel himself more at ease if he could carry a line with him from any acquaintance of yours, I offered my services for that purpose. In doing this I am conscious that I have been transferring the act of intrusion from this gentleman to myself—and

---

[2] The second of these is probably Letter 41; the first appears not to have survived.

that I may stand in more need of an apology than he would have done: but on the whole I resolved to run the hazard of this; trusting that your knowledge of the unalterable regard and veneration which I must feel for you will be a surety for me that I cannot mean to take an undue liberty; and thinking it better that I should seem to have miscalculated the privilege which I may claim in virtue of having been once honored with a place in your [friendship *scratched through*] good opinion than that this gentleman should be obliged to leave the country (as he is now on the point of doing) without having it in his power to gratify a wish to which with his feelings and knowledge he must naturally attach so much importance.

[*Close and signature cut off.*]
[*Address:*] William Wordsworth Esqr. / Rydal Mount
    For the Gentleman at the Red Lion
        with Mr. De Quincey's Compliments

CHAPTER FOUR

◿ RECONCILIATION

Somehow De Quincey pulled himself together, reduced his consumption of opium from 8,000 to 1,000 drops a day, and took Margaret belatedly to church on February 15, 1817. They were married, says the Register, "in the presence of John Simpson, Geo. Mackereth"—the bride's father and the parish clerk. There is no mention of the Wordsworths. But curiously enough, Mary Armitt declared, in a book published posthumously in 1916 and drawing upon memories of those who could remember the Wordsworths, "Little Dora Wordsworth signed the register." [1] Dora, not yet thirteen at the time of the wedding, would hardly have been expected to be an official witness, but does Miss Armitt repeat a garbled local tradition about some association of the Wordsworths with De Quincey's nuptials? Dorothy wrote that the ceremony took place on the day of her return to Rydal. Could it have been delayed waiting for her to come back? She did not say that she was there, although she said De Quincey was "utterly changed in appearance." In 1881, when alterations were contemplated on Grasmere Church and William Wordsworth, Jr., was applied to for information on the past state of the edifice, he wrote, "The loft, if I remember was enclosed on the day of Mr. de Quincey's marriage at which I was present." [2] Since he was then not yet seven, perhaps too much weight should not be put on the evidence of his memory. Still, he was De Quincey's godson, and it would have been appropriate for him to have attended the ceremony. Perhaps the Rydal Mount family swallowed their disapproval after events had come to such a pass, and at least went to see Peggy made a decent woman.[3]

De Quincey's answer to all head-wagging, in an 1818 letter to his mother, was "In justice to my wife, I must say that she is all I could desire, and has in every way dignified the position in which she stands to me." [4] His treatment of this period in his 1821 *Confessions* is an interesting example of defensive coloration, written perhaps partly for the Wordsworths' benefit. The year 1816, he says, "was a year of brilliant water." He calls upon a painter to picture his happiness in Dove Cottage, in a room "populous with books," before a good fire and with "a lovely young woman" presiding over his tea table:

no, dear M., not even in jest let me insinuate that thy power to illumine my cottage rests upon a tenure so perishable as mere personal beauty; or that the witchcraft of angelic smiles lies within the empire of any earthly pencil.

Up to the middle of 1817, he declares, he judged himself to be "a happy man." Then he sank for four years under "the Circean spells of opium." [5] It was during these four years of "torpor" that relations with the Wordsworths were re-established, or at least revitalized; that, probably with William's aid, De Quincey was launched upon a career as a periodical writer through the editorship of the *Westmorland Gazette*—none of which is mentioned in the *Confessions*.

The first definite evidence of renewed contact between Dove Cottage and Rydal Mount is a stiffish letter of De Quincey's to Wordsworth on March 25, 1818. It began formally, "My dear Sir," and ended conventionally, "Your faithful Servant." In the course of it De Quincey announced

his intention of troubling the poet with another letter upon
an unspecified subject mentioned to him by a Mr. Irving
at Wordsworth's desire. The implication is that their exchange was solely by correspondence and third parties. The
ostensible reason for De Quincey's presuming to address
Wordsworth was to report an incident in the first of three
campaigns which the radical Henry Brougham waged in his
unsuccessful efforts to capture one of the Parliamentary
seats for Westmorland County which had long been controlled by the Tory Lowther family: when Brougham arrived in Grasmere, "the Church Bells were rung"! De
Quincey had intended to ask the rector, the Reverend
Thomas Jackson, to forward two papers which he was
writing in support of the Lowthers, but now he would have
nothing to do with the rector's help, and wondered whether
Wordsworth could assist him.

There can be no doubt about the sincerity of De Quincey's
political opinions and his real interest in this election. He
was characteristically a John Bull Englishman, loyal to
Church and state; he even remarked once that future arche-
ologists could dig him up as an example of a fossil Tory.[6]
Most of the conservatives were outraged at Brougham's
"rabble-rouzing" attack upon a seat which had not been
contested since 1774, and De Quincey's vehement participation in the campaign was to be expected. Since he had married into the family of a radical " 'Statesman," it was all
the more natural that he should reassert himself as a Tory
gentleman. Still, one suspects a certain calculation in this
overture to Wordsworth. The poet was not, as De Quincey
recognized, on the Lowther Political Committee; and because of his official position as Distributor of Stamps for
Westmorland County he had to be guarded in his political
activity—why address him? Furthermore, when Wordsworth informed him that Mr. Jackson was not culpable in
the incident of the bells, De Quincey quickly veered by saying that he would give one paper to the rector, but would
still like to have Wordsworth's help with the other.

De Quincey's application had plausibility, since, although
the poet was not actually on the Committee, his loyalty and

influence were patent. Indeed, his whole household espoused
the Yellow cause: even eight-year-old Willy, as his father
wrote to Viscount Lowther with a grin on March 16, was
"a complete Yellow, having got the jaundice, poor Lad, so
that he has no occasion for Ribbons, though he wears them."
Mary wrote that Wordsworth himself was "so engrossed"
that he could not attend to anything else. On February 21
he had published two letters in the *Kendal Chronicle* signed
"A Friend of Truth"; and he had also printed in the *Chronicle* (February 14), in the *Carlisle Patriot* (March 7), and
as a broadside called "to the Freeholders of Westmorland" (February 28), versions of parts of a major effort,
a pamphlet entitled *Two Addresses to the Freeholders,* the
"Advertisement" of which was dated the day after De
Quincey's opening letter.[7] How much of this De Quincey
knew is made doubtful by a reference in his April 8 letter
to the work of "A Friend of Truth" as if he had no suspicions that Wordsworth was the author. He must have
known enough to have had grounds for thinking that the
poet's support might get his own efforts prominently published. Perhaps he also hoped that Wordsworth might read
and revise his tract.

Probably De Quincey was primarily interested, however,
in refurbishing relations with the poet. Back in 1808 he had
learned that the safest common ground with Wordsworth
was politics. The poet might be impatient of the younger
man's opinions on poetry or nature, but both men were
sound Tories with a liberal leaven and could without reservations join forces against the vulgar upstart Brougham.
Wordsworth was thoroughly roused in defense of principle
and patron (Lord Lonsdale, head of the Lowther clan,
had helped him get his stamp distributorship). The poet
would be glad of any aid, and, we recall, he thought
De Quincey a *"remarkably"* able writer. In that opening
letter De Quincey said frankly that he expected to send
Wordsworth another on "some private concerns." Possibly
he was already thinking of enlisting Wordsworth's support
in getting the editorship of the new newspaper which the
conservatives were projecting as a balance to the Blue

Kendal Chronicle. For the poet had been in the thick of
the newspaper business since February—trying to influence
the editor of the *Chronicle,* writing for it and urging his
friends to do the same if "only to keep others out," attempting to get control of the paper for the Lowther
interests, and, when that course seemed impossible, looking about for an editor for the new journal.[8] The situation
was ripe for reconciliation in the common cause. De Quincey
was obliging and humble, even offering to submit to editorial alteration by any member of Wordsworth's family.
His only pride now was in his soundness of political principle—and his wife's.

Certainly De Quincey felt the need to disassociate himself from the radicalism of the Simpsons, and if possible to
purge Peggy also of that stain. How strongly he was im-
pelled to breathe more intellectual, aristocratic air is apparent in his April 14 letter, in which he spoke a little
pathetically of the pleasure of delivering himself of feelings
for which he could "look for little general sympathy." He
hastened to add, however, that his wife had generously
accompanied him in his views, and in spite of all the efforts
of her family to influence her, had "uniformly behaved"
in a fashion which might be expected "where the heart is
not habitually malignant nor the understanding greatly
abused." In short, Peggy was one of nature's noblewomen,
of a sort which Wordsworth, of all people, should appreciate. Thus with a faintly "I-told-you-so" defense of
Peggy, De Quincey strove to rehabilitate himself with
Wordsworth.

To these overtures Wordsworth responded promptly
and, evidently, in a friendly fashion. Only four days separated De Quincey's first and second letters of this exchange,
so that William must have answered almost immediately,
even though he was in Kendal or preparing to go there.
The close has been cut from De Quincey's second letter
and supplied in another hand on the third as "Your faithful friend & servant," but by the fourth (April 2), he was
signing confidently, "Very faithfully and affectionately
yours." Wary of Wordsworth's old inattentiveness to his

long and involved letters, he now cautiously repeated his
questions at the head with some such remark as, "Nothing
in this letter requires an answer, except the two following
questions" (Letter 50). For he could not keep his letters
or his essays within bounds, and was somewhat worried at
the impression he was making. The promised paper, or the
paper which he produced (it seems not to have been one of
the two mentioned in his first letter), was an analysis of
Brougham's speech at Kendal on March 23.[9] Characteristically it grew under his hands. He promised it by Tuesday,
and then sent only part on Wednesday, saying desperately
that it could be altered, or printed, or burned. Wordsworth
liked it, and it was published, probably about the middle of
April, as *Close Comments upon a Straggling Speech.* Significantly De Quincey dragged Peggy into his thanks: "It was
the very highest gratification to my wife and myself . . .
to find that what I had then sent was honored by your approbation" (Letter 48). This same letter expressed his per-
turbation "at the recollection of one word" in the paper
and attempted to justify his writing anonymously. With the
proofs he sent a brief note of corrections, and the next day
a long letter of afterthoughts. He was much relieved when
Wordsworth wanted to publish part of that letter also.

Things were going on nicely, although the two former
friends seem not to have come together personally at once.
In early April Wordsworth sent by his son John, De Quincey's old Latin pupil, a copy of the just-published *Two Addresses to the Freeholders.* De Quincey read it "twice and
very carefully," and, in a letter of April 8, judiciously
praised it as luminous and powerful. He added neatly that
Wordsworth dignified the local contest by giving it national
significance and making it worthy of his efforts, and—the
finest touch—that he himself held the same views, "as was
to be expected from any reflective man who should have
had the happiness which I had for so many years to benefit
by your conversation" (Letter 50). In this letter he also
mentioned "Miss Wordsworth's Report," which suggests
that he had seen the accounts of Brougham's speech Dorothy had written from Kendal; [10] he may have been at Rydal

Mount. By April 14 he felt free to ask to borrow Coleridge's *Sibylline Leaves,* and judged the time was ripe to
seek the poet's help in getting the editorship of the *Westmorland Gazette.* In this he was most circumspect, asking
whether Wordsworth knew any reason why he should not
apply, and presupposing assistance only if the poet preferred no other candidate. He frankly admitted that he was
not competent to undertake the mechanical or business parts
of the enterprise, and he forthrightly recognized that the
poet might have some reservations about his punctuality
and perseverance, but assured him that he had reformed
since he "last had the happiness to associate with" Wordsworth. The word "last" was inserted as an afterthought, in
token of De Quincey's confidence that a new association was
beginning. Finally, he declared his intention to contribute
everything in his power to support the paper, whatever the
outcome of his application, to which end he had been "finishing" the letters on the critical attacks upon Wordsworth
which he began in 1815. That, no doubt, was intended as
an earnest of his reformation—and perhaps as an implication that the editor could be serviceable to the poet. He had
also, he said, made some translations of Kant and Jean
Paul and would "very soon set about" some amusing essays,
so that he should have "some stock to begin with." His next
letter, on April 19, continued to demonstrate his fertility
and usefulness: he urged that the Tories do something for
the victims of a quarry accident before the Broughamites
stepped in; he was working anxiously on two more papers;
he tactfully suggested printing part of Wordsworth's
pamphlet as a handbill. It was a brave attempt; De Quincey
spread his wares as fetchingly as possible.

Maybe Wordsworth was inclined to prefer another's
interests or, more probably, was not eager to use his influence for De Quincey. After the *Convention of Cintra* affair,
we remember, he had pronounced definitely that De Quincey
was "not fitted for smooth and speedy progress in business."
Anyway, more than a month before De Quincey's application
Wordsworth had written for nominations to the chiefs of the
Courier, the *Sun,* and the *New Times;* and ultimately an

editor was imported from London, under whom the *West-morland Gazette* began with a self-righteous fanfare of intention to "support the established Institutions of the Country," on May 23, 1818.[11] Possibly news of this turn of events accounted for the apparent disruption after April 19 of the renewed correspondence which had produced nine letters from De Quincey in little more than three weeks. He must have been disappointed not to have been named editor; his principles and abilities seemed to make him a natural choice, and he sorely needed the money. Peggy was about to bear his second child—Margaret, born June 5. Of course, the cessation of letters may mean not pique but merely that the two men had returned to face-to-face communication. And possibly out of this closer association Wordsworth exerted himself to help De Quincey to get the editorship after all.

For in less than six weeks the imported editor "disgusted" the proprietors "in every way," and, as De Quincey grandiosely wrote to his uncle, "the principal gentlemen of the country then addressed an application"[12] to him—his pride making him not the petitioner but the petitioned. What, if anything, Wordsworth had to do with this is not clear. That the poet still had doubts as to the suitability of the appointment is apparent from his announcement to Lord Lonsdale: "The Editorship of the new Kendal Paper has passed into the hands of a most able man; one of my particular Friends; but whether he is fit, (I mean on the score of punctuality) for such a service, remains to be proved—*His* attainments and abilities are infinitely above such a situation."[13] It is interesting to note that then, when the disgraced daughter of a " 'Statesman" had been less than a year and a half mistress of Dove Cottage, Wordsworth described De Quincey to the first gentleman of the county as "one of my particular Friends." Did the poet mean merely to assure the Lowthers that he would be able to exercise strong influence on the new editor, or had the erring disciple been completely reinstated?

Whatever Wordsworth's role in getting De Quincey the position—and at the very least he made him a candidate by getting *Close Comments* published—he certainly seems to have tried to help him on the job. Obviously the stiff, epistolary relationship gave away to intimate conversation under pressure of the *Gazette* business, if it had not done so before. On September 27 De Quincey wrote to apologize for "not having presented" himself at Rydal Mount "last Sunday" because of illness. His letter makes it clear that the two men had discussed the paper and Wordsworth had given some advice about its conduct. If we can judge by the tone of the first issue which De Quincey edited (July 18, 1818),[14] the previous editor may have "disgusted" in part by his relative moderation toward the Brougham adherents; for the new policy was vehemently partisan. At first De Quincey devoted his energies faithfully to the cause, and produced a fairly routine provincial party paper. Soon, however, he was riding his hobby horses with assize reports, metaphysical speculations, and economic analyses. Wordsworth clearly protested against this esoteric tenor, as appears from De Quincey's reply blaming his assistant for the prominent display of a metaphysical piece, for he himself would not have treated the poet's advice so lightly as to repeat an error of which he had complained before. The editor had also—as the Lonsdale correspondence shows—become even too obstreperous in his attacks on the Broughamites, and Wordsworth had complained about that.

Indeed, Wordsworth must have frequently complained and advised. His letters to Viscount Lowther [15] sound almost as if the poet thought of himself as virtual editor of the *Gazette*. At least he assumed, inaccurately, that the editor was in his pocket. On September 22 he told his lordship, for instance, that "it seemed best not to notice" one of Brougham's pamphlets in the *Gazette*—as if the decision were his. A week later he wrote, "I have had a conference with the Editor of the *Gazette* about a rascally letter to you which appeared in the last *Kendal C*[hronicle]—and still more rascally notices of it by the Editor of that Journal. We have agreed upon the mode of noticing both, which he has undertaken to do." On October 6 he was again determining policy: "Two rules *we* ought to lay down; *never* to retort by attacking private character; and never to notice the *particulars* of a personal calumny. . . . What the Editor of the *Gazette* said in his last number upon this subject was not quite what I wished and we agreed upon, but I hope it would do no harm." He thought a "spirited article" of October 10 "a little too strong perhaps in the expression." On October 13 he assured his lordship that the Editor was "prepared to act as you wish in respect to private conduct," and on October 23 reassured: "I entirely concur with you in your observations on the *Westnd Gaz:* and on the desirableness of letting its election politics subside. The Editor I am sure would treat with deference any observations coming from me on this subject." With this motive he will "take care to see the Editor" before leaving for Lowther.

For all his deference, however, De Quincey proved less than tractable. As he bragged to Woodhouse later, "I so managed it as to preserve my independence." [16] Wordsworth's position was obviously awkward. The Lowthers, his patrons, were dissatisfied and were looking to him to do something with his very "particular friend." Viscount Lowther wrote his father on October 21: "I think our own Kendal paper is now getting too libellous," and even added, "the last week's specimen is certainly a most blackguard production." [17] Lowther protested to the poet, and he in turn wrestled delicately and rather futilely with an editor zealous of his independence. On November 8 Wordsworth complained crossly: "I much fear that the Editor will hurt the character of his paper by making too many promises, and then failing frequently to perform them." The poet was in the humiliating position of not always being able to make his protests heard: "I called several times lately on De Quincey," he wrote on December 6, "before I could see him." He went on portentously, "I fear that from one cause or another the *Gazette* is sinking." Patiently, two days later, "I have frequently urged De Quincey to adopt this plan [of terminating long-winded discussions]; he acknowledges the propriety of it; but he has no firmness—I shall be at him again upon the subject."

Thus Wordsworth was ever "at" De Quincey. The phrase

is revealing. Probably he had been "at" him in something
of the same fashion about the impropriety of marrying
Peggy. When Wordsworth cared about things, he worked
at them—a trait commendable in his nature, but sweeter in
the stomach than in the mouth. One can understand how De
Quincey found it hard to swallow, how he later complained
to Hessey of the poet's "certain ways . . . of annoyance." [18] De Quincey developed a defensive shell; and the
note of explanation, between apology and braggadocio,
which dulled the later letters of the *Convention of Cintra*
episode, sounds also in the *Westmorland Gazette* days. This
tone pervades the last surviving letter written to Wordsworth during De Quincey's editorship (June 14, 1819), in
which he apologized for a reprehensible article written by
his assistant. More apologies are evident from Sara's remark to Thomas Monkhouse that some disgusting letters
had appeared in the *Gazette,* but "Mr. de Q. did not know
of them being put in till too late." [19] Clearly De Quincey
was often in difficulty with the Wordsworths over the paper;
and his assistant in Kendal, Mr. Kilner (who got most of
the pay and, apparently, despite De Quincey's alleged regeneration of punctuality and perseverance, often had to get
out the issue himself), was a convenient whipping boy.

More welcome aid, undoubtedly, than Wordsworth's advice was his allowing some of his poems to appear in the
Gazette. Six numbers print poems of his, most of which had
already been published and were not signed in the *Gazette.*
On February 6, however, appeared a letter from the poet
to the editor: "Having observed three original Sonnets of
mine announced as making a part of the contents of the last
number of Blackwoods Edinburgh Magazine, you will oblige
me by reprinting them in your journal from my own M.S.,
in which they have undergone some alteration since they
were presented by me to Mr. Westall, with liberty to make
what use of them he thought proper." A fourth sonnet,
hitherto unpublished, Wordsworth offered "as a small acknowledgement of your civility, should you think proper to
insert the foregoing." [20] Such contributions were of assistance to De Quincey, but cannot be taken as indicating any

peculiar favor, for Wordsworth accorded a similar privilege to the next editor.

Wordsworth was, however, being friendly, as is further evidenced by his sending a copy of his *Peter Bell*, which De Quincey acknowledged with apologies for delay, and thoughtful comments, on June 14. Wordsworth was also trying to serve De Quincey in another way. In May, 1819, he wrote to ask Southey's interest with the editor of the *Quarterly Review* to procure for De Quincey the reviewing of pamphlets on the bullion question. Southey replied that he was sorry the *Quarterly* would be closed to De Quincey's views "because if De Quincey could bring his reasonings before the public through a favourable channel I think he would go far towards exploding a mischievous error." [21] Wordsworth apparently even enlisted Lord Lonsdale's influence in this project, for on June 16 he wrote thanking the earl for his "exertions and intentions on behalf of Mr De Quincey's introduction to the *Quarterly Review*."

This *Quarterly* business reflects Wordsworth's and Southey's approval of the *Gazette* essays on "Paper of the Bank of England," and suggests that the poet saw some reason to be proud of his "particular friend." According to De Quincey's account to his uncle—undoubtedly a rosy version—he had compelled himself "to work so much" that the circulation of the paper was now "much increased." It is a fact that the journal made a profit under his regimen, something that had not happened again by 1826, when Viscount Lowther complained of the "indifferent" hands into which the editorship had fallen.[22] And, although De Quincey's pages were too often filled by the easy expedient of copying Assize Reports—on the specious grounds that few things could be so morally edifying to his readers—his editorials were above the standard of a provincial journal.

But these were the dark days of the "Pains of Opium." When Wordsworth called several times at Dove Cottage without being able to see De Quincey, and feared that "from one cause or another" the *Gazette* was sinking, he certainly meant—and was charitable in not saying—that the editor was in an opium stupor. The columns of the weekly began to carry frequent notices of promised articles deferred until the next issue, and to apologize for difficulties occasioned by the editor's "distance from the press." The proprietors urged in vain that he move to Kendal to remedy that "inconvenience," and at last on November 5, 1819, respectfully accepted his resignation. To Viscount Lowther Wordsworth reported without comment in December: "De Quincey has left the *Gazette*." The reaction of the Wordsworth circle is recorded by Sara: "Mr. de Q. has given up the Editorship of the *Gaz.* & we have given it up also." On first blush this looks like striking loyalty; it may, however, reflect chiefly economy: the Wordsworths had been getting the paper free, and they now expected to have to pay for it. When the journal continued to come anyway, they finally wrote to De Quincey asking him to have it stopped, for fear they would suddenly be presented with a retroactive bill.[23]

The *Gazette* episode had certainly provided the occasion for a renewal of the old intimacy of discussion between poet and protégé, but it had also provided new friction and frustration. In the last weeks of the editorship, relations do not seem to have been very close. Dorothy wrote in September: "Mr. Gee will dine with us to-day and perhaps Mr de Quincey. He has been invited, but we never see him now." [24] Was Peggy invited?

Circumstances were forcing De Quincey to find another axis than Rydal Mount. The end of the *Westmorland Gazette* job was the end of his last excuse for staying on at the Lakes, where he had by now practically all expenses and no income. The guinea a week the editorship had netted him was not much, but without it his regular income was only the £18 a year from his share of the rent on a family warehouse. He was already living on loans from his mother, his sister, his uncle, and even John Wilson, who finally protested early in 1821 that he was drawn to the edge of bankruptcy by De Quincey's bills.[25] Southey, of course, was able to stay in Keswick while supporting himself by writing for the *Quarterly Review* and other distant journals. De Quincey toyed with similar activity. Wilson had for some time been urging him to write for *Blackwood's,* and John Murray had in 1818 sent him a twenty-six volume set of Schiller to review for the *Quarterly*.[26] Later De Quincey tried for a while to contribute to the *London Magazine* from Westmorland, but he simply could not work by remote control for long. Southey was a confident, methodical man; De Quincey was a diffident, labyrinthine one, who always foresaw difficulties and possibilities which had to be resolved by editorial conference before he could proceed to write, and who had some sort of compulsion to keep his copy until the last instant. Thus he was away in Edinburgh for two months at the end of 1820; from 1821 through 1825 he was often in London, miserable when he was away from his family, frustrated when he was away from his publisher; and from 1826 he spent most of the time in Edinburgh. The era which began when he ran down the hill with the Coleridge boys and came suddenly upon that diamond-paned cottage, a shrine which was to be associated with his sweetest and his bitterest memories—that era was ended. The intimacy was over, and the storm and stress of rupture was over, and the effort of reconciliation was over. The sequel is routine, until De Quincey's art and journalism brought back the old days again.

The general attitude of the Wordsworths toward De Quincey, from the end of the *Westmorland Gazette* episode until he began to publish revelations they considered impertinent, was rather that of a busy family toward a harmless, ne'er-do-well relative. According to their temperaments and moods they mocked or regretted his shortcomings, but on the whole they tolerated him, were friendly—even charitable—toward him, but never expected much of him or involved themselves closely with him. And this sort of antiseptic relation was to De Quincey—with his history of discipleship and "one of the family" intimacy—probably the cruelest of all. There was the sort of casual contact reflected in the poet's sending Viscount Lowther, on May 27, 1820, a piece of information which had been "told Mr. De Quincey." There was the kind of neighborliness which enabled Thomas Monkhouse, Mary's cousin, to keep his carriage in De Quincey's coach house when he visited Rydal Mount in the spring of 1822—but a neighborliness not close enough for De Quincey to know Monkhouse's first name or his exact relationship to the family. There was the curiosity keeping tabs on interesting movements, as demonstrated by Dora's writing on October 17, 1825, "the poor little Man is returned—he reached the Nab Thursday last." [27] And there was the detached amusement of Sara's report to the Wordsworths, then touring on the Continent, of De Quincey's renting a second house:

Mr de Quinceys Books have literally turned their master & his whole family out of doors—He is *arranging* them—so being strewed about & he meditating a journey to Edin[h] he thought the safest way, as 'his wife did not understand books' (as he expressed it to Mr Wm) & they the maids *would be dusting,* was to take another house—and now they are safely lodged at Fox Ghyll which he has taken for 6 months. I predict that there they will remain unless unsettled by an earth-quake or a second accummulation of Books (September 21, 1820; *SH*, p. 209).

It is noteworthy that even in writing to the family Sara used the formal "Mr" instead of the old nicknames.

Her prophecy about the Opium-Eater's tenure at Fox Ghyll (a comfortable house about a mile from Rydal Mount) was not quite accurate, although his six months did stretch to over four years. Much of the time Mary Wordsworth seems to have been wishing him away. She suggested that her cousin Thomas Monkhouse take the house (February 18, 1821), and wrote to him on November 5, 1821: "Mr. de Q's family are still at Fox Ghyll—he in London—but I should hope, for Mr. Blakeney's sake that that house may be ready for you, if you should prefer it, before you want one." Mary did not like Blakeney, the landlord, at all; but she took a darker view of De Quincey. When Mrs. Luff was negotiating to buy Fox Ghyll, Mary's comment was, "And how to get Quincey out after all." When the purchase finally went through, she wrote skeptically on December 10, 1824: "the de Q's are to leave [the house] early in the Spring (i.e. provided the O. E. arrives from London, whence he has been expected for weeks, & is able to move himself & Family out of it—by the bye Mrs de Q is confined of her 5th)—" [28]

Connected with Fox Ghyll, however, is another, warmer story giving insight into the relations with the Wordsworths. It concerns an ass which apparently belonged to the Wordsworths but had been given or lent to the De Quinceys. The beast, De Quincey said, was an "excellent ass—barring his folly," but undoubtedly "the most 'outward' ass in existence," for it kept running away to Ambleside. Therefore he wrote Dorothy a spirited, involved letter (Letter 55) to accompany the animal being returned, but tacked on a surprising postscript in which he said he would keep the ass and call on the Wordsworths the next day. In spite of its light, friendly tone, the letter begins on a defensive note—"Bridget Huddleston has not any authority for saying what she did" —and ends with an awkward apology for having written instead of Peggy, who joined in "kind regards." One suspects an empty front of relations between the women.

William, however, seems to have continued kind and helpful. Sara wrote to Thomas Monkhouse in May, 1821, "Mr de Quincey is still in your favorite Fox Ghyll, with which William came in today in raptures." One surmises that the poet had walked over to see De Quincey. About this time he gave him a letter of introduction to Sergeant Talfourd,[29] which De Quincey carried to London in June, and which helped to open the pages of the *London Magazine* to him.

De Quincey for his part was, despite the reconciliation, not quite in charity with his Rydal Mount neighbors. The sense of grievance which becomes blatant in his later writing he clearly took with him to London in 1821, although he tried to repress it. For Crabb Robinson distastefully described De Quincey then as "querulous, very strongly impressed with his own excellence, and prone to despise others," [30] but seems to have recorded no disparagement of Wordsworth, as he almost surely would have done had De Quincey been overtly critical. Neither do Richard Woodhouse's reports of the Opium-Eater's conversations, acid

with surprising attacks upon Wilson, give any hint of dissatisfaction with Wordsworth. True, De Quincey did pass on
as examples of groundless gossip stories that he was himself
the father of Cathy Wordsworth, and that William and
Dorothy had unnatural relations.[31] Perhaps he got a certain
satisfaction out of subtle subversion of the proud and
mighty; but he was vehement in denying the calumnies, and
explained how they could have arisen innocently from his
partiality for Cathy, and from William's habits of taking
long rambles with his sister and of kissing the women of his
family on meeting or parting. He not only was characteristically profuse in his appreciation of Wordsworth the poet
but even took occasion to defend the character of the man
in the ludicrous business of double standards in candles. This
trivial anecdote, which originated with Charles Lloyd, had
Wordsworth parading his economy by blowing out one of
two candles at Lloyd's house, but ostentatiously ordering a
servant to bring in six tapers when Lord Lowther visited
his own home. Lloyd told the story at Greta Hall (whence
it promptly got back to Rydal Mount), to De Quincey, and
to Hazlitt. The latter, to the intense irritation of the Wordsworths, told the world in his "Table Talk" in the November
London Magazine. De Quincey sorted out fact and fiction
for Woodhouse, who wrote:

The anecdote told by Hazlitt . . . is true. Wordsworth was the person, and Mrs. Lloyd was the friend at whose house he snuffed out
one of the candles. The rest of the story, respecting the order to the
servant when the nobleman dined with Wordsworth, is a fabrication
for the sake of effect. The Opium-Eater, to whom Lloyd told it, knowing from the character of Wordsworth that it could not be true, cross-
examined Lloyd and ascertained its incorrectness. Wordsworth would,
in fact, scorn to be thought to interfere with the domestic management of his establishment, and would despise any man who should
do so.[32]

There is, however, one interesting piece of evidence
that De Quincey unbosomed himself to Woodhouse—or
feared that he had. In April, 1822, Thomas Monkhouse,
who had been visiting the Wordsworths, offered to take
letters or parcels to London for De Quincey. He, however,

was "wretchedly ill" and had nothing ready; but he sent a letter to Hessey, across the top of which he put the warning: "Mr. Monkhouse is a *Relative* (I know not what) of Wordsworth's." And at the end he emphasized the caution:

Mr. Monkhouse will perhaps call on you: if so, do not forget that he is a great friend—admirer—and further near *relation* of W. W: of whom (in certain * ways he has of annoyance) I wish *I* could say yt—"he never more will trouble you—trouble you."

The asterisk refers to a note under the signature: "which I mentioned to Woodhouse: who possibly to you." Obviously De Quincey was alarmed lest something he had said get back to the poet. Obviously, also, he still nursed his grudge. Perhaps he influenced or shared the view of Wordsworth which John Wilson expressed to Alexander Blair on May 30, 1825, immediately after having mentioned De Quincey: "The Stamp-Master is well & as mean as ever—but pleasant & pompous." [33]

On his frequent trips back to Rydal or Grasmere, De Quincey seems sometimes to have had contacts with the Wordsworths, and sometimes not, depending upon his health and spirits. Edward Quillinan, who was later to be Wordsworth's son-in-law and who was De Quincey's neighbor at Spring Cottage in 1821, recorded in his journal: "he remained in bed, I understood, all day, and only took the air at night, and then was more shy than an Owl." Mary noted laconically on November 29, 1822, "The Seer continues in close retirement," and the same month Dorothy wrote, with more cleverness than feeling for De Quincey's difficulties: "Mr de Q is here shut up as usual—the house always blinded—or left with but one eye to peep out of—*he* probably in bed—We hear nothing of him." He was sick, and trying in vain to work, as Hessey's letter of October 7 shows: "De Quincey's Preface was not complete—I have had another Letter from him promising the *end* by *next* post, but it is not come yet—He is very ill he says—his letter is quite affecting." [34]

Sometimes, when De Quincey was in one of his reclusive moods, it appears that the overtures were made by the Wordsworths. In the winter of 1823 the combination of

opium, "care, and wretchedness" made him "never set foot
out of doors" for two and a half months. On December 22
he wrote: "I have refused to see every soul who called (3
nights ago I was 'not at home' to Wordsworth and an old
friend whom I had not seen for 5 or 6 years)." [35] This may
be the same occasion to which De Quincey refers in an undated letter to Wordsworth beginning "I feel so much pain
at not having been able to express my sense of the favor
you did me in calling" (Letter 57). The language is rather
formal, as is that in which De Quincey goes on to say that,
although he has been much tied down writing for the *London
Magazine,* he hopes by Tuesday to have it in his power to
pay his respects. One wonders whether it may not have been
at least partly the accompanying friend, William Jackson,
to whom De Quincey owed the honor of Wordsworth's
visit.

In more ebullient moods, which usually coincided with
some financial relief, De Quincey made more effort to keep
up a semblance of the old association. Sara wrote to Quillinan in November, 1825, that the Opium-Eater was there
"in great force, his Mother having given him £300 to pay
his debts." [36] He was with his family at Nab Cottage and
evidently had some contact with nearby Rydal Mount, for
Sara reported his conversation with Dorothy and revealed
the Wordsworths' old desire to use De Quincey's talents:
"We want him to review M. J. J.'s book & give her *'a lift'*
poor thing! but if he is really *disposed* I fear we must not
look for his production before doom's day." The next month
Dorothy wanted another work reviewed, and had more
hope:

No one is more able to do it well . . . but he is a sad procrastinator,
and, however willingly he may promise, I cannot depend upon him—
but I will limit him as to time, and with a hope that the work may be
done I will not send the parcel with this letter, as I intended when
I began to write to you (*LY,* I, 232).

The tone of this is the warmest since before Peggy came
into the picture. De Quincey is indeed a "sad procrastinator," but Dorothy seems to think that she has some powers

of wheedling. "I will limit him as to time" sounds like the
remark of a wife or sister.

Dorothy appears to have assumed that the old free relationship had been re-established, because she wrote to
Crabb Robinson confidently on July 2, 1825: "if Mr De
Quincey ever does find his way back to Rydal, we can borrow
the Magazines from him." [37] By October, however, when
De Quincey had found his way back, events had taken a
turn which naturally increased Dorothy's faith in her influence over the Opium-Eater. That summer Margaret fell
into a state of depression and wrote heart-rending letters
which greatly disturbed her husband. He feared for her life,
and yet he was helplessly tied to London. In his need he
wrote to Dorothy on July 18, asking her to go over and
drink tea with Margaret, speak a word of comfort to her,
take her a few old newspapers, and try to get her to eat some
solid food. For these simple things he implored Dorothy,
conjuring her by the memory of Cathy: "Oh! Miss Wordsworth,—I sympathised with you—how deeply and fervently—in your trials 13 years ago . . . do not refuse me
this service." With all allowance for De Quincey's agitation, which may have heightened the language of his plea,
there can be no doubt that he was asking for something
unusual, that it would be extraordinary for Dorothy to visit
Margaret. But Dorothy must have done so, and established
some closer connection with Nab Cottage to help account for
the relative warmth of November relationships.

The exhilarating £300 from De Quincey's mother, although followed soon by another £100, did not, as he put
it, "liberate" him. He relapsed into such low spirits that in
the winter of 1825 he was able only "3 or 4 times in as
many months to bear going into the smallest company—
such for instance as that of Rydal Mount." Relations with
the Wordsworths were, obviously, on the "company" level;
but they continued. By the following June De Quincey was
writing to Wilson of having heard of him from Wordsworth
"some time ago." Dorothy also appears to have kept up her
attentions to Peggy, for when she returned to Grasmere in
November, 1826, after a nine-month absence, she promptly

visited Dove Cottage, where the De Quincey family was once more settled. She sent the father—again in Scotland—a comforting and gracious report on the fine appearance of the children and good spirits of the mother, but suggested delicately that the family might better be moved to Edinburgh. Was there any polite fabrication in the odd postscript: "My Brother and Sister do not know of my writing: otherwise they would send their remembrances." [38] Perhaps for Mary, probably not for William.

In July, 1827, De Quincey was back in Westmorland, and a tourist who witnessed the rush-bearing ceremonies at Grasmere church on July 21 reported: "In the procession I observed the 'Opium Eater,' Mr. Barber, an opulent gentleman residing in the neighbourhood, Mr. and Mrs. Wordsworth, Miss Wordsworth and Miss Dora Wordsworth." [39] Samuel Barber was on friendly terms with the Wordsworths, and that they were all in one party is not certain but probable. A measure of De Quincey's place—however casual and inferior—in the Wordsworth circle is the fact that in 1828 Christopher Wordsworth sent him a gift in care of the poet, most likely a copy of his recently published *King Charles the First, the Author of Icon Basilike*. William replied simply, "Mr De Quincey is, & has been long in Edinburgh—he shall have your present when he returns." [40]

For a brief period the association of Wordsworth and De Quincey seemed to be taking on a somewhat different character—that of established neighbors and fellow freeholders. In 1829 De Quincey took steps toward acquiring a permanent residence less than a mile from Rydal Mount, by buying Nab Cottage from his father-in-law.[41] It was a curious paper transaction by which De Quincey, who not only had no money to buy a farm but even was heavily in debt, took over the estate of John Simpson, who was also heavily in debt, and borrowed on the land enough to give them both momentary ease. This attractive scheme obviously had to come to an accounting, and neither of the men could meet his obligation. De Quincey's mother paid two years' interest on the mortgage in 1832, but her help was a hopeless finger in the dike; the next year Nab was put up for auction and became a part of Rydal Manor. What Wordsworth thought of this culmination may possibly be reflected in Crabb Robinson's later distortion that De Quincey "made his father-in-law sell his little estate for his benefit & father & family were brought literally to the parish." [42] When he first moved into the Nab, however, the Wordsworths expressed interest in their new neighbor, and possibly even made gestures of friendship which were slightly reciprocated.

At all events, the Rydal Mount family thought the business newsworthy, but one gathers that they did not get their information firsthand. Wordsworth wrote to the Reverend William Jackson on April 10: "Mr. de Quincey is returned but I have not seen him he has bought the Nab estate—" [43] Not only had the poet not seen his former disciple, but he seems not even to have been sure he was back, for two days later Dora sent Quillinan a different version. Her letters suggest the Wordsworths' attitude toward the Opium-Eater at that time—curious, interested, and amused; not unkind, perhaps, but with the condescending superiority of sensible people:

Father who is just come in from a walk on the Terrace bids me transcribe a passage from my Mother's letter—which *he* says (*indeed indeed not I*) may be useful to you in your character of the Man of business—"Mr. Johnson (a Kendal Attoy. with whom she journied as far as Kendal) told me Mr. de Quincey is expected in a fortnight —he had received a letter from him in which he tells him he shall receive another letter by and by in answer to one sent ½ doz: years before—that he is beginning to reply to letters received in 18*12*—& his will come in due course"—
Mr. de Q– has been in Edinburgh *two* years Father says; coming home every month, & then every week—at last (about 3 months ago) his wife went to see after him and now I suppose somebody must go to bring the pair home—Mr. de Q. is about buying the Nab Estate.[44]

On June 16, however, the poet wrote with almost an overtone of welcome, "Mr de Quincey the opium eater is expected to resume his abode among us in a few days." Actually, De Quincey had already been at the Nab for three days, but was down with a fever. When Wordsworth learned this, he was sympathetic, and even seemed to have been looking forward to his old disciple's company: "Mr de Quincey I am sorry to say admits no one on account of illness. . . . This grieves me much, as he is a delightful Companion and for weightier reasons, he has a large family of young Children with but a slender provision for them." [45]

Wordsworth wrote "admits no one" with undoubted conviction, for his family seems to have made several overtures. Maria Jane Jewsbury, the ubiquitous "MJJ" of the annuals and a close friend of Dora, was then in the last week of a visit at Rydal Mount. She called at the Nab, probably with Dora—to meet a friend of her hostess, or to visit an old associate of the Kelsalls she knew in Manchester, or just to get a glimpse of the Opium-Eater. Whether she saw him is not certain, but Dora definitely did not when she went by to leave Miss Jewsbury's card after her departure, and even Wordsworth himself was refused admittance, as he had been before in 1823. This Dora thought worth narrating to Maria Jane: "Father called on Mr de Quincey the other evening but was not admitted." With cynical impatience she added on July 17, "Mr de Quincey's 'tomorrow' for calling at Rydal Mount [has] not yet arrived." [46]

On July 19 De Quincey wrote to thank the poet and his son John for the "favor" of their calls, but it appears that they were not admitted from his going on to say that he will be sorry if he has missed the pleasure of seeing John—his old pupil, little Johnny, now strangely dignified as "Mr. John Wordsworth." Although De Quincey ended by hoping "to come over" in the course of a week, the closing "Ever yours most truly" does not suggest any very easy companionship. And we know practically nothing about any further contact between the two men. Edward Quillinan assumed communication between the Mount and the Nab when, in a letter of November 19, he told Dora that she "had better transcribe for Mr. De Quincey" a curious story which Sir Edgerton Bridges had sent him from Geneva of a "person here calling himself *De Quincey Mee*" and introducing him-

self as the author of the *Opium-Eater*.[47] The general character of De Quincey's seclusion and Wordsworth's detach-
ment, however, are obliquely displayed in the poet's report to
his daughter that Mr. Barber had told them that "Chauncey
Hare who has been prowling about this neighbourhood for
some time had at last succeeded in forcing himself for three
hours upon the Opium Eater." [48]

Throughout this post-*Gazette* period the Wordsworths
continued to be interested in De Quincey's writings. Although no report of the poet's reactions to the *Confessions*
seems to have survived, and no copy of the work was in the
Rydal Mount library when it was sold in 1859, Quillinan
at least had a copy, which was for a time at Rydal. Interestingly, when Dora made a "List of Mr Quillinan's books sent
to Rydal" in June, 1833, she put "Opium Eater" fifth on the
list, right after Wordsworth's own *Poems* and *Excursion*.[49]
In 1827 Sara was even excessively laudatory of another work:

> We are busy reading a novel 'Walladmoor' translated from the
> German by De Quincey—freely as he says—for much of it is his
> own—& much has been left out. It is well worth reading—as the
> style & descriptions are far very far beyond anything in merit that you
> meet with in such publications—seldom indeed anywhere—for every-
> thing that he does must be clever (*SH,* 354).

According to Francis Jacox, the author-translator twenty-
five years later found it "gratifying" to reckon Dora Wordsworth among the admirers of the novel. Quite possibly De
Quincey presented a copy to her; it was scarcely the kind of
book the Wordsworths would buy. More admiration came
from the poet himself in a letter to Crabb Robinson (January 27, 1829) : "In the same number of Blackwood is an
Article upon Rhetoric, undoubtedly from De Quincey. Whatever he writes is worth reading." [50] Whatever the personal
relations, each man continued to value the other's work.

If De Quincey did indeed "come over" and renew his
association of "delightful" conmpanionship during his flirta-
tion with being a landowner at the Nab, it was certainly the
last time. He probably never saw the poet again. By the

middle of 1830 he had moved his family to Edinburgh, and, although he kept the lease on Dove Cottage until early 1835, his sojourn in the Wordsworth country was ended. If De Quincey's "tomorrow" for calling never arrived, the fault must have been his: William at least seems to have been friendly enough.

Rydal Mount continued to hear of De Quincey, no doubt, from John Wilson and other Edinburgh friends. Cyril Thornton sent in 1833 an anecdote of the strange ways of the Opium-Eater which Dora passed on to Quillinan in a curiously unfeeling way: "Cyril . . . tells us he has made many fruitless attempts to see the Opium Eater who has discovered a new mode of procuring a cheap dinner for his family—he buys game which is too bad for other folks & thus dines them all for one shilling." [51] The Wordsworths heard of the death of De Quincey's wife in 1837, and when they were in Bath in 1839 they even visited his mother and sister—apparently with great amity, for Mary at least intended a second call. Of the first conversation with old Mrs. Quincey—she had long since dropped the "De"—Mary most annoyingly says it "must remain to be chatted about by Aunty's good fire." The talk, however, can safely be assumed to have been censorious. Jane De Quincey was no admirer of her brother, and Mary recorded sarcastically, "She told me that they had often wanted to send the children to school, but their father would not consent—and said they *were highly educated.*" [52] Mary was undoubtedly thinking of "Kinsey" in his posture as schoolmaster to Catharine and John.

In such indirect ways the orbits of Wordsworth and De Quincey still brushed each other. There is no evidence of continued attraction at the centers. Only one letter from De Quincey to Wordsworth after the Grasmere period survives —an impersonal letter of introduction for an acquaintance. It is unlikely that there were many more. De Quincey had almost ceased to exist to the Wordsworths as a man; he remained as a gadfly.

LETTERS, 1818–1848

44. *To William Wordsworth*

Ms. Dove Cottage. Pub. PMLA, *LV (1940), 1113–1114. Qtd. Eaton, p. 234.*

[Grasmere]
[March 25, 1818]

My dear Sir,

I take the liberty of reporting a fact to you which, for the advantage of the Lowther cause,[1] ought to be made known to their Committee, since, connected with other circumstances (which at more leisure I will state to you in a second note), it proves that whether through carelessness or design that cause is betrayed in Grasmere by those to whom the support of it has been confided.— —On the arrival of Mr. Brougham this morning, and during his stay here, *the Church Bells were rung.* And this insult to the house of Lowther (in their own manor surely it must be thought so) was not offered without the knowledge of Mr. Jackson;[2] and had at the least his allowance; for I myself sent him word by Barbara Lewthwaite[3] as early as yesterday morning that Mr. Brougham's party were attempting for this purpose to obtain the Church keys from George Walker.— —That Mr. Jackson should have any adequate sense of the contest, I never expected: but he knows what is fidelity to a cause, and what is treachery; at least when it takes the shape of an overt act—committed or allowed. I for my part feel so much disgusted at his double dealing—that I do not now mean (as I had done) to use his assistance for getting two papers[4] of mine laid

---

Letter 44:

[1] See above, pp. 280 ff.

[2] The Reverend Thomas Jackson, from 1811 to 1822 rector of Grasmere, served the church in Langdale, where he lived, and acted as steward to Lady Fleming of Rydal Hall. He was a vice-president of the Kendal Lowther Committee. His son, William Jackson, Fellow and later Provost of Queen's College, Oxford, had been assisting his father as curate of Grasmere, and performed De Quincey's marriage ceremony in 1817, but was probably at this time in Oxford (*MW*, p. 34; *SH*, p. 129).

[3] Barbara Lewthwaite seems, sooner or later, to have taken Mary Dawson's place as De Quincey's servant.

[4] The one paper which is known to have emerged was sent to Wordsworth on April 1 and 2 and published about the middle of the month as a pamphlet,

before the Committee. Nevertheless, having taken great pains with one
of these papers, I am anxious to have it published: but I do not know
what other course to adopt for obtaining the sanction of the Committee.
You, I suppose,—from your official station,[5]—are not on the Committee; and, for the same reason, you may not choose to interfere so far
as to give my paper the weight of your recommendation. But, if this
be so, perhaps you will do me the favor of pointing out to me the
proper mode of communicating it.

When I have more leisure, I shall trouble you with a letter relating
to some private concerns of my own: in that letter I shall take an opportunity of speaking upon a subject mentioned to me at your desire
by Mr. Irving [6]— —which I have thought of more or less every day
since, and never without sorrow and astonishment. I have now heard
from Mr. Wilson [7] on that subject; and can at length speak authori-

---

Close Comments upon a Straggling Speech—a reply to Brougham's March
23 speech at Kendal. This paper, however, shows considerable dependence
upon the *Kendal Chronicle's* March 28 report, and was probably a later
development; on April 9 and 19 De Quincey still spoke of sending the two
papers mentioned earlier. For the text of *Close Comments,* as well as a full
discussion to which I am indebted, see John Elwin Wells, "Wordsworth and
De Quincey in Westmorland Politics, 1818," *PMLA,* LV (Dec., 1940), 1080–
1128.

[5] Wordsworth had been since March, 1813, Distributor of Stamps for Westmorland County, and had been warned against political activity (A. Aspinall,
Politics and the Press [London, 1949], p. 356 *n.*).

[6] Perhaps James Irving of Edinburgh, who on Nov. 21, 1816, and Feb. 1,
1817, wrote Wordsworth inquiring about De Quincey (Dove Cottage Mss.)
and also told Wordsworth that Brougham was the author of the *Edinburgh
Review* article on *Christabel* (see Letter 48).

[7] Probably John Wilson (see Letter 35, note 6). The "subject" was probably Wordsworth's suspicion that Wilson had had a share in the brutal attacks on his "Letter to a Friend of Robert Burns" in the *Edinburgh Monthly
Magazine* and its successor, *Blackwood's:* "Observations on Mr. Wordsworth's Letter" (June, 1817), "Vindication of Mr. Wordsworth's Letter"
(Oct.), and "Letter Occasioned by N's Vindication of Mr. Wordsworth"
(Nov.). Apparently Irving sent Wordsworth the first "Observations," suggesting a defense (Dove Cottage Mss.); he may later have been commissioned
to make inquiries through De Quincey, who had been in Edinburgh with
Wilson in 1814–1815 and possibly in 1817, and was believed by the Words-
worths to be writing for *Blackwood's* at least as early as May, 1819—as
Sara Hutchinson says in the same context in which she declares *"we know*
[Wilson] writes both *for* and *against"* Wordsworth (*SH,* p. 155).

tatively from him—so far as his name has been connected with it. Meanwhile, for the business of this present letter, I have not thought it a necessary introduction (nor indeed have I time at this moment) to say anything on that point; hoping that on a public matter, and for the purpose I have in view, the profound interest I feel in the issue of the present contest will stand in the place of all other apology.

I remain, my dear Sir,
Your faithful Servant
Thomas De Quincey.

Grasmere
> Wednesday night, March 25.

P.S. I find that a female servant of Mr. Jackson's attended to hear Mr. Brougham's Speech at the Red Lion—wearing Mr. Brougham's color, with the permission (she says) of her master.

45. *To William Wordsworth*

Ms. Dove Cottage. Pub. PMLA, *LV (1940), 1115–1116. Qtd. Eaton, pp. 234–236.*

[Grasmere]
[March 29, 1818]

2 Questions:—Your address in Kendal, if you stay till Tuesday?
Does Mr. Brougham sit for a close Borough?

My dear Sir,

As it appears from your note that, in my charge against Mr. Jackson, I proceeded upon an erroneous assumption—viz. that he had the command of the Bells,—the main ground I had for suspecting his fidelity, and by consequence the main ground I had for declining his assistance to myself, is done away; for, as to the injury which he has occasioned to the cause hereabouts by overbearing language and insinuations, in all that he does but act according to his known character; and, as he will not practice forbearance in his own affairs, he cannot be expected to do more for the Lowthers. I am left therefore where I was; and, as Mr. Jackson volunteered to send my papers, I ought to put one into his hands: I have however a second which for these reasons I would willingly send through yours;

first and chiefly,—with a view to your revisal of what I have written:

secondly,—for your influence with the Committee;—thinking that my paper would be of some use among the deluded yeomanry, I would wish to have it not merely sent to the Carlisle Patriot but also printed as a Hand-bill: [1]

thirdly,—for your influence in obtaining for me, through your friend in Kendal, a few copies of the Hand-bill for this neighbourhood. For these reasons I would wish, as I have said, to send it through your hands; but I find that I cannot have it ready for this evening: by Tuesday morning however, if you stay till that time in Kendal, I will engage to have it in your hands; but for this purpose I must beg to have your address in Kendal.

I fear that I may have made my paper too long; and have labored to make it shorter: but the question, treated according to it's whole compass, will not let itself be abridged below a certain point.—One thing in it, and only one, I have expressed without certain knowledge: I have spoken of Mr. Brougham as sitting for a *close* Borough (which I believe he does): I have not laid any stress upon it; but I have said it:—now, is this so? [2]

I accused Mr. Jackson the other day of double-dealing: and I fear that those, who overrate my influence at the Nab, may—in reference to the conduct of that family—think that I lie open to the same charge: one word therefore on this subject:—John Simpson [3] is, I am sorry to say it, a rank Jacobin; not from any delusion of his judgement, but as a pure malignant towards the nobility—gentry—clergy—magistracy—and institutions of the land. I understand that you condescended to talk with him; giving him credit no doubt for conscientious scruples in regard to the Lowthers; but in that you did him too much honor. I have talked with him for years upon politics; so that I know his temper in that point; and have found all efforts at giving him better feelings to be weaving Penelope's web; and have accordingly abjured all such conversation with him for ever. His wife and eldest son share with

---

Letter 45:

[1] Suggests De Quincey knew that Wordsworth's letter in the *Patriot* of March 7 had appeared substantially as the broadside "To the Freeholders of Westmorland," dated Feb. 28, 1818.

[2] No such statement appears in *Close Comments,* but curiously it does in Wordsworth's *Two Addresses* (*Prose Works,* I, 247).

[3] De Quincey's father-in-law (see above, p. 225).

him, and perhaps go beyond him, in rancorous Jacobinism; and are ready at this moment to abet Mr. Brougham with all their might; though they were not noticed by him: whilst (as my wife this morning reproached her mother) they *have* been noticed by the heads of the other party as to rank and as to intellect in having had attentions from Lord Lowther and yourself.

[Close and signature cut off.]

Grasmere
 Sunday evening, March 29.

[*Address:*] William Wordsworth Esqr. / Rydal Mount

46. *To William Wordsworth*

Ms. Cornell. Pub. PMLA, LVI (1941), 597. Heading and closing cut off and supplied by another hand.

⟨Grassmere [*sic*] ½ past 4 o'clock Wednesday
morng. April 1. 1818⟩

My dear Sir,
 With my utmost diligence I have not been able to finish this paper in time for this morning's post; about one quarter of it remains here. It has grown under my hands; and I fear has already outgrown it's title: but that, or anything else, you or Miss Wordsworth can alter— if you think it worth that trouble. Such as it is, it is at your service; and all; or any part of it, may be printed or burned—as you think fit. The remainder I will send by the next post.
 ⟨In a great hurry as you will suppose
    Your faithful friend & servant
     Thomas de Quincey⟩

47. *To William Wordsworth*

Ms. Dove Cottage. Pub. PMLA, LV (1940), 1116–1117.

I have written a short answer to Mr. Clarkson's letter [1]—as given in the Kendal Chronicle of last Saturday; do you think any is wanted?

Letter 47:
 [1] Thomas Clarkson (1760–1846), indefatigable abolitionist and friend of the Wordsworths, lived near Ipswich at Playford Hall, where Sara Hutchin-

Grasmere
Thursday, April 2,—1818.

My dear Sir,

I send you the remainder of my Comments:—I was not able, from accident, to send it earlier. The whole paper would easily divide itself into two if you think it too long; and either part might be printed— accordng to your judgement.

It occurs to me that in my hurry I forgot to supply some words wanting in a Foot-Note allusive to Mr. Brougham's [*torn: ?attack*] upon you: the omission was, I believe, in the first line which should [*torn: ?read t*]hus—'By the side of Mr. Brougham's weightier offences it is not much to charge him with slighting the courtesies of private life—.' [2] If the omission was not in that line, you will easily discover it.

I remain, my dear Sir,
Very faithfully and affectionately yours,
[*Signature cut off.*]

[*Address:*] William Wordsworth Esqr. / Mr. Cookson's / Kendal
[*Stamp:*]   Kendal Penny Post

48. *To William Wordsworth*

Ms. Dove Cottage. Pub. PMLA, *LV (1940), 1117–1118.*

Grasmere
Saturday evening, April 4,—1818.

My dear Sir,

I am a good deal disturbed at the recollection of one word in my Paper (which escaped me in my hurry and the indignation I felt at Mr.

---

son was then visiting. Although not an elector in Westmorland, he had lived in Ullswater and was known in the district. He wrote a reasoned letter (printed in the *Kendal Chronicle* for March 28) in support of Brougham on the grounds that the antislavery cause needed his services in Parliament. (See A. L. Strout, "Thomas Clarkson—as Champion of Brougham in 1818," *N & Q,* CLXXIV [June 4, 1938], 398–401.) Dorothy regretfully called the letter "a feather in their caps,—a beautiful—a delightful letter" (*MY,* II, 811).

[2] A note to the third comment in *Close Comments* (p. 7) begins as here indicated.

Brougham's scurrilous attack upon you coupled with his monstrous effrontery in asserting of his own party that they were clear of all personalities in their writings though provoked to them by your example) : the word I mean is *'Slanderer'*; I describe him, in his *ci-devant* character, as 'Mr. Brougham the anonymous Slanderer in reviews.' Now, though in my opinion every contributor to the Edinburgh Review may be justly held a party to the malice and defamatory spirit which prevades that work, yet I have no certain knowledge that Mr. B. is further chargeable with slander or detraction than on this way of accounting each member of the conspiracy answerable for the acts of the whole. One most malignant article leveled at Coleridge (I think on occasion of his Christabel) has indeed, as Mr. Irving informed me, been generally ascribed to Brougham;[1] but from the internal evidence I was myself persuaded that it was Hazlitt's. If this be so, I should be very sorry to use an expression which in the judgement of many may leave me open to a retort as being myself an anonymous slanderer. At any rate, when writing anonymously, I would be (as I know you would wish all your friends to be) more especially anxious about the accuracy of my words of accusation or disparagement : and therefore, if it be *now* possible to alter this (supposing that you have not already altered it), I would beg that it might be put thus—'Mr. Brougham the contributor to slanderous Reviews'—or 'Mr. B. the Senator, not able to forget &c., speaks like the old intriguer of that name in scurrilous Reviews'; or in any better way of expressing it that may occur to Miss Wordsworth or yourself; or, as an Erratum, it might be noticed at the end thus—'For *Slanderer* read *Scribbler* in a slanderous Review.'[2]

It seems adviseable to write anonymously for two reasons; first, be-

---

Letter 48:

[1] Brougham did contribute many slashing reviews to the *Edinburgh Review,* but the authorship of this one in the Sept., 1816, number is still debated. It has also been attributed, in part at least, to Francis Jeffrey and Thomas Moore as well as Hazlitt. See P. L. Carver, "The Authorship of a Review of *Christabel* Attributed to Hazlitt," *JEGP,* XXIX (1930), 562–578; Elisabeth Schneider, "The Unknown Reviewer of *Christabel:* Jeffrey, Hazlitt, Tom Moore," *PMLA,* LXX (June, 1955), 417–432; Hoover H. Jordan, "Thomas Moore and the Review of *Christabel,*" *MP,* LIV (Nov., 1956), 95–105.

[2] The passage appeared: "Mr. B., the Senator, speaks—as Mr. B., the anonymous Trader in Reviews, writes" (*Close Comments,* p. 3 ; cf. pp. 7, 10).

cause otherwise it is probable that one may be accused (perhaps really suspected) of designing to advertise oneself to the notice of Lord Lonsdale; Secondly, because a real signature will be sure (especially since the license given by Mr. Brougham's example) to converge upon itself, and serve as a *conductor* to, the whole body of foul-mouthed wrath which at present for the most part spends itself harmlessly upon the Lowther party in general. Nevertheless,—excepting this single word *Slanderer*,—there is nothing in my Paper which I would scruple to acknowledge. But I should be grievously ashamed to be thought valiant by favor of a mask beyond what I would have been if speaking under my own name.

I have feared that your more important engagements may have prevented your revising my Paper with any minuteness; and on that consideration I have troubled you with this application.

I remain, my dear Sir,

Yours most affectionately and faithfully,

Thomas De Quincey.

[*Above salutation:*] P.S. I received your note acknowledging the receipt of my first packet by the messenger who took my second to the post—that is to say, not until yesterday morning. It was the very highest gratification to my wife and myself, that we could reap from it, to find that what I had then sent was honored by your approbation.

[*Address:*] William Wordsworth Esqr. / Mr. Cookson's / Kendal

49. *To William Wordsworth*

Ms. Dove Cottage. Pub. PMLA, LV (*1940*), *1118–1119.*

[Grasmere]
Tuesday night April 7 [1818]

My dear Sir,

In the greatest possible hurry I return you the Proof—very ill corrected, I fear, but according to my power.

    1. The addition which I have made in the margin of p. 5 [1] is not necessary manifestly; is it at all useful?

Letter 49:

[1] Probably the reference, not incorporated, to Brougham's association with the Whigs in the effort to repeal the Leather Tax (see Letter 50).

2. The two corrections in p. *6* are neither of them to my mind: would *'is involved'* be better than *'lies hid'?*

3. p. 7 (in the note) :—Brougham has *avowed* his writing in the Ed. Rev. (as I learn from you) by incorporating it with his Col. Pol.²

4. *Sansculottism,* p. *12*,³ cannot be understood fairly perhaps (in it's connexion) but of the Kendal *mob*—not of freeholders: but should it be qualified with the word *pauper?* The paragraph seemed to me to run down too suddenly to a close; and I have added a sentence accordingly; but I could not turn it to my satisfaction.

I remain
Most affectionately yours,
Thos. De Quincey.

For a particular reason I have desired the Printer to return the Proof: I suppose there can be no objection to this.

50. *To William Wordsworth*

Ms. Dove Cottage. Pub. PMLA, *LV (1940), 1119–1124. Qtd. Sackville-West, pp. 129–130.*

P.S. *Nothing in this letter requires an answer, except the two following questions:*

1.—Do you know the age, or thereabouts of Lord and Col. Lowther? —The Brougham party are now attempting, in Grasmere, to represent them as mere boys. I have ventured in one case to say that Col. L. having been in the retreat to Corunna in 1808–9 (which fact I drew from a very excellent letter,¹ dated I think *'Parish of Orton',* in the Kendal Chron. some weeks ago), must be nearly 27; as it is not easy to suppose him under 17 at that time, when the whole subaltern duty of his regiment (it seems)

---

² Brougham's *An Inquiry into the Colonial Policy of the European Powers* (London, 1803), 2 vols.

³ The passage reads: "I believe that they will take their chance of ruin with Lord Lonsdale and the property of the County rather than safety with Mr. B. and his Sansculloterie."

Letter 50:

¹ By Wordsworth, signed "A Friend of Truth," dated "Orton Parish," in the *Kendal Chronicle* for Feb. 21. (For text see Wells, *PMLA,* LV, 1085–1090.)

fell upon him; if even the Army regulations admit of his being
so young.

2.—Have you Brougham's *'Colonial Policy'?* And, if so, can you do
me the favor of lending it to me for a day or two?

Grasmere
Wednesday afternoon, April 8 [-9]—1818.

My dear Sir,

Yesterday I was so much jaded in mind and body by having sate up
the whole of the preceding night, without one half hour of rest,—for
the dispatch of some private business now pressing upon me which
causes me a little anxiety,—that I could not at all satisfy my own
mind in the corrections which I attempted to make in the Paper; and
such even as I could make exhausted my time too fully to allow me a
minute for acknowledging in a proper manner the receipt of your
Pamphlet.[2]

With respect to *that,*—I have not yet time to speak minutely: having however read it through twice and very carefully,—I may now
venture in general to add my thanks for it, as a person deeply interested
in the cause which it luminously explains and so powerfully supports,
to the previous thanks which I sent through your son John for your
kindness to myself individually in communicating it to me: (I say
communicating; because I do not know whether you meant to lend it
to me, or to give it; but I shall presume it to be a gift, unless I hear
that too few copies have been printed to allow of your giving it conveniently:)— —The view which you take of the question at issue in
this contest, by raising it from a merely municipal question to a question highly national (and still further important in the light of 'an
attempt' *'To effect a total change in the character of County Elections'*) must be thought by all your friends to justify your taking part
in a contest which, if it's relations to the public welfare were not more
than ordinary, might seem to fall below the level of your intellectual
duties: this view is the same as that which from the very first I have
myself taken of it; as was to be expected from any reflective man who
should have had the happiness which I had for so many years to
benefit by your conversation. I made notes of all that presented matter
of question to my own mind—as I read; and whatever in these notes

---

[2] *Two Addresses to the Freeholders of Westmorland,* dated March 26
("Advertisement") and April 4 ("To the Reader").

seems, on second thought, worth troubling you with—I will communicate in a day or two.

With respect to the *corrections* in my Paper,—though perhaps in a fugitive paper of this nature it is not of much importance whether a line here and there be more or less happily expressed, and the main point to be aimed at is no doubt to avoid all misrepresentation and also whatever can colourably be misrepresented as misrepresentation,—yet, —on the bare chance that you may not have returned the Paper to the Printer by this morning's post, and also to supply what I left deficient in my explanations of last night,—I add a few notes on that point:

I.—p. *5:* If the sentence, which I added about Lord Althorpe, has not been wholly struck out by you (as would perhaps be better), it might be shortened thus; *'joint-heir with yourself to that immortality towards which you soar upon wings of Leather.'* [3] I added this sentence under the ludicrous impression which I retained (as of a *Parturiunt Mortis*) from Miss Wordsworth's Report of B's annunciation to the people of the Leather-Tax Repeal in the light of a great patriotic service.—

II.—p. *6:* Neither *conscience,* nor *consciousness,*—in my way of understanding you,—is exactly the expression;—but *'the recollections which his conscience must furnish';* or something to that effect: [4]

III.—p. *12:* By 'Sansculotterie' I meant to carry on the same reference as I designed to make by the expression of *'mob with or without breeches';* [5] that is, a reference to the rabble who welcomed Mr. B. to Westmorland and made the greater part of his audience; to them also I meant the *'imis'* of the Latin quotation [6] to refer: and my reason for saying last night that perhaps the connexion in which it stood might

---

[3] The passage does not appear. It was undoubtedly to go in the following parenthetical remark: "Beware Mr. Brougham, that the Oppositionist, Earl Spencer, does not hear this, or he will call you a conceited coxcomb, not forgetting that his own Son, Lord Althorp, when the Foxites were in power, held the same office [as Lord Lowther, who had been attacked for being on the public payroll]!"

[4] The pamphlet reads: "With how little ceremony Mr. Brougham treats his own consciousness, when he would raise his reputation as a public man at the expense of that of Lord Lonsdale. . . ."

[5] See Letter 49, note 3. *Close Comments* reads: "thanks be to a discerning mob whether with or without breeches—there *is* a Brougham." None of the revisions De Quincey suggests here were made.

[6] No such quotation appears in the pamphlet.

disallow any misreference—was that the French expression is almost directly paraphrased beforehand by the English expression, and will therefore naturally be referred to the same class of persons:—it occurs to me however at this moment that possibly by the expression *'take their chance of safety'* you suppose me to allude to the hypothetical consignment of their votes at the *Election;* but the truth is, *that* way of understanding the words never struck me before; and I alluded to a chance derived from general political bias and attachment, in which a *Sansculotterie* even really such may be spoken of as one of the parties; in the other way of understanding the words I fear the term *is* objectionable. The next sentence about *perishing with the Lowthers* is certainly better out—as too violent, unless understood with more allowance than must be looked for; my meaning in it was to give the sense of the Latin passage by anticipation: perhaps it might be altered better in some such way as this—(than by the substitution I proposed last night in the margin)—*'We are not yet come to such a masquerade of congruities and decorum in our political relations—as that, if the State be to owe her forward movement to the measures of Revolutionary Reformers, she would not rather remain stationary in the condition secured to her by the political system of the Lowthers:'* but this is of little importance.

———————

What *you* say of Brougham—that you 'firmly believe that he is a man who would stop at nothing to make himself of more consequence than he now is,'—[7] therein speaking no doubt from all possible sources of information,—*I,* who draw my belief in this point from no source besides his own vagrant harangues, do also firmly believe. The violence and frantic intemperance of these has, I confess, gone much beyond what I expected: for, as he did not want any fresh recommendations with the mob, he might safely (I thought) have attempted *now* to conciliate the gentry; whereas on the contrary—even as if he prided himself in their enmity,—he has throughout his rambles abused by wholesale every class, order, division and subdivision, of people in this county—from the Lord Lieutenant downwards—expecting only the yeomanry (whose votes he may have thought likely to be influenced by his speeches), and the Rabble who constituted his audience. To this as a fact, if it were not from the first proposed to himself as an aim, he seems even himself

———————

[7] Wordsworth does not say this in the pamphlet sent over by John; perhaps it was in an accompanying note.

latterly to have adverted; for, in no other view apparently than to
provide against the charge of having abused *every* body whom he had
mentioned, does he in his Penrith harangue fly off suddenly to a long
éloge of the twelve judges [8] (who, I hope, would not be ready to return his civility): either this must have been done by way of set-off
to his *general* abusiveness, or as a palliation *specially* fitted to his abuse
of the magistrates in the same speech; for connexion it has none, unless
a mere verbal one, more than a panegyric on the twelve tribes of Israel
would have had with the course of his harangue.—It grieves me to
think that any man of education (more especially that one who, I
suppose from you, is a man of ability and real knowledge) should be
capable of such truly unprincipled conduct perpetrated in so malignant
a manner: from the countenance given to plebian envy and the insur-
rectionary doctrines sown up and down the country by this *Member
of Parliament* (is it possible, I am on the point of exclaiming, that he
can really be a member of Parliament?) what a precious crop of dis-
organizing feelings and actions must we expect to reap! The injury
done to every kind of social restraints upon the lowest class must be
incalculable—far beyond any good, I fear, that will ever properly be
referred to Mr. Brougham as it's author:—on a Sunday morning
from our windows we can hear the carriers opposite (who, by the
bye never cared to read newspapers during the liveliest periods of the
War against Bonaparte) not reading merely but shouting aloud in
pure phrenzy of insolent exultation and sympathy those passages in
the speeches which are leveled at the gentry—but above all those
leveled at the clergy. Even *their* minds cannot sink lower in vulgarity
of abuse than to represent the entire gentry of the county as meeting
at Lowther Castle to *'lick the dust'* beneath the feet of Lord Lonsdale
—and that nobleman as willing to countenance this 'cringing' and
having *'such appetite as not to reject it.'* [9] Surely Mr. B. cannot have
any of the customary feelings of a gentleman; else, for his own sake,

---

[8] According to the April 4 *Carlisle Patriot*, Brougham in his April 1 speech
at Appleby praised the circuit judges who "lend themselves to no faction,
and will not crouch to any person," contrasting them with local magistrates.

[9] The *Kendal Chronicle* for April 4 reported Brougham as saying at Penrith on March 31: "For aught I care, they [party-serving magistrates] may
lick the dust until even they are sick of crawling, then let them be as meek,
fawning, as crouching as they are offensive and domineering to the rest of
his Majesty's people: such grovelling only sullies themselves, and if those
for whose gratification it is intended, have such appetite as not to reject it,
I have no reason to interfere."

he would not have imagined as a bare possibility an intercourse of this kind going on at Lowther—or anywhere indeed as practiced at this day by any considerable body of English people of education: it is quite superannuated malice; and to Lord Lonsdale, whom from your report of him I have always collected to be a man of real dignity of nature, must be specially inapplicable.

By the bye, whilst I think of it from it's connexion with this subject of personal abuse,—let me mention that I (who know next to nothing of his character) felt much disgusted at the way in which Mr. Hasell was treated at Mr. Brougham's Kendal dinner—both by Mr. B. himself and by the old buffoon Mr. Wybergh: [10] not only is he sneered at as a *'decent'* country-gentleman fit for nothing but fox-hunting &c.; and the very notion of his sitting in parliament treated as insupportably ridiculous; but (which is the point that chiefly moved my disgust) a young gentleman, admitted to be scarcely beyond a boarding-school age—a *Hobbledehoy*—whose *only* fault it seems is that he is not impudent enough—is solemnly propounded by Mr. B.[11]—and in the most conceited manner the flattery is accepted as no more than a reasonable homage by old Wybergh—propounded as *'every way well qualified'* to fill that very station which it was held up to the mockery and the scoffs of the company as an insupportable jest to suppose could be ever *'dreamed-of'* by a man of mature age; against whose pretensions however nothing is *produced* except a habit which he has in common with most country-gentlemen, and which at the worst can be no more a disqualifying habit for him than Mr. Curwen's or Mr. Coke's stall-feeding &c. for them.[12]—I know nothing of the parties in this business; but in the whole tone of it there seems to me private

---

[10] Edward W. Hasell of Dalemain was chairman of the Appleby Lowther Committee and later officially placed in nomination the name of Viscount Lowther. The Lowthers were said to have offered one of the two Parliamentary seats to him, rather than run two members of their own family. At the Kendal dinner on March 23 Thomas Wybergh, who later nominated Brougham, made fun of the possibility: he "had always found him [Hasell] an honest decent country gentleman; but he never once dreamed that he wished to be a Member of Parliament" (*Carlisle Patriot*, March 28, 1818).

[11] Brougham had toasted Frederick Lawson, a young man in his early twenties then traveling on the Continent, as "every way worthy of the honor" of sitting in Parliament. Wybergh had replied that his "only fault . . . was too much modesty."

[12] John C. Curwen (see Letter 16, note 4) and Thomas Coke, Whig M.P.'s for Carlisle and Norfolk, respectively. Coke, later Earl of Leicester of Holkham, was a famous agricultural reformer.

malice, at least on the part of Wybergh, and something deeper than mere difference in politics. Of Wybergh I do not know even—who and what he is; so ignorant am I of the county; and I know almost as little of Hasell: but a decent man of Martindale, a kinsman of my wife's, (which man, by the bye, had just then been crammed with the vilest falsehoods in relation to yourself and Ld. Lonsdale by Mr. Edmonds of Ambleside [13]) told me, on calling here some weeks ago, that Mr. Hasell was much beloved amongst his tenantry: and therefore, out of pure hatred to insolence like this,—as nobody has yet stepped forward to interpose a word between Mr. H and their scoffs,— unless I hear from you that he is on some account or other not a respectable man,—I will take an opportunity of retorting a word or two in reference to him on the old zany Wybergh.[14]

A short answer to Mr. Clarkson's 'Letter' I will send you to-morrow: [15] two other papers, which I mentioned in a former note as having for some time in preparation, shall be in your hands within a few days.[16]

I thank you for giving me an opportunity of correcting the Press errors (which, by the bye, were much fewer than in most London printing) ;—and I remain

Your very faithful and affectionate servt.,

Thomas De Quincey.

[*Across front under address:*] An answer is requested to the two questions which stand at the head of the first page of this letter.

N.B. Up to the word 'importance' in the middle of the second page was written yesterday afternoon, and designed to have been sent over in post-time; but this was prevented by the heavy rain; and the remainder has been added to-day—Thursday April 9.

[*Address:*] William Wordsworth Esqr. / Rydal Mount

[13] An attorney who was master of ceremonies at Brougham's Kendal dinner of March 23.

[14] Wybergh got his appellation from such remarks as his hit at Lowther's clerical supporters: "he presumed each of these Gentlemen was a GREAT GUN, or at least a *Minor Canon*" (*Kendal Chronicle*, Feb. 7, 1818).

[15] Probably that which appeared in the *Carlisle Patriot* for April 25, signed "One of the Old School."

[16] If these materialized and were published, they are not positively identifiable. Wells suggests that an article signed "X" in the May 23 *Westmorland Gazette,* and a series of later papers in the same journal signed "Philadelphus Alter," may be by De Quincey (*PMLA*, LV, 1123 *n.*).

51. To William Wordsworth

Ms. Dove Cottage. Pub. PMLA, *LV (1940), 1124–1126; in part, Eaton, pp. 236–238.*

Grasmere

Tuesday afternoon, April 14,—1818.

My dear Sir,

What I wrote to you on Thursday last—is entirely at your disposal for any purpose: such alterations as may be necessary—every one of your family can easily make: the name of Mr. Edmonds it will of course be adviseable to strike out; but perhaps it does not stand in a part of the letter which you thought of printing. I am happy that in this way you have reconciled me to the length of my letter; for it was in truth so unconsciously long that after I had sent it I grew disturbed to think that I should have made so heavy a demand on your time and attention for no specific purpose in view—beyond that of communicating what I felt so deeply; and, if I had had leisure, I should have written on the following day to apologize: the fact is—that, having little opportunity of expressing my thoughts and feelings on important subjects . . . and on this particular subject meeting with nobody among the few whom I see to consider the contest in it's just importance, I felt a pleasure in delivering myself from the burthen of feelings which press strongly upon me—and in which, as I said, I can look for little general sympathy. When I say this however, let me do justice to my wife; and let me acknowledge that from the very first she has accompanied me in my view of the case with a generous warmth of feeling—according to her humble pretensions in point of knowledge and experience; and just now with so much more of warmth as may be expected from her lively gratitude for the honor done to me by yourself and the Committee. Indeed, long before this particular movement of jacobinical violence, she had learned to feel justly on this subject; and, in spite of repeated attempts from her family to win her over to their way of thinking, uniformly behaved and expressed herself on all points referring to the traitorous efforts for nursing discontent and disrespect towards the government &c. in that manner which may be always expected I suppose where the heart is not habitually malignant nor the understanding greatly abused.

I learned a fact on Saturday night from Mr. Jackson which leads me to trouble you with an application—one main purpose of which, I acknowledge frankly, respects my private advantage.—I have long wondered why the new Kendal Paper [1] should not, at so important a time, be set in motion; and once before endeavoured without success to learn the cause: but on Saturday night Mr. Jackson informed me that *one* cause at least of the delay was the want of an Editor: I understood him that this post had been offered to you; and that you had refused it. Now,—if this be so, and if the post be still undisposed of,—do you know of any reasons which should make it imprudent or unbecoming in me to apply for it? If you do not, and there should be no other person whose interests in this case you are inclined to prefer,—I feel confident that you will do me the kindness to assist me in obtaining it with your recommendation. I must mention however, which possibly may be alone sufficient to defeat my application, that in about a year I shall be under the necessity of resigning the place; having an intention then or soon after to remove finally to London for the prosecution of my profession as a lawyer.[2] That part of an editor's duties which respects the mechanical and commercial management of a Paper—I should certainly not be competent to undertake; but perhaps this department could be conducted by some clever compositor or other person about the Press; and at any rate, with advice from a judicious man of business, I could learn even this part (which, in a place no larger than Kendal, cannot be very intricate) ; and, in respect to the Selection of articles from the London Papers and the Political Comments on them, I trust that I should be able to satisfy the wishes of the patriotic subscribers. In one point you may still feel some doubt of my competence to do so—judging from your former knowledge of me; in punctuality, I mean, and power of steady perseverance: but in this I am altered since I last [last *inserted*] had the happiness to associate with you; and, among other grounds of remorse, I have suffered too much in conscience on account of time left unimproved or misemployed—ever to offend in that way again, even upon calls of less importance than this would be. I do not suppose that the profits of Editorship, as connected with a Kendal Paper (and that too under the disadvantage of opposing an established rival),

---

Letter 51:

[1] See above, pp. 281–290. The *Kendal Chronicle* had on Feb. 28 reported "a deep laid plan" to start a Lowther paper.

[2] See above, p. 223.

can be very considerable; but a trifling emolument would at this time
be very useful to me; and I should be happy to draw *that* from an
employment that would be on other accounts agreeable to me—and
which, from the peculiar service and duties imposed upon it as it's
distinguishing purpose, I should look upon as truly a service of honor.
In humble testimony of my respect for this purpose, I shall at any
rate (let the event of the application be what it may) think it a duty
to contribute everything in my power to support the Paper; and in
this view, by way of *literary* support, I have been finishing that course
of Letters on the value of the attacks made by the critics of the day
upon your Poems[3] which I wrote in part at Westhay when I was
last there—viz. in February 1815—but which was afterwards abandoned from the tremendous interest at that time revived to the political affairs of Europe by the escape of Bonaparte from Elba; in
connexion with which interest it appeared to me that any other of a different nature must suffer greatly, if it could at all co-exist with it.
My wife has also already copied out for the Press one, and will soon
have copied out more, of some translations which I have made and
am going to make from the minor works of Kant: I have also adapted
to the taste of English readers some translations from John Paul:[4]
and I shall very soon set about a collection of Essays—rendered amusing by anecdotes &c.—for the Dalesmen of Westmorland: So that on
the whole I should have some stock to begin with.

I remain, my dear Sir, with many thanks for the kind attentions
with which you have honored me,

[*Close, signature, and part of address cut off.*]
[*Address:*] [Will]iam Wordsworth Esqr. / Rydal Mount
           [Apri]l 15

[conven]iently favour me for a day or two with Coleridge's
'Sibylline [? *Leaves*']

---

[3] See above, p. 216.

[4] De Quincey is here forecasting much later activity. The *Westmorland
Gazette* printed his article on "Immanuel Kant & Dr. Herschell" on Sept. 8,
1819; but De Quincey published translations from Kant in the *London Maga-
zine* in 1824 and *Tait's Edinburgh Magazine* in 1833, and translations of
"Analects from Richter" in the *London* in 1821 and 1824 (M, XI, 273–293;
IX, 428–444; XIV, 46–93).

52. *To William Wordsworth*

Ms. Dove Cottage. Pub. PMLA, LV *(1940), 1127–1128.*

Grasmere
Sunday morning—half past 5 o'clock, April 19. [1818]

My dear Sir,

I have a few miscellaneous Queries and Remarks for your consideration—which, being pretty much disconnected, I present *as* disconnected by separating them into numbered items.

I.—Would not Ld. Lonsdale be inclined to do something if the case were made known to him, for the family whose Father and Second Son have just now perished in the Patterdale Quarry? [1] I believe, the Quarry is farmed under his lordship: and we are told on Patterdale authority that a Widow and seven Children, of whom the eldest has been severely injured in searching for his father, are left by this disaster in a state of great indigence. I should be happy, in my place and according to my means, to offer something—if a subscription were set on foot from any authentic quarter. It would surely be a pity that the Brougham party should be allowed to step-in as leaders in such a service; which, for ostentation's sake, perhaps they will.

II.—I scarcely know how to express the sense which I have of the disproportionate honor done by the Committee to my Paper. It seems but fit that I should acknowledge their condescension in a formal letter of thanks:—But what is the regular mode of conveying such acknowledgements? Would they properly take the shape of a letter to yourself, since the Paper passed through your hands?

III.—Do you not suppose that, by dating his parting address from *Brough,* Mr. Brougham meant to insinuate to the ignorant some connexion between that place and his family; as, on a former occasion apparently between Brougham Castle and his family? [2]—To be sure, he was *at* Brough: but why was it pre-arranged that he should be at Brough as his place of closing exhibition?—It seems to me that in all

---

Letter 52:

[1] On April 11 a man named Leck and his son were killed by a fall of slate in a quarry at Hartsop.

[2] Brougham took a "native son" tone and claimed to be descended from the ancient lords of Brougham Castle; but his family's holding in Brougham manor dated from the eighteenth century only, and he himself was born in Edinburgh.

this he does but keep up that ostentatious show of importance which I could not but read in his invariable London date—'*House of Commons*'. Perhaps in this last-mentioned case indeed, he might have another motive: of the half-blood at least I have always understood that Mr. B. is Scotch—and that his education was Scotch: with Scotch '*discreetness*' therefore possibly he lodges in such a street in London as it might not seem altogether 'comme il faut' that a Candidate for a County should assign as his place of residence.

IV.—This parting Address—and the Kendal Paper of Sat. April 4— I beg *earnestly* that you will allow me to keep until to-morrow: I have not yet had time to take a copy of either; and my wife has been for some days too much indisposed to attempt it: but I have much and imminent need of them; and you may be assured that they shall be most religiously taken-care-of.

V.—I have two papers, mentioned heretofore, nearly ready to send you; both are laboured carefully; and one especially; in that one I have been minutely anxious for the fidelity of all the statements—for the soundness of the arguments—for the accuracy of the expressions— and for the comprehensiveness of the whole survey taken.

VI.—I cannot but recommend to your notice that *modest* passage (*modest,* I call it, considering that your Pamphlet had been sometime published) in an attack made (in the Kendal Chronicle of Sat. April 11) on Mr. Harrison's Narrative of the K. Riots [3] where it is asserted that 'not one, from the elaborate "Freeholder" (yourself, I presume) down to "A True Briton," has yet—fairly grappled with the question at issue, the Parliamentary influence' (meaning, it is supposed, influence in returning members to Parliament) 'of the Earl of Lonsdale.' (By the bye, in making this the question at issue—or any part of it—he not only speaks merely from his own *ad libitium* view of the case, which is never presented under this aspect to the mob—nor will be; but he is absolutely disowned herein as a ground of *general* opposition to the Lowthers by the *fact* of the B. party submitting at all to the return of one member on the Lowther interest, and also by the express *verbal* admission in many papers of the B. party that *thus far* they submit chearfully and conscientiously: an admission of this

---

[3] Long analysis by "A Kendal Ward Man" of "An Impartial Narrative of the Riotous Proceedings which took place in Kendal, on Wednesday, the 11th February, 1818, collected from the observation of eye-witnesses, by T. [Thomas] Harrison."

extent is good surely for the whole of the constitutional question of right, though it may fail of satisfying the question of provincial expedience as affected by the L. influence.)—I mention this not out of any respect for the attack here cited (which is not only altogether in a bad spirit—making most ungentlemanly and malicious references to Mr. Harrison's profession [4] and to his origin; but also fails, I think, in a way really laughable to establish any substantial partiality in Mr. H.; and manifestly wishes by raising a prodigious dust about *Ale and Cheese—Cheese and Ale,* to blind the unthinking reader into a forgetfulness of the real and sole question of any importance— "Were, or were not, the Kendal Riots [5] produced by the inflammatory mis-statements of the Brougham party?["]); but I mention it for the sake of suggesting to you the propriety of printing in the shape of a Hand-bill that part of your Pamphlet which relates to the interference of Press in Elections.[6]

I remain, my dear Sir,
Very affectionately yours,
Thos. De Quincey.

53. *To William Wordsworth*

Ms. Dove Cottage. Unpub. Qtd. Eaton, p. 241.

Grasmere
Sunday evening, September 27. [1818]

My dear Sir,

I write to you for various purposes.

First,—let me apologize to you for not having presented myself at R. Mount last Sunday: it was not the rain which would have prevented me from coming, but a most tormenting affection of the head which first attacked me last Tuesday night but one, and has never left

---

[4] Thomas Harrison was a surgeon-apothecary, Alderman of Kendal, and member of the Lowther Central Committee.

[5] The occasion of the "riots" was the entrance of the Lowthers into Kendal. The Broughamites were accused of having piled up stones in advance, the Lowther supporters of having precipitated trouble by bringing in canal laborers to swell the crowds. Windows of two inns were "nearly all broken," and one man was seriously injured.

[6] *Prose Works*, p. 253.

me since: sometimes it has driven me half frantic: all the tooth-aches I ever experienced are a joke to it; and my spirits in consequence have been unspeakably depressed—not merely mechanically from the complaint, but also through my fears that it might turn out to be *Hydrocephalus*. My eldest sister died of that complaint:[1] she indeed was only eight years old; but you know it *may* attack an adult.

Secondly, to this infernal torment it was owing that I made no appearance in the Paper of yesterday. I had during the week compelled myself to make up the Paper; nearly the whole was of my selection: I had even written some articles which would, I trust, have bothered the Broughamites beyond their slender powers of patience to endure. But, when it came to correcting and transcribing these articles on Tuesday night, I was so overcome by pain that I could not do it.

Thirdly,—this mention of the Paper reminds me to apologize for the metaphysising art. which occupied the chief place in the penultimate Paper;[2] or rather for having placed it in that situation. The truth is, that was not my doing: it was a mistake of Mr. Kilner's:[3] I meant it to have been thrown into a corner. For I am and always have been convinced that the leading art. should be in a popular tone on a popular subject: and, if I were not so convinced, I should yet not have treated your advice so lightly as to repeat (and in an aggravated way, inasmuch as it was much longer) the very error of which you had so justly complained before.—No man in future will ever have to tax me with obscurity: I hope to be too intelligible for the peace of the Broughamites.

Explanations over,—I now come to Questions:

1. Do you know the history or origin of that insinuation against lord Lowther in yesterday's Chronicle made by a scoundrel who signs himself *Birch?*[4]—I do not purpose to notice this fellow further than

---

Letter 53:

[1] Elizabeth, d. 1791 (see M, I, 38–45).

[2] The Sept. 19 leader was "Review of the Comments Published in the 'Kendal Chronicle,' upon an essay in the 'Westmorland Gazette' of August 29," two full columns investigating syllogistically the theory of taxation.

[3] John Kilner, subeditor resident in Kendal, who after De Quincey's resignation was described on the masthead as printer and publisher.

[4] Letter dated St. Bee's School, Sept. 22, 1818, and signed "Birch," accusing Lord Lowther of personal abuse and of having "taken offence at the complexion of the Grand Jury" because there were *"only fourteen* yellows to nine blues."

thus: in an art. against the Editor of the Chron. I shall assert that he has disgraced his Paper (if that be possible) by admitting into it an *irrelevant* charge (irrelevant to his public character) against lord Lowther, and an unproved charge made in a sneaking way—as if, being such, it could be any fair counter-part or set-off to the open and un-answerable charges alleged at the Appleby Dinner against the *public* character of lord Thanet.[5] Now of course it would greatly assist me if you could enable me to add that the charge was a false one. But most probably you will not know the circumstances of the case.

2. What is the name of that Arch in Cambridge about which the tradition is—that it is to fall when a greater man than lord Bacon passes under it? [6]

At your leisure I will request an answer to these two questions; and and I remain, my dear Sir,

[*Signature and part of address cut off.*]
[*Address:*] [William Words]worth Esqr. / [Ry]dal Mount

54. *To William Wordsworth*

Ms. Dove Cottage. Unpub.

Monday June 14,—1819.
Grasmere

My dear Sir,

I ought to take shame to myself for not having earlier acknowledged

---

[5] Sackville Tufton, ninth Earl of Thanet (1767–1825), hereditary Sheriff of the counties of Westmorland and Cumberland with seats at Appleby Castle and Brougham Castle, was a prominent Whig. The Tory forces claimed Brougham was his cat's-paw. As Sheriff he was responsible for selecting juries, and Lowther had said at Appleby (according to the *Gazette* for Sept. 12) that some prominent Lowther men had been left off the Grand Jury: "Whether this was a mistake, or pitiful electioneering spite, I am unwilling to express my opinion." On Oct. 3 De Quincey assured Birch that these re-marks "were not, in any blameable sense of the term, personalities," since they dealt with public acts.

[6] There was a gatehouse to the old Grandpont, later Folly Bridge, in Oxford, which was traditionally Friar Roger Bacon's study, and was sup-posed to fall when a greater man than he passed under it. This, however, was torn down in 1779. Apparently De Quincey transferred the legend to Francis Bacon, who was at Trinity College, Cambridge.

your kindness in sending me a copy of Peter Bell.[1] The truth is—I began a letter of acknowledgement some time ago, and have advanced some way in it: but my old habit of procrastination interrupted it. I thought it right to shew that I had read the improved Poem attentively: and had intended therefore to express my feeling with respect to the various alterations from that M.S. copy of Mr. Coleridge's which I read in 1807.—In general the alterations in the Prologue strike me as being greatly for the better: but, for some of the slighter alterations in the body of the Poem, I cannot but say that on a first and second reading they appear to me to have injured the effect. However no doubt you went upon sufficient reasons; and perhaps on further study of the passages I may come to see your reasons.—With respect to the Poem as a whole, I need not at this day express to you my fervent admiration of it. In common with all Englishmen who know anything on the subject of Poetry,—I feel more and more how great a debt of gratitude is owing to you for the vast services which you have rendered to the literature of the country and eventually to the interests of Human Nature.

I was not the author of that answer to the three Ambleside Correspondents which you may have observed in the Gazette of last Saturday;[2] and I cannot sufficiently express my sense of Mr. Kilner's presumption in putting forth such a rebuff to three persons possibly of age and respectability. Besides the incivility of throwing a doubt upon their veracity (*"If* what they say be true")—how does it follow that,— because there was 'intemperance,' i.e. drunkeness,—therefore the Brougham party are to be screened in any outrage? I think very differently. I abhor that spirit, which governs so many of the Lowther party, of false and stupid candor and 'liberality.' The Blues do all they can against us: they never spare us: they leave their tradesmen on account of their party: and we are going on candoring and candoring until we shall candor away all our strength. On this particular occasion I do not know what took place: but Mr. Jackson told me

Letter 54:

[1] Wordsworth's dedication of *Peter Bell* to Southey is dated April 7, 1819.
[2] The June 12 number carried as a filler in very small type the following: "We have to acknowledge our obligation to *three* Correspondents for the communication respecting the Boat-launching at Low Woods.—If the incidents they mention did really occur, the whole was an exhibition of folly and intemperance, and therefore unworthy of notice."

that *you* could tell me what was fit to be noticed in the Gazette. Mr. Partridge,[3] I think, said the same.—The Gazette is established in part for the sake of exposing such things, as is evident to any man. And I am resolved that next week I will call the attention of the Public to the absurd policy of many Lowtherites; and, if I hear that it would be worth while, to this case. How can we expect to be furnished with true accounts of things,—or that the enthusiasm of the party should be maintained, if an ignorant lad who is perhaps making love to a blue girl shall be permitted to stifle the representations of three correspondents at once.—if you have an opportunity, I will trouble you to let me know what *did* happen—provided you think it right that any notice should be taken.

I purpose bringing out my sketch of an essay on the Bank Question immediately.[4]

> I remain, my dear Sir,
> Your faithful servant,
> Thomas De Quincey.

[*Address:*] William Wordsworth Esq. / Rydal Mount

55. To Dorothy Wordsworth

Ms. Dove Cottage. Unpub.

[?Fox Ghyll]
[?1821–2]

My dear Madam,

Bridget Huddleston[1] has not any authority for saying what she did—but it is probable that she heard somebody say that the ass was no more than a loan to us: which in fact I myself supposed.—

—Who told her this, I know not: but the truth is that I meant, if the rain had not been so heavy, to have come over this morning to

[3] Of Ambleside.

[4] De Quincey had printed discussions of the "Paper of the Bank of England" on Feb. 6, 27; March 20, 27; April 3, 10, 17; and May 22. Perhaps he intended to collect them in pamphlet form. Later in life he published papers on economic subjects, and in 1844 *The Logic of Political Economy.*

Letter 55:

[1] "Miss Huddlestone" was among the intended guests at De Quincey's Christmas Eve party in 1814 (see p. 226).

Rydal Mount to concert something about the poor foolish creature.
For on the one hand he is said to be a most excellent ass—barring
his folly: and yet on the other we understand him to be a nuisance to
all Ambleside from the ease with which he gets into gardens.—Here
they find it impossible ever to keep him for 2 days: for, to feed him
with hay, they are obliged to keep him near the house—where, besides
opening gates, he has found out a way of jumping down to the road
from the fields immediately adjoining:—and in the stable at present
they have no room for him (he has a shed to retire to). This same
B.H. brought him home once before from the boys of Ambleside who
were sadly abusing him: he then staid only 1 day and a part of another
before he absconded (he took advantage of the dusk). This might be
6 weeks ago: and in that interval several other people have brought
him back from the same tormentors.—

For the present we send him to you: but before you resolve upon
having him shot, in the case of Mr. Jackson's declining him, I should
be glad to confer with you about him: for at Grasmere we might
have a better chance of securing him: which on every acct. we should
be glad to do; for all agree that he is a most excellent creature if he
had but more *conduct*—in fact, if he were not the most 'outward' ass
in existence.

To spare your messenger's time, I have written instead of my wife,
who begs to join me in kind regards.

                    Affectionately yours, my dear Madam,
                         Thos. De Quincey.

On reading your note again I observe that B.H. represented us as
meaning to send the ass to your house again: which is a mistake: we
never had any intention of the sort, unless we should first understand
that you could do something with it better for it's own comfort—and
it's character at Ambleside. We send it now only to give it a chance
of escaping it's Amb. tormentors until some plan is arranged.

P.S. A fresh plan has now been devised, in consequence of which
we keep the ass for the present: and I will call to-morrow.

[*Address:*] Miss Wordsworth / Rydal Mount

56. To William Wordsworth

Ms. Dove Cottage. Unpub.

[?Fox Ghyll]
Sunday September 14. [?1823]

My dear Sir,

I beg to introduce to you Mr. Carne, a gentleman who has lately returned from Palestine, Upper Egypt &c. (last from Greece). He is passing hastily through the country; and has not time, I am sorry to say, to see the most interesting parts of the lakes: but could not allow himself to leave them without putting himself to some inconvenience to wait upon you.—He takes the greatest interest in your works: and I was sure that you would have much pleasure in conversing with a traveler so lately from the seat of war in Greece &c.

I am very sorry that a prodigious pressure of writing to meet a temporary necessity has prevented me from having the pleasure of accompanying him, as he could not stay beyond this day and to-morrow at the Coach hour.

I am, dear Sir, yours more faithfully,
Thos. De Quincey.

[*Address:*] William Wordsworth Esqr. / Rydal Mount

57. To William Wordsworth

Ms. Dove Cottage. Unpub. Qtd. Sackville-West, p. 188.

[?Fox Ghyll]
[?December 22, 1823]

My dear Sir,

I feel so much pain at not having been able to express my sense of the favor you did me in calling—that I think it right to explain that the load of labor, under which I groan, has continued to make it impossible for me to get out for one half hour even (excepting one afternoon that I went over to Town End [1] for a book).—When I am not utterly exhausted, I am writing: and all is too little; so unpro-

---

Letter 57:

[1] That is, Dove Cottage (see Letter 17, note 3). De Quincey had moved his family to Fox Ghyll in 1820, but he continued to keep most of his books at Dove Cottage.

ductive as to quantity is such ungenial labor.—Mere correction of proofs indeed, and corresponding with London on business, is almost enough to fill up my time: for, if all that I have lately written— were published at once, it is a literal fact that I should *more* than fill the London Mag.[2] myself.—Tuesday,—to my relief in one point though to my great embarrassment in another, there is no post: and I shall therefore have it in my power to pay my respects to you if you are at home.

I understand that Mr. William Jackson[3] was so good as to call with you about 3 days ago. If you see him, I wish that you would be so kind as to let him know in what way I am situated. To-morrow however, if he is in the neighbourhood, I shall endeavour to make my excuses to him personally.

I would not have troubled you with this account of my own private affairs, but for the consciousness of the strange appearance which my behaviour in this particular must otherwise wear.

I am, my dear Sir,
Most faithfully yours,
Thos. De Quincey.

Sunday evening.

I believe that in 2 or 3 days I may be under the necessity of going to London: which I mention beforehand, in case [*torn*] should have any letters or other commands for me.

[*Address:*] William Wordsworth Esqr. / Rydal Mount

58. *To Dorothy Wordsworth*

Ms. Dove Cottage. Pub. Eaton, pp. 307–308.

[London]
Saturday, July 16,—1825.

My dear Madam,

I am at this time in great agitation of mind, and I solicit your assistance in a way where you can give it effectually.—Call, I beg and pray you, my dear Miss Wordsworth, on my poor wife—who suffers

---

[2] He had been contributing to the *London Magazine* since his *Confessions* appeared there in Sept. and Oct., 1821.

[3] See Letter 44, note 2.

greatly from a particular case of embarrassment affecting me just
now. What this is, and how it arose, I began to explain in a very
long letter: but repeated interruptions from the Press have not allowed
me to finish it. Suffice it however here to say—that in a few weeks I
shall be free from all distresses of the kind which have so long
weighed upon me. Meantime, she writes me the most moving and
heart-rending letters—not complaining, but simply giving utterance
to her grief. In her very last letter she concludes by begging me "not
to take her grief amiss": and in fact she disturbs my fortitude so much,
that I cannot do half what I else could. For my fear is—that being
thrown entirely upon herself, with no soul (unless her eldest sister)
to speak a word of comfort to her—she will suffer her grief to grow
upon her, and in her present uncomfortable situation will fret herself
to illness. If that should happen, I know what I must look for next:
and I shall never have any peace of mind, or a happy hour, again.
Assure her that all will be well in a very few weeks; and the greater
part in a fortnight. What a sad thing then that she should give way
to a momentary pressure, just at the time when I have first a prospect
of for ever getting over any pressure of that kind.—Oh! Miss Wordsworth,—I sympathised with you—how deeply and fervently—in your
trials 13 years ago: [1]—now, when I am prostrate for a moment—and
the hand of a friend would enable me to rise before I am crushed,
do not refuse me this service. But I need not conjure you in this way:
for you are full of compassion and goodness to those whose hearts
are overburthened with long affliction.—What I wish is—that you
would give my wife the relief of talking over her distress with one
whom she can feel to be sympathising with her.—To do this with the
less constraint, perhaps you will be so good as to go over and drink
tea with her. And let me know, if you please, how she is in health:—
Direct to me—To the care of Chas. Knight Esqr.,[2] Pall Mall East,—
London.

Say whatever you can think of to raise and support her spirits: beg
her not to lie down too much, as she is apt to do in states of dejection,
but to walk in the fields when it is cool; and to take some *solid* food,

---

Letter 58:

[1] Probably refers to the deaths of Thomas and Catharine Wordsworth.

[2] De Quincey was for a few months living with Knight, proprietor of
Knight's Quarterly Magazine, in which he published a translation of a
German story, "The Incognito: or Count Fitz-Hum" (M, XII, 417–433).

which she is very apt to neglect.—She is amused by newspapers: perhaps you could lend her a few just for the present, until I am able to send one down.

Having written so much of my longer letter, I shall finish and send it on Monday or Tuesday. I must beg you to excuse my putting you to the expense of 2 letters: which, in any other circumstances, I would not have done.

If I had any chearful news from home,—I am *now* in a condition to extricate myself in 28 days.

God bless you, my dear Miss Wordsworth,—stand my friend at this moment.

[*Close, signature, and most of address cut off.*]
[*Address:*] [Miss Wordswor]th / [Ryda]l Mount / Ambleside

59. *To William Wordsworth*

Ms. Cornell. Unpub.

Rydal Nab
July 19, 1829

My dear Sir,

I write to thank you and Mr. John Wordsworth [1] for the favor of your calls,—a thing which I ought to have done long ago, and should have done but for the great disgust I have connected during my late illness with the very sight of pen and ink.

My illness was a fever caught, I believe from a fellow passenger on the Edinburgh Mail upon the 12th of June: for 18 days after I arrived at this place (June 13) this fever utterly prostrated me, and during all that time I was able to take only a little lemonade or ginger beer. Hence, or from the malady itself, I was left so weak as to be scarcely able for a fortnight to crawl from room to room; and have not yet felt myself strong enough, though otherwise perfectly well and in good spirits, to go more than a few yards behind the house.

I trouble you with this account of myself only to explain why I have not hitherto acknowledged the favor of yours and Mr. John

---

Letter 59:

[1] Wordsworth's oldest son and De Quincey's former pupil, "Johnny," now an ordained clergyman.

Wordsworth's call. I should be very sorry to find that I have missed the pleasure of seeing Mr. J. Wordsworth; but hope that this will not be so. In the course of this week I shall certainly be able to come over: and meantime I beg my best regards to him;—and remain, my dear Sir,

Ever yours most truly,
Thos. De Quincey.

[*Address:*] William Wordsworth Esqr. / Rydal Mount

60. *To William Wordsworth*

Ms. draft. Craig Papers. Pub. Japp, I, 352.

[?Edinburgh]
September 12, 1848

My Dear Sir,

Under circumstances which oblige me to write in a hurry,—I take the liberty of introducing to your notice an accomplished young Grecian, Mr. Neocles Jaspis Mousabines. He honors your name and services to [*struck out:* what is highest and most durable in literature] this generation; and, from my personal intercourse with him, I can undertake to say—that he has been powerfully and unaffectedly impressed by the study of your works. Equally master of modern Greek and English, as regards both writing and speaking, he may probably find or make opportunities for diffusing his own deep impressions amongst the more intellectual of his countrymen. I have ventured, therefore, to suppose that you may find a pleasure in conversing with him; whilst, on the other hand, Mr. Mousabines is prepared to understand—that from the pressure of strangers on your time, or from [your] state of health, or from accidents of personal convenience, you may find a difficulty in doing so without meaning any sort of slight to himself.

Ever my dear Sir,

Your faithful friend and servant,
Thomas de Quincey.

[*Address:*] Wm. Wordsworth, Esq. / Rydal Mount

CHAPTER FIVE

AFTERMATH

Although personal contact between the two men was probably finished after 1830, De Quincey was not through with Wordsworth. From a master and friend, the poet was eventually transformed into a literary property. The Opium-Eater had moved to Edinburgh to live by writing for *Blackwood's* and *Tait's* magazines, and, as pressures for copy built up, it became inevitable that he would sooner or later exploit his relationship with the Lake poets. Under the circumstances, it is remarkable that he delayed as long as he did.

It was not until 1839 that De Quincey took up Wordsworth as a subject, but he was considering the possibility as early as 1822, when he wrote to Hessey that he was working on a "sort of *Ana*" which would include "History—Criticism—Human Life—Love—Marriage—Courtship—Polit. Econ.—Literature—Anecdotes of lit. men—Mathematics—Morals—Coleridge—Wordsworth—Myself in childhood in ref. to Educ.—Germ. Literature—&c. &c. &c. &c." [1] He did draw briefly on his private knowledge of Coleridge in an uncomplimentary description of a discreetly anonymous "eminent living Englishman" for his 1823 "Letters to a

Young Man whose Education has been Neglected," but his earliest frank exploitation of his literary friendships was an 1829 essay on "Professor Wilson" in the *Edinburgh Literary Gazette,* in which Wordsworth appeared only as the friend in whose house he met Wilson.[2] He began to get closer home in a four-part essay on "Samuel Taylor Coleridge," which he rushed out for *Tait's* soon after Coleridge's death (September, October, November, 1834; January, 1835).

This expedition into biographical reminiscence should have warned him to walk very gently around Wordsworth. His essay had been, by any standards and especially those of advancing Victorianism, most indiscreet. He charged Coleridge with taking opium for the "luxurious sensations," accused him of plagiarism, and discussed frankly his marital misery.[3] About this last he was defensive, and showed, in a passage which he later deleted, that the sore spot of the Lakers' treatment of Peggy was still raw. After praising Sara Coleridge as a "virtuous wife, and a conscientious mother," he suddenly broke out:

Meantime, I, for my part, owe Mrs. Coleridge no particular civility: and I see no reason why I should mystify the account of Coleridge's life or habits, by dissembling what is notorious to so many thousands of people. An insult once offered by Mrs. Coleridge to a female relative of my own, as much superior to Mrs. Coleridge in the spirit of courtesy and kindness, which ought to preside in the intercourse between females, as she was in the splendor of her beauty, would have given me a dispensation from all terms of consideration beyond the restraints of strict justice (*Lit. Rem.,* I, 177 f.).

The "insult" was an "intemperate" letter written by Mrs. Coleridge to "one whom she did not know by sight" (obviously Peggy was not welcomed at Greta Hall) over a book or manuscript which De Quincey, absent in London, had failed to return. In this injured mood De Quincey tells all, even: "Coleridge, besides, assured me that his marriage was not his own deliberate act; but was in a manner forced upon his sense of honor, by the scrupulous Southey, who insisted that he had gone too far in his attentions to Miss F— [Fricker] for any honorable retreat." Well, Coleridge was

dead, but Sara and Southey were not, and there were many
left to be "given pain" by such forthrightness.

Coleridge's family was understandably outraged. His
daughter wrote charitably: " 'the dismal degradation of pe-
cuniary embarrassments,' as he himself expresses it, has induced him to supply the depraved craving of the public for
personality." [4] But brother-in-law Southey grew practically
apoplectic when Carlyle merely asked if he knew De Quincey:

"Yes, sir," said Southey with extraordinary animosity, "and if you
have opportunity, I'll thank you to tell him he is one of the greatest
scoundrels living!" I laughed lightly, said I had myself little acquaintance with the man, and could not wish to recommend myself by that
message. Southey's face, as I looked at it, was become of slate colour,
the eyes glancing, the attitude rigid, the figure altogether a picture
of Rhadamanthine rage,—that is, rage conscious to itself of being just.
He doubtless felt I would expect some explanation from him. "I have
told Hartley Coleridge," said he, "that he ought to take a stout cudgel,
proceed straight to Edinburgh, and give De Quincey, publicly in the
streets there, a sound beating—as a calumniator, cowardly spy, traitor,
base betrayer of the hospitable social hearth, for one thing!" [5]

In 1836 the Coleridge family even tried to get Cottle to
leave out of his *Early Recollections* the account of De Quincey's generous loan to Coleridge of £300, on the grounds
that by writing such articles he had forfeited the right to
favorable mention. There was sputtering also at Rydal
Mount. Dora wrote Quillinan about the "atrocious article"
and added: "Poor Hartley says he will 'give it him' & I
do hope he will—for such unprincipled wretches do deserve
to be shewn up & without mercy—Aunt Sara burns with
indignation against the little Monster—whom she never
liked over well." Sara herself told Quillinan, with an ironic
flick, "If you see *Taits* you will have seen a series of infamous
Articles upon poor Coleridge by his Friend the Opium
Eater." [6]

Both women probably followed the lead of Wordsworth,
who was enough incensed by De Quincey's strung-out essay
—even the fourth part was marked at the end "To be con-

cluded in our next"—to try to put a stop to it. He wrote to Joseph Henry Green, Coleridge's literary executor, in January, 1835:

This notice is, in most points, relating to Mr C's personal *Character*, highly offensive, & utterly unworthy of a Person holding the rank of Gentleman in english society. It is not to be doubted that the Writer was honoured by Mr C's confidence, . . . and how he had abused that confidence, & in certain particulars perverted the communications made to him, is but too apparent from this obnoxious publication. The Article in question is one of a promised series; & upon this account more particularly, & holding our Friend's memory dear, I venture to submit, whether or no it would be adviseable for you, in the capacity of Executor, to address to Mr de Q; or to the Ed: of the Mag: a letter of caution, or remonstrance, as in your judgement may seem most likely to put a check upon communications so injurious, unfeeling, & untrue. Much indeed of this notice is false in its statements, & unjustifiable in its inferences to that degree, that I should have been sure the writer was not in intimate connection of friendship with Mr C., had I not personal knowledge, & proofs from Mr C's own letters, to the contrary. In justice to Mr. de Q. who was an inmate during the space of 7 Months in my own house, I must say that I did not observe any traces of *malevolent* feeling towards *Mr* C., & that the Writer extols his intellectual powers as much as the most ardent of his Admirers, if discreet & judicious, would do.[7]

Apparently De Quincey could seduce a neighboring farmer's daughter, marry her, and become a confessed opium addict—and still be a "particular friend" and a "delightful companion." But once he sank to publishing personal materials gained through the intimacies of friendship, he had forfeited the right to be an English gentleman, and Wordsworth wanted nothing to do with him. He begged Green to consider his letter as "strictly confidential": his name was not to be mentioned in the matter. If he had really been so much concerned for Coleridge's memory, he might have perceived that writing to De Quincey himself would have been more likely to be effective.

The protestations of the Wordsworth clan may, however, have been a shade disingenuous, and William was probably not concerned entirely with the memory of his dear friend

Coleridge. For De Quincey had naturally brought the Wordsworths into his discussion of S.T.C. The poet was probably irked that De Quincey should have quoted Southey as saying "that he highly disapproved both of Mr. Wordsworth's theories and of his practice." Even if it could be argued that the Laureate's opinions on poetry were to some degree public property, it was definitely going too far to write thus intimately: "Wordsworth disliked in Southey the want of depth, or the apparent want, as regards the power of philosophic abstraction. Southey disliked in Wordsworth the air of dogmatism, and the unaffable haughtiness of his manner." [8] Most certainly Wordsworth was exercised at the account of Coleridge's difficulties with his wife, which laid some of the blame, although quite innocently, on Dorothy. De Quincey did not name her, indeed, but the meaning was clear enough:

A young lady became a neighbour, and a daily companion of Coleridge's walks, whom I will not describe more particularly than by saying that intellectually she was very much superior to Mrs. Coleridge. That superiority alone, when made conspicuous by its effects in winning Coleridge's regard and society, could not but be deeply mortifying to a young wife. . . . no shadow of suspicion settled upon the moral conduct . . . : the young lady was always attended by her brother; she had no personal charms. . . .

Still, it is a bitter trial to a young married woman to sustain any sort of competition with a female of her own age for any part of her husband's regard, or any share of his company (M, II, 159 f.).

This analysis no doubt had some truth—Dorothy was at least half in love with Coleridge, and poor Sara was always being unfavorably compared by her discontented husband with some woman on the other side of the fence: Mary Evans, Charlotte Brent, Dorothy Wordsworth, and Sara Hutchinson. But De Quincey himself recognized that the basic trouble was "simply incompatibility of temper and disposition," and he even declared that Coleridge would have quarreled with "*any* wife, though a Pandora sent down from heaven to bless him" [9]—although he did not put this last sentiment into his essay until the 1854 revision. Dorothy's

particular petty *pièce à trois* was, then, symptomatic only—
why drag it into bright isolation, especially now that Dorothy
was ill and sinking into senility? The whole tone could not
have set well with the chaperone brother.

Whether or not Green wrote to De Quincey or Tait, as
Wordsworth suggested, the last essay in the series of four
on Coleridge shows clearly that the writer had become aware
of criticisms. Maybe De Quincey did learn a lesson from
the Coleridge essay: he stayed away from such personalities
for nearly four years. His first attempt at a paper on Wordsworth, an unpublished open letter to William Tait dated
May 16, 1838, took a relatively safe tack—"concerning the
Poetry of Wordsworth." This letter is practically devoid
of overt biographical comment, although perhaps there are
such implications in the proposal that Tait publish a volume
of selections of Wordsworth's poetry, for which De Quincey would furnish an introduction! Apparently he anticipated
no objections from the poet to his performing such an office.
This may mean, however, no more than that he was not even
in close enough touch with Rydal Mount to know what a
"little monster" his Coleridge articles had made him.

By 1838, however, three factors combined to make De
Quincey feel free to write about Wordsworth. One was that
his series in *Tait's Magazine,* "Sketches of Men and Manners from the Autobiography of an English Opium-Eater,"
was obviously marking time at the point in his life where it
began to parallel Wordsworth's. Another was that his financial situation was desperate. In 1837 and 1838 he was
changing residence constantly to avoid arrest for debt, moving as often as three times within a month.[10] He was once
seized, and would have been jailed had not the publisher
Adam Black agreed to pay his debt on condition that he
write articles on Pope and Shakespeare for the *Encyclo-
paedia Britannica.* Nine persons were dependent upon him,
and the family was down to one meal a day. In such straits
he could not afford to be nice about the sacredness of intimate revelations. He had to have entertaining copy, and
what he knew about the Lake poets was interesting—Crabb

Robinson said "scandalous, but painfully interesting." [11]
The last factor was that on August 7, 1837, Margaret died
of typhus fever.[12] De Quincey was grief-stricken and somewhat bitter. His one original short story, *Household Wreck*,
written about this time, is a pathetic narrative of a good
woman and her helpless husband who are victims of social
injustice. One senses a deep involvement on the author's
part. Some of the same intensity comes into the Wordsworth
articles when De Quincey touches upon his wife. Peggy dead
became more of a martyr to the injustices of the Wordsworths than Peggy alive, and the sorrowful and angry husband aimed sharp barbs at Rydal Mount, especially at the
ladies.

Tait's for January, 1839, carried an essay entitled "Lake
Reminiscences: No. I. William Wordsworth." Wordsworth
was also the subject of Nos. II and III in February and
April; No. IV, in July, was "William Wordsworth and
Robert Southey"; and No. V, in August, "Southey, Wordsworth, and Coleridge." Articles on the lesser celebrities of
the Lakes—Lloyd, Wilson, and others—appeared on into
1840, often with references to the Wordsworths, and including an account of the death of Cathy.[13]

The "Lake Reminiscences" on Wordsworth are both biographical and autobiographical. De Quincey began with his
impressions on first meeting the Wordsworths in 1807, then
went back to fill in such information about their lives as he
knew. This was far from complete and too often vague and
inaccurate. Such a passage as the following is typical of his
handling of dates and events:

Somewhere about this period [1794–1795], also, (though, according to my remembrance of what Miss Wordsworth once told me, I
think one year or so later,) his sister joined him; and they began to
keep house together: once at Race Down, in Dorsetshire; once at
Clevedon, on the coast of Somersetshire; then amongst the Quantock
Hills, in the same county, or in that neighborhood; and, at length, at
Alfoxton, a beautiful country house, with a grove and shrubbery attached, belonging to Mr St Aubyn, a minor, and let (I believe) on
the terms of keeping the house in repair. Whilst resident at this last
place it was, as I generally understood, and in the year 1797 or 1798,

that Wordsworth first became acquainted with Coleridge; though, possibly, in the year I am wrong (*Lit. Rem.,* I, 342 f.).[14]

Of course De Quincey made no pretensions to scholarly accuracy in biographical details. He did regret, in an unpublished section of his essay, his lack of more definite information, but explained it in a manner creditable both to his feelings and to his subject:

I therefore, who might from Coleridge have learned every particular about Wordsworth's life, had felt so exclusive a concern about his mind and intellectual being, and should have been so ashamed that my friendship for him and his family could be supposed to stand upon any other than the purest intellectual interest, that I threw away my opportunities almost unconscious of their existence.[15]

His impressions rather than his "facts" were the real meat of his essay, and they were undoubtedly the most objectionable to the Wordsworths. What he said was so frank—even when it was complimentary it was so personal that it seemed taking a liberty. He was perhaps too hearty in "admiring" Dorothy; he must have been nauseous in remarking that there was "even an unsexual character to her appearance." Of Mary he reported unequaled "sunny benignity—a radiant gracefulness," but also "a considerable obliquity of vision," which *"ought* to have been displeasing or repulsive" although "it was not." William "walked like a cade," his legs were decidedly unornamental, and even Dorothy was mortified by his appearance from behind: "How very mean he looks." [16] De Quincey presumed to "notice a defect in Miss Wordsworth's self-education" and suggest that "if she had been, in good earnest, a writer for the press," she would not have "yielded to that nervous depression . . . which . . . has clouded her latter days." He permitted himself such character judgments as, "I do not conceive that Wordsworth could have been an amiable boy; he was austere and unsocial, I have reason to think, in his habits; not generous; and, above all, not self-denying." He indulged in such impertinent speculations as "some of us have sometimes thought [him] a lover disappointed at some earlier period

by the death of her he loved." He revealed that Dorothy
once told him "in a whispering tone" that William at one
time suffered from a "nervous affection," the remedy for
which was to play cards every night. He enviously catalogued
Wordsworth's "good luck" in having incumbents and relatives with estates die off at convenient moments, and face-
tiously concluded "had I happened to know of any peculiar
adaptation in an estate or office of mine, to an existing need
of Wordsworth's—forthwith, and with the speed of a man
running for his life, I would have laid it down at his feet.
'Take it,' I would have said—'take it—or in three weeks I
shall be a dead man.' " [17]

Realizing that all this might open him to a charge of
"pique or illiberality," De Quincey went on at the end of his
first essay to a frank admission:

I shall acknowledge, then, on my own part—and I feel that I might
even make the same acknowledgment on the part of Professor Wilson
—(though I have no authority for doing so)—that to neither of us,
though, at all periods of our lives, treating him with the deep respect
which is his due, and, in our earlier years, with a more than filial
devotion,—nay, with a blind loyalty of homage, which had in it, at
that time, something of the spirit of martyrdom, which, for his sake,
courted even reproach and contumely; yet to neither of us has Wordsworth made those returns of friendship and kindness which most
firmly I maintain that we were entitled to have challenged. More by
far in sorrow than in anger—sorrow that points to recollections too
deep and too personal for a transient notice—I acknowledge myself to
have been long alienated from Wordsworth; sometimes even I feel a
rising emotion of hostility—nay, something, I fear, too nearly akin to
vindicative hatred (*Lit. Rem.,* I, 293 f.).

There it was, out in the open, for the world to read, and—
probably more important—for Wordsworth to read. De
Quincey proceeded to spell out the case of a man who had
identified himself with another's battles and griefs, and was
himself deserted when he needed support. The general
reader could hardly make much of this, but the Wordsworths
would know that the reference was to De Quincey's marriage.[18]

Margaret's specter literally haunts the essay. At the beginning she inspires a mysterious vision De Quincey had of his future in the vale he was entering to visit the poet. When he is describing the excessive reverence which made it difficult for him to approach Wordsworth, he explains: "People there were in this world whose respect I could not dispense with: people also there *have been* in this world (alas! alas!) whose love was to me no less indispensable. Have it I must, or life would have no value in my eyes." [19] The poignant parallel between Wordsworth and Peggy burns: the two things that have been really important in his life, and one blights the other. When he mentions Wordsworth's marriage, he wonders how it ever came to pass, because the poet could not have been a passionate lover, could not have surrendered himself to a suitor's homage, might even have told his mistress to hold her tongue. The comparison with De Quincey's own love swells out immediately:

I could not, perhaps, have loved with a perfect love, any woman whom I had felt to be my own equal intellectually; but then I never thought of her in that light, or under that relation. When the golden gate was opened, when the gate moved upon its golden hinges that opened to me the paradise of her society—when her young, melodious laughter sounded in my too agitated ear—did I think of any claims that *I* could have? Too happy if I might be permitted to lay all things at her feet. . . . Empty, empty thoughts! vanity of vanities! Yet no; not always; for sometimes, after days of intellectual toil, when half the whole world is dreaming—I wrap my head in the bed-clothes . . . and then, through blinding tears, I see again that golden gate (*Lit. Rem.,* I, 347 f.).

Oh, Wordsworth, he seems to imply, you objected that she was an ignorant girl—but how little that mattered you could never understand. These passages indicate how close to the surface at the time of writing was De Quincey's grief, and how inextricably his wife was entwined with the Wordsworths in his thoughts. It is significant that all three of these passages referring to Margaret were excised in later revisions. When his sorrow was fresh, however, fidelity to Peggy's memory almost required him to make it quite clear that, though he admired the poet, he lamented a weakness in the man.

Another, even more cryptic, charge against Wordsworth —also cut out in revision—came unexpectedly toward the end of the rather light-hearted account of the poet's good fortune in having legacies and stamp distributorships fall into his lap:

Yet, William Wordsworth, nevertheless, if you ever allowed yourself to forget the *human* tenure of these mighty blessings—if, though wearing your honors justly—most justly, as respects A. and B., this man and that man—you have forgotten that *no* man can challenge such trophies by any absolute or meritorious title, as respects the dark powers which give and take away—if, in the blind spirit of presumption, you have insulted the less prosperous fortunes of a brother, frail, indeed, but not dishonorably frail, and in his very frailty—that is, in his failing exertions—and for the deficient measure of his energies, (doubtless too much below the standard of reasonable expectations,) able to plead that which you never cared to ask—then, if (instead of being sixty-eight years old) you were 68/2, I should warn you to listen for the steps of Nemesis approaching from afar (*Lit. Rem.*, I, 358 f.).

Thus the frail brother took a sort of public vengeance, pathetic and tasteless. De Quincey did not seem to mind how he revealed himself in chalking Wordsworth's faults. Most petty and tawdry is his remark, in a late "Lake Reminiscence," on Thomas Wilkinson, to whose spade Wordsworth addressed a poem: "for some reason that I never could fathom, he was a sort of pet with Wordsworth. Professor Wilson and myself were never honoured with one line, one allusion from his pen; but many a person of particular feebleness has received that honour." [20]

The chief basis for De Quincey's major charge against the poet, that of ingratitude, was his own sympathy and support when "the finger of scorn was pointed at Mr. Wordsworth from every journal in the land." It strengthened his case, then, to emphasize his admiration for Wordsworth's poetry and the ridicule of others. Thus he worked in an attack on Jeffrey for his imperceptiveness in damning "There was a Boy," [21] and regularly throughout his writings exaggerated

the poet's unpopularity and his own uniqueness in recognizing Wordsworth's merits. True, he often tried to get support by including Wilson in the appreciation, in order to
include him in the grievance.[22] But frequently De Quincey
proclaimed hyperbolically, "I only in all Europe," "me *only*
in all this world," "I, therefore, as the very earliest (without one exception)." [23] He insisted on Wordsworth's lack of
fame in the Lakes, exploiting the least detail: "it is another
and striking proof of the slight hold which Wordsworth,
&c. had upon the public esteem" that Elizabeth Hamilton,
author and learned lady, spent six months in the area without seeking an introduction. Wordsworth, he asserted, had
"no admiring circle; no applauding coterie ever gathered
about him"; indeed, from 1809 to 1820, "The neighbouring
people, in every degree 'gentle and simple,' literary or half-
educated, who had heard of Wordsworth, agreed in despis-
ing him." He remembered, inaccurately, that the French
traveler, M. Simond, did "not vouchsafe to mention such a
person as Wordsworth." When De Quincey entered Oxford,
Wordsworth's "name was absolutely unknown." He gloated
that he was sending worshipful letters in 1804, "when no
man, beyond one or two in each ten thousand, had so much
as heard of either Coleridge or Wordsworth, and that one,
or those two, knew them only to scorn them, trample on
them, spit upon them." He even went so far as to maintain
that "men, so abject in public estimation . . . had not
existed before, have not existed since, will not exist again." [24]
In all this De Quincey was probably honest, as he was in
more modest terms correct. One suspects, however, that he
hammered on the idea partly because he took pride in his
critical acumen in recognizing Wordsworth, but also because—perhaps subconsciously—he got satisfaction in mag-
nifying his wrong by making the ingratitude which could
allow it all the more monstrous.

How the Wordsworths would react to all this was not
difficult to predict. Basil Montagu had cut Hazlitt for writing something about him in the *Liberal,* and Crabb Robinson
had broken off "all acquaintance" with Henry Southern
merely for allowing something about a friend to be printed

in the *Westminster Review*. William's stuffiness about vio-
lations of confidences of the hearth had already appeared in
other connections. He had written to Charles Lloyd on February 20, 1822, bitterly accusing him of ungentlemanly conduct in being the source of the candle anecdote quoted by
Hazlitt in the *London Magazine:* "The particulars upon
which you *grounded* this representation came to your knowledge as a guest invited to my table, and therefore could not
have been repeated in any miscellaneous society with a view
to lower my character, without a breach of the rules of
gentlemanly intercourse." [25] When Chauncey Hare Townsend's essays came out in *Blackwood's,* Wordsworth sput-
tered: "The Revd. Chauncey Hare Townsend is as pretty
a rascal as ever put on a surplice." The great aggravation
was: "I have occassionally seen him upon very friendly
terms, both at Cambridge, where I had dined with him,
at Keswick and at my own House where he has slept—
and where he was cordially received twice while this attack upon my person and writings was in process." [26] Moreover, as Wordsworth pontificated to Lloyd, "Such silly
tales throw no light upon the character they are brought
forward to illustrate—what light they may throw upon that
of those who repeat, or listen, to them, I should be loth to
trouble myself to ascertain."

How much worse for such tales to be told by one who had
lived so closely with the family as had De Quincey! When
the *Tait's* articles appeared, Wordsworth refused to read
or even hear anything of them. Crabb Robinson reported:

I was with Words. one day when the advertisement of one of his
[De Quincey's] papers was read. He said with great earnestness: "I
beg that no friend of mine will ever tell me a word of the contents of
those papers" & I dare say he was substantially obeyed. It was a year
or two afterw[ard]s (for these papers went on for a long time & were
very amusing) however, that I ventured to say: "I cannot help
telling one thing De Q. says in his last number in [these] very words
—that Mrs. W. is a better wife than you deserve." "Did he say
that? . . . That is *so* true that I can forgive him almost anything else
he says." [27]

But of course he could not really forgive De Quincey. His smoldering resentment shows in a marginal comment he made on the manuscript of the life of himself written by Barron Field. Field had objected to De Quincey's revelations as "unwarrantable exposures, especially as published during their lifetime." The poet noted:

Not so much as published during their lives as published or intended to be published at all. The Man has written under the influence of wounded feelings as he avows, I am told; for I have never read a word of his infamous production nor ever shall. My acquaintance with him was the result of a letter of his own volunteered to me. He was 7 months an inmate of my house; by what breach of the laws of hospitality, that kindness was repaid, his performance, if rightly represented to me, sufficiently shows. A man who can set such an example, I hold to be a pest in society, and one of the most worthless of mankind.[28]

Crabb Robinson, who prided himself on a rational fair-mindedness, recognized some palliation of De Quincey's *"impertinent reminiscences."* "There is a considerable part of these articles which published thirty years hence would be read with pride & satisfaction by your grand-children— I dare say the unhappy writer means to be honest." [29] Robinson went on, however, "But as you most truly remarked— It is not *what* he writes that excites your indignation but that he should write *anything*—Praise is an insult at such a time and in such a manner." If De Quincey hoped to make any impression on Wordsworth as to the justice of his grievance, he failed dismally. The poet would still have nothing to do with "fending and proving."

Wordsworth's last preserved reference to his apostate disciple demonstrates that, although he still respected De Quincey's talents, he would have nothing to do with him personally. In 1847 the poet wrote to John Wilson about a glossary of local names for *A Guide through the District of the Lakes:* [30] "I am still of opinion that it is very desirable that they should be looked over by Mr De Quincey if he could be got at." The wry implication of "if he could be got at" is emphasized by the hasty addition, "but on no account whatever let them be sent to him without previously taking a correct copy, otherwise it is great odds Mr N's MS would be lost." Then a postscript underlines his desire not to be brought into the matter personally: "I repeat what I said to you at Rydal that if application *be* made to Mr. de Q. my name must on no account be used in the business." [31]

One unsevered link remained, however, between Wordsworth and the Opium-Eater—the poet's *Convention of Cintra* pamphlet with De Quincey's notes and long postscript. The poet wrote in 1840 that he thought "with some interest upon its being reprinted hereafter," [32] but would not issue it again as long as the Duke of Wellington was alive. Since the Duke outlived the poet, the interesting problem did not arise of whether Wordsworth would have continued to accept his collaborator. Possibly his distaste for facing the equities of this matter had as much to do with Wordsworth's delay as did his respect for the Duke.

It is easy to have some sympathy for Wordsworth. When we remember his overlooking a *mésalliance* and an unsavory dissipation to try to help the dilatory editor of the *Westmorland Gazette;* when we recall that on several occasions Wordsworth's neighborly intentions were frustrated because De Quincey was "too ill" to see him, but that he persisted in well-doing, we can understand how the poet thought his "fault was only that of bearing with him . . . far more tenderly" [33] than he ought. How ironical that De Quincey's charge of ingratitude should be so bitterly topped. He clearly had, however, some premonitions of how Wordsworth would view the *Tait's* articles. Uneasiness is evident in the defensive declaration toward the end of the first essay that "Commensurate with the interest in the poetry will be a secondary interest in the poet—in his personal appearance, and his habits of life, *so far as they can be supposed at all dependent upon his intellectual characteristics*" (*Lit. Rem.,* I, 293). Even more defensive is an awkward explanation which appears in a context that has obviously been cut:

I should not have noticed this trait in Wordsworth's occasional manners, had it been gathered from domestic or confidential opportunities.
But, on the contrary, the first two occasions on which, after months'
domestic intercourse with Wordsworth, I became aware of his possible
ill-humour and peevishness, were so public, that others, and those
strangers, must have been equally made parties to the scene. This scene
occurred in Kendal (M, II, 286).

De Quincey's letters to Tait likewise tell an interesting
story of his awareness of the problem and his concern with
it, despite the economic pressures for copy. On March 9 he
wrote to the editor, "The part I am now upon in the acct.
of W.W. is deeply indebted to my knowledge of his private
Memoirs: I violate no confidence, but at the same time I tell
what no man could tell, for Coleridge only, besides myself,
had ever been allowed to read this most interesting part of
his works." [34] He was referring to *The Prelude,* which was
not to be published until after Wordsworth's death—and it
was probably no small part of the poet's grievance that De
Quincey printed passages from memory. After he had sent
off the articles, De Quincey began to have qualms about the
propriety of some of his revelations. In great agitation he
wrote to Tait in Feb. 20, 1839.

The publication of this paper about Wordsworth and Miss Wordsworth will do me very great injury besides giving very great pain. I
would not for all the world appear in the light of one who took advantage of an accidental discovery to expose an infirmity so common
(and, except for the degree and except for the connection with philosophic pretension, so venial) as an occasional burst of ill-temper.

Evidently Tait had already argued about the expense of
making revisions at this late date, for De Quincey went on
passionately to justify himself, asserting that he had always
expected to be able to revise these essays, and before this
had caused very little trouble about revisions. So serious was
the matter, that he was even willing to pay the expense himself!

This cause of De Quincey's anxiety was probably the

section near the beginning of the third essay on Wordsworth which told of a quarrel between brother and sister.[35] The passage was cut out, but De Quincey continued to have trouble with Tait for not allowing him the reconsideration he thought necessary to this delicate subject. On July 10 he even threatened "to set myself right in public opinion by publishing my disavowal of the article as an article corrected or deliberately warranted by myself. Every man is entitled to the benefit of his second thoughts." He looked upon himself, he said, "as very seriously injured." It was probably also Tait to whom he addressed a letter on January 16, 1840: "But let me again assure you solemnly that, from the facts made known to me since that paper was written, it will lead to consequences (if not corrected) which must oblige me to state the circumstances publicly." [36] We cannot be sure what this paper was, but *Tait's* published in March, 1840, an article on Charles Lloyd from which some anecdote about Wordsworth was simply cut out and asterisks put in its place. The text reads: "One evening*****A pang of wrath gathered at my heart." The newly learned facts may have had something to do with Lloyd's insanity or Dorothy Wordsworth's breakdown. That De Quincey was in close enough touch with the Wordsworths to know about Dorothy is tenderly indicated at the end of the third essay on the poet: "Farewell, Miss Wordsworth! . . . it may sometimes cheer the gloom of your depression to be assured of never-failing remembrance, full of love and respectful pity." [37]

After he had done his best with Tait, and the "Lake Reminiscences" on Wordsworth had appeared, De Quincey was no doubt conscious of various states of shock and titter in literary circles. Defensively he wrote to T. N. Talfourd on March 5, 1840:

if . . . you ever look into my Autob. sketches in Tait, bear in mind that I disown them. They were not written, as will be thought, in monthly successions and with interval sufficient: but all at once 2 years ago; in a coffee-room of a mail coach inn; with a sheriff's officer lurking near; in hurry too extreme to allow of reading them over even once; and with no other revision. (Quoted with permission from the

original manuscript in the Carl H. Pforzheimer Library, Misc. MS
104.)

Perhaps the remarkably outspoken exposition of his complaints against Wordsworth, which in October, 1840, De
Quincey attached oddly to a *Tait's* essay on "Walking Stewart," was intended as a sort of public justification and clari-
fication of his position. He there set forth with devastating
directness his version of the situation: the poet's preternatural pride and exclusiveness initially prevented any close
bonds between the men, and—as was inevitable in an atmosphere where efforts at explanation were dismissed, and
where there were women—clouds of misunderstanding
gathered. He told the story of Mary Dawson's misrepre-
senting his instructions on the use of Dove Cottage in his
absence,[38] and then—to prove that he was not alone in this
experience with Wordsworth—he claimed that Wilson was
also estranged from the poet, gave an account of Coleridge's
break with William, and ended with a few examples of
Wordsworth's stubborn *Einseitigkeit*.

In all this Peggy was not mentioned; there was only a
passing allusion to later injuries "still more irritating, because they related to more delicate topics." [39] At least part
of De Quincey's point, it seems, was that the split was inevitable and had begun long before his marriage. Possibly
he regretted covert references in "Lake Reminiscences"
which could give support to gossip that he was simply
piqued because Mrs. Wordsworth refused to receive his
"peasant girl" wife (as Sara Coleridge called Peggy).[40] Although he was certainly disingenuous in putting so much
blame on Mary Dawson, he was to some extent setting the
record straight—poor Peggy was not solely to blame either.
It is interesting that, once again in defense of Margaret,
De Quincey attacked Wordsworth.

Perhaps he was also answering in this essay rumors
which had reached him of the Rydal Mount wrath at his
breach of the laws of friendship, for he found occasion to
declare flatly that Wordsworth "most assuredly . . . drew
such a picture of Coleridge, and of his sensual effeminacy,

as ought not to have proceeded from the hands of a friend." [41] At least the charge has an amusing "you're another" aspect, although the circumstances were not parallel. Wordsworth would have pointed out that he did not publish his picture.

De Quincey had his last word during the poet's lifetime in his essay "On Wordsworth's Poetry," published in *Tait's Magazine* for September, 1845. He had half-launched upon the subject, we recall, back on May 16, 1838, in an open letter to William Tait "concerning the Poetry of Wordsworth"; but he meandered off into so many digressions that the editor did not publish it. By 1845, when he took up the topic again, Wordsworth had been Poet Laureate for two years and was certainly fair game for a serious critical article. Commenting at the outset that this was his first attempt at an "examination of any man's writings," although he had "retraced fugitive memorials of several persons celebrated in our own times," De Quincey wryly noted that sound criticism was more difficult, but personal recollections were more dangerous:

of men and women you dare not, and must not, tell all that chance may have revealed to you. Sometimes you are summoned to silence by pity for that general human infirmity which you also, the writer, share. Sometimes you are checked by the consideration that perhaps your knowledge of the case was originally gained under opportunities allowed only by confidence, or by unsuspecting carelessness. Sometimes the disclosure would cause quarrels between parties now at peace. Sometimes it would inflict pain, such as you could not feel any right to inflict, upon people not directly but collaterally interested in the exposure. Sometimes, again, if right to be told, it might be difficult to prove (M, XI, 294).

This is rather delicious. The implications are clearly that he could, if he would, have told much more; that he had indeed exercised great care and screened his revelations through several different logical sieves. To the victims the effect could only have been to add insult to injury. But De Quincey was not done yet. He went on:

And seldom, indeed, is your own silent retrospect of close personal connexions with distinguished men altogether happy. . . . "Put not your
trust in the intellectual princes of your age"; form no connexions too
close with any who live only in the atmosphere of admiration and
praise. The love or the friendship of such people rarely contracts itself
into the narrow circle of individuals. You, if you are brilliant like
themselves, or in any degree standing upon intellectual pretensions,
such men will hate; you, if you are dull, they will despise. Gaze, therefore, on the splendour of such idols as a passing stranger. Look for a
moment as one sharing in the idolatry; but pass on before the splendour
has been sullied by human frailty (M, XI, 295).

In the context of an essay "On Wordsworth's Poetry," by
one who had been a friend and admirer of the Laureate,
this was almost to repeat the specific statement of grievance
in the first part of the "Lake Reminiscences" essay on
Wordsworth.

The criticism which followed this introduction was, especially at the beginning, not so favorable to the poet as
was De Quincey's wont. Wordsworth's "theory of Poetic
Diction," as expressed in the Preface to the *Lyrical Ballads,*
De Quincey blasted as injudicious, an "obstacle purely self-
created" to his fame, and "not true in a double way": only
part of "the very language of men" was available to poetry,
and that only to special kinds of poetry. He had here nothing good to say about the Preface and upbraided Wordsworth for his failure to illustrate his points adequately. Yet
in another place he called the Preface "the subtlest and . . .
the most finished and masterly specimen of reasoning" in
all criticism.[42] In the 1845 critique he proceeded to find
great fault with *The Excursion,* not only because of its
"*undulatory* character" and prolix colloquial form but also
because its first book is "in a wrong key, and . . . on a
false basis." He scornfully asked why all the fuss—could
not the Wanderer simply have advised Margaret to write
to the War Office and locate her soldier husband, instead
of indulging in "sloth, and the habit of gadding abroad"?[43]
Really, she should be charged with homicidal negligence in
the death of her baby!

But De Quincey deeply admired Wordsworth's poetry, and outweighing this carping is much sensitive and appreciative comment on his "complex and oblique" dealing with "a passion . . . passing under the shadow of some secondary passion," and his bringing "many a truth into life, both for the eye and for the understanding, which previously had slumbered indistinctly for all men." Here, as regularly, De Quincey saw Wordsworth as primarily a poet of the profound truths of the human heart, and in this department—says the closing sentence of the essay—"there is little competition to be apprehended by Wordsworth from anything that has appeared since the death of Shakespere." [44]

Perhaps De Quincey continued to believe that this faith, which he had championed long and effectively, entitled him to some vestige of the privileges that had once been his. At any rate, although he obviously worried about the freedom of his writing of his Lake friends, and undoubtedly heard at least indirectly some repercussions from Rydal Mount, he does not seem to have considered that he had done anything to sever such relations as continued to exist between them. On September 12, 1848, as we have seen, he wrote without apology a note introducing a Mr. Mousabines to the poet, signing himself, "Your faithful friend and servant" (Letter 60). When he came to revise his articles for his *Selections* in 1854, he did not make much effort to remove the objectionable sections. He did, of course, cut out his elaborations of personal grievance, and he also left out reference to Wordsworth's walking like a cade; but most of the omissions seem really to have been those which involved himself, Peggy, and Wilson. He even added gratuitously in his 1854 revision of the 1834 essay on Coleridge, in the context of the skating artistry of the German poet Klopstock, "the poet of the 'Excursion' sprawled upon the ice like a cow dancing a cotillon." [45]

A curious footnote to the affair was written the same year, when the ardent American Wordsworthian, Professor Henry Reed, visited Rydal Mount. His sister-in-law, Anne Bronson, recorded: "De Quincey's spite against Wordsworth has been explained since we have been here. It seems that De Quincey, after living some years with a sort of housekeeper—the mother of several of his children, saw fit, at last, to marry her; and then wanted Mrs. Wordsworth to visit this woman—which she refused to do. In revenge for this De Quincey wrote as he did, of Wordsworth." [46] Miss Bronson had been talking to Crabb Robinson, increasingly garrulous at 79, and this garbled "explanation" sounds like his work. If it came from Mary, De Quincey was undoubtedly right about her hostility. It is a harsh last word from Rydal, surely.

By this time Wordsworth was dead and Dorothy almost so. When she died the next year, De Quincey noted the fact in a letter to his daughter without show of feeling: "On Tuesday last I saw announced the death of Miss Wordsworth at the age of eighty-four." [47] De Quincey himself was then seventy, and at last was all passion spent.

Their relationship, however, survives both Wordsworth and De Quincey, for it lives on in their writings—not only in the narrative fragments we have pieced together here, but also in mutual influences. Literary and intellectual influences, particularly in contemporaries subject to many of the same forces, are difficult to pin down; but it seems fair to say that De Quincey's output would have been very different if Wordsworth had not entered his life. Wordsworth, the older, more established man, naturally owed much less to the influence of his disciple. Still, there is evidence that the current ran both ways.

The poet was more subject to suggestions from his friends than is perhaps generally recognized: Coleridge, Sara Hutchinson, Crabb Robinson, Barron Field, and Edward Quillinan, for example, all were responsible for revisions in Wordsworth's poetry. How much poetic criticism De Quincey presumed to contribute is doubtful. In his 1838 open letter to William Tait on Wordsworth's poetry, he complained that the poet was too susceptible to suggestion, and had thereby "half-ruined some dozens of his finest passages by 'cobbling' them as it is called." [48] Consistency

should have kept De Quincey from tinkering himself. He
was not, however, backward about expressing to the poet
his reservations about "cobbling": in his 1819 letter on
Peter Bell he said frankly that some of Wordsworth's alterations seemed to him "to have injured the effect." Possibly, in the early years of closer association, he was more
explicit in his criticism, and he may have left more marks
on Wordsworth's verse than are now decipherable. At least
he pointed out to the poet that the allusion to "Father
Adam" in "The Redbreast Chasing the Butterfly" was obscure, and, as he reported in *Tait's* for March, 1837, "in
consequence of what I then said, he added the note of reference to Milton which will be found in the subsequent editions." [49]

There are, however, marks enough of De Quincey's influence and assistance in Wordsworth's prose writings. Of
course, Wordsworth, during the publication of *The Convention of Cintra* in 1809, had called on De Quincey for
footnotes, the appendix on Sir John Moore, punctuation
and "alterations" where necessary. We remember that in
1815 the poet wrote anxiously wanting to know whether
De Quincey approved the phrasing of the Preface to the
new edition of his *Poems*. And, according to what the young
man told Crabb Robinson, he persuaded Wordsworth to
leave out of that Preface an attack upon Jeffrey.[50]

Although such evidence as can be adduced is susceptible
to different interpretations, it is not unlikely that De Quincey influenced Wordsworth's thinking as well as his phrasing. As early as 1809 he sent to the poet from London the
Earl of Selkirk's *A Letter Addressed to John Cartwright,
Esq. . . . on the Subject of Parliamentary Reform,* an attack on democratic suffrage such as Wordsworth probably
would not have appreciated ten years earlier (see Letter
32 above). De Quincey's conservative politics—he had been
shocked at hearing Wordsworth and Southey talk "treason"
when he first met them in 1807—may have encouraged the
poet's gradual hardening into a Tory pattern. It is also at
least interesting to note that Wordsworth, in the spring of
1833, wrote to Alexander Dyce, "The tenth sonnet of

Donne, beginning 'Death, be not proud,' is so eminently characteristic of his manner, and at the same time so weighty in thought, and vigorous in the expression, that I would entreat you to insert it, though to modern taste it may be repulsive, quaint, and laboured." For De Quincey, who seems to have felt even more strongly that Donne was "a man yet unappreciated," had expressed similar sentiments in 1818, when he printed in the *Westmorland Gazette* the same sonnet, as worthy of "high place," and urged that a selection of Donne's work be published.[51]

Whatever the accounting in various specific ideas, of Wordsworth's enduring influence on De Quincey there can be no doubt. Among the scraps of the disciple's posthumous papers are such notes as this: "I happen'd this evening (Saturday, August 3rd, '44) to be saying of W. W. to myself: 'No poet is so free from all cases like this, viz. where all the feelings and spontaneous thought which they have accumulated coming to an end, and yet the case seeming to require more to finish it, or bring it round, like a peal of church bells, they are forced to invent, and form descants on rapture never really felt.' " A similar undated note preserves this insight: "Wordsworth is always recording phenomena as they are enjoyed; Coleridge as they reconcile themselves with opposing or conflicting phenomena." Perhaps there is more personal feeling behind his jotting down, probably in 1844, "W. W.'s social phil. is surely shallow." [52] Thus De Quincey "happened" to be thinking about Wordsworth.

Indeed, to read De Quincey's writings is to find references to Wordsworth almost *passim*. Even in "On Murder Considered as One of the Fine Arts" De Quincey remarks that a certain murderer "carried his art to a point of colossal sublimity, and, as Mr. Wordsworth observes, has in a manner 'created the taste by which he is to be enjoyed.' " More than two hundred such allusions are scattered through his works from beginning to end. He several times quotes as the finest single verse in English literature a line from the fourth of Wordsworth's "Poems on the Naming of Places" (l. 38): "Sole-sitting by the shores of old romance." Wordsworth's opinion is cited on everything from Walking Stewart's eloquence to Barbara Lewthwaite's beauty. His theories as to the character of Westmorland valleys, the distinguishing feature of tarns, and the proper derivation of "Blentarn" are quoted with respect. But De Quincey's children's reactions to the death of a bird made him doubt the truth of "We Are Seven," and recollections of his own boyish feelings at the funeral of his sister brought forth criticism of *The Excursion*'s contention that "unsteady faith" in immortality was the cause of grief at the death of loved ones. His seeing Wordsworth under every bush becomes almost ludicrous when he discovers the portrait of Milton in Richardson's edition to be "a likeness nearly perfect of Wordsworth." [53]

De Quincey's references to Wordsworth's poetry, and his frequent quotation from memory, reveal how attentive he was to it. In 1819 he acknowledged the poet's present of a copy of *Peter Bell* by judicious references to his memory of the version he had read in 1807. In 1839 he quoted at some length—and understandably misquoted— passages from the still unpublished *Prelude,* which he had seen or heard read more than twenty years before. A memory so charged was bound to give forth unannounced, and perhaps even unrecognized, echoes. We are startled as at a parody when we read what De Quincey did with the eminently Wordsworthian doctrines of solitude, silence, and reverie: "He naturally seeks solitude and silence, as indispensable conditions of those trances, or profoundest reveries, which are the crown and consummation of what opium can do for human nature." [54] For the jarring "opium" substitute something like "external nature," and the sentiment seems a fair enough reflection of the mystical side of the poet.

Other echoes of Wordsworth may be heard in De Quincey's favorite "Pariah" characters, which perhaps owe something to the poet's various Solitaries, and in De Quincey's respect for childhood. Consider his assertion:

I maintain steadfastly that into all the *elementary* feelings of man children look with more searching gaze than adults. . . . children have a specific power of contemplating the truth, which departs as they enter the world. It is clear to me, that children, upon elementary paths which require no knowledge of the world to unravel, tread more firmly than men; have a more pathetic sense of the beauty which lies in justice.[55]

This reads like a gloss on Wordsworth's "Seer blest" in the "Intimations" ode.

Naturally, much of Wordsworth's reverential attitude toward man's funded life, the haunting and nourishing past, appears also in De Quincey's writings. De Quincey's analysis of Coleridge's relation to his past reflects that poet's "Dejection" but is also rich with the flavor of Wordsworth's "Intimations" ode, *The Prelude,* and "Composed upon an Evening of Extraordinary Splendour and Beauty"; it is thoroughly Wordsworthian in its burden, its phraseology, its imagery:

Phantoms of lost power, sudden intuitions, and shadowy restorations of forgotten feelings, sometimes dim and perplexing, sometimes by bright but furtive glimpses, sometimes by a full and steady revelation, overcharged with light—throw us back in a moment upon scenes and remembrances that we have left full thirty years behind us. In solitude, and chiefly in the solitudes of nature, and, above all, amongst the great and *enduring* features of nature, such as mountains, and quiet dells, and the lawny recesses of forests, and the silent shores of lakes, features with which (as being themselves less liable to change) our feelings have a more abiding association—under these circumstances it is that such evanescent hauntings of our past and forgotten selves are most apt to startle and to waylay us. These are *positive* torments from which the agitated mind shrinks in fear; but there are others *negative* in their nature—that is, blank momentoes of powers extinct, and of faculties burnt out within us (M, II, 204 f.).

De Quincey's whole exploitation of his own past undoubtedly owes something to Wordsworth's example of introspection and psychological analysis of the "hiding places" of man's power. His autobiographical dream visions came avowedly from a qualified "child is father of the man" view of life and art, as he makes clear in the Introductory Notice to his 1845 "Suspiria de Profundis":

An adult sympathizes with himself in childhood because he *is* the same, and because (being the same) yet he is *not* the same. He acknowledges the deep, mysterious identity between himself, as adult and as infant, for the ground of his sympathy; and yet, with this general agreement, and necessity of agreement, he feels the difference between his two selves as the main quickeners of his sympathy. . . . Some of the phenomena developed in my dream-scenery, undoubtedly, do but repeat the experiences of childhood; and others seem likely to have been growths and fructifications from seed at that time sown (Elwin, pp. 452 f.).

Such a crucial moment from his past as that described in the following passage from the *Confessions* resembles in tension and significance a Wordsworthian "spot of time":

all through the hours of night, I have continued motionless, as if frozen, without consciousness of myself as an object anywise distinct from the multiform scene which I contemplated from above. . . . The town of Liverpool represented the earth, with its sorrows and its graves left behind, yet not out of sight, nor wholly forgotten. The ocean, in everlasting but gentle agitation, yet brooded over by dove-like calm, might not unfitly typify the mind, and the mood which then swayed it. For it seemed to me as if then first I stood at a distance aloof from the uproar of life; as if the tumult, the fever, and the strife, were suspended; a respite were granted from the secret burdens of the heart,—some sabbath of repose, some resting from human labours. Here were the hopes which blossom in the paths of life, reconciled with the peace which is in the grave; motions of the intellect as unwearied as the heavens, yet for all anxieties a halcyon calm; tranquility that seemed no product of inertia, but as if resulting from mighty and equal antagonisms; infinite activities, infinite repose (M, III, 395).

The modulations are typically De Quinceyan, and he is characteristically more interested in "mighty and equal antagonisms" than in the creative process; but the figure of the ocean as typifying the mind is reminiscent of Wordsworth's great Snowdon vision of "The perfect image of a mighty Mind" (*The Prelude* [1805], XIII, ll. 66–98).

The recorded places of De Quincey's power were in experiences tinged like Wordsworth's with "beauty and fear":

standing by the bedside of his dead sister Elizabeth when
he was six years old, sitting in the weakness of near-death
on a Soho doorstep by Ann of Oxford Street when he was
seventeen, lying on the grave of Cathy Wordsworth in
nympholeptic despair when he was twenty-seven, watching
in horror as a mysterious wandering Malay bolted a gift
of opium at his cottage door when he was about thirty-one.
These events, half-visionary despite their painful reality,
had dreamy reincarnations that colored the gorgeous
phantasmagoria of the *Confessions*, "The Afflictions of
Childhood," "The Daughter of Lebanon," "Levana and
Our Ladies of Sorrow," and "The Dream Fugue." The
Malay became the focus of Oriental nightmares; Elizabeth, Ann, and Cathy each had her own visionary manifestation, and merged with the nameless lady of "The
Vision of Sudden Death" through the various transforma-
tions of threatened innocence in "The Dream Fugue"—all
with the extravagant distortion of space and time which
De Quincey attributed to opium.[56] His "spots of time" did
not, perhaps, so much enshrine "the spirit of the Past / For
future restoration" (*The Prelude*, XII, ll. 285–286), as
feed the eidetic imagery of his vaunted and feared dreaming faculty. Wordsworth, at least by the time De Quincey
knew him, rarely reached such bravuras of reverie. They
were, however, not unrelated to his experiences when "the
eye was master of the heart" (*The Prelude* [1805], XI,
l. 172), and when

> There came among those shapes of human life
> A wilfulness of fancy and conceit
> Which gave them new importance to the mind;
> And Nature and her objects beautified
> These fictions, as in some sort in their turn
> They burnish'd her. From touch of this new power
> Nothing was safe.
> (*The Prelude* [1805], VIII, ll. 519–525)

De Quincey acknowledged taking from Wordsworth such
specific details as the image of the "mighty wheel of day
and night" in "Levana and Our Ladies of Sorrow," [57] and

we have seen how he may have borrowed larger motifs; even more interesting is the analogy between *The Prelude* and the *Confessions*. Both are personal histories with general applications, as the subtitles suggest: "The Growth of a Poet's Mind" and "Extract from the Life of a Scholar." Both follow the lines of the regeneration myth: Wordsworth's recovery from the sloughs of rationalism and De Quincey's supposed escape from the opium bonds which, in fact, he could never quite throw off. Both are selective autobiographies, with emphasis upon childhood experiences, chronicling only the events which seem to their authors to have been significant in the development of their minds and the coloring of their thoughts. The "Mind of Man" is declaredly the "main region" of Wordsworth's song ("Prospectus," ll. 40–41), and the "majestic intellect" in the "shadowy world of dreams" (M, III, 384, 215) is assertedly the center of De Quincey's interest. Just as Wordsworth undertook *The Prelude* in part to examine his equipment as a poet, De Quincey was to some degree intent upon explaining his development as a dreamer—an office which he believed had divine origins. His dream passages are in what he called "impassioned prose," what has as well been called prose poetry. It is not impossible that De Quincey had something like a prose *Prelude* in mind when he wrote the *Confessions*.

Wordsworth's ideas also served De Quincey well in his scattered literary criticism, as he frankly admitted in 1823: "for most of the sound criticism on poetry, or any subject connected with it that I have ever met with, I must acknowledge my obligations to many years' conversation with Mr. Wordsworth." [58] He credited the poet with some of his most significant theories, particularly his famous distinction between the Literature of Knowledge and the Literature of Power, and his conception of "confluent" style:

In saying this, we do but vary the form of what we once heard delivered on this subject by Mr. Wordsworth. His remark was by far the weightiest thing we ever heard on the subject of style; and it was this: that it is in the highest degree unphilosophic to call language or diction "the *dress* of thoughts." And what was it then that he would substitute? Why this: he would call it "the *incarnation* of thoughts." Never in one word was so profound a truth conveyed (M, X, 229 f.).

Apparently he also drew upon Wordsworth in other instances which he did not acknowledge, perhaps because he did not recognize his source. At least Wordsworth thought so, for he wrote to Crabb Robinson that the essay on "Rhetoric" contained "some things from my Conversation —which the Writer does not seem aware of." It is hard to certify originality when two minds are much together. One of the ideas common to both men which appears in this essay is disagreement with Samuel Johnson's designation of "metaphysical" poets.[59] There are others.

However, De Quincey was never content with mere passive acceptance: subtle modification was an inalienable right of his mind. Wordsworth's famous definition of poetry as the "spontaneous overflow of powerful feeling recollected in tranquility" became in De Quincey's statement the "spontaneous overflow of real unaffected passion, deep, and at the same time original, and also forced into public manifestation of itself from the necessity which cleaves to all passion alike of seeking external sympathy." [60] Wordsworth declared "a Poet writes under one restriction only, namely, the necessity of giving pleasure to a human Being." De Quincey asserted, "a poet in the highest departments of his art may, and often does, communicate mere knowledge, but never as a direct purpose, unless by forgetting his proper duty." [61]

De Quincey may also have taken up Wordsworth's opinions of specific writers, or have been strengthened in his own original verdicts. There is, for example, agreement in deprecating Samuel Johnson's style and on such opposites as the poetry of George Crabbe and James Macpherson. Wordsworth wrote to Samuel Rogers on September 29, 1808—just before De Quincey arrived at Allan Bank—of "Crabbe's *verses:* for *poetry* in no sense can they be called," declaring that "nineteen out of 20 of Crabbe's Pictures are mere matters of fact; with which the Muses have just about as much to do as they have with a Collection of medical reports, or of Law cases." [62] De Quincey fulminated to Woodhouse along similar lines:

His [Crabbe's] pretensions to poetry were not nothing, merely, but if they were to be represented algebraically, the negative sign must be prefixed. All his labours and endeavours were unpoetical. Instead of raising and elevating his subjects, he did all he could to make them flat and commonplace, to disrobe them of the garb in which imagination would clothe them, and to bring them down as low as, or even to debase them lower than, the standard of common life. Poetry could no longer exist if cultivated only by such writers as Crabbe (*De Quincey and His Friends,* p. 92).

De Quincey had for Ossian "such a scorn as every man that ever looked at Nature with his own eyes, and not through books, must secretly entertain. Heavens! what poverty: secondly, what monotony: thirdly, what falsehood of imagery!" In 1815, when Wordsworth and De Quincey were still fairly intimate, Wordsworth made, in his "Essay Supplementary to the Preface," similar strictures against the falseness of observation in Ossian: "From what I saw with my own eyes, I knew that the imagery was spurious." [63]

Many of these ideas were, of course, in the air, and could have been derived from other sources than Wordsworth. Coleridge too expressed the idea, almost a commonplace in criticism, that a "poem is that species of composition, which is opposed to works of science, by proposing for its *immediate* object pleasure, not truth." Southey likewise shared the reservations noted above about the felicity of the designation "metaphysical" poets. Consider also this agreement on *Paradise Regained:* Coleridge (1810): "however inferior its kind is to 'Paradise Lost,' its execution is superior"; Wordsworth (Robinson's report, 1836): "He spoke of the *Paradise Regained* as surpassing even the *Paradise Lost* in perfection of execution, though the theme is far below it and demanding less power"; De Quincey (1838): in *Paradise Regained* "the execution is more highly

finished," but "the compass being so much narrower . . .
inevitably the splendours are sown more thinly." [64]

De Quincey was not, however, disposed to accept all of
Wordsworth's ideas. For instance, he once credited Wordsworth with unveiling "the great philosophical distinction
between the powers of *fancy* and *imagination*," but his own
definition of the imagination appears to be closer to Coleridge's, and the whole concept—so significant to Wordsworth—was relatively unimportant in his thinking. He also
came to prefer Coleridge's view of "Poetic Diction" to
Wordsworth's, although he was not satisfied with what
either had written on the subject.[65] Again, Wordsworth told
Aubrey de Vere that it was wrong to speak of Shakespeare
"as if even he were perfect. He had serious defects."
De Quincey, one of the foremost Bardolaters of the age,
may have prompted the poet's complaint. For he proclaimed that Shakespeare's work, like the works of nature,
were "to be studied with entire submission of our faculties,
and in the perfect faith that in them there can be no too
much or too little." [66]

In view of the differences in their temperaments and the
disruption of their personal relations, diversity of opinion
between De Quincey and Wordsworth was natural enough
—so natural that their manifold agreements loom more
significant. The later "hostility," which De Quincey admitted to, might in a small mind have even taken the form
of deliberate contradiction of things Wordsworthian. That
it did not is a tribute to both men and a token of the enduring importance of their association, particularly to the
younger man, who remained to the end something of the
disciple, albeit a discontented and irreverent one.

NOTES

CHAPTER ONE
"APPROACH"

1. *Confessions of an English Opium-Eater, in Both the Revised and the Original Texts, with its Sequels, Suspiria de Profundis and the English Mail-Coach*, ed. Malcolm Elwin (London, 1956), p. 352. (Future references to the *Confessions* will be to this convenient edition, and will be indicated as Elwin); manuscript in the possession of Misses Maude de Quincey and Clare Craig (hereinafter cited as Craig Mss.), quoted by Horace A. Eaton, *Thomas De Quincey* (London, 1936), p. 68. (When manuscript sources which I have consulted are also available in print, I hereafter add the printed reference in parentheses. Sometimes there are slight variations, especially in punctuation, which some of De Quincey's editors have normalized.)

2. Elwin, pp. 164, 16ç.

3. *De Quincey's Writings* (Boston; Ticknor and Fields, 1859), *Literary Reminiscences*, I, 294. (This edition is regularly cited for references to the original magazine version of works revised by De Quincey for his *Selections Grave and Gay*, these volumes as *Lit. Rem.*); Wordsworth's marginalia in Barron Field's Ms. life of Wordsworth (British Museum Add. Ms. 41,325, fol. 15).

4. Craig Mss. (A. H. Japp, *Thomas De Quincey: His Life and Writings* [London, 1890], pp. 53 f. [hereinafter cited as Japp]).

5. *The Collected Writings of Thomas De Quincey*, ed. David Masson (London, 1896), I, 383, 396 (hereinafter cited as M).

6. M, I, 56, 32.

7. It is revealing that De Quincey pictured himself as "scarcely seven" when he was past eight, and William as "five or six years" older, when he was probably less than four (M,

CHAPTER ONE (*Continued*)

I, 59, 84, 119). Unless William was a premature child, he could hardly have been born before late July, 1881 (Eaton, p. 3).

8. *De Quincey Memorials,* ed. A. H. Japp (London, 1891), I, 8–10, 19, 38, 60 f.; II, 94 (hereinafter cited as *Memorials*).

9. Elwin, p. 351.

10. Craig Mss. (Japp, p. 40; Eaton, p. 50.

11. M, III, 258.

12. M, I, 320; "Life and Manners," *De Quincey's Writings,* p. 164; M, I, 394.

13. For the letters to Wordsworth, see Letters 1–7; M, III, 302. References to De Quincey's letters to the Wordsworths which are reprinted here will normally be given hereafter parenthetically by letter number. This account is substantiated by an 1804 letter (Letter 4) and an 1834 essay (M, II, 138 f.). An 1835 essay claims he first wrote to Wordsworth in 1802, but did not send a letter until the next year (M, II, 59).

14. Richard Woodhouse, "Notes of Conversation with Thomas De Quincey," *De Quincey and his friends,* ed. James Hogg (London, 1895), p. 72; M, I, 153.

15. Japp, pp. 26, 28 n.

16. M, XIV, 368 f.; I, 192.

17. *A Diary of Thomas De Quincey for 1803,* ed. H. A. Eaton (London, 1927), pp. 181 f.

18. Craig Mss. (in part Japp, pp. 36, 33); *Memorials,* I, 42, 44, 47 f.; Eaton, p. 275 n.

19. M, I, 193; *Diary,* pp. 182, 181 f.

20. *Diary,* p. 152; M, II, 129.

21. *Diary,* pp. 207, 209, 191 f., 154.

22. See above, Letter 1.

23. *Diary,* p. 188.

24. M, III, 36.

25. *The Early Letters of William and Dorothy Wordsworth (1787–1805),* ed. E. de Selincourt (Oxford, 1935), p. 333 (hereinafter cited as *EL*).

26. Oct. 14, 1803, *Collected Letters of Samuel Taylor Coleridge,* ed. E. L. Griggs (London, 1956), II, 1013 (hereinafter cited as *STC*).

27. M, III, 36.

28. *EL,* p. 369.

29. *EL,* p. 370. Wordsworth was referring to *The Prelude* and the never-completed *Recluse.*

30. See Mary Moorman, "Wordsworth's Commonplace Book," *N & Q,* CCII (Sept., 1957), 400–405.

31. *The Letters of William and Dorothy Wordsworth, The Middle Years,* ed. E. de Selincourt (Oxford, 1937), I, 159 (hereinafter cited as *MY*).

32. *EL,* p. 373.

33. M, III, 379 f., 389.

34. M, II, 230 f.

35. This letter seems to have been lost, but in a note to her brother when she forwarded the April 6 letter Dorothy said that she had written to De Quincey (*MY,* I, 18), and De Quincey acknowledged it on June 9. William wrote from London on May 5 (*MY,* I, 22 f.).

36. Craig Mss., Japp, and Eaton give these dates incorrectly as 1805.

37. Japp, p. 75; M, XI, 321.

38. *MY,* I, 159; Thomas Carlyle, *Reminiscences,* ed. J. A. Froude (London, 1881), I, 256; M, V, 19 n.

39. M, II, 232.

40. *MY,* I, 23, 29, 124.

41. M, III, 35, 38.

42. M, II, 140; British Museum Add. Ms. 35,344, fol. 204.

43. M, II, 150.

44. Craig Mss. (Japp, p. 91); M,

II, 163; *Memorials,* II, 113. Cottle told the story of De Quincey's loan in his *Early Recollections Chiefly Relating to the Late Samuel Taylor Coleridge* (London, 1837), II, 125–131.

45. *Minnow among Tritons. Mrs. S. T. Coleridge's Letters to Thomas Poole,* ed. Stephen Potter (London: Nonesuch Press, 1934), p. 8.

46. *MY,* I, 156.

47. M, II, 235, 303.

CHAPTER TWO
"OPPORTUNITY"

1. "The Lake Poets: William Wordsworth and Robert Southey," *Tait's Magazine* (July, 1839), reprinted in M, II, 303–332; *MY,* I, 155.

2. M, II, 306–307. Both of these quoted passages were cut out by De Quincey when he revised the article for his *Selections.*

3. *MY,* I, 159; M, II, 322; *Selections Grave and Gay* (Edinburgh, 1854), II, 322. In his letter of March 25, 1808, he said he heard only the introduction on the way to Penrith, the rest in London (Letter 8).

4. *Peter Bell,* 133; M, III, 315.

5. M, II, 154; XIII, 335; I, 41 f.

6. M, II, 62; Craig Mss., Sept. 15, 1807 (Japp, p. 90; M, II, 306).

7. M, II, 328.

8. *MY,* I, 175.

9. M, II, 188; *STC,* III, 47, 51–53; *Memorials,* I, 138–139.

10. British Museum Add. Ms. 47, 520, fol. 72; *STC,* III, 48; James Gillman, *The Life of Samuel Taylor Coleridge* (London, 1838), I, 251.

11. *STC,* III, 53; *MY,* I, 184, 207.

12. *MY,* I, 179.

13. British Museum Add. Ms. 47, 521, fol. 5.

14. *MY,* I, 210. For De Quincey's account of the tragedy, see M, XIII, 125–149. For Dorothy's, see *George & Sarah Green, a Narrative,* ed. Ernest de Selincourt (Oxford: Clarendon Press, 1936).

15. *De Quincey and His Friends,* ed. James Hogg (London, 1895), p. 101.

16. *MY,* I, 234; M, II, 190.

17. See Letter 19 and Letter 31, p. 178; Cornell Lib. Wordsworth Coll., No. 2223.

18. *MY,* I, 233 f., 245.

19. *MY,* I, 247, 257.

20. British Museum Add. Ms. 41, 325, fol. 15; M, II, 190, 359.

21. *The Letters of Sara Hutchinson from 1800 to 1835,* ed. Kathleen Coburn (London, 1954), p. 12 (hereinafter cited as *SH*). Joanna was Sara's sister, Wordsworth's sister-in-law.

22. M, V, 19 *n.; SH,* p. 11.

23. *MY,* I, 261.

24. British Museum Add. Ms. 34,046, fol. 78; *STC,* III, 177.

25. *SH,* p. 15 (cf. *MY,* I, 262; *The Letters of Mary Wordsworth, 1800-1855* (ed. Mary E. Burton [Oxford, 1958], p. 6), hereinafter cited as *MW; MY,* I, 327.

26. M, III, 359; *Diary,* p. 173; Craig Mss. (Japp, p. 91).

27. *Lit. Rem.,* II, 341; *The Posthumous Works of Thomas De Quincey,* ed. A. H. Japp (London, 1891), II, 16.

28. M, II, 312. (In revising the essay for his *Selections* De Quincey cut out the buttery knife story); see Letter 31, p. 178.

29. M, II, 322.

30. *MY,* I, 253, 250.

31. *Lake Poets,* p. 96; Foster Collection, Victoria and Albert Museum, F 48.D. 32; see also *The Life and*

CHAPTER TWO (*Continued*)

Correspondence of Robert Southey,
ed. C. C. Southey (London, 1850),
III, 179.

32. *MY,* I, 243, 245; *Life of Southey,* III, 197, 180; *MY,* I, 250, 258.

33. *MY,* I, 255; *STC,* III, 164, 206;
see John Edwin Wells, "The Story
of Wordsworth's 'Cintra,' " *SP,*
XVIII (1921), 26–29; *Lake Poets,* p.
158; Eaton, p. 159 n.

34. *MY,* I, 260, 276; see Letter 35.

35. *STC,* III, 134; Wells, *SP,*
XVIII, 25–26.

36. *MY,* I, 266; *STC,* III, 174.

37. *MY,* I, 329. The house was
then known as Longman, Hurst,
Rees, and Orme.

38. *MY,* I, 272.

39. M, I, 9. Curiously, he called
his works *Selections Grave and Gay,*
adapting a phrase he had used in
1809, when he wrote Dorothy that
he sent her "everything—grave and
gay" (Letter 13).

40. Dove Cottage Mss.

41. *MY,* I, 310; see end of Letter
26.

42. *STC,* III, 214; *MY,* I, 290, 266,
271.

43. *MY,* I, 263 (misdated March
26), 268 (misdated March 27), 274,
275, 279, 285, 267, 271.

44. *MY,* I, 274.

45. Wells, *SP,* XVIII, 59.

46. *MY,* I, 260, 263, 262.

47. *MY,* I, 264, 272.

48. *MY,* I, 267–278.

49. *MY,* I, 267.

50. *MY,* I, 266–272, 273. De Selincourt makes the first letter March
27, but Dorothy's postscript is dated
"Sunday afternoon," which fell on
the 26th.

51. *MY,* I, 276.

52. *MY,* I, 267.

53. *MY,* I, 281–284.

54. *MY,* I, 286, 316.

55. *MY,* I, 315.

56. British Museum Add. Ms. 34,-
046, fol. 98; *STC,* III, 205.

57. *MY,* I, 320.

58. *MY,* I, 279, 288.

59. *MY,* I, 313.

60. *MY,* I, 313 f.; see above, p. 58.

61. *MY,* I, 296, 309.

62. *MY,* I, 314.

63. *MY,* I, 319, 321.

64. De Quincey's notes and drafts
of the postscript show as many as
six versions of some parts (Cornell
Lib. Wordsworth Coll., No. 2804).

65. *MY,* I, 311 f.

66. *MY,* I, 316 f.

67. *MY,* I, 313, 320.

68. *MY,* I, 323.

69. *MY,* I, 323, 331; British Museum Add. Ms. 34,046, fol. 107;
STC, III, 214; *Life of Southey,* III,
246; Cornell Lib. Wordsworth Coll.,
No. 3117.

70. Wells has analyzed De Quincey's changes in the punctuation, *SP,*
XVIII, 65 f.

71. *MY,* I, 282, 287, 300.

72. *MY,* I, 312, 305.

CHAPTER THREE
"ESTRANGEMENT"

1. *MY,* I, 313, 333, 336.

2. *Lit. Rem.,* I, 261 f.; *MY,* I,
310 f.; 330.

3. *STC,* III, 286.

4. *MY,* I, 344.

5. M, I, 203 f.; VIII, 298 n.

6. M, III, 282; II, 438; *MY,* I, 294.

7. *MY,* I, 346; M, II, 191.

8. *MY,* I, 393; Wedgwood Museum; Craig Mss.; *MY,* I, 411.

9. M, II, 382.

10. *MY,* I, 344.

11. *Memorials,* II, 29–51; see Eaton, pp. 281–285, 420 f.

12. Southey spent two nights at Dove Cottage in December, 1810; De Quincey visited for a week at Greta Hall in April, 1811, and in May asked Southey to get four books for him from London. He mentions seeing Southey at Easedale in 1812, got letters of introduction from him in the same year for a family friend, and in 1813 sent through the Wordsworths news of a discovery in a London bookshop which he thought might interest Southey. In 1814 Southey wrote to Cottle that he had heard of him through De Quincey. M, II, 318; Japp, p. 133; *Unpublished Letters of Thomas De Quincey and Elizabeth Barrett Browning,* ed. S. Musgrove, Auckland (New Zealand) Univ. Coll. Bull., No. 44 (1954), pp. 4, 13; M, II, 345; *Memorials,* II, 138 n.; Letter 41, above; Joseph Cottle, *Reminiscences of Samuel Taylor Coleridge and Robert Southey* (London, 1847), p. 386.

13. *SH,* p. 28.

14. Letter to Sara Hutchinson, August, 1811 (in the possession of Miss Joanna Hutchinson); *Memorials,* II, 79; Musgrove, pp. 11–13.

15. *SH,* p. 22; Mary L. Armitt, *Rydal* (Kendal, 1916), p. 677.

16. M, II, 443; *MY,* I, 335; *SH,* p. 27.

17. See Letter 31, p. 178; *MY,* I, 395.

18. *MY,* II, 502 f., 525.

19. *Henry Crabb Robinson on Books and their Writers,* ed. Edith J. Morley (London, 1938), I, 103 (hereinafter cited as *Books*).

20. *MY,* II, 503. On June 11 Wordsworth wrote to Catherine Clarkson "with a full heart; with some sorrow, but most oppressed by an awful sense of the uncertainty & instability of all human things" (Cornell Lib. Wordsworth Coll., No. 2304).

21. *Books,* I, 104.

22. *M,* II, 433, 445; Cecilia H. Hendricks, "Thomas De Quincey, Symptomatologist," *PMLA* (Sept., 1945), LX, 828–840.

23. M, II, 372, 378; Cornell Lib. Wordsworth Coll., No. 2223; April, 1836, letter in *The Correspondence of Henry Crabb Robinson with the Wordsworth Circle, 1808–1866,* ed. Edith J. Morley (Oxford, 1927), I, 298 (hereinafter cited as *Circle*).

24. M, X, 48 n.; *Lit. Rem.,* I, 313.

25. M, X, 229 f.; Cornell Lib. Wordsworth Coll., No. 2808. For discussion of De Quincey's indebtedness to Wordsworth's ideas, see below, pp. 357–365.

26. M, II, 389; *Lit. Rem.,* I, 320 n.

27. *Works of the Ettrick Shepherd,* ed. Rev. Thomas Thomson (London, 1874), I, 464.

28. *Blackwood's Magazine,* XVI, 592; Lockhart to his wife, Aug. 25, 1825 (*Familiar Letters of Sir Walter Scott,* ed. David Douglas [Edinburgh, 1894], II, 341); *Memorials,* II, 38.

29. M, III, 198, 204.

30. "Personal Recollections of Thomas De Quincey," *De Quincey and His Friends,* ed. James Hogg (London, 1895), p. 156.

31. *M,* III, 199.

32. M, III, 206, 205.

33. M, III, 202.

34. *MY,* II, 629–630.

35. *Books,* I, 161; *MY,* II, 652; *Memorials,* II, 109 (misdated 1816).

36. *Lit. Rem.,* I, 316.

37. *Books,* I, 137.

38. M, II, 440.

39. Cornell Lib. Wordsworth Coll., No. 2808.

CHAPTER THREE (*Continued*)

40. M, III, 197.
41. Dove Cottage Mss.
42. *MY*, II, 488.
43. *MY*, II, 778.
44. M, III, 201–202.
45. Craig Mss. (*Memorials*, II, 157).
46. *MY*, II, 652.
47. *MW*, pp. 24–25; M, III, 387.
48. M, III, 398.
49. Dr. William's Library Mss.
50. *MY*, II, 779; *SH*, p. 310; *Books*, I, 187.
51. British Museum Add. Ms. 47, 511, fol. 36. See *STC*, III, 296 f.
52. British Museum Add. Ms. 47,520, fol. 84.
53. *Books*, I, 160.
54. *MY*, II, 779; M, III, 409; XIII, 238 f.
55. British Museum Add. Ms. 37,215, fol. 27 f.; Armitt, pp. 699 f.
56. *The Works of Charles and Mary Lamb*, ed. E. V. Lucas (London: Methuen, 1905), VI, 494; Sept. 13, 1807 (British Museum Add. Ms. 47,509, fol. 45).
57. Edward Sackville-West suggested that Peggy met De Quincey more than halfway (*A Flame in Sunlight* [London: Cassell, 1936], p. 150). Possibly, but De Quincey's 1803 *Diary* records visits to a "fat whore's" (p. 194), and Lamb thought De Quincey ought to gargle his mind for talking of Margaret with "speculative proflicacy" (*Works*, ed. Lucas, VI, 507).
58. Eaton, p. 217.
59. Japp, p. 135.
60. National Lib. of Scotland Ms. 2522, fol. 29 (*Memorials*, II, 39).
61. *Memorials*, II, 116.
62. Houghton Lib. Mss., Eng. 56 / National Lib. of Scotland Ms. 599,

fol. 121 (pages numbered 57–58 and 58–59 by De Quincey).
63. *Memorials*, II, 110; *Circle*, I, 90; *Works*, ed. Lucas, VI, 506.
64. *MY*, II, 778–779; *SH*, p. 88.
65. Elwin, pp. 51–52.
66. *Memorials*, I, 285; M, II, 297.
67. M, II, 238–239, 302.
68. M, II, 239, 294; *MY*, II, 639.
69. *MW*, p. 11; Mary Dawson married John Fisher on Nov. 8, 1817.
70. July, 1824, pp. 22–23.
71. M, III, 178; *Wordsworth and Reed*, ed. L. N. Broughton (Ithaca: Cornell University Press, 1933), p. 226.
72. M, II, 368–369.
73. *MY*, II, 628.
74. *MY*, II, 728–729; *Books*, I, 194, 187.
75. *Books*, I, 195.
76. Eaton, pp. 282–283.
77. Cornell Lib. Wordsworth Coll.
78. M, III, 45.
79. *Lit. Rem.*, I, 297.
80. M, XIII, 132.
81. M, II, 246.
82. *Books*, I, 187, 195; *Circle*, I, 90.

CHAPTER FOUR
"RECONCILIATION"

1. Mary L. Armitt, *Rydal* (Kendal, 1916), p. 679.
2. *MY*, II, 778 f.; copy of rough draft of a letter dated April 12, 1881, to Rev. H. M. Fletcher, supplied me by Mrs. H. D. Rawnsley.
3. The Wordsworths' reactions are probably reflected in Mary Lamb's writing, "I am very sorry for Mr. De Quincey," and Charles Lamb's calling it "a delicate subject" (*Works of Charles and Mary Lamb*, ed. E. V. Lucas [London,

1905], VI, 506 f.). Sara Hutchinson noted astringently, "I have no news from this neighbourhood that will amuse you—except that Mr De Quincey is at length married to his rustic beauty" (*SH*, p. 106). An autograph letter dated Oct. 20, 1852, and signed by initials which may be "JGL," offers "a few bits of De Quincey's history," in which it claims that after Margaret's pregnancy became apparent "W. W. & his womankind" tried "to get a marriage accomplished but the hero wd not—he again bolted" (National Lib. of Scotland Ms. 45, foll. 25–28). But this "history" is inaccurate in so many details that little credence can be given this one.

4. *Memorials*, II, 116; not in the Craig Mss. draft, and possibly a concoction of Japp's; but it matches De Quincey's mother's answer (*Memorials*, II, 123).

5. Elwin, pp. 405, 411, 418.

6. *M*, XI, 403 f.; *M*, V, 195.

7. Lonsdale Mss.; *MW*, p. 40; John E. Wells, "Wordsworth and De Quincey in Westmorland Politics, 1818," *PMLA*, LV (Dec., 1940), pp. 1084–1096.

8. A. Aspinall, *Politics and the Press, c. 1780–1850* (London, 1949), p. 356. Plans for the new paper were "exposed" in the *Kendal Chronicle* on Feb. 28, and officially announced in the *Carlisle Patriot* on April 11.

9. Wells, *PMLA*, LV, p. 1098.

10. *MY*, II, 808–810.

11. Aspinall, p. 358.

12. Japp, p. 153.

13. Lonsdale Mss.

14. Charles Pollitt, *De Quincey's Editorship of the Westmorland Gazette* (Kendal and London, 1890), p. 4.

15. Quotations from Wordsworth's letters to the Lowthers are from Lonsdale Mss. unless otherwise noted.

16. R. Woodhouse, "Notes of Conversations with Thomas de Quincey," *De Quincey and His Friends*, ed. James Hogg (London, 1895), p. 75.

17. Aspinall, p. 358.

18. April 22, 1822 (British Museum Add. Ms. 37,215, fol. 7).

19. *SH*, p. 152. The first installment of "'Letters from the Lakes,' translated from the German of Philip Kemperhausen, written in the summer of 1818," appeared in the *Gazette* for Feb. 20 and 27, copied from *Blackwood's* for January.

20. Sept. 12, 1818: "The Two Thieves" and "Description of a Female Beggar"; Oct. 17: "The Affliction of Margaret"; Oct. 24: "She dwelt among the untrodden ways" and "I travell'd among unknown men"; Oct. 31: "Sonnet Written in November, 1813"; Feb. 6, 1819: "Pure element of waters," "At early dawn," "Was the aim frustrated," and "One, who was suffering tumult in his soul" [previously unpublished]; Sept. 25: "Captivity." See A. L. Strout, "De Quincey and Wordsworth," *N & Q*, CLXXIV (June 11, 1938), 423.

21. *MY*, II, 846 f.

22. Japp, p. 154; Aspinall, p. 361.

23. *SH*, p. 169; *The Letters of William and Dorothy Wordsworth: The Later Years*, ed. E. de Selincourt (Oxford, 1939), I, 259 (hereinafter cited as *LY*).

24. *MY*, II, 854.

25. Eaton, p. 254; *Memorials*, II, 41.

26. Japp, p. 154.

27. Letter to Monkhouse, April 20,

CHAPTER FOUR (*Continued*)

1822 (Joanna Hutchinson Mss.);
Dove Cottage Mss.

28. *MW*, pp. 76, 82, 115; Dove
Cottage Mss. (Armitt, p. 685).

29. *SH*, p. 221; M, III, 127.

30. *Books*, I, 275.

31. Houghton Library Mss.

32. *De Quincey and His Friends*,
pp. 77 f.

33. British Museum Add. Ms. 37,
215, fol. 6 f.; Brotherton Lib. Mss.,
University of Leeds (Elsie Swann,
Christopher North [Edinburgh:
Oliver and Boyd, 1934], p. 232).

34. Dove Cottage Mss.; *LY*, I, 97;
The Keats Circle, ed. Hyder E.
Rollins (Cambridge, Mass.: Harvard
University Press, 1948), II, 424.

35. Letter quoted in catalogue of
Francis Edwards, London bookseller, 1923.

36. *SH*, p. 310.

37. *Circle*, I, 142.

38. Quoted with permission from
the original manuscript in the Carl
H. Pforzheimer Lib., Misc. Ms. 200
(June 10, 1826); *LY*, I, 259.

39. Anon., *The Rushbearing*
(London, 1889), p. 17.

40. British Museum Add. Ms. 46,
136, fol. 37.

41. See Armitt, pt. VII, and, for
a more charitable view, Eaton, pp.
320–322.

42. *Blake, Coleridge, Wordsworth
. . . Selections from the Remains of
Henry Crabb Robinson*, ed. E. J.
Morley (Manchester: Longmans,
Green, 1922), p. 58.

43. Cornell Lib. Wordsworth
Coll., No. 2349a.

44. Dove Cottage Mss.

45. *Some Letters of the Wordsworth Family*, ed. L. N. Broughton

(Ithaca: Cornell University Press,
1942), pp. 22, 24.

46. *Letters of Dora Wordsworth*,
ed. Howard P. Vincent (Chicago:
Packhard and Co., 1944), pp. 84, 48,
57.

47. Dove Cottage Mss.

48. *LY*, I, 468.

49. Dove Cottage Mss.

50. *De Quincey and His Friends*,
p. 233; *Circle*, I, 201.

51. Dove Cottage Mss.

52. *MW*, pp. 186, 230, 226.

CHAPTER FIVE
"AFTERMATH"

1. April 20, 1822 (British Museum Add. Ms. 37,215, fol. 6).

2. M, X, 16 f.; V, 262.

3. M, II, 185, 143–148, 158–161.

4. *Memoir and Letters of Sara
Coleridge*, ed. Edith Coleridge
(London, 1873), I, 115 f.

5. Thomas Carlyle, *Reminiscences*, ed. J. A. Froude (London,
1881), II, 315 f.

6. "Mr. Cottle and the Quarterly
Review: Second Preface to the 2nd
500 of J. Cottle's *Early Recollections*," p. 17; Dove Cottage Mss.
(Oct. 1, 1834); *SH*, p. 438.

7. Latymer Mss.

8. M, II, 173 f.

9. M, II, 161.

10. Eaton, pp. 372–381.

11. *Books*, I, 273.

12. The Wordsworths were late
hearing about it; Dora informed
Quillinan on April 20, 1838 (Dove
Cottage Mss.).

13. M, II, 229–445.

14. Actually, it appears that Dorothy and William kept house together briefly at Windy Brow, Kes-

wick, in 1794; settled from 1795 to
1797 at Racedown, where they paid
no rent; from 1797 to 1798 lived at
Alfoxden, on the edge of the Quantock Hills, a home belonging to Mr.
St. Albyn, "a minor," for which
they paid £23 a year rent. Wordsworth had met Coleridge in 1795,
and it was as a result of a visit to
him at Nether Stowey that the
Wordsworths settled at nearby Alfoxden (Mary Moorman, *William
Wordsworth* [Oxford: Clarendon
Press, 1957], I, 245, 267, 324 f., 400).

15. Houghton Lib. Eng. Ms. 56.

16. M, II, 239; *Lit. Rem.*, I, 275;
M, II, 237; *Lit. Rem.*, I, 282; M,
II, 243. De Quincey defined a cade
as "some sort of insect which ad-
vances by an oblique motion."

17. M, II, 300 f.; *Lit. Rem.*, I, 312
("above all" cut out in revision);
Lit. Rem., I, 353, 360.

18. *Lit. Rem.*, I, 297.

19. *Lit. Rem.*, I, 266.

20. M, II, 419.

21. *Lit. Rem.*, I, 295, 316.

22. An undated letter of De
Quincey's to Tait reassures the editor: "Prof. W. is not concerned as
Defendent but as joint plaintiff with
myself . . . . he will be highly
pleased" (Nat. Lib. of Scotland Ms.
1670, No. 110).

23. M, III, 302, 283, 439 *n*.

24. M, II, 419, 439, 379, 60; III,
42.

25. Dr. Williams's Lib., London,
H. C. Robinson Mss. 1828, fol. 57;
1827, fol. 20; Cornell Lib. Wordsworth Coll., No. 2322. See above,
pp. 294 f.

26. *Blackwood's Magazine*, Sept.–
Dec., 1829; *LY*, I, 448.

27. *Blake, Coleridge, Wordsworth*, ed. E. J. Morley (Man-

chester: Longmans, Green, 1922), p.
58.

28. British Museum Add. Ms. 41,
325, fol. 15.

29. August 27, 1839 (Dr. Williams's Lib. Mss.).

30. This glossary was supplied to
the 1853 edition by Mr. Nicholson,
Kendal publisher. (I owe this identification to Mrs. Beatrix Hogan.)

31. Dove Cottage Mss.

32. *Wordsworth and Reed*, ed. L.
N. Broughton (Ithaca: Cornell University Press, 1933), p. 36.

33. To Barron Field (British Museum Add. Ms. 41,325, fol. 15).

34. Letters in the possession of
Mr. M. Ronald Brunkenfeld, New
York City.

35. Houghton Lib. Eng. Ms. 56.

36. National Lib. of Scotland Ms.
1670, fol. 64.

37. M, II, 388, 302.

38. M, III, 200 ff. See above, p.
219.

39. M, III, 203.

40. Letter to Thomas Poole, June
6, 1819 (British Museum Add. Ms.
35,344, fol. 47).

41. M, III, 203.

42. Thomas De Quincey, *Posthumous Works*, ed. A. H. Japp (London, 1891–1893), II, 210. For a discussion of De Quincey's criticism of
Wordsworth, see my *Thomas De
Quincey: Literary Critic* (Berkeley
and Los Angeles: University of
California Press, 1952).

43. M, XI, 307.

44. M, XI, 301, 315, 322.

45. M, II, 171.

46. *Wordsworth and Reed*, p.
226.

47. Japp, p. 376.

48. Cornell Lib. Wordsworth Coll.
Cf. M, VII, 72 *n*.

CHAPTER FIVE (*Continued*)

49. M, III, 28.

50. *MY,* II, 629; *Books,* I, 161.

51. *LY,* II, 652; M, XI, 110; Pollitt, pp. 70–71.

52. *Posthumous Works,* I, 293 f.

53. M, XIII, 12; III, 407 *n.;* VII, 72 *n.;* XI, 307 *n.;* III, 96, 404 *n.;* XIII, 127, 128 *n.,* 135 *n.;* Elwin, p. 471; M, II, 248.

54. Elwin, pp. 274–275 (M, III, 394).

55. Elwin, pp. 491 f.

56. Elwin, p. 468 (M, XIII, 338).

57. M, XIII, 363 *n.*

58. M, X, 48 *n.*

59. *Circle,* I, 201; M, X, 101; *The Poetical Works of William Wordsworth,* ed. E. de Selincourt (Oxford, 1952), II, 417.

60. M, I, 194.

61. M, XI, 215.

62. M, X, 128; *Books,* I, 103; *MY,* I, 244.

63. M, III, 148; *Poetical Works,* II, 423.

64. See Meyer H. Abrams, *The Mirror and the Lamp* (New York: Norton, 1958), chap. XI; *Biographia Literaria,* ed. J. Shawcross (Oxford, 1907), II, 10; see Samuel Johnson, *Lives of the English Poets,* ed. G. B. Hill (Oxford, 1905), I, 67; *Diary . . . of Henry Crabb Robinson,* ed. T. Sadler (London, 1872), I, 163; *Books,* II, 479; M, IV, 113–114 *n.*

65. M, X, 72. See my "De Quincey on Wordsworth's Theory of Diction," *PMLA,* LXVIII (Sept., 1953), 764–778.

66. *Prose Works,* III, 488; M, X, 394.

INDEX